# The Turning Point
# in the Gospel of Mark

# The Turning Point
# in the Gospel of Mark

A Study in Markan Christology

GREGG S. MORRISON

☙PICKWICK *Publications* • Eugene, Oregon

THE TURNING POINT IN THE GOSPEL OF MARK
A Study in Markan Christology

Copyright © 2014 Gregg S. Morrison. All rights reserved. Except for brief quotations in critical publications or reviews, no part of this book may be reproduced in any manner without prior written permission from the publisher. Write: Permissions, Wipf and Stock Publishers, 199 W. 8th Ave., Suite 3, Eugene, OR 97401.

Pickwick Publications
An Imprint of Wipf and Stock Publishers
199 W. 8th Ave., Suite 3
Eugene, OR 97401

www.wipfandstock.com

isbn 13: 978-1-61097-760-9

*Cataloging-in-Publication data:*

Morrison, Gregg S.

    The turning point in the Gospel of Mark : a study in Markan christology / Gregg S. Morrison.

    xiv + 268 p.; 23 cm. —Includes bibliographical references.

    ISBN 13: 978-1-61097-760-9

1. Bible. Mark—Criticism, interpretation, etc. 2. Bible. Mark—Theology. 3. Jesus Christ—Person and offices—Biblical teaching. 4. Jesus Christ—History of doctrines—Early church, ca. 30–600. I. Title.

BS2585.52 M68 2014

Manufactured in the U.S.A.

For Laura

# Contents

*List of Tables* | ii

*Foreword* by Francis J. Moloney, SDB | iii

*Preface* | vii

*Abbreviations* | x

1. Introduction | 1
2. Surveying the Possible Turning Points | 40
3. A Look at Another Approach | 80
4. Reading Peter's Confession and the Transfiguration Together | 98
5. Converging Lines in Markan Christology | 165
6. Conclusion | 229

*Appendix 1: The Narrative Flow of the Gospel of Mark* | 237

*Appendix 2: Summary of Major Commentators and Mark's "Turning Point"* | 239

*Appendix 3* | 242

*Bibliography* | 245

# Tables

| | | |
|---|---|---|
| Table 1 | Teaching to Disciples and Others | 57 |
| Table 2 | Shared Vocabulary and Syntactical Construction: Mark 8:27—9:1/9:2–13 | 84 |
| Table 3 | Thematic Links between Twin Pericopae | 90 |
| Table 4 | Comparison of Mark's Passion Predictions | 133 |
| Table 5 | Georg Strecker's Passion and Resurrection Predictions | 135 |
| Table 6 | Dorothy Lee's Diptych Approach to 8:27—9:13 | 152 |
| Table 7 | C. Clifton Black's Tripartite Structure to Mark's Gospel | 189 |
| Table 8 | Variants for Son of God in Mark 1:1 | 220 |
| Table 9 | Mark's Christological Images and the Kingdom of God | 232 |
| Table 10 | The Janus Effect on Mark's Christology | 234 |

# Foreword

The Gospel of Mark emerged as the most studied of the Synoptic Gospels once the burgeoning interest in source criticism established that Mark had to be the earliest of the four Gospels. Other points of view were still argued, generally in an attempt to maintain the long-standing tradition that Matthew was the "first Gospel." But widespread support of Markan priority raised other questions for the early critics. For the greater part of the second half of the nineteenth century, Mark was seen as the best source for recovering the Jesus of history. If Mark was the earliest witness, he had to be closest to the "facts." Many regarded the very sequence of Mark's narrative as a reasonably accurate report of Jesus' public life and ministry, a "framework" for his life story. He conducted an initial large-scale mission in Galilee, journeyed to Jerusalem into conflict, the episode in the Temple, his arrest, trial, and eventual execution.

As is well known, the combination of Albert Schweitzer's survey of the nineteenth-century quest for the historical Jesus, and Wilhelm Wrede's study of the use of the so-called "messianic secret" in the Gospels, brought that era to an end. In a new critical atmosphere, across the first half of the twentieth century the form critics had little respect for Mark's skills as an author. Most regarded him as an editor of received traditions, and some regarded his editorial work as very clumsy. Rudolf Bultmann even suggested that he was not in control of his sources. The dominance of this negative appreciation of Mark as an author and an early Christian theologian came to a timely end across the second half of that century, and into the third millennium. In many ways the so-called redaction critics returned to the initial insights of Wrede, who had claimed that Mark was an early Christian theologian. An initial trickle of interest in Mark as a theologically motivated creative author has become a veritable flood. The contemporary literary interest in biblical narrative has led many to turn to a study of the Gospel of Mark, finding there a sophisticated and inspired story of Jesus that demands respect as a unified narrative.

*Foreword*

Gregg Morrison's study, *The Turning Point in the Gospel of Mark: A Study in Markan Christology*, should take its rightful place in this "veritable flood." An important element in the interpretation of a narrative text is the determination of its literary structure. On the basis of *elements within the narrative itself*, finding a "skeleton" upon which the flesh of a narrative hangs, is a crucial first step in any literary reading of a text that is a "story" or, in the case of the Gospels, a biography. The importance of this initial step must not be underestimated. In the end, the visible "shape" of the narrative is what the reader, or the listener, sees or hears. The impact of the story as a whole plays a determining role in what they think its various parts might mean. Gregg Morrison's book makes an important contribution to this aspect of Markan studies.

Since the beginning of an interest in the Gospel of Mark as a narrative, to be read as a whole and not as a collection of disparate elements, the scene that reports the confession of Peter at Caesarea Philippi and its aftermath (Mark 8:27–33) has played a major role in the determination of its literary structure. Even an initial reading of the Gospel indicates that—in terms of Mark's narrative rhetoric—something important happens at that stage of the unfolding story. A character in the narrative confesses Jesus as "the Christ" for the first time (v. 29), even though the reader has been informed of this truth from the very first line (1:1). Jesus responds to that confession with a command to silence (8:30), and tells his disciples that he is the Son of Man who must suffer, die, and on the third day rise again (v. 31). He says this openly, even though they are not able to accept it (vv. 32–33). Most would claim that the narrative has turned an important corner. Immediately following this episode, after the transfiguration, a voice from heaven announces that Jesus is a beloved Son, and that the disciples must listen to him (9:7).

Morrison's study opens with a helpful overview of the scholarly discussion of the literary structure of the Gospel of Mark, from Wrede to the present day. Against that background, Morrison develops his own case. He claims that the centerpiece of the Markan narrative is to be found in Mark 8:27—9:13, and that it plays a "Janus" role, looking both backward and forward across the story. Too often literary structures are developed on the basis of "interpreted meaning" of passages. These interpretations inevitably are the result of a certain subjectivity. Morrison shows, on the basis of a careful, and possibly more objective, linguistic, and philological analysis of his so-called Janus section, that the choice of language, rhetoric, and especially terms used about Jesus, can be found at the beginning, the center, and the end of the

*Foreword*

story. In order to gather the beginning and the end, however, one must see the centerpoint as *both* the episode at Caesarea Philippi (8:27–38) and the subsequent event of the transfiguration (9:2–13), swiveling around the perennial *crux interpretum* of 9:1.

The second half of the book moves away from the explicitly literary issues surrounding the interpretation of the Gospel of Mark, to reflect upon more theological themes. Again within the context of a precious survey of past and present interpretations of the Christology of the Gospel of Mark, Morrison discusses the role of the Markan use of the Christ, the Son of God, and the Son of Man. In a progressive strengthening of his case concerning 8:27—9:13 as the "Janus" moment in the story, he shows that christological issues have determined Mark's use of Messiah, Son of God, Son of Man, and kingdom at the beginning, in the middle, and at the end of the story. The case for a Janus-effect has been made cumulatively through study of the narrative rhetoric, the verbal parallels, and Mark's christological claims. Morrison's suggestions concerning the role and meaning of 9:1 are very helpful. Scholarship is traditionally called to decide *when* some who are standing there with Jesus "will not taste death before they see that the kingdom of God has come with power." Most opt for *either* the transfiguration, that immediately follows, *or* the resurrection, that ends the narrative, *or* the end of all time, promised in 13:24–37. At the center of the Janus passage, 9:1 is the swivel around which 8:27—9:13 turns, and thus the single verse around which the whole narrative swings. On these grounds, Morrison suggests that it may direct the reader to all these eventualities.

In addition to his own helpful Janus-moment thesis concerning the Markan literary structure, Morrison provides lucid surveys of the many suggestions surrounding the literary structure of the Gospel, between the extremes of those who suggest that there is no clear-cut literary structure, to those who wish to divide the Gospel into smaller units that interrelate. A similar survey is found in the latter part of the study where early, modern, and contemporary studies of the Markan Christology are presented. This book not only makes a contribution to Markan scholarship in terms of its own original proposal about the literary structure of the Markan narrative and its Christology; but also provides people interested in the Gospel of Mark with valuable surveys of the history of scholarship that are chronological, logical, fair, and clearly written.

I had the privilege of directing Gregg Morrison's original doctoral dissertation, defended at the Catholic University of America, Washington DC,

v

in November, 2007. His post-doctoral life and ministry rendered impossible the task of immediately preparing his dissertation for publication. Over six years we have discussed possible timelines for a publication in the context of the challenge of Gregg's work loads, family obligations, and many other factors. This has led to a distance of seven years between the original defense of his dissertation, and its eventual publication. *Would that this were the case with many other doctoral dissertations.* The difference in the quality of what Gregg has provided for publication and the original dissertation is very great. What he argued then is still argued in the book that follows. But like most dissertations, in the original form of this book every footnote was lengthy, and not a stone was left unturned. Some of those overturned stones made little or no contribution to the debate, but they had been published, and Gregg had to read them! He was then—and remains now—a *passionate* bibliophile. One example will indicate what I mean. Quite recently, as I was reading Gregg's work on the Son of Man in Mark, I mentioned to him that I had just published an article on Jesus and the Son of Man. An immediate email arrived in response: "I read it last night!"

I admire this aspect of his work, as it is but one indication of his broader "passion" for the Word of God in whatever form it comes to us. However, as for all of us who seek to interpret the New Testament within the Christian church, there are two dimensions that a "passion" for the Word of God must address. Maintaining the balance is not simple. On the one hand, there is a scholarly passion to ensure that every textual, historical, literary, and theological possibility is discussed and evaluated, no matter how significant or insignificant any single one of them may or may not be. This thoroughness is the stuff of what is normally regarded as scholarly discourse. On the other hand, however, there must be a passion to make a critical analysis of the Word of God "relevant." In my opinion, Gregg's focus upon the literary structure and the Christology of the Gospel of Mark addresses two major "relevancy" issues: How do I read it, and what does it mean?

Pickwick Publications have rendered considerable service to Markan scholarship by publishing this fine book. It is no longer yet another published dissertation, but a mature reflection on major issues that surround contemporary interpretation of the Gospel of Mark.

*Francis J. Moloney, SDB, AM, FAHA*
Australian Catholic University
Fitzroy, Victoria 3065, AUSTRALIA.

# Preface

My interest in the academic study of the Gospel of Mark began in the summer of 1994 at Beeson Divinity School under the fine teaching of J. Norfleete Day. The course textbook for that summer was William L. Lane's commentary on Mark in the NICNT series. I remember reading Lane and becoming intrigued by Mark's literary strategy. I sensed that Mark was "up to something" with his opening line (1:1) and the carefully placed "confessions" of Peter (8:29) and the centurion (15:39). Though nearly eight years would elapse before returning to a serious study of Mark's Gospel, my curiosity with this Gospel did not diminish. Much of what is contained in these pages is my effort to come to grips with Mark's narrative and what he was up to.

During the 2002–2003 academic year, I returned to the formal study of Mark in consecutive doctoral seminars at The Catholic University of America. Those two seminars were memorable for many reasons and I am grateful to all my colleagues in those classes for I learned a great deal from each of them as we examined the text together. I especially want to acknowledge Sherri Brown, Daniel C. Claire, Kelly R. Iverson, and Christopher W. Skinner for their friendship, which was nurtured during those two semesters—friendships that continue despite our distances. Chapter 3 was essentially my seminar paper for the second of those seminars and Sherri, Dan, Kelly, and Chris have each, in their own way, encouraged me with this current work and their probing questions and interaction have made it a better book (though the flaws remain with me). The professor for those seminars was Francis J. Moloney, SDB. The debt of gratitude I owe Father Moloney is immeasurable. Much of what one might read in these pages can be traced back to him in one way or another even though we may differ on certain matters. He was a terrific *Doktorvater* and he continues to be a cherished and valued friend. I especially appreciate him writing the Foreword to this work. I wish also to thank my readers of the original dissertation (which was defended in late 2007), Frank J. Matera and the late

*Preface*

Francis T. Gignac, SJ, for their time and energies on my behalf. I would be remiss if I did not acknowledge and thank all my former teachers, especially those New Testament scholars I was privileged to work with at some point: Joseph A. Fitzmyer, Luke Timothy Johnson, Steven J. Kraftchick, Robert Kysar, and Frank S. Thielman.

The bulk of the research for this work was accomplished at four libraries: The Catholic University of America's John K. Mullen of Denver Memorial Library and The Woodstock Theological Library, Georgetown University, both in Washington DC; the Davis Library at Samford University, Birmingham, Alabama; and the Start-Kilgour Memorial Library at Simpson University in Redding, California. I wish to thank the staff of each library, especially the invaluable personnel working in the Interlibrary Loan departments. In addition, I served on the faculty of the latter two and wish to thank my colleagues at Beeson Divinity School, Samford University, and the Department of Theology and Ministry at Simpson University for their encouragement and support. I also would like to thank my students at those institutions for their engaging questions and interest in my work. I should extend my thanks as well to members of my Sunday School class at Shades Mountain Baptist Church, who on more than one occasion have heard me give my take on Mark's Gospel.

While this monograph was being researched, written, and (later) revised, I sat under three pastors: Danny Wood, John R. Hutchinson, and Bill Randall. I am grateful to each of them for their preaching ministry and for their friendship. However, I could never have undertaken this project were it not for my former pastor, mentor, and friend, Charles T. Carter. His interest in my work means a great deal to me and I appreciate the wise counsel he has supplied over the years. Suffice it to say, he is a pastor and friend *par excellence*.

Embarking on doctoral studies is not an endeavor one can do alone. Neither is returning to a manuscript for revision after being away from it (and the academic world) for several years. Without the support of friends and family, I doubt very seriously if I would have made it. I am grateful to friends Lev and Vicki Bragg and Steve and Kim Hancock for their prayers and encouragement. I also wish to thank several friends who helped (in large and small ways) along the way: Jonathan Bass, Dave and Sue Belcher, John Bell, Charles and Gladys Dunkin, Dick and Jayne Edge, Randel and Sheila Everett, James Earl Massey, Ken and Dea Mathews, William W. McDonald, Hal Parrish, Randy Pittman, David E. Potts, Jim Pounds, and

Turner Waide. I also appreciate the support and friendship of my current professional colleagues: Bill McDonald Jr., Thomas J. Maddox, and Vaughn P. Stough.

In addition, I have been blessed by the support of my family. A man could hardly find better in-laws than Arthur and Carolyn Edge. I love and appreciate them very much. It is also nice to have a sister-in-law and two brothers-in-law as friends—Jennifer and Bill McMahon and Art Edge. I am also very blessed to have two extraordinary parents, Warren and Joyce Morrison. No one has encouraged me, prayed for my well-being, and sacrificed for my education more than the two of them. Mom and Dad, thank you. I love you.

When this work was first completed as a doctoral dissertation, the happiest two people were probably my children: Scott (then age eight) and Katherine (then age four). They are now age fourteen and ten, respectfully. They both have been very supportive of my work and I am grateful. Scott and Katherine, your mom and I love you very much and we are so proud of you both.

This work is dedicated to my wife, Laura. We were married while I was in graduate school. The first decade of our married life included some form of graduate work—either hers or (mostly) mine. I would say that is going above-and-beyond the call of duty. Laura has been a constant source of encouragement for me while I researched and wrote the original dissertation and, especially, lately as I have endeavored to revise it. She did many, many things that lightened my load and I am grateful. Her patience was steady throughout the process. Her love was never ending. She is my best friend. Laura, I love you.

*Christmas 2013*

# Abbreviations

| | |
|---|---|
| **AB** | Anchor Bible |
| **ABRL** | Anchor Bible Reference Library |
| **ACNT** | Augsburg Commentaries on the New Testament |
| *AcOr* | *Acta orientalia* |
| **AGAJU** | Arbeiten zur Geschichte des antiken Judentums und des Urchristentums |
| **AnBib** | Analecta biblica |
| *BBR* | *Bulletin for Biblical Research* |
| **BDAG** | Walter Bauer et al. *Greek-English Lexicon of the New Testament and Other Early Christian Literature.* 3rd ed. Chicago: University of Chicago Press, 2000. |
| **BDB** | Francis Brown, S. R. Driver, and Charles A. Briggs. *Hebrew and English Lexicon of the Old Testament.* Oxford: Clarendon, 1907. |
| **BETL** | Bibliotheca Ephemeridum theologicarum Lovaniensium |
| *Bib* | *Biblica* |
| *BJRL* | *Bulletin of the John Rylands University Library of Manchester* |
| *BK* | *Bibel und Kirche* |
| **BNTC** | Black's NT Commentaries |
| *BT* | *Bible Translator* |
| *BTB* | *Biblical Theological Bulletin* |

*Abbreviations*

| | |
|---|---|
| *BZ* | *Biblische Zeitschrift* |
| **BZNW** | Beihefte Zeitschrift für Theologie und Kirche |
| *CBQ* | *Catholic Biblical Quarterly* |
| **CBQMS** | Catholic Biblical Quarterly Monograph Series |
| *CTM* | *Currents in Theology and Missions* |
| *DTT* | *Dansk teologisk tidsskrift* |
| **EBib** | Études bibliques |
| **EKKNT** | Evangelisch-katholischer Kommentar zum Neuen Testament |
| *EvQ* | *Evangelical Quarterly* |
| *ExpTim* | *Expository Times* |
| **FB** | Forschung zur Bibel |
| **FRLANT** | Forschungen zur Religion und Literatur des Alten und Neuen Testaments |
| **GBS** | Guides to Biblical Scholarship |
| **GNS** | Good News Studies |
| **HNT** | Handbuch zum Neuen Testament |
| *HS* | *Hebrew Studies* |
| **HTKNT** | Herders theologischer Kommentar zum Neuen Testament |
| *HTR* | *Harvard Theological Review* |
| **IBC** | Interpretation: A Bible Commentary for Teaching and Preaching |
| **IBT** | Interpreting Biblical Texts |
| **ICC** | International Critical Commentary |
| *Int* | *Interpretation* |
| **JAAR** | *Journal of the American Academy of Religion* |
| **JBC** | R. E. Brown et al. (eds.), *The Jerome Biblical Commentary* |

*Abbreviations*

| | |
|---|---|
| *JBL* | *Journal of Biblical Literature* |
| *JR* | *Journal of Religion* |
| *JNST* | *Journal for the Study of the New Testament* |
| **JSNTSup** | Journal for the Study of the New Testament Supplement Series |
| *JSOT* | *Journal for the Study of the Old Testament* |
| **JSOTSup** | Journal for the Study of the Old Testament Supplement Series |
| *JTS* | *Journal of Theological Studies* |
| **KEK** | Kritisch-exegetischer Kommentar über das Neue Testament |
| **LCL** | Loeb Classical Library |
| **LD** | Lectio divina |
| **LNTS** | Library of New Testament Studies |
| **MNTC** | Moffatt New Testament Commentary |
| *Neot* | *Neotestamentica* |
| **NIBC** | New International Biblical Commentary |
| **NICNT** | New International Commentary on the New Testament |
| **NIGTC** | New International Greek Testament Commentary |
| *NJBC* | R. E. Brown et al. (eds.), *New Jerome Biblical Commentary* |
| *NovT* | *Novum Testamentum* |
| *NTG* | New Testament Guides |
| *NTS* | *New Testament Studies* |
| **PNTC** | Pillar New Testament Commentary |
| *RevExp* | *Review and Expositor* |
| **SBLABS** | Society of Biblical Literature, Archaeology and Biblical Studies |
| **SBLDS** | Society of Biblical Literature Dissertation Series |
| *SBLSP* | *Society of Biblical Literature Seminar Papers* |

| | |
|---|---|
| **SBLSS** | Society of Biblical Literature Semeia Studies |
| **SBLSymS** | Society of Biblical Literature Symposium Series |
| **SBS** | Stuttgarter Bibelstudien |
| **SBT** | Studies in Biblical Theology |
| *SE* | *Studia Evangelica* |
| **SNTSMS** | Society for New Testament Studies Monograph Series |
| **SNTSU** | Studien zum Neuen Testament und seiner Umwelt |
| **SP** | Sacra Pagina |
| **SPB** | Studia postbiblical |
| **THKNT** | Theologischer Handkommentar zum Neuen Testament |
| *TJ* | *Trinity Journal* |
| **TU** | Texte und Untersuchungen |
| ***TWNT*** | *Theologisches Wörterbuch zum Neuen Testament* |
| **TynBul** | *Tyndale Bulletin* |
| *USQR* | *Union Seminary Quarterly Review* |
| *VT* | *Vetus Testamentum* |
| **WBC** | Word Biblical Commentary |
| *WTJ* | *Westminster Theological Journal* |
| **WUNT** | Wissenschaftliche Untersuchungen zum Neuen Testament |
| *ZNW* | *Zeitschrift für die neutestamentliche Wissenschaft* |
| *ZTK* | *Zeitschrift für Theologie und Kirche* |

# 1
# Introduction

THE QUESTION I WILL confront in this monograph is whether there is a turning point in the Gospel of Mark, that is, a pivot on which the entire narrative turns. A second and related question is: If such a pivot exists, then what is it? I believe there exists such a turning point in the Gospel of Mark and I hold it to be (broadly stated for now) in Mark's middle section (8:22—10:52).[1] I am not alone in this determination. Several scholars have observed a major climax and turning point in this section of the narrative. The second question—what precisely is the turning point?—is more difficult to answer and constitutes the burden of this book. If, as I will argue, the author constructed the Gospel with a decisive midpoint in mind, then how or in what way does the presentation of the turning point have an impact on the primary objective in writing, namely, the presentation or identity of Jesus?[2] To put it another way, what is the relationship of the narrative's turning point to Markan Christology?

---

1. It is generally acknowledged that the Gospel of Mark is anonymous. Determining the identity of the author is beyond the scope of this work. I will refer to the author as "Mark" (without the use of the quotation marks) only for ease and to facilitate reading. In so doing, I am not making a statement for or against any particular author. For the various proposals regarding authorship, see the major commentaries and especially Black, *Images of an Apostolic Interpreter*, 1–73.

2. Not everyone holds the primary purpose of the Gospel of Mark to be the identity of Jesus. Gundry (*Mark*, 1), for example, sees the Gospel as an apology for the cross: "The Gospel of Mark contains no ciphers, no hidden meanings, no sleight of hand . . . Mark's meaning lies on the surface. He writes a straightforward apology for the Cross." Evans (*Mark 8:27—16:20*, xi) has written a commentary that is "in essential agreement with Gundry's interpretation" [of the purpose of the Gospel]. In support of my conclusion, see Hooker, *The Gospel According to Saint Mark*, 19: "The gospel is about 'good news about Jesus Christ,' and the whole book is focused on the figure of Jesus." More recently, Maloney (*Jesus' Urgent Message for Today*, 42) agrees: "To summarize the Christology of Mark's Gospel is very difficult since almost the entire narrative focuses on Jesus' identity."

The Turning Point in the Gospel of Mark

In order to introduce this topic, I need to establish the context for determining *the* turning point in the Gospel, which will involve an examination of the structure or sequencing of the Gospel. After reviewing the proposals surrounding the various ways to outline the Gospel, I will examine the literary device of "turning point," including how the question of gospel genre influences the discussion. Finally, I will provide a general overview of the plot of Mark's Gospel, which will serve to introduce my proposal for the identification of Mark's turning point.

## THE STRUCTURE OF MARK'S GOSPEL

Interpreters interested in the structure of Mark's Gospel have searched diligently for a coherent organizing principle in order to make sense of the narrative. Coming up with a conclusive outline or structure to the Gospel of Mark is difficult.[3] One reason may be the seemingly disjunctive manner in which Mark assembled the materials at his disposal. Eusebius, for example, says that Papias claimed that (according to "the Presbyter") Mark did not arrange the stories of Jesus in any particular order.[4] Toward the end of the nineteenth century, Martin Kähler insisted that all the Gospels are "passion narratives with extended introductions."[5] Accordingly, scholarly opinion

---

See also Kingsbury, *Christology of Mark's Gospel*, ix.

3. The late Robert Guelich (*Mark 1:1—8:26*, xxxvi) noted that "[o]ne might well despair of finding any structure or outline for Mark's Gospel based on consensus. The suggestions are as diverse as the individual commentators." More recently, Marcus (*Mark 1–8*, 62) agrees: "Of the making of many Markan outlines, there is, seemingly, no end."

4. Eusebius, *Hist. eccl.* 3.39.15. The actual quote (from Kirsopp Lake's translation in *The Ecclesiastical History*, 297) is: "And the Presbyter used to say this, 'Mark became Peter's interpreter and wrote accurately all that he remembered, not, indeed, in order, of the things said or done by the Lord. For he had not heard the Lord, nor had he followed him, but later on, as I said, followed Peter, who used to give teaching as necessity demanded but not making, as it were, an arrangement of the Lord's oracles, so that Mark did nothing wrong in thus writing down single points as he remembered them. For to one thing he gave attention, to leave out nothing of what he had heard and to make no false statements in them.'" For a helpful discussion of Papias and his observations, see Black, *Images of an Apostolic Interpreter*, 82–94.

5. Kähler, *The So-Called Historical Jesus*, 80, n.11. While the phrase quoted above is well known, Kähler's subsequent sentence in the footnote is less familiar: "Mark 8:27 to 9:13, the group of events from Peter's confession at Caesarea Philippi to the transfiguration on the mountain, show clearly where the emphasis lies for the narrator." In many ways, as I hope to show below, this monograph seeks to develop Kähler's lesser-known phrase.

regarding the structure of the Gospel abound.[6] While it is possible to oversimplify matters, the Gospel of Mark has generally been outlined in one of four ways: (1) topographically, along geographic movements in the Gospel; (2) thematically, highlighting a particular theme or the development of a theme such as Christology, discipleship, or faith; (3) topically, with Jesus' teaching and healing ministry as the first major section and Jesus' death and resurrection as the second; or (4) rhetorically, seeking some literary or persuasive device by which to distinguish the material.[7]

## Topographical Outlines

One of the first commentators of Mark's Gospel in the twentieth century, Benjamin W. Bacon, divides the material topographically.[8] Simply stated, he sees two major divisions of material: Part I relates to Jesus' Galilean ministry (1:1—8:26) and Part II concerns Jesus' Judean ministry (8:27—16:8). More recently, James R. Edwards shares the view of Bacon by stating that the narrative falls naturally into the same two halves.[9] Vincent Taylor expands this twofold structure into six major divisions (after a prologue) in his outline of the Gospel: (1) the Galilean ministry (1:14—3:6); (2) the height of the Galilean ministry (3:7—6:13); (3) the ministry beyond Galilee (6:14—8:26); (4) Caesarea Philippi and the journey to Jerusalem (8:27—10:52); (5) the ministry in Jerusalem (11:1—13:37); (6) the passion and resurrection narrative (14:1—16:8).[10] Many other commentators use topography as a means of examining the makeup of the Gospel.[11]

---

6. There are several good surveys of the various proposals for the structure of Mark. For a now rather dated overview (with helpful chart), see Baarlink, *Anfängliches Evangelium*, 73-83, esp. 75-78. More recent surveys include Cook, *Structure and Persuasive Power of Mark*, 11-86 and Larsen, "The Structure of Mark's Gospel," 140-60.

7. My four categories are similar to that of Larsen ("The Structure of Mark's Gospel," 143-55), who proposes the following: (1) topography/geography; (2) theological themes; (3) *Sitz im Leben* of the recipients; and (4) literary factors.

8. Bacon, *Beginnings of Gospel Story*, vi-vii.

9. Edwards, *Gospel according to Mark*, 20-21.

10. Taylor, *Gospel According to St. Mark*, 105-13.

11. Others who divide the Gospel topographically include Bryan, *A Preface to Mark*, 83; Cranfield, *Gospel According to Saint Mark*, 15; Guthrie, *New Testament Introduction*, 86-87; Harrington, "The Gospel According to Mark," 598; Hauck, *Das Evangelium des Markus*, vii-x; Klostermann, *Das Markusevangelium*, 1; Kümmel, *Introduction to the New Testament*, 82-83; Lührmann, *Das Markusevangelium*, vii-ix; Schnelle, *History and Theology of the New Testament Writings*, 204-5; and Swete, *Gospel According to St. Mark*.

## The Turning Point in the Gospel of Mark

Using topography as the signal feature in developing a Markan outline is not, however, without problems, especially within the portrayal of Jesus' Galilean ministry (1:14—8:26). For example, in the so-called parable chapter (Mark 4), Jesus teaches in a boat alongside the sea (4:1–9). In 4:10, when he was alone, those around him with the Twelve (οἱ περὶ αὐτὸν σὺν τοῖς δώδεκα) ask about the parable he had told at the seashore. His response to this inquiry has been given the label "parable theory," for in it Jesus sets forth the essence of his teaching in parables: to *you* (plural) the secret (τὸ μυστήριον) of the kingdom has been given, but to those on the outside (τοῖς ἔξω) everything is in parables (4:11–12). Jesus then explains in allegorical fashion the meaning of the parable of the sower (4:13–20) and continues with no mention of a change of venue by offering three additional parables: a light under a bushel (4:21–25), the growing seed (4:26–29), and the mustard seed (4:30–32). In 4:33, the narrator explains that with many such parables he spoke *to them* (αὐτοῖς). A reader would naturally assume that the "them" to whom Jesus was speaking was the Twelve and those around him in the private setting of 4:10–12. There has, after all, been no mention of a change in Jesus' location in the narrative or any reentry of others into the conversation. Yet 4:34 indicates that he (Jesus) did not speak *to them* (αὐτοῖς) without a parable, *but* privately to his own disciples he explained everything. There is a distinct contrast between the "them" in 4:33–34 and the disciples in 4:34. A reader would assume that the subsequent three parables (4:21–32) were spoken only to the disciples and those with Jesus (in private), but the closing statement indicates a shift whereby others (presumably the crowd) must have heard Jesus speak these parables since he explained everything privately to the disciples (something that is only mentioned in regards to the parable of the sower, 4:13–20). Has there been a change of location that the narrator has not identified? Should a reader assume geographic consistency unless given reasons to believe otherwise? Geography or topography, in this case, is an impediment to a precise understanding of the nature of Jesus' parables.[12]

---

Using the geographic schema in a different manner is Marxsen (*Mark the Evangelist*, 54–116). Marxsen assumes that Mark's geographic scheme does not represent history; rather, it represents the theological/redactional understanding of the author and thus provides the key to the Gospel.

12. Marcus ("Blanks and Gaps in the Markan Parable of the Sower," 247–62, esp. 249) argues that these confusing "stage directions" form a narrative "blank," an inadvertent failure on behalf of the author to supply necessary information or an accidental transmission of confusing narrative signals.

*Introduction*

Another topographical dilemma in the Galilee cycle occurs in Mark 6. In 6:45, Jesus instructs his disciples to get into a boat and go to Bethsaida while he remained behind to pray (6:46). The precise location of their whereabouts is uncertain—the text (6:31, 35) simply indicates that they were at a "lonely place" (ἔρημος). Based on the details of the pericope (6:30–44, the feeding of the five thousand), it is clear that Jesus and his disciples were on the "Jewish side" of the Sea of Galilee. During the night, as Jesus was alone on the shore praying, the disciples were getting nowhere in the boat because of the wind (6:48). Seeing their struggle, Jesus came to them walking on the water. When he got into the boat with them the wind ceased, confusing the disciples (6:51–52). The narrative then states (rather awkwardly) "when they had crossed over, they came to land at Gennesaret, and moored to the shore."[13] The disciples (now with Jesus) land not at Bethsaida—the intended destination according to 6:45 but rather Gennesaret, which does not actually represent a "crossing over" the sea—at least not in the Markan sense. Gennesaret is on the northwest, or Jewish, shore of the Sea of Galilee while Bethsaida is on the northeast (i.e., Gentile) shore. Paul J. Achtemeier attributes this geographic confusion to the rearrangement of traditional material by the author.[14] Werner H. Kelber offers a similar explanation:[15] "In the pre-Markan miracle catena the story of the walking on the sea, introduced by reference to departure for Bethsaida (6:45), was directly linked with the story of the blind man of Bethsaida (8:22–26), likewise introduced by reference to Bethsaida (8:22). Mark displaced the latter because he considered it the journey to the south." Elizabeth Struthers Malbon suggests that the geographical discrepancy is attributable to the fear

---

13. So the *RSV*. The Greek is καὶ διαπεράσαντες ἐπὶ τὴν γῆν ἦλθον εἰς Γεννησαρὲτ καὶ προσωρμίσθησαν. The issue is what the prepositional phrase ἐπὶ τὴν γῆν modifies, the adverbial participle διαπεράσαντες or the proper noun Γεννησαρέτ. The syntactical position of the phrase (i.e., following the participle διαπεράσαντες) suggests a translation of "and after crossing over upon the land they came to Gennesaret . . ." Such a translation, however, does not account for the presence of προσωρμίσθησαν (they were moored to shore). The author of the Gospel of Matthew apparently sees this tension and attempts to smooth the awkward syntax by shifting the prepositional phrase so that it follows the verb ἦλθον (see Matt 14:34).

14. Achtemeier, "Toward the Isolation of Pre-Markan Miracle Catenae," 265–91, esp. 283.

15. Kelber, *The Kingdom of God in Mark*, 58. In a later work (*Mark's Story of Jesus*, 37), Kelber is misleading when he states, "After arrival on the Gentile side, Jesus performs a vast number of healings at Gennesaret (6:53–56)." A reader would get the impression that Gennesaret is on the eastern/Gentile side of the Sea of Galilee when in fact it is not.

of the disciples to move out beyond their comfort zone and go to Gentile land. The language is stressed: Jesus *made* (ἠνάγκασεν) his disciples get into the boat and go to the other side (6:45). The Greek implies that Jesus is asking them to do something against their will. Yet, to Malbon, Jesus is asking them to do precisely what he has already done—move beyond his own people and tradition into Gentile territory.[16] The disciples launch out in the boat but are unable to make any progress because the wind was against them. They react to Jesus approaching them on water with fear (6:50) and surprise (6:51)—two reactions that represent failure. Their failure is highlighted by their return to the Jewish side of the sea (6:53). The story of the disciples' failure illustrates the concerns many scholars have "when trying to use topography to determine sub-points within a section."[17]

# Thematic Outlines

Other interpreters have attempted to identify a coherent theme such as Christology, faith, or discipleship, or they address the structure of the narrative from the perspective of rhetorical motifs and/or other narrative features. Jack Dean Kingsbury stresses the identity of Jesus (and the "problem" of the secrecy motif) as the major focus of Mark's Gospel. In so doing, he argues that Mark's presentation of Jesus is that of the Davidic Messiah-King, the Son of God, who is also Son of Man.[18] Kingsbury then divides the Gospel into three main parts. The first part (1:1–13) comprises frame material and the beginning of the narrative proper, where John introduces Jesus' identity. The second part (1:14—8:26) depicts Jesus ministering through preaching, calling disciples, teaching, healing, and exorcizing demons in and around Galilee. The third part (8:27—16:8) treats Jesus' journey to Jerusalem and his suffering, death, and resurrection.[19] The driving feature of Kingsbury's analysis is Mark's presentation of Jesus—each part imparts information on the author's view of Jesus.[20] He offers an understanding of Jesus that attempts to take seriously the cryptic "secrecy" motif, which occupies a central place

16. Malbon, *Narrative Space and Mythic Meaning*, 28.
17. Larsen, "Structure of Mark's Gospel," 144.
18. Kingsbury, *Christology of Mark's Gospel*, 55.
19. Ibid., 50–51.
20. For another division of the Gospel of Mark along christological lines, see Wright, *The New Testament and the People of God*, 390. His division is quite broad: Part 1: Who Jesus Is (1:1—8:38); Part 2: Jesus Is Going to Die (9:1—16:8).

*Introduction*

in the narrative, and to deal with the so-called "corrective Christologies."[21] Kingsbury's Christology, which will be discussed in greater detail in chapter 5, presents Jesus as the Davidic Messiah-King who is Son of God and Son of Man. Christology, no doubt, is a crucial theme in the Gospel of Mark. Yet it is not the sole theme of importance to this author and consequently, along with the other motifs that will be mentioned below, cannot be the *exclusive* organizing principle by which the narrative is constructed.

The conversion of the Twelve, however, is not only a major theme in the Gospel of Mark, but "the organizing principle by which Mark structures his Gospel," according to Richard V. Peace.[22] Mark has chosen to write this account of the life and ministry of Jesus for evangelistic purposes from the perspective of the Twelve—and in particular their step-by-step process of turning—with the hope that "his readers will follow this same path of discovery as the Twelve and so become, like them, disciples of Jesus."[23] Conversion—which involves repentance, faith, transformation—is the theme that plays "the controlling part" in the unfolding of the Gospel of Mark. This process of turning describes the gradual turning from a misunderstanding of who Jesus is to a complete and radically new understanding.[24] Peace proposes an outline that highlights this theme of conversion. He divides the Gospel into two parts (1:16—8:30; 8:31—15:39). The two parts are subdivided into six units, each of which highlights two features: (1) the title by which the Twelve come to understand Jesus; and (2) the facet of conversion that Mark points out in this unit.[25]

---

21. The corrective Christologies of which Kingsbury speaks hold that in the mind of the Evangelist the titles Son of God and Messiah/Christ were defective. He was offering a "corrective" or alternative by his presentation of Jesus as Son of Man. See Kingsbury, *Christology of Mark's Gospel*, 25–45. On the messianic secret motif, see esp. Wrede, *Messianic Secret*; Tuckett, ed., *Messianic Secret*; Räisänen, *The "Messianic Secret" in Mark*; and Telford, *Theology of the Gospel of Mark*, 41–54.

22. Peace, *Conversion in the New Testament*, 107.

23. Ibid., 110.

24. Ibid., 112.

25. Ibid., 115–16. Peace defends the validity of this structure in four ways: "(1) by showing that each unit has an independent literary structure that consciously sets it apart from the other units; (2) by showing that each of the proposed transition points between units bears similar stylistic characteristics indicating that it was Mark's intention to shift at that point to a new topic; (3) by showing that Mark has bracketed each unit so as to identify it as a unit of material that is to be interpreted together; and (4) by showing that Mark carefully uses the titles for Jesus so that no title used by 'the people' until the unit in which Jesus is revealed to possess that title."

The Turning Point in the Gospel of Mark

Peace employs these features in the following outline:[26]

1. Prologue: The preparation of Jesus for ministry (1:1–15)
2. Part I: The discovery that Jesus is the Messiah (1:16—8:30)
    A. Unit One: Jesus the teacher (1:16—4:34) [*Embracing the Word*]
    B. Unit Two: Jesus the prophet (4:35—6:30) [*Faith*]
    C. Unit Three: Jesus the Messiah (6:31—8:30) [*Repentance*]
3. Part II: The discovery that Jesus is the Son of God (8:31—15:39)
    A. Unit Four: Jesus the Son of Man (8:31—10:45) [*Discipleship*]
    B. Unit Five: Jesus the Son of David (10:46—13:37) [*Repentance*]
    C. Unit Six: Jesus the Son of God (14:1—15:39) [*Repentance*]
4. Epilogue: The conclusion of Jesus' ministry (15:40—16:8)

There is much to be said for Peace's outline and discussion of structure. First, Peace's emphasis on conversion does not ignore christological concerns. As each unit heading emphasizes, Jesus in Mark is depicted as teacher, prophet, Messiah, Son of Man, Son of David, and Son of God. Two of these titles—Messiah and Son of God—remind a reader of the opening line of the Gospel (1:1).[27] Second, as I will argue later, Christology and discipleship (of which Peace has put forward an important aspect with the emphasis on conversion) are one and the same. When one understands the identity of Jesus properly, the natural response is to follow in discipleship. Finally, the major divide in Peace's outline occurs at 8:30 after the so-called confession of Peter and response by Jesus. It is this (and the subsequent) pericope that I propose is the key scene in Mark's Gospel. Peace (for different reasons than I) sees the importance of this passage in the larger Markan story.

The narrow theme of faith is chosen as the Gospel's principle organizing feature in Christopher D. Marshall's work, *Faith as a Theme in Mark's Narrative*.[28] In this work, the Gospel is structured not sequentially but

---

26. Ibid., 123–24. I have added the italicized material in order to highlight the aspect of conversion that Peace suggests.

27. There is, of course, a significant textual issue in 1:1, namely, the inclusion of the title "Son of God" (υἱοῦ θεοῦ). This textual issue will be discussed in greater detail in chapter 5.

28. Marshall, *Faith as a Theme in Mark's Narrative*.

along rubrics related to the narrative's logic: the call to faith (1:14–15); the place of miracles in the call to faith (1:27, 44; 2:10, 12; 3:3–6; 4:40–41; 5:19; 6:2–3; 7:36–37); faith and the powerless (2:1–12; 5:21–24, 35–43; 5:24–34; 9:14–29; 10:46–52); faith and discipleship (1:14–20; 10:46–52; 13:5–6, 21–23; 9:42; 11:20–25); and the nature of unbelief (from adversaries, 2:1–12; 6:1–6a; 11:27–33; 15:27–32; from disciples, 4:35–41; 9:14–29).[29] Marshall suggests that Mark's purpose is best understood pastorally—namely, "to instruct and strengthen the faith of his readers by involving them in the story of Jesus in such a way that those features of his teaching and example that Mark has chosen to narrate are experienced as directly relevant to their present needs."[30] Thus, faith becomes the dominant hermeneutical lens through which the entire Gospel should be read.

Christology, conversion, and faith are not the only themes that have been used by interpreters to outline the Gospel of Mark. Ernst Best has championed the theme of discipleship in Mark.[31] Best articulates his study of Mark in three parts: Part I, the Disciple and the Cross (8:27—9:1; 9:2–8, 9–13, 14–29, 30–32, 33–50; 10:1–12, 13–16, 17–31, 32–34, 35–45; 8:22–26/10:46–52); Part II, The Disciple and the World (1:16–20; 2:14; 3:13–19; 6:6b–13, 30; 14:28; and 16:7); and Part III, The Disciple and the Community (14:27–28; 6:34 and the community in general).[32] As does Marshall, Best argues that the main purpose behind Mark was pastoral: "to build up his readers as Christians and show them what true discipleship is," namely, following Jesus.[33]

Another motif that interpreters propose as the primary organizing principle of the Gospel is that of rejection and misunderstanding.[34] Eduard Schweizer observes a threefold pattern in the Gospel of Mark that involves (1) a calling to follow Jesus; (2) rejection of Jesus' call; and (3) a transitional summary statement by the narrator.[35] This pattern in the first half of the Gospel is thus:

29. Ibid., vii–viii.
30. Ibid., 6.
31. Best, *Following Jesus*. Schweizer ("Portrayal of the Life of Faith in the Gospel of Mark," 387–99) argues that "following Jesus" is a metaphor that unveils the profound relations between believer and the living Lord. A more recent work—focusing on the disciples (not necessarily discipleship as Best's work does)—is Shiner, *Follow Me!*
32. Ibid., 6–7.
33. Ibid., 12.
34. Larsen, "Structure of Mark's Gospel," 146.
35. Schweizer, "Portrayal of the Life of Faith," 388.

The Turning Point in the Gospel of Mark

1. Calling to follow Jesus
   - Disciples (1:16–20)
   - Selection of the Twelve (3:13–19)
   - Sending of the Twelve (6:7–13)
2. Rejection
   - By Pharisees (3:6)
   - By his fellow citizens (6:1–6a)
   - By disciples (8:14–21)
3. Transitional Summaries
   - Jesus' healing (3:7–12)
   - Jesus' teaching (6:6b)
   - Opening of blind eyes (8:22–26)

In the middle section of the Gospel (8:27—10:52), there are three predictions regarding Jesus' suffering, death, and resurrection (8:27–32a; 9:30–32; 10:32–34). Each of the predictions is followed by a misunderstanding of the disciples and a call to follow Jesus (8:32b—9:1; 9:33–50; 10:35–45). The final scene of Jesus opening the eyes of Bartimaeus (10:46–52) forms another transitional pericope. The concluding section of Mark's Gospel (according to Schweizer) deviates from this pattern by presenting two main concerns—the temple in Jerusalem (11:1—13:37) and the passion/resurrection of Jesus (14:1—16:8). Schweizer's point is clear: "Even those who would disagree about some of the details would agree on *three main points* made by this structure of the whole Gospel: (1) Jesus is, throughout the Gospel, rejected by men . . . ; (2) man is called to follow Jesus . . . ; and (3) Jesus cannot be understood without his cross."[36]

In some ways, each of these key themes—whether it is Christology, conversion, faith, discipleship, or rejection/misunderstanding—does identify a primary concern of Mark. Yet precisely because *each* of these themes is present in the narrative, it is hard to choose *one* of them as dominant. Themes in Mark are interconnected with one another.[37] One would

---

36. Ibid., 389; emphasis original.

37. I am reminded of the landmark study of Robert Tannehill, whose essay "The Disciples in Mark" ushered in the narrative-critical perspective into Markan studies. One might think that if the disciples carry a primary role in Mark, then discipleship

*Introduction*

be hard pressed to look at discipleship alone without taking into account Mark's presentation of "Who is this?" (4:41). Rejection and misunderstanding by those with an interest in Jesus—Pharisees, fellow citizens, and disciples—would not be as forceful as a motif if it were not juxtaposed to the faith of others (primarily minor characters).[38] Especially in a narrative, as opposed to an epistle, themes are not applied rigidly, but move in and out of the narrative, giving the entire presentation texture. As Dewey observes, "A scholar's outline of Mark tells us more about which aspect of the Gospel narrative is his or her focus than it does about Mark's structure."[39]

## Topical Outlines

A number of commentators outline the Gospel along topical lines, with Jesus' healing and teaching ministry as the first major section and Jesus' death and resurrection as the second.[40] In many ways, such a manner of outlining Mark's Gospel dates back to the Gospel's first commentator—an unknown person referred to as "Pseudo-Jerome."[41] Though this author does not mention an "organizing principle" as I have been describing, he does exhibit a heightened interest in the miracles of Jesus, which he uses as a structuring element for the Gospel.[42] For example, he comments: "Mark

would be a dominant theme. However, this work was supplemented two years later with Tannehill's "Gospel of Mark as Narrative Christology." Thematic studies, while valuable, cannot be given exclusive pride of place.

38. On the faith of the minor characters, see esp. Malbon, "Major Importance of the Minor Characters," 58–86; repr., Malbon, *In the Company of Jesus*, 189–225. See also Williams, *Other Followers of Jesus*.

39. Dewey, "Mark as Interwoven Tapestry," 235.

40. For this treatment, see esp. Blomberg, *Jesus and the Gospels*, 115–25; Gnilka, *Das Evangelium nach Markus*, 1:32; Grundmann, *Das Evangelium nach Markus*, v–viii; Hare, *Mark*, 7–8; Hurtado, *Mark*, xxiv; Lagrange, *Évangile selon Saint Marc*, lix–lxx; Lane, *Gospel according to Mark*, 29–32; Malley, "Gospel According to Mark," 21–61, esp. 23–24; Mann, *Mark*, 87–93; Schweizer, *Good News According to Mark*, 7–10; and Williamson, *Mark*, 150–63.

41. Pseudo-Jerome, *Expositio quattuor Evangeliorum*, PL 30:531–90. For an English translation of this work, see Cahill, ed., *The First Commentary on Mark*. On the identification of this work as "the first Markan commentary," see Cahill, "Identification of the First Markan Commentary".

42. See Cahill's observations (*First Commentary*, 5) in his Introduction to the English translation of the commentary. He notes that the author of this commentary structured the Gospel according to fifteen miracles (*virtutes* in Latin) of Jesus, omitting from the list

arranged the passages of the Gospel in view of the Gospel itself and not for their own sake. He did not follow the order of the story but followed the order of the mysteries. This is why he tells the story of the first miracle as occurring on the sabbath."[43] Thus, a configuration device used by an early commentator of Mark's Gospel was the various miracles of Jesus. Such an observation is indeed helpful, but it can hardly be the primary organizing element Gospel since the last (i.e., fifteenth) *virtus* performed by Jesus (according to Pseudo-Jerome) occurs in Mark 10 with the healing of Bartimaeus. How would such a proposal outline the last six chapters?

A more recent example of a topical treatment, though not one focusing on the mighty deeds of Jesus, is the work by John R. Donahue and Daniel J. Harrington.[44] They divide the Gospel into three major sections, each described by the content of the section. The first major section (1:1 [*sic*]—8:22) is entitled "Jesus as the Anointed Son of God Proclaims in Galilee the Imminence of God's Reign in Powerful Words and Deeds." The second section (8:27—10:45) is entitled "Journey to Jerusalem Where Jesus, as God's Son, Is the Son of Man Who Must Suffer, Die, and Rise Again. His Life Is a Ransom for Many." The final section (11:1—16:8) is entitled "Jesus in Jerusalem: Conflict of Kingdoms; Farewell Address of Jesus; Passion, Death, and Resurrection." This outline is but one example of many that focuses upon the content of the Mark's message, and while often such outlines observe geographic movements in the Gospel, the content-driven outlines tend to group the various pericopae around the movement and work of the Gospel's central character, Jesus.[45]

The strength of such a topical approach is that the outline proposed closely follows the text of the Gospel, which in turn follows the life and ministry of Jesus from his initial appearing (1:9) to his burial (15:46). There

the cure of the woman (Mark 5:25) and the walking on water (Mark 6:48).

43. Cahill, *First Commentary*, 38.

44. Donahue and Harrington, *Gospel of Mark*, 46–50. Though Donahue and Harrington opt for this type of outline, they do observe the difficulty in choosing one overriding structure: "It might be best to think of Mark as a series of overlays that comprise multiple structures and modes of composition" (47).

45. Interpreters who combine topographical and topical elements in outlining the Gospel include Brown, *Introduction to the New Testament*, 127; Elwell and Yarbrough, *Encountering the New Testament*, 90; Gould, *Gospel According to St. Mark*, xiii–xvi; Guelich, *Mark 1:1—8:26*, xxxvii; Horsley, *Hearing the Whole Story*, 14; Johnson, *Writings of the New Testament*, 169–78; Johnson, *Gospel According to St. Mark*, 24–26; Juel, *Mark*, 23–26; Lohmeyer, *Das Evangelium des Markus*, 5–6; Nineham, *Gospel of St Mark*, 27–29; and Painter, *Mark's Gospel*, ix–xiv.

*Introduction*

is no abstract attempt on the part of the interpreter to "reduce" the Gospel to a single discernable theme or to categorize the material under the broad category of geography. In this linear form of presentation, very little substantive material risks being lost or subsumed under a false title. To many, this "life of Jesus" approach (to borrow a phrase from the [first] quest for the historical Jesus) is appealing, especially given the Evangelist's interest in Jesus' passion.[46] One is reminded again of Kähler's observation that the Gospel is a passion narrative with an extended introduction.

However, Mark's Gospel is not simply a collection of stories about Jesus loosely strung together as if it resembled a "string of pearls."[47] Rather, it is a well-crafted story from a gifted storyteller.[48] As a result, the author uses literary techniques such as foreshadowing, intercalation, hinge passages, and *inclusiones* to tell the story of Jesus.[49] Many of these features provide clues to a more appropriate manner of structuring the Gospel. It is to these literary features that I now turn.

## Literary and Rhetorical Outlines

The rise in literary analysis as it relates to biblical criticism not only gave rise to thematic studies of Mark's Gospel but also accounts for an increased tendency to look for rhetorical or other narrative-related clues in the text by which to discern a structure.[50] While there is confusion over the governing principles of rhetorical criticism versus narrative criticism, the basic

---

46. For an examination of the "quest for the historical Jesus," see Schweitzer, *Quest of the Historical Jesus*.

47. Schmidt, "Die Stellung der Evangelien in der allgemeinen Literaturgeschichte, 50–134, esp. 127.

48. For a discussion of Mark as storyteller, see Best, *Gospel as Story*, 128–33; and Moloney, *Storyteller, Interpreter, Evangelist*, 47–121.

49. Dewey ("Mark as Interwoven Tapestry," 225) offers a helpful list of these devices: "theme, manifest content, particular aspects of content such as setting, geography, or characters, form-critical type, and rhetorical devices such as key and hook words, inclusios, intercalations and frames, parallel and chiastic repetitions." "These means," she adds, "may be used to structure a single episode, to interrelate a few episodes, or to interconnect an entire narrative."

50. For narrative criticism and the Gospel of Mark, see Malbon, "Narrative Criticism," 23–49; Rhoades, "Narrative Criticism and the Gospel of Mark," 411–34 (now available in Rhoades, *Reading Mark*, 1–22); and Rhoades, "Narrative Criticism: Practices and Prospects," 254–85 (also now available in Rhoades, *Reading Mark*, 23–43). On Mark's literary world, see Tolbert, *Sowing the Gospel*, 35–79.

notion is that rhetorical critics focus on the orality of a work—especially the rhetorical convention of persuasion—while narrative critics focus on the written text.[51] There is, of course, considerable overlap between the two. For example, Duane F. Watson positions rhetorical criticism as "a historical enterprise standing between ahistorical literary criticism and historical criticism."[52] From another perspective, Mark Allan Powell similarly situates the discipline of narrative criticism as one that "focuses on stories in biblical literature and attempts to read these stories with insights drawn from the secular field of modern literary criticism. The method is eclectic, drawing from such related fields as structuralism and rhetorical criticism, with the goal of determining the effects the stories are expected to have on their audiences."[53] Here I am not proposing to examine either of these fields in depth. Rather, I am interested in the ways in which these methods aid in addressing the structure of Mark's Gospel. In other words, each method commonly employs devices or techniques—whether the focus is written or oral—that may function as an organizing principle by those looking into the structure of the Gospel. What follows is a brief survey of some of these devices and their relationship to the Gospel of Mark.[54]

## *Literary Devices*

One of the earliest literary devices came not, however, from a literary or narrative critic but from a form critic, Karl L. Schmidt. Schmidt was the first to notice Mark's penchant for "summary statements" (*Sammelberichte*).[55] *Sammelberichte* are opening or closing statements added to individual stories that tie these stories together but are otherwise, according to Schmidt,

---

51. Larsen, "Structure of Mark's Gospel," 149, 153.

52. Watson, "Rhetorical Criticism, New Testament," 399–402, esp. 400.

53. Powell, "Narrative Criticism," 201–4, esp. 201.

54. See also Collins, *Mark*, 85–93, for a discussion of compositional and structural devices.

55. Schmidt, *Der Rahmen der Geschichte Jesu*, 320. See also Hendrick, "The Role of 'Summary Statements' in the Composition of the Gospel of Mark," 289–311; and Larsen, "Structure of Mark's Gospel," 150–51. Scholars continue to debate which passages constitute specifically the *Sammelberichte*. Possible examples include: 1:14–15, 21–22, 32–34, 39, 45; 2:1–2, 13; 3:7–12; 4:1–2; 5:21; 6:6b, 12–13, 30–33, 53–56; 10:1. Others who recognize summary statements in the Gospel include Egger, *Frohbotschaft und Lehre*; and Perrin and Duling, *The New Testament*, 239–40. For critiques of this approach, see esp. Hall, *Gospel Framework*.

*Introduction*

historically worthless.⁵⁶ Statements summing up many things, especially the activity of Jesus, are key elements of Mark's narrative structure. One noteworthy example of the decisive role summary statements plays in the narrative regards the Prologue and in particular its precise limits. Leander Keck argues that 1:14–15—which offers the detail of the activity and message of Jesus—goes more properly with the preceding material (1:1–13) than subsequent material.⁵⁷ Keck's primary reason is the noun τὸ εὐαγγέλιον, which occurs in 1:1 and 1:15, forms as it were an *inclusio* (another literary device to be discussed below).⁵⁸ In addition, the handing over (παραδοθῆ ναι) of John the Baptist in 1:14 is theological information presented to the reader and so "fulfills the word of John about Jesus, while at the same time it rounds out the over-arching interest in τὸ εὐαγγέλιον."⁵⁹ Thus, the *Sammelberichte* of 1:14–15 looks back, in Keck's view, not forward. In many ways, Keck's view was contradictory to the more established view set forth by R. H. Lightfoot, which held the Prologue to end at 1:13. Lightfoot's argument was one of content: "only in verses 9 to 13 do we learn that He is Jesus from Nazareth of Galilee, and that He, Jesus of Nazareth, is the unique or only Son of God."⁶⁰ One critic, Frank J. Matera, builds on the work of Lightfoot but offers an insightful literary reason why the extent of the Prologue ends at 1:13.⁶¹ He suggests that in vv. 1–13, the narrator communicates privileged information about Jesus and John the Baptist that is crucial in properly understanding the Gospel message. The additional information (see primarily 1:2–3, 10, 12–13) "is communicated *only* to the reader; none of the human characters within the narrative (Jesus excepted) is privy to it."⁶² In contrast, the characters in the story are privy to the information set

---

56. Ibid., 17.

57. Keck, "Introduction to Mark's Gospel," 352–70. Others who share this view include Pesch, *Das Markusevangelium*, 1:71–74; Marcus, *Mark 1-8*, 137–39; and Boring, "Mark 1:1–15 and the Beginning of the Gospel," 43–81.

58. Keck, "Introduction to Mark's Gospel," 359–60.

59. Ibid., 361.

60. Lightfoot, *The Gospel Message of St. Mark*, 15–20, esp. 17. Lightfoot's reasoning became very influential. Among those holding to this view include Cranfield, *Gospel According to St. Mark*, 33–60; Lane, *Gospel According to Mark*, 39–40; Schweizer, *The Good News According to Mark*, 28–41; and Taylor, *The Gospel According to Mark*, 151.

61. Matera, "The Prologue as the Interpretive Key to Mark's Gospel," 3–20, esp. 5.

62. Ibid., 5. Emphasis original.

forth in the summary statement of 1:14–15. According to Matera, this is "the most telling clue to the extent of the Prologue."[63]

Francis J. Moloney identifies four "textual markers" (1:1; 1:14–15; 8:31; and 16:1–4) that alert the reader that the author is "up to something."[64] These textual markers permit a reader to begin to plot the literary design of the author. Moloney proposes a fourfold outline[65]:

1. Prologue: The beginning (1:1–13)

2. Who is Jesus? (1:14—8:30)

    - Jesus and the Jews (1:14—3:6)

    - Jesus and his own (3:7—6:6a)

    - Jesus and the disciples (6:6b—8:30)

3. The suffering and vindicated Son of Man: Christ and Son of God (8:31—15:47)

    - On the way from blindness to sight (8:31—10:52)

    - The symbolic end of Israel and the world (11:1—13:37)

    - The crucifixion of the Son of Man, the Christ, and the Son of God (14:1—15:47)

4. Epilogue: A new beginning (16:1-8)

Several scholars propose the literary technique of intercalation or "sandwiching" as a key structural device.[66] Intercalations or sandwiches

---

63. Ibid., 6.

64. Moloney, *Gospel of Mark*, 16–20. Moloney notes that "narrative units are not separated by brick walls. One flows into the other, looks back to issues already mentioned, and hints at themes yet to come" (19). Similarly Carson, Moo, and Morris (*Introduction to the New Testament*, 89) suggest that the Markan narrative is punctuated by six "transitional paragraphs" or statements (1:14-15; 3:7-12; 6:1-6; 8:27-30; 11:1-11; 14:1-2), which divide Mark's account into seven basic sections. While not "markers" in the above sense, Pesch (*Naherwartungen*, 54–67) observes an ancient literary symmetry in the Gospel, with the first three major sections (1:2—3:6; 3:7—6:29; 6:30—8:26) corresponding to the final three sections (8:27—10:52; 11:1—12:44; 14:1—16:8) except for chap. 13, which carries for the Evangelist a special place. See also Pesch, *Das Markusevangelium*.

65. Moloney, *Gospel of Mark*, 20.

66. Edwards, "Markan Sandwiches"; Shepherd, *Markan Sandwich Stories*; Shepherd, "The Narrative Function of Markan Intercalations"; and van Oyen, "Intercalation and Irony in the Gospel of Mark." As we will see later, Kee (*Community of the New Age*, 75) rejects a single manner of outlining Mark's Gospel because of "the thematic complexity

*Introduction*

are "literary conventions with theological purposes. Each sandwich unit consists of an A¹-B-A² sequence, with the B-component functioning as the theological key to the flanking halves."⁶⁷ Shepherd identifies twenty different Markan passages in which scholars have determined to be intercalations. Based on consensus of these commentators, he identifies six passages as clearly representing this technique:⁶⁸

1. Jesus' Relatives and the Beelzebul Controversy (Mark 3:20–35)
2. Jairus and the Woman with the Hemorrhage (5:21–43)
3. The Mission of the Twelve and the Beheading of John the Baptist (6:7–32)
4. The Cursing of the Fig Tree and the Cleansing of the Temple (11:12–25)
5. The Passion Plot and the Anointing (14:1–11)
6. Peter's Denial and Jesus' Trial (14:53–72)

Another literary device commonly employed by Markan commentators to address the overall structure of the Gospel is that of chiasms.⁶⁹ A chiasm is a concentric schema whereby "the crosswise repetition of one or several elements" is place around a central (usually significant) element in the center.⁷⁰ This schema resembles the sandwiching technique referred to above. Bas M. F. van Iersel notes that this was common *compositional* device in the first-century Greco-Roman world, so much so that schoolchildren had to learn the alphabet both forward and backwards.⁷¹ This device can be applied at the microlevel, that is, within a single episode, at the mesolevel (a combination of episodes), or at the macrolevel (an entire

---

of Mark." However, he does note with appreciation the significance of Mark's interpolation technique (see 54–56).

67. Edwards, *Gospel According to Mark*, 11.
68. Shepherd, *Markan Sandwich Stories*, 388–92.
69. On the use of chiasms in Markan studies, see Dewey, *Markan Public Debate*, 48; Humphrey, *He is Risen?*, 4; Rhoades, Dewey, and Michie, *Mark as Story*, 51–55, esp. 53; and Scott, "Chiastic Structure," 17–26. A more popular work that relies on a chiastic structure is Dart, *Decoding Mark*.
70. Van Iersel, *Mark*, 68–86, here 71. See also van Iersel, *Reading Mark*, 18–30.
71. Ibid., 70–71. See also Stock, "Chiastic Awareness and Education in Antiquity."

composition).⁷² Thus, van Iersel's macrostructure of Mark's Gospel (after the title of 1:1) is as follows:⁷³

[A]  Prologue, the wilderness (1:2–13)

[B]  Prospective hinge (1:14-15)

[C]  *Galilee* (1:16—8:21)

[D]  Frame: blind (seeing) (8:22-26)

[E]  The Way (8:27—10:45)

[D′] Frame: blind (seeing) (10:46-52)

[C′] *Jerusalem* (11:1—15:39)

[B′] Retrospective hinge (15:40-41)

[A′] Epilogue, the tomb (15:42—16:8)

A final literary device underscores an altogether different technique. Ben C. Witherington, working within a socio-rhetorical model, suggests a macrostructure of the Gospel corresponding to the questions in the narrative (1:27; 2:7, 15, 24; 4:41; 6:2; 7:5) culminating with Jesus' question to the disciples in 8:27.⁷⁴ The remainder of the narrative (8:27—16:20) seeks to answer that question ("Who is Jesus?") and the attendant question—What is Jesus' mission? In brief, Witherington's outline is divided into four parts: (1) the questions—who and why (1:1—8:27); (2) the "who" question answered (8:27-30); (3) what is the mission? (8:31; 9:31; 10:32); and (4) mission accomplished (11:1—16:20).⁷⁵ The questions all focus on the identity of Jesus; thus, the major concern of the Gospel, according to Witherington,

---

72. Van Iersel, *Mark*, 72–76. The bold print (original) observes the topographic elements of the Gospel, which has previously been noted. For a discussion of the notion of van Iersel's "hinge passages," see pp. 83–84. See also Stock, "Hinge Transitions in Mark's Gospel."

73. Ibid., 84. See also Standaert, *L'Évangile selon Marc*, 38–109.

74. Witherington III, *Gospel of Mark*, 36–39. Robbins ("Socio-Rhetorical Criticism," 165–209, esp. 165) defines socio-rhetorical criticism as "a textually-based method that uses programmatic strategies to invite social, cultural, historical, psychological, aesthetic, ideological and theological information into a context of minute exegetical activity." While I will "categorize" other socio-rhetorical outlines in the section to follow, Witherington himself seems to suggest that his model should be viewed under the auspices of literary techniques since the "original reader would have read it aloud to himself" (16).

75. Witherington III (*Gospel of Mark*, 44–49) sees the Gospel concluding with the so-called "longer ending" (16:9–20).

is Christology. As we have seen before, it is hard to separate themes and outlines neatly. Here is one more example of a commentator using a literary device (questions) to punctuate the overarching theme of the Gospel (Christology).[76]

## *Rhetorical Devices*

As mentioned above, rhetorical approaches to a biblical text focus on oral rather than written concerns. This is not the place to discuss, much less critique, rhetorical criticism as a discipline.[77] Rhetorical criticism is complex and evolving within the broader field of biblical criticism. As has already been noted, it shares the stage with narrative or literary criticism on some points while (in its modern or "new rhetoric" form) it overlaps with the emerging disciplines of text linguistics, semiotics, reader-response criticism, discourse analysis, and speech-act theory, among others.[78] At this point, four approaches from many possible "rhetorical" subdisciplines will be discussed. I hope this simple survey will be sufficient to show that structural concerns are often inseparable from hermeneutical concerns.

**a.** *A Classical Approach.* Benoît H. M. G. M. Standaert employs the common fivefold division of classical rhetoric in his outline of the Gospel of Mark:[79]

- *Exordium* (1:1–13)
- *Narratio* (1:14—6:13)
- *Probatio* (6:14—10:52)
- *Refutatio* (11:1—15:47)
- *Conclusio* (16:1–8)

One easily sees Aristotelian influence on Standaert's work.[80] An interesting and surprising feature emerges, however, in that Standaert couples

---

76. For another commentator that stresses the asking of rhetorical questions as a storytelling (though not necessarily a structural) technique, see Fowler, *Let the Reader Understand*, 131–34.

77. For a helpful essay on this discipline, see Wuellner, "Where is Rhetorical Criticism Taking Us?"

78. Watson, "Rhetorical Criticism," 401.

79. Standaert, *L'Évangile selon Marc*, 42. See also Stock, *Call to Discipleship*, 49.

80. Aristotle, *The "Art" of Rhetoric*.

this classical rhetorical division with the literary analysis of concentric compositions and genre analysis of ancient drama.[81] The combination of rhetoric, literary, and genre analysis makes Standaert's proposal unique among Markan commentators.

**b.** *A Linguistic Approach.* John G. Cook's *The Structure and Persuasive Power of Mark* offers an example of the study of Markan structure from the perspective of text linguistics.[82] As the name implies, "text linguistics" originates from the procedure that whole texts are analyzed rather than single components (i.e., sentences).[83] It is a discipline that has its origins in a secular field (not biblical criticism) and goes under several different rubrics depending on the perspective under review: semantics (the relationship between a sign and its meaning), pragmatics (the relationship between a sign, its meaning, and its users), semiotics (the observance of signs), or speech act (the use of language to "do something").[84] The vocabulary associated with text linguistics is sophisticated, and an attempt to explain this methodology is not within the scope of my work.[85] Regardless of the sophistication of this method of inquiry, the resulting outline is virtually the same as has been described above in many of the other categories. Cook uses the linguistic device of "text part" to distinguish the Markan material. In fact, he uses several layers or "frames" to discuss these text parts: Frame 00 contains the editor's title (or "name label"); the frame labeled 0 contains the title of the work; Frame 1 contains the narrator's description of characters and events; and Frames 2, 3, and 4 are used for words found in the mouths of the various characters in the narrative. Classification of these final three frames (Frames 2–4) is determined based on the type of communication. A frame that includes characters speaking to characters is Frame 2. If a character tells a story in which the members of the story communicate with one another, then that results in a classification notation of Frame 3. When a speech in Frame 3 itself indicates

---

81. Standaert, *L'Évangile selon Marc*, 174.
82. Cook, *Structure and Persuasive Power of Mark*.
83. Ibid., 1.
84. Ibid., 87–89, 351.
85. For a general discussion of this method, see Baldinger, *Semantic Theory*. For a discussion for applicable to the study of Mark's Gospel, see Boers, "Reflections on the Gospel of Mark"; and Danove, *Linguistics and Exegesis in the Gospel of Mark*.

*Introduction*

a communication, that communication will be classified in Frame 4.[86] This technique produces the following summary outline:[87]

Frame 00: Superscript ("Gospel according to Mark")

Frame 0: Prologue (1:1)

Frame 1:

- Text Part 1: John and Jesus in the wilderness (1:2-13)
- Text Part 2: Jesus' ministry in Galilee and environs (1:14—8:26)
- Text Part 3: Jesus' journey to Jerusalem (8:27—10:52)
- Text Part 4: Jesus in Jerusalem and environs (11:1—16:8)

Despite the particularized *verba*, this approach in effect simply yields another topographical outline.

**C.** *Ancient Drama Approach.* Mary Ann Beavis employs what she calls a "reader oriented" approach. In this approach, she ignores repetition and any other so-called textual marker and opts for a structure based on the alternation of blocks of narrative and teaching. "The overall structure of the Gospel thus resembles that of a five-act hellenistic play, with the place of the four choruses taken by teaching scenes" (the first of which—4:1-34, especially vv. 11-12—is foundational).[88] The five-act sequence can be visualized in this manner:

1. 1:1—3:35 (Narrative: Prologue, controversies); 4:1-34 (Teaching: Parables [*See!*])
2. 4:35—6:52 (Narrative: Miracles); 6:53—7:23 (Teaching: Clean and unclean)
3. 7:24—9:29 (Narrative: Revelations); 9:30—10:45 (Teaching: Discipleship)
4. 10:46—12:44 (Narrative: Jerusalem, controversies); 13:1-37 (Teaching: Apocalyptic discourse [*Hear!*])
5. 14:1—16:8 (Narrative: Passion, empty tomb)

86. To find the meanings of these various frames, see ibid., 122-25, and 139-42.

87. The summary outline is contained in Appendix 2 of Cook's work (*Structure and Persuasive Power*, 343-47). The full linguistic outline comprises most of the book (see pp. 172-283).

88. Beavis, *Mark's Audience*, 163-65.

The Turning Point in the Gospel of Mark

The primary strength of Beavis's outline is her attention to the Hellenistic literary culture in which the Gospel was composed and the interplay between the narrative and didactic elements of the Gospel. The idea of Mark resembling a Hellenistic play is found frequently in the literature (see below), but usually in discussion on genre, not structure. Two recent commentators have, like Beavis, observed the resemblance to a Greek play and have outlined the Gospel in three or more "acts." Richard T. France, after acknowledging the author's heading and prologue, divides the gospel into three acts centered around the physical presence of Jesus: (1) Galilee (1:14—8:21); (2) On the Way to Jerusalem (8:22—10:52); and (3) Jerusalem (11:1—16:8).[89] Similarly, Marcus focuses on the length of the various pericopae and proposes a structure made up of six major sections—all of approximately equal length[90]—divided into three acts. His outline looks like this:[91]

1. 1:1–15—Prologue (15 verses, 248 words)
2. 1:16—8:21—Act I: Jesus' Earthly Ministry (290 verses, 4,813 words)
    a. 1:16—3:6: First Major Section—Honeymoon and Beginning of Opposition (64 verses, 1,095 words)
    b. 3:7—6:6a: Second Major Section—The Struggle Intensifies (118.5 verses, 1,958 words)
    c. 6:6b—8:21: Third Major Section—Feasts (107.5 verses, 1,760 words)
3. 8:22—10:52—Act II: Fourth Major Section—"On the Way" (117 verses, 2,076 words)
4. 11:1—15:47—Act III: Jerusalem Ministry (231 verses, 3,828 words)
    a. 11:1—13:37: Fifth Major Section—Teaching (113 verses, 1,963 words)
    b. 14:1—15:47: Sixth Major Section—Dying (118 verses, 1,865 words)
5. 16:1–8: Epilogue (8 verses, 136 words)

---

89. France, *Gospel of Mark*, 13–14.
90. Except for the first section (2:1—3:6), which is about half the length of the others.
91. Marcus, *Mark 1–8*, 64. Marcus does not specify whether his word count is based on the number of words in Greek or English.

**d.** *"New" Rhetorical Approaches.* Watson observes that there is a "new rhetoric" on the scene now. This approach "redefines rhetoric as argumentation with a persuasive intent and focuses on the audience/readers of rhetoric. This historical and social situation that produced speech and in which it was enacted becomes central. Rhetoric is a liaison between text and social context, assessing the latter through the former."[92] A primary proponent of this approach in New Testament studies is Vernon K. Robbins.[93] In 1984, he published a sociorhetorical interpretation of Mark under the title *Jesus the Teacher*.[94] Robbins's stated goal for such an investigation is "to read the Gospel of Mark in the context of a wider range of literature from the Mediterranean world…both within and outside Jewish and Christian circles of influence."[95] Robbins favors certain "stylistic traits," which lead to a three-step progression that, in turn, is an elaboration of 1:1. The three-step progressions are: (1) Jesus goes to a new place with the disciples; (2) he engages in a special interaction; and (3) as a result of this interaction, he summons his disciples anew. This pattern of behavior on the part of Jesus is repeated and serves to differentiate the various stages of development in Mark's narrative.[96] This three-step progression allows Robbins to see six major sections (in addition to an introduction and conclusion). Robbins's outline, entitled "The Gospel of Jesus Christ, the Son of God" (an obvious reference to 1:1; see above), is as follows:[97]

Introduction: Jesus and John the Baptist (1:1–13)
1. Jesus and the Gospel of God (1:14—3:6)
2. The Healing Son of God (3:7—5:43)
3. The Rejected Prophet (6:1—8:26)
4. The Suffering, Dying, Rising Son of Man (8:27—10:45)
5. The Authoritative Son of David (10:46—12:44)
6. The Future Son of Man and the Dying Messiah-King (13:1—15:47)
Conclusion (16:1–8)

---

92. Watson, "Rhetorical Criticism," 401.
93. He examines this method in *Exploring the Texture of Texts*.
94. Robbins, *Jesus the Teacher*.
95. Ibid., 12.
96. Ibid., 19–51, esp. 20–26. See also his "Summons and Outline in Mark."
97. Ibid., 27.

Other "new rhetorical" interpreters employ different features to outline the Gospel.[98] Ched Myers, for example, sees the three apocalyptic movements or what he calls "pillar stories" of Jesus' baptism, transfiguration, and crucifixion as "anchors" in Mark. "At the level of the narrative, each moment is fundamental to the regeneration of plot: the baptism opened the subversive mission of the kingdom, the transfiguration deepened it by confirming the second call to discipleship. Golgatha becomes the 'practice' of the first two moments: 'baptism' (which according to 10:38 is a metaphor for political execution) and 'cross' (8:34)."[99]

The overarching strength of these literary or rhetorical models is the close attention *to the text* of Mark. Such an emphasis is not far from the goals of this present work, but one has to wonder whether these tools alone can successfully get at the heart of the *author's* developmental structure.[100]

## Outline "Alternatives"

In his 1975 commentary, Paul J. Achtemeier observes: "A satisfactory solution to the problem of the outline of Mark thus remains to be found. Perhaps this is due to insufficient attention to the narrative of Mark on the part of scholars, or perhaps it is due to the fact that Mark himself did not shape his Gospel with any such central point in mind, but rather moved, section by section, to the chronological as well as theological climax of his Gospel."[101] Since that time, there has been a plethora of analyses of Mark's Gospel from the perspective of narrative criticism—most of them, as noted above, choosing some method of division for the structure of the Gospel.[102] However, a few interpreters of Mark continue to argue that the

---

98. Vena ("The Rhetorical and Theological Center of Mark's Gospel," 327–45, esp. 328–29) combines a "new rhetorical" emphasis with the literary device of chiasm—the center or fulcrum of the chiasm being 8:34—9:1, Jesus' call to suffering and discipleship. The broad pattern of his outline is: A (1:1–13); B (1:14—7:23); C (7:24—10:52); B′(11:1—14:31); A′ (14:32—16:8).

99. Myers, *Binding the Strong Man*, 390–91. Another example of a sociopolitical reading is Waetjen, *Reordering of Power*. Waetjen is less concerned about providing an overall outline for the Gospel and instead concentrates on offering a reading the text of Mark's Gospel in light of the historical sociology.

100. For a helpful discussion on the author, see Hirsch, *Validity in Interpretation*, 1–23.

101. Achtemeier, *Mark*, 40.

102. For example, see Rhoades et al., *Mark as Story*. For a recent scholarly examination

*Introduction*

Gospel has no discernable outline, or at least not a linear outline as is often proposed. Robert H. Gundry argues that "the Gospel of Mark presents only a loose disposition of materials governed by little more than the initiatory character of John the Baptizer's ministry and its locale in the wilderness at the Jordan River, the charismatic character and Galilean locale of the bulk of Jesus' ministry, and the finality of Jesus' passion and resurrection and their locale in Jerusalem . . . Mark presents a collage, not a diptych or a triptych or any other carefully segmented portrayal of Jesus."[103] Edwin K. Broadhead refuses to present an outline in his brief commentary on Mark, choosing instead to address what the Gospel is not (an oral presentation, visual, bare historical report, a story of the gods, a psychological profile, or a modern biography) versus what it is—"a narrative account of Jesus' ministry and death, set in sequential order."[104] Similarly, William R. Telford simply presents several structures for consideration without offering one as dominant.[105]

Two interpreters—Howard Clark Kee and Joanna Dewey—do not go as far as Gundry or Broadhead but are pessimistic about whether Mark's Gospel has a single *linear* outline. Kee pays close attention to the key themes in the Gospel such as kingdom, discipleship, and eschatology. Yet he suggests "no simple outline can do justice to the thematic complexity of Mark."[106] Instead, he suggests that these themes "run like a great fugue throughout the Gospel."[107] Dewey argues persuasively that Mark's Gospel does not have a discernable linear outline but is rather like an "interwoven tapestry" made up of "overlapping structures and sequences, forecasts of what is to come and echoes of what has already been said."[108] She further concludes that this nonlinear compositional style is a characteristic feature

---

of this work, see Iverson and Skinner, eds., *Mark as Story: Retrospect and Prospect*.

103. Gundry, *Mark*, 1045–46.

104. Broadhead, *Mark*, 139; emphasis supplied.

105. Telford, *Mark*, 101–4. Of the few structures Telford presents, he especially mentions Schweizer (101), van Iersel (103), and Edwards (104).

106. Kee, *Community of the New Age*, 75.

107. Ibid.

108. Dewey, "Mark as Interwoven Tapestry," 224. Dewey gets this "interwoven tapestry" motif from Johnson, *Commentary on the Gospel According to St. Mark*, 24, whose metaphor for the structure of Mark's Gospel was an "oriental carpet with crisscrossing patterns."

of aural narrative (but submits that we can continue to study the Gospel using literary analysis).[109]

## TURNING POINTS AND THE GENRE OF MARK

Outlines and turning points, however, are two different things. The issue at hand with regard to Mark's Gospel is, regardless of how one outlines or breaks the material into constituent parts, does the Markan *narrative* have a similar decisive turning point?

## Nature of Turning Point

Before addressing the Markan turning point, it is necessary to revisit the definition of turning point and examine it in the context of literary criticism. In the work commonly known as *The Poetics* (Περὶ Ποιητικῆς in Greek, derived from the work's first two words), Aristotle deals with the gist of drama (δρᾶν, which for him means it presents people who μιμοῦνται δρῶντας, lit. representing or imitating actions), especially its development of plot—a matter of considerable importance if the work is to be a success (*Poet.* 1.1). Before defining plot (μῦθος), Aristotle carefully distinguishes two kinds of δρᾶν—the actions of people doing good things (τὰς καλὰς ἐμιμοῦντο πράξεις), which he calls "tragedy" (τραγῳδία) and the actions of lesser people doing common or lesser things (οἱ δὲ εὐτελέστεροι τὰς τῶν φαύλων), which he calls "comedy" (κωμῳδία) (*Poet.* 3.8). Tragedy is the imitation of an action that is great and complete in itself and does not employ mere narration or recital (ἐπαγγελία). It evokes empathy and fear (ἐλέου καὶ φόβου) to the observer (*Poet.* 6.2–4). Every tragedy has six constituent parts:

1. Plot (μῦθος)
2. Character (ἤθη)
3. Style (λέξις)
4. Thought (διάνοια)
5. Appearance (ὄψις)
6. Music (μελοποιία)

109. Ibid., 224, 236.

*Introduction*

Plot (μῦθος), according to Aristotle, is the most important—something he calls the soul (ψυχή) of a tragedy—and is defined as the putting together or the arrangement of the matters (σύνθεσιν τῶν πραγμάτων) (*Poet.* 6.8, 20).[110] Plot is further developed to contain two movements of sorts: the first phase, which he calls complication (πλοκή) and the second phase, which often goes by the label dénoument (λύσις) (*Poet.* 18.3). Two of the most important elements in bringing an emotional effect to the observers in this movement from complication to dénoument are "reversals" or (περιπέτειαι) and "recognitions" (ἀναγνωρίσεις). These are moments in the drama where the course of action that one is seeing in the first phase suddenly changes direction or course and generally involve some sort of recognition moment with respect to the characters. These two notions—reversal and recognition—come very close to what many contemporary literary critics label "climax" or "turning point."[111] Aristotle's *Poetics* is important in analyzing the structure of a tragedy in particular, but also that of any piece of literature that seeks to tell a story.

At the turn of the nineteenth century, the German literary critic Gustav Freytag analyzed the structure of a five-movement play in a manner that has since been referred to as "Freytag's Pyramid."[112] The first three movements—introduction, inciting moments, rising action—"rise" as the pyramid image suggests. The fourth movement is the apex of the pyramid, which Freytag called the climax. The final two movements—falling action and catastrophe—parallel the rising of the pyramid with the so-called falling side of the pyramid. Both Freytag and the vast majority of literary analysis since the time of Aristotle see this moment of climax as a crisis point or turning point in the drama.

Freytag's fivefold movement (or Aristotle's threefold) creates what many scholars simply refer to as the beginning, middle, and end of a

110. The modern literary critic Meyer Howard Abrams (*Glossary of Literary Terms*, 159) defines plot similarly: "The plot in a dramatic or narrative work is constituted by its events and actions, as these are rendered and ordered toward achieving particular emotional and artistic effects." In addition to the definition of Abrams, Culpepper (*Anatomy of the Fourth Gospel*, 79–80, esp. 80) presents five other definitions of plot, but considers Abrams's "a concise synthesis of most of the elements of the other definitions."

111. To modern literary critics, a turning point is the observable moment when—in the development of a plot—there is a definite change in direction and a reader begins to be aware that the story/plot is moving toward its end. See Cuddon, *A Dictionary of Literary Terms*, s.v. "turning point," 950. Aristotle's definition of περιπέτεια is "a change of the situation into the opposite" (*Poet.* 11.1).

112. Freytag, *Technique of the Drama*, 114–40.

narrative or play. Aristotle observed this early on: "A whole is what has a beginning and middle and end. A beginning is that which is not a necessary consequence of anything else but after which something else exists or happens as a natural result. An end on the contrary is that which inevitable [sic] or, as a rule, the natural result of something else but from which nothing follows; a middle follows something else and something follows from it. Well-constructed plots must therefore not begin and end at random, but must embody the formulae we have stated" (*Poet.* 7.3–7 [Fyfe, LCL]).

Aristotle's *Poetics* or Freytag's pyramid is helpful in analyzing any piece of dramatic literature, whether ancient or modern, drama or comedy. But is the document we call "the Gospel of Mark" a drama? It would not be judged by most to be a comedy.[113] So what is the genre of Mark's Gospel and how does genre aid (if at all) in the understanding of the so-called turning point?

## Genre and Turning Point

Examination and attempts at making an ironclad classification of the genre of Mark's Gospel is not new within NT scholarship.[114] At one time or another, the Gospel has been identified with almost every conceivable genre of ancient literature: Homeric-type epic poems,[115] ancient biography or *bios*,[116] Jewish novel,[117] Jewish midrash,[118] Hellenistic novel,[119] Greek tragedy,[120] apocalyptic historical monograph,[121] Ancient Near Eastern

---

113. But see Via, *Kerygma and Comedy in the New Testament*.

114. On genre in general, see Hirsch, *Validity in Interpretation*, 68–126; and Fowler, *Kinds of Literature*. On the nature of genre applied to gospel studies, see Burridge, "About People." For a discussion of genre and Mark's Gospel, see esp. Bryan, *Preface to Mark*, 9–26; and Guelich, "The Gospel Genre."

115. MacDonald, *The Homeric Epics and the Gospel of Mark*.

116. Burridge, *What Are the Gospels*. See also, Talbert, *What is a Gospel?*

117. Vines, *Problem of Markan Genre*. These novels include canonical/deuterocanonical books such as Judith, Esther, Daniel, and Tobit.

118. Sabin, *Reopening the Word*.

119. Beavis, *Mark's Audience*, 31–44; Tolbert, *Sowing the Gospel*, 48–83; Tolbert, "The Gospel of Mark," 45–56, esp. 52–53.

120. Bilezikian, *Liberated Gospel*; Hooker, *Beginnings*, 1–22; Standaert, *L'Évangile selon Marc*, 373–494, esp. 385–92.

121. Collins, *Is Mark's Gospel a Life of Jesus?* This work can now be accessed in Collins, *The Beginning of the Gospel*, 1–38.

*Introduction*

combat myth,¹²² oral performance,¹²³ and apologetic tract.¹²⁴ Others hold that Mark's Gospel is *sui generis*—a new type of literature without previous parallel.¹²⁵ It is not necessary for me to choose one genre as dominant. In saying this, I am not saying that genre is not important. I believe it is. What kind of book a reader thinks he or she is reading can and often does shape the manner in which he or she reads.¹²⁶ However, the more appropriate question to ask, especially in light of my interest in the narrative turning point, is what do these various genres have in common and how will the answer to this question aid in the quest of ascertaining the Gospel's turning point? Here I will survey briefly five of the genres referred to above—Greek tragedy, Hellenistic novel, apologetic tract, Jewish midrash, and Graeco-Roman biography—and show that in each case, plot is the common feature.

## *Greek Tragedy*

Since the 1920s, New Testament scholars have compared the Gospel of Mark with ancient Greek tragedies.¹²⁷ In many ways, it is the easiest of these examples to show the mutual element of plot given the Aristotelian definition. Gilbert C. Bilezikian has argued most extensively that Mark's Gospel was written within the milieu of Greek tragedy since tragedy was one of the dominant literary strategies in the Roman empire of the first century.¹²⁸ All the features of Greek tragedy articulated by Aristotle in *Poetics*, for example, are present in Mark: the Gospel narrates the actions of a

---

122. Miller, "The Kingship of Jesus," 1–16, esp. 7–9.

123. Shiner, *Proclaiming the Gospel*.

124. Roskam, *Purpose of the Gospel of Mark*, 217–38, esp. 236.

125. Achtemeier, *Mark*, 4–5, 42; France, *Gospel of Mark*, 4–15; Lane, *Gospel of Mark*, 1; and Donahue and Harrington, *Mark*, 13–16. Guelich (*Mark 1:1—8:26*, xxii) sees the Gospels belonging *formally* to the broad category of Hellenistic biography, while *materially* they are *sui generis*.

126. Marcus, *Mark 1–8*, 64.

127. The early work includes Riddle, "The Martyr Motif in the Gospel According to Mark"; Carré, "The Literary Structure of the Gospel of Mark"; Burch, "Tragic Action in the Second Gospel"; and Bundy, "Dogma and Drama in the Gospel of Mark." The latter three are cited by Frederick C. Grant in his 1943 Cole Lectures (published as *The Earliest Gospel*, 133) as he advocates this point: "Some scholars have seen in Mark the pattern of a Greek tragedy, and indeed with some probability."

128. Bilezikian, *Liberated Gospel*, 33–50, esp. 50. Weeden (*Traditions in Conflict*, 17) remarks that Mark "approximates the style of Greek drama." See also, Inch, *Mark as Tragedy*, 71–168.

good person (Jesus); the observer experiences the emotional effects of fear and empathy; the plot develops along the standard formula of (1) complication (1:1—8:26); (2) crisis (8:27–8:30); and (3) dénoument (8:31—16:8). Bilezikian's reading of Mark's Gospel in light of this paradigm yields the following summary: "The action in the Gospel of Mark follows a course identical to the one recommended by Aristotle for Greek tragedies. In the language proper to dramatic composition, it can be said that the first half of the Gospel constitutes the complication, the recognition at Caesarea Philippi is the crisis, and the remainder of the Gospel is the denouement."[129]

Whether the author consciously tried to mimic the Greek tragedy is hopelessly unprovable; rather, if one can study the structure, language, and plot of the Gospel narrative and detect similarities in design, then it holds that the "movement" of Mark's plot resembles the Greek tragedy. And if it resembles it, then we are in a better position to examine the interim climax or crisis point in the story.

## Hellenistic Novel

Another form of literature that Mark's Gospel has been compared to is the Greek ancient novel. Mary Ann Tolbert has been an especially strong advocate for this form and has labeled her suggestion of it as "a new hypothesis for genre" of Mark's Gospel.[130] She notes that while only five complete novels have survived, fragments from many others exist—some which can be dated as early as the first century BCE.[131] Two of the five, Xenophon's *Ephesian Tale* and Chariton's *Chaereas and Callirhoe*, can be dated broadly from 100 BCE to 50 CE, well within the time frame with which Mark would be familiar.[132] These novels are all erotic novels, that is, their basic plot centers on the familiar work of the god Eros. Clearly, the Gospel of Mark does not fit this pattern. However, Tolbert argues that when read closely, Mark does share features with this ancient literary form, especially in terms of plot. Tolbert writes:

---

129. Bilezikian, *Liberated Gospel*, 55.

130. Tolbert, *Sowing the Gospel*, 59.

131. Ibid., 62. The five are Chariton's *Chaereas and Callirhoe*, Xenophon's *An Ephesian Tale*, Longus's *Daphnis and Chloe*, Achilles Tatius's *Leucippe and Clitophon*, and Heliodorus's *An Ethiopian Tale*. For these, see Reardon, *Collected Ancient Greek Novels*.

132. Tolbert, *Sowing the Gospel*, 62.

*Introduction*

> The literary heritage of the Greek novel combines Greek drama and historiography. As prose writing, it takes its basic narrative structure from historiography but blends manners, style, and concerns of drama and epic into its stories. The ancient novel is 'fundamentally drama in substance and historiography in its outward form.' The major characters in the novels are often historical persons of earlier periods or the fictional sons and daughters of actual historical figures. The action takes place in real cities and involves practices and groups that truly existed (e.g., shipwrecks, pirates, slavery, crucifixion). This essential historiographic form gives verisimilitude to the conventionalized and formulaic plots themselves. The internal dynamics of the plots owe much to drama and epic: brief, dramatic scenes, dialogue with narrative summaries interspersed, episodic development, beginnings with minimal introduction or *in medias res*, central turning points, and final recognition scenes. The ancient novel, then, like the modern novel, is a remarkably synthesizing genre, pulling together a great variety of earlier forms and adapting and diluting them for a larger audience.[133]

Talbert dismisses this as a possible explanation of the genre of Mark because of the fictitious nature of the story. "Both history and biography, however legendary, claim to speak of actual people and real events."[134] However, Tolbert never claims—nor do I—that the Gospel of Mark is fictitious. Rather, she simply argues that Mark's Gospel shares many of the same characteristics with these novels. I simply want to observe is that one of these characteristics is plot development.

## *Apologetic Tract*

A relative newcomer on the genre scene—as it relates to Mark—is that of an apologetic tract. Hendrika H. Roskam argues that Mark was written to a specific Galilean community in the period shortly after the Jewish Revolt. This Christian community is currently experiencing hardship and is becoming increasingly subject to severe threats and persecution. The author of Mark's Gospel has written "to confirm them in their faithfulness to the Christian message, so that they will be strong enough to endure the

---

133. Ibid., 64–65. The quote is from Perry, *The Ancient Romances*, 140.
134. Talbert, *What Is a Gospel?*, 17.

hardships they are experiencing."[135] The evangelist Mark writes this tract using the story of Jesus' life (and death) as a model, a model that resembles closely ancient biography. But it is not biography per se because Mark's overall *purpose* in writing is apologetic; he simply uses this biographical form "to argue his case ... and thus to give his arguments more cogency."[136] So, how does this "apologetic writing in biographical form" deal with plot development?

Roskam argues that while Mark's structure is ostensibly chronological, the narrative itself is constructed in such a way as to highlight Mark's apologetic arguments.[137] Thus, she concludes: "The Gospel's story as a whole is, so to speak, a narrative argument against the accusation of subversiveness that might be addressed to the Markan Christians. Although the Gospel has a chronological and geographic framework, the *sequence of events* in the Gospel is not so much determined by time or location, as by the evangelist's apologetic line of reasoning."[138] As with Greek tragedy and the Hellenistic novel, the "sequence of events" or plot is under the control of the author.[139]

## *Jewish Midrash*

Marie Noonan Sabin asks an important question in the study of Markan genre: what was the cultural frame of reference that produced the composition of Mark?[140] Her answer to this question is that Mark's Gospel is first and foremost a religious document. What type of genre might communicate best in a Jewish religious context? Sabin's answer is midrash.[141] Sabin struggles, as do many, with a precise definition of Jewish midrash. It is clearly the Jews' "most ancient way of interpreting the Bible."[142] But it is

---

135. Roskam, *Purpose of the Gospel of Mark*, 236.

136. Ibid.

137. Ibid., 232. See pp. 145–211 for the detailed development of how the narrative structure parallels Mark's apologetic concerns.

138. Ibid., 233; emphasis supplied.

139. Though speaking about Greek tragedy (not biography or apologetic tracts) and the Fourth Gospel, Bryant (*Dialogue and Drama*, 256) concurs: "An author must decide how and where to begin, how to articulate a plot and limit its action to a coherent series of events in which one calls the next into being. Writers learn this art by emulating the writing of others."

140. Sabin, *Reopening the Word*, 10.

141. Ibid., 13.

142. Ibid.

*Introduction*

also more. She explores midrash as theological imagination, a way of reading, a way of writing, and as a way of reading life. What is of interest to us is the penultimate exploration: midrash as a way of writing—something she suggests motivated the author of Mark's Gospel. At a minimum, midrashic writing attempts to link one biblical text with another and usually does so through allusions, echoes, catchwords, and the like or juxtaposes different texts in an effort to hear the "double voice" of Scripture. Rabbis would employ this method in creating homilies. These homilies would tie together different passages of Scripture for the purpose of stimulating discussion or to open the door for theologizing. The tying together of different passages became an art for the rabbis. "[These verses] were linked together by the homilist so as to form a narrative 'journey,' a 'plot-like' structure from [one part of Scripture to another]."[143] It is not unreasonable, Sabin poses, to think that Mark's narrative thus "flows from this midrashic tradition."[144] Without passing judgment on that issue, the point here is that a midrashic understanding of the Gospel of Mark sees the author engaged in a "plot-like journey [like that] of the synagogue homily."[145]

## *Graeco-Roman Biography*

In many ways, this final category is the most difficult to make a connection that plot is the common thread among the various genre studies of Mark. Richard A. Burridge has written the most exhaustive study on the Gospels as ancient biographies or βίοι.[146] His study of these works identifies four generic features that are common to this form of literature: opening features, subject, external features, and internal features.[147] The one that concerns us is the internal features, that is, setting, content, style, tone, mood, attitude, occasion for writing, and the author's intent or purpose. In Burridge's discussion of this last item, authorial intent, his study reveals several common features such as informative, didactic, apologetic and polemic. One addition value, he observes, is entertainment value: the ability of an author to hold the audience's attention.[148] The employment of vari-

143. Ibid., 19.
144. Ibid., 23.
145. Ibid., 22.
146. Burridge, *What Are the Gospels*.
147. Ibid., 107.
148. Ibid., 182. See also, Burridge, "About People," 137: "Furthermore, we must not

33

ous literary techniques, such as "dramatic and tragic motifs," was used by these ancient authors.[149] With the notion of "drama" or "tragedy," we are back where we started with Aristotle and the primary elements of tragedy. Ancient biographies, after all, like Gospel or tragedies, or epic poems, or novels, or even midrash involve the recounting of a story—historical or imagined. It is in the nature of *story* where plot—how one sequences the events that are being described or related—comes into play.

## Mark's Milieu

I have resisted choosing a single genre for Mark's Gospel because as many of these examples suggest, there are *elements* of each of them in Mark. If there were not, scholars would have no trouble eliminating them as possible candidates. Mark, in composing a *Gospel* (εὐαγγέλιον) did so within the context of the literary milieu of the day. Mark was probably familiar with or at the very least aware of many different types of literature.[150] As I have shown, the common thread that ties disparate type of literature together is the notion of plot. Even if one is dealing with the account of a historical figure, such as ancient βίος, the *narrative* or story must be interesting enough to be read or, if performed, interesting enough to hold the attention of the audience. Or take the rather obscure apologetic tractate. My review of Roskam's thesis demonstrates that plot serves the larger purpose. Jo-Ann Bryant states it nicely with respect to John's Gospel: "The gospel as a literary form may indeed be *sui generis*, but the methods of representing time, setting, action, and characters [and I would add plot] found in the Fourth Gospel [and I would add Mark's Gospel] are not."[151] Whatever writers want to do, whether ancient or modern, they want to communicate. In so doing, one is constantly negotiating the tensions inherent between what one

---

forget that much ancient biography was written to entertain the audience, which is best exemplified by the anecdotes about Euripides preserved in Satyrus, or by the satirical undercurrents included in Lucian, who was a professional entertainer, in his *Demonax*, not to mention the literary skill of Plutarch's or Tacitus's writings."

149. Burridge, *What Are the Gospels*, 182.

150. Bilezikian (*Liberated Gospel*, 50) concurs: "The probability of Mark being familiar with one of the dominant literary forms of the culture in whose language he composed his own work cannot be lightly dismissed."

151. Bryant, *Dialogue and Drama*, 256.

*Introduction*

wants to say (i.e., purpose) with how best to say it (i.e., style) so that one's audience grasps and reacts accordingly.[152]

## PLOT AND THE GOSPEL OF MARK

So what is Mark's emphasis? Plot—the ordering or sequencing of events—is as we have seen the lifeblood of any story. In this closing section, I want first to revisit one key point made by Aristotle concerning plot; second, to use that key piece of information to lay out briefly the narrative flow of Mark's Gospel; and finally, based on that narrative flow, to state what I believe is Mark's overall purpose.

First, Aristotle observed that a good story has three parts: a beginning, middle, and end (*Poet.* 7.3–7). In the Aristotelian concept of plot development, the beginning is called the "complication phase." Action in this phase centers on the potential tragic situation of the hero. This is followed by a series of events that lead to a climax, usually a recognition scene that occurs near the middle of the narrative. In this section, often the true nature of the main character, which has been veiled thus far, is revealed with greater clarity. The situation of the hero or main character, however, changes for the worse in the final phase. The complicating factors that characterized the beginning phase, which were brought to a head in the middle phase, now are dealt with decisively.

From the survey of Markan outlines above, it is quite clear that—regardless of the manner in which the material is broken into constituent parts—Mark's Gospel follows this pattern. If one believes Mark keyed these movements to the geographic movement of Jesus, one is left with a "beginning" in and around Galilee (1:1—8:26), a "middle" on the way to Jerusalem (8:27—10:52), and an "end" in Jerusalem (11:1—16:8). If one prefers another, more literary method (like van Iersel's chiastic structure), there is still a discernable beginning, middle, and end.

This middle phase, what Aristotle referred to as the περιπέτεια, the "great reversal" or "turning point," is seen by most interpreters as occurring

---

152. I think Collins ("Mark and His Readers: The Son of God among Jews," and "Mark and His Readers: The Son of God among Greeks and Romans") touches on this in her two articles that deal with the manner in which Mark's title Son of God would have been heard among the different readers: Greeks and Romans on the one hand and Jews on the other. Readers (or hearers) understand things in their own contexts. Good authors will try to anticipate how their work will be understood and write accordingly.

in or around 8:22 or 8:26 and continuing to 10:45 or 10:52. But this is a broad range of possible turning points. More precision is needed in isolating Mark's περιπέτεια.[153]

Second, using this key Aristotelian concept of beginning, middle, and end, I want to suggest a narrative flow for Mark's Gospel. A "narrative flow" is not the same thing as plot, but addressing the flow of a story should aid in discerning the plot and purpose of a work. I suggest that Mark's Gospel is a very balanced Gospel (Appendix 1 depicts this narrative flow). The story's beginning (i.e., Prologue) is matched by a corresponding ending (i.e., Epilogue).[154] Approximately one-fourth of the way into the story, Jesus is seen teaching in parables alongside (or on) the Sea of Galilee (4:1–34). This represents a significant teaching section in the Gospel.[155] It is paralleled with the only other uninterrupted block of teaching material, which occurs at approximately the three-fourth's mark of the Gospel—the so-called Olivet Discourse (13:4–37).[156] Between these two blocks of teaching material, at approximately the half-way mark, sits the "middle section" (8:22—10:52), which consists of "the turning point" (8:27—9:13), flanked by two blind miracles (8:22-26; 10:46-52).[157] Linking these major markers (i.e., beginning, middle, and end) are various episodes that keep the narrative moving.[158]

Finally, as the graphic in Appendix 1 illustrates, at each of these three phases, the identity of Jesus comes into view. In the beginning phase, his identity as Messiah/Christ is seen in the opening line of the Gospel (1:1).[159] The divine voice from heaven appears in 1:11 referring to Jesus as "my beloved son." Jesus himself, after forgiving and healing a paralytic, refers to himself with the cryptic phrase, Son of Man. These same three titles—Messiah, Son of God, and Son of Man—are found in each of the following phases. In the middle section, Peter confesses Jesus to be the Christ (8:29) to which Jesus sternly speaks of the impending suffering, death, and resurrection of "the Son of Man" (8:31). In the subsequent Transfiguration scene

---

153. For a recent full-scale commentary that relates Aristotle's *Poetics* to the structure of the Gospel, see Collins, *Mark*, 85–93, esp. 92–93.

154. This, in the graphic display, is highlighted by the use of diamond-shaped boxes.

155. One only needs to compare the "red letters" in Mark to that of Matthew's Gospel (or John's) to see that Mark is low on sustained, uninterrupted blocks of Jesus teaching.

156. Appendix 1 highlights this feature with square-shaped boxes.

157. The "turning point" is marked with an oval-shaped circle in Appendix 1, while the blind miracles are square-shaped boxes that "touch" the oval.

158. Hence the arrows pointing forward to the conclusion of the story.

159. Many MSS also have "Son of God" in this verse.

(9:2–13, which I will argue goes with Peter's confession), the divine voice from heaven reappears summoning Peter, James, and John to listen to "my beloved Son" (9:7). This repetition of christological titles occurs again in the Passion Narrative, which could be labeled the final phase. At the trial of Jesus (14:61–62), the high priest asks Jesus, "Are you the Christ, the Son of the Blessed?" To which Jesus replies, "I am" (ἐγώ εἰμι). He continues, "and you (plural) will see the Son of Man seated at the right hand of Power, and coming with the clouds of heaven" (14:62). At this strategic final scene, Jesus concurs with what many in the story (and certainly the readers) have known—he is the Messiah, Son of God (i.e., Blessed One), and Son of Man. Whatever else may be on the mind of Mark, he is attempting—based on this plotting of the account of Jesus—to reveal the true nature of Jesus.[160]

But in Mark's Gospel a correct understanding of who Jesus is can never be divorced from the question "what does this mean?" In the narrative, recognition of Jesus' true identity carries responsibilities. Jesus' call is a demanding call: he calls people to follow him. This is what happens in the calling of the first disciples (1:16–20): Simon and Andrew leave their fishing nets and immediately follow him. Two other would-be disciples, James and John, not only leave their boats, but they leave their father in the boat in order to follow Jesus. The essence of what it means to "follow Jesus" is found in another calling scene (3:13–19). Here Jesus calls "whom he desired" and they came to him and he appointed Twelve to be "with him" (μετ' αὐτοῦ). Lest one think that being "with Jesus" is easy, the very Twelve that first heard and responded to this call would abandon him in his moment of greatest need, as Roman soldiers came to arrest him (14:50). The language is startling: "they all left him and fled" (καὶ ἀφέντες αὐτὸν ἔφυγον πάντες). To flee is the opposite of being "with" someone. Mark's presentation juxtaposes Christology (who is Jesus?) with discipleship (what does this mean?). They are indeed two sides of the same coin.

# CONCLUSION

In this introductory chapter, I have tried to make three points. The first is that many have attempted to provide *the* outline for the Gospel of Mark, but somehow Mark's Gospel resists nice, neat, concise outlines—even

---

160. See the disciples question in 4:41: τίς ἄρα οὗτός ἐστιν ὅτι καὶ ὁ ἄνεμος καὶ ἡ θάλασσα ὑπακούει αὐτῷ; (Who then is this that even the wind and the sea obey him?).

though the geographic strand is tempting. The nature of narrative is much more complex and does not lend itself to precise divisions. Kee's image of fugue or Dewey's depiction as "interwoven tapestry" is closer to Mark's design. Second, narratives—as stories—do not resist, however, literary devices, such as turning points. This is true regardless of the genre in which one writes since authors want most desperately to communicate. Finally, I believe that Mark worked from a cultural context that would have allowed him to concentrate on the "lifeblood" of a good story—plot. This plot, which is presented in a balanced fashion, is concerned chiefly with Jesus and one's proper response to him. What does this have to do with the notion of turning point?

As mentioned above, the majority of commentators see the central or middle section of Mark's Gospel (8:22—10:52) as crucial in the development of Mark's story of Jesus. Yet, when one reviews the secondary literature on this topic there is hardly any agreement as to precisely which pericope in the central section is the so-called turning point. A few commentators suggest that Jesus' question to the disciples in 8:21 ("Do you not yet understand?") is meant to serve as the conclusion to the first half of the narrative. The vast majority of interpreters see Peter's confession of Jesus as "the Messiah" (8:29) as the pivot on which the entire narrative turns. Others, however, see Jesus' response to Peter and the disciples in 8:30 ("He warned them not to tell anyone about him") and the subsequent prediction ("The Son of Man must suffer . . .") as the critical point.

The purpose of this monograph is threefold: first, to survey the various analyses of the turning point in Mark's Gospel by looking in detail at the central section, especially 8:27—9:13, and pointing out the textual features to which the interpreters rely on in arriving at their conclusions; second, to offer another approach in search of an interim climax in the Markan narrative; and finally, to assess this approach's impact on Markan Christology. Specifically, based on linguistic and thematic links in the narrative, I will argue that the twin pericopae of Peter's confession (8:27—9:1) and the Transfiguration (9:2–13) *together* function as the turning point of the Gospel and serve in a Janus-like manner enabling the reader to see the author's true intention: the identity of Jesus and the significance of that reality for Jesus' disciples. Peter's confession faces backward toward the Prologue (1:1–13)—especially the opening line (1:1)—and serves to answer the disciples' basic question, "Who then is this that even the wind and sea obey him" (4:41)? The declaration by God on the mountain faces forward

*Introduction*

and introduces or foreshadows the last word about Jesus, namely that he is the Son of God (15:39). In the midst of these two statements *about* Jesus, Jesus responds to Peter and the disciples by identifying himself as Son of Man (8:31). Christologically, the images of Jesus as Messiah, Son of Man, and Son of God converge and present Jesus, the crucified, as king, ushering in the kingdom of God in power (9:1). When one is confronted with this Jesus—after calculating the costs (8:34–38)—the only wise decision, according to the Markan story, is to follow in discipleship.

Five chapters follow that attempt to articulate in detail the thesis stated above. In the following chapter, I will survey the many possible turning points (e.g., 8:21, 29, 30, etc.) and address why exegetes have these as the watershed moments in the narrative. My own proposal, the so-called Janus approach, will be set forth in chapter 3. If Peter's confession and the story of the Transfiguration together function as the turning point of the Gospel, then it must be shown that the two pericopae were meant to be read together. I will set forth thirteen grammatical or linguistic links, eight thematic correlations, and one suggestion from Synoptic studies that suggest that these two pericopae go together. Setting forth these links is the purpose of chapter 4. In a chapter entitled "Converging Lines in Markan Christology" (chapter 5), I will deal with the christological notions of Messiah/Christ, Son of God, and Son of Man in its immediate context (8:27–9:13) and in the wider context of the Gospel as a whole. While each of these terms is used elsewhere in the Gospel, why is it here that they take on such heightened importance, so much so that the entire narrative turns on these disclosures of Jesus' identity? In the final chapter (chapter 6), I will summarize the essential argument of this monograph and set forth its findings as it relates to Synoptic studies in general and to Markan studies in particular.

# 2
# Surveying the Possible Turning Points

IN THE PREVIOUS CHAPTER, I set forth several preliminary issues in determining the turning point in a Gospel narrative. These issues involve the internal structure of the Gospel, the nature of a turning point, and the genre of the Gospel—and especially plot as the common feature among several divergent genres of the ancient world. The primary purpose of this chapter is to survey the many possible turning points of Mark's central section and address reasons why each could be the pivot on which Mark's narrative turns. Before addressing these various possible turning points, however, two preliminary issues must first be addressed. First, I have used the phrase "turning point" (or its Greek equivalent περιπέτεια) to indicate the point of significant change in the Gospel of Mark. Who was the first to use this phrase with respect to Mark's Gospel? Has its use always been in direct relationship to the Markan narrative? In the first part of this chapter, I will address these questions and how scholarship on the notion of turning point has evolved from its earliest use to the present. The second preliminary issue that warrants attention relates to Mark's middle section. If the turning point in the Gospel occurs in the middle section, as I have suggested, then a brief overview of this portion of the Markan story will lay the groundwork for the rest of the chapter (and for my proposal in chapter 3). The primary objective of this chapter—surveying the potential turning points—will be achieved by an analysis of the prospective περιπέτειαι under three main headings: (1) no turning point; (2) a single turning point; and (3) more than one turning point.

*Surveying the Possible Turning Points*

# HISTORY OF TURNING POINT LANGUAGE

## The Early Uses and Historical Criticism

As we have seen, Aristotle is one of the first to associate turning point (περιπέτεια) as an important element of plot development in any poetic work. When it comes to the study of the Gospel of Mark, William Wrede was the first person to use the label "turning point." In 1901, he penned *Das Messiasgeheimnis in den Evangelien*, which addressed the so-called messianic secret in the Gospels.[1] Wrede lived and worked in a time where the "liberal lives of Jesus" was commonplace in the academic study of the "historical Jesus" and in Gospel studies in general. Wrede was interested, as were others, in whether (and if so how) Jesus viewed himself as Messiah.[2] His contention was that since Jesus repeatedly commands people to silence when confronted with his personhood, Jesus could not "have spoken of his messianic coming in the way the Synoptists report. The messiahship of Jesus, as we find it in the Gospels, is a product of community theology correcting history according to its own concepts."[3] Wrede's views on the messianic secret did not command scholarly agreement (due mainly to Schweitzer's critique), but his views did open up an otherwise neglected notion of secrecy in Mark's Gospel.[4] In Wrede's analysis of this secret motif in Mark's Gospel, the middle section—in particular the story of Peter's confession—played an important role. Part One of Wrede's work shows the importance he places on Mark's central section:

> At his baptism by John, Jesus receives the Spirit and obtains the testimony from on high that he is God's son. With this, according to Mark, Jesus' life as Messiah begins. Next to this fundamental event the decisive point [*entscheidende Punkt*] is the confession of his messiahship by Peter, 8.27ff. In Jesus' last period, not long before

---

1. Wrede, *Das Messiasgeheimnis in den Evangelien* (English translation, *The Messianic Secret*). The following references are to the English translation.

2. Wrede, *The Messianic Secret*, 1. This viewpoint has now been well documented and has even achieved proper scholarly nomenclature—Jesus' "messianic consciousness."

3. Schweitzer, *Quest of the Historical Jesus*, 303.

4. A detailed review of Wrede's work is beyond the scope of this chapter. What is important for our discussion is to examine his sense of Mark's central section. For discussions (including critiques) of *Das Messiasgeheimnis*, see especially Schweitzer, *Quest for the Historical Jesus*, 296–314; Tillesse, *Le secret messianique dans l'Evangile de Marc*, 9–34; Martin, *Mark*, 84–106; Tuckett, ed., *Messianic Secret*; and Räisänen, "Messianic Secret" in *Mark*, 38–75.

he sets out on the decisive journey [*entscheidende Wanderung*] to Jerusalem, there dawns on the disciples at Caesarea Philippi an understanding they have not so far had; and one which in a sense they ought not to have...This dawning of messianic awareness on the part of the disciples accordingly appears in fact as epoch-making [*Epoche*] in Jesus' public life. In this connection it becomes at the same time evident that Jesus thought it important that there should be no forcing of the correct evaluation of his person but that it should be allowed to mature gradually in people's minds.[5]

As my parenthetical insertions indicate, the language Wrede employs is not the unambiguous *Wendepunkt* (turning point), though words like *Epoche* and phrases like *entscheidende Punkt* and *entscheidende Wanderung* come close. However, in an appendix that develops further the statements made above, Wrede does use the word *Wendepunkt*. In a paragraph where he critiques the work of Bernhard Weiss and Johannes Weiss, he refers to Peter's confession (8:29) as a *Wendepunkt*: "The crux of the criticism leveled by [B.] Weiss lies in his utilization of the gospel of John. From John 6.14–15 (where it is desired to make Jesus a king after the feeding) he reads a 'catastrophe', a turning point [*Wendepunkt*] in the life of Jesus and he then interprets Mark 8.27ff. according to John 6.66ff.: Jesus refuses to unfurl the messianic flag and thereby he loses the sympathies of the people but the disciples swear loyalty to him."[6] Wrede's acknowledgement that Weiss' catastrophe is "a turning point in the life of Jesus" is the earliest known reference to turning point and the Gospel's portrayal of Jesus' life.

Within a few years of Wrede's publication, American scholar Benjamin Wisner Bacon published a commentary on Mark's Gospel in The Modern Commentary series.[7] Bacon divided the Gospel into halves at 8:27 and refers to the scene at Caesarea Philippi as "the most definite milestone of the Gospel," "the culminating point," "an epoch-making point of the Gospel."[8] It is worth noting that Bacon's emphasis on Caesarean pericope is from a narrative perspective—he calls Peter's confession an "epoch-making point

---

5. Wrede, *Messianic Secret*, 11.

6. Ibid., 253. In making this "catastrophic" observation, Wrede cites Weizsäcker, *Untersuchungen über die Evangelische Geschichte*, 454; and Weiss, *Das Leben Jesu*, 2:263–67. While employing a similar term "crisis" [*krisis*], neither Weizsäcker nor Weiss use *Wendepunkt*. Wrede appears to be the first to use this term as it relates to any pericope in the Gospel of Mark.

7. Bacon, *Beginnings of Gospel Story*.

8. Ibid., 103–4.

*of the Gospel*." Wrede labeled Peter's declaration a "turning point in the *life of Jesus*." A few years later, Marie-Joseph Lagrange not only confirmed Bacon's sense of the turning point being associated with the Gospel, he calls attention to Peter's confession (which he holds is 8:27) as a *péripétie*.[9]

By 1921 and the publication of Rudolf Bultmann's groundbreaking work, *Die Geschichte der Synoptischen Tradition* (ET: *The History of the Synoptic Tradition*), the source critical approach of Wrede was giving way to form criticism.[10] Bultmann's work is divided into three major sections: (1) the tradition of the sayings of Jesus; (2) the tradition of the narrative material; and (3) the editing of traditional material. The final section contains a detailed discussion of the three Synoptic Gospels from the perspective of the "narrative material and the compositions of the Gospels." Bultmann is critical of Mark's skill as an editor. Nevertheless, he makes an important observation regarding the same pericope in Mark that Wrede emphasized:

> Mark is not sufficiently master of his material to be able to venture on a systematic construction himself. The one actual section—apart from the preface and period in Jerusalem—is the confession of Peter in 8$^{27\text{ff}}$. Of course, not in the sense that the ministry as a whole was given a new turn (in this Wrede is quite right) but only in so far as the esoteric instruction about the new conception of Messiahship began at this point. So it is an epoch for the reader only, not for the life of Jesus; for Mark has neither depicted the recognition of Jesus as something newly won by him, as the fruit of his ministry or of his estimate of the outward and inward situation, nor has he pictured the recognition by the disciples as the outcome of some development.[11]

Interestingly, Bultmann recognizes the *Wendepunktliche* nature Peter's confession *for the reader only* and not for Jesus. Bultmann's comment distances him from Wrede and even Bacon. Wrede focused on the impact of Peter's confession on the life of Jesus. Bacon focused on the impact of Peter's confession in the Gospel itself, that is, within the narrative world of the Markan story. Bultmann's view moves away from the historical Jesus and even the narrative to the *reader*. Observing the various referents for the turning point highlights the inherent tension present in Gospel studies:

---

9. Lagrange, *Évangile selon Saint Marc*, lxiv. My citation is from the 1947 revised edition.

10. Bultmann, *Die Geschichte der Synoptischen Tradition*. My citations come from the ET, *History of the Synoptic Tradition*.

11. Ibid., 350.

*readers* seek understanding about a person, *Jesus*, through a text written by an *author* who can no longer be consulted.

Two years after Bultmann's publication, Elias Bickermann authored an article in *ZNW* entitled "*Das Messiasgeheimnis und die Komposition des Markusevangeliums.*"[12] Based on his reading of several OT passages, Bickermann speaks of a dual or bilateral turning point (*Wendepunkt*): an inner (*innerer*) and an outer (*äußerer*) one.[13] This dual *Wendepunkt* speaks of the phenomenon we have seen at work, namely, the turning point in the life of Jesus versus the turning point of the Markan narrative. Bickermann argues that the inner and outer turning point converge at the confession of Peter in 8:27–30 and thus function as the key recognition scene (borrowing from Aristotle) in the Gospel: "*So ist auch die Szene bei Caesarea Philippi eine Erkennungsszene und die Handlung im Markusevangelium ist* ἡ πεπλεγμένη πρᾶξις, *wo* ἡ μετάβασις μετὰ ἀναγνωρισμοῦ ἐστιν."[14]

In the ten-year period encompassing 1933 to 1943, Frederick C. Grant penned two books of significance in the study of the Synoptic Gospels, *The Growth of the Gospels* (1933) and *The Earliest Gospel* (1943).[15] In the earlier work, Grant focuses on the origin, development, transmission, and interrelationships of the four canonical Gospels. He discusses the literary structure of each of the Gospel and emphasizes the priority of Mark. In the discussion on Mark's structure, he recognizes Mark's emphasis on "the early proclamation of the good news by Jesus" (which leads to the "climax" of Peter's confession) and the significance of the "long way" to the cross in the second half of the Gospel.[16] He positions Peter's confession together with the Transfiguration and indicates, "Peter's confession (viii. 27–30) marks the turning point in the Gospel."[17] Grant's later book addresses similar questions about the early Christian tradition and its relationship to Mark's Gospel. In a study of the question about whether the tradition Mark uses has its origins in Jerusalem or Galilee, Grant acknowledges the pattern of Greek tragedy emphasizes the resurrection as the decisive moment *in*

---

12. Bickermann, "Das Messiasgeheimnis und die Komposition des Markusevangeliums," 122–46.

13. Ibid., 123.

14. Ibid., 132.

15. Grant, *Growth of the Gospels* (reprint, *The Gospel: Their Origin and Growth*); Grant, *The Earliest Gospel*.

16. Grant, *Growth of the Gospels*, 103.

17. Ibid., 119.

*Jesus' life*: "Some scholars have seen in Mark the pattern of Greek tragedy, and indeed with some probability. In that pattern, the course of action from Caesarea to the still-anticipated *Parousia* leads on steadily to the grand *katastrophê*, resulting in the divine *peripéteia*: the Resurrection is an episode indispensable to the total action, but still an episode."[18] Two items should be noted: first, Grant affirms the pattern of Greek tragedy in the Gospel of Mark. Indeed, this viewpoint had a small following during this period.[19] Second, because of the historical interests of Grant, there is still emphasis on the life of Jesus and his divine περιπέτεια. Yet in his earlier work, Grant affirms the sense of a *literary* turning point at Peter's confession. Grant is the last to refer to περιπέτεια in a dualistic fashion. Subsequent scholars who mention a turning point or points do so from the perspective of written Gospel, not the historical Jesus.

## The Later Uses and Literary Criticism

The notion of a turning point in Mark's Gospel remained relatively dormant until the mid 1970s, when Gilbert Bilezikian's work, *The Liberated Gospel*, ushered in a revival in comparing the Gospel with Greek tragedy.[20] Of course, during the period that Bilezikian was revising his work, a revolution of sorts was taking place in biblical studies. The "old" source and form criticism that dominated the study of the New Testament prior to the Second World War had given way to redaction criticism with its interest in the theological vantage point of the authors/editors. No sooner had that been digested by the scholarly guild when "new theories" of biblical interpretation began to appear, methods that paid attention to the social and cultural contexts and the New Testament documents as literary compositions.[21] As

---

18. Grant, *Earliest Gospel*, 133.

19. Grant cites the following scholars who see Mark resembling a Hellenistic tragedy: Carré, "The Literary Structure of the Gospel of Mark"; Burch, "Tragic Action in the Second Gospel"; and Bundy, "Dogma and Drama in the Gospel of Mark." To those, we may mention one other in that time period: Riddle, "The Martyr Motif in the Gospel According to Mark."

20. Bilezikian, *Liberated Gospel*. This was a revision of Bilezikian's doctoral dissertation, presented at Boston University's School of Theology, some twenty years earlier (1953). There is one brief mention of "turning point," only as a heading of a section in Johnson, *Gospel According to St. Mark*, 25.

21. The towering figures in these days with respect to sociocultural studies in Mark are: Kee, *Community of the New Age*; Kelber, *Oral and Written Gospel*; and Robbins, *Jesus*

# The Turning Point in the Gospel of Mark

Peter Bolt has suggested, "what was occurring was a shift from studying the Gospels (or, indeed the whole Bible) under the paradigm of 'history' to studying them under the paradigm of 'literature.'"[22] In this milieu, Bilezikian argued that "for Mark the supreme act of Christian liberation may well have been to proclaim the universal relevance of a very Jewish story by telling it in the manner of a Greek tragedy."[23] To observe an Aristotelian structure—of beginning, middle, and end—was not only natural but also required. Bilezikian reads Mark through the lens of Aristotle's *Poetics* and, accordingly, highlights the phase between the plot's "complication" and its "dénoument." The "crisis point" or the hinge between the initial phase and the dénoument is Peter's confession: "In the Gospel the confession of Peter constitutes a *turning point* in the action. The dramatic tension created by the complication of the incognito presence of the Messiah is partly relaxed when the disciples recognize, on their own and against seemingly contrary evidence, the real identity of Jesus."[24] From this point forward, due in part to the increased attention on the narrative of the Gospel, the use of "turning point" language in the central section of Mark (usually Peter's confession) is common.[25]

---

the Teacher. The early advocates of literary or narrative criticism of Mark's Gospel include: Perrin, "The Christology of Mark"; Tannehill, "The Disciples in Mark"; Tannehill, "The Gospel of Mark as Narrative Christology"; and Rhoads and Michie, *Mark as Story*. The second edition of the last work was published as Rhoads, Dewey, and Michie, *Mark as Story*, in 1999. There is now a third edition, which was published in 2012. All references to *Mark as Story* in this monograph will correspond to the second edition. For a collection of essays that interact with Rhoads, Dewey, and Michie's work, see Iverson and Skinner, eds., *Mark as Story: Retrospect and Prospect*.

22. Bolt, "Mark's Gospel," 397.

23. Bilezikian, *Liberated Gospel*, 31.

24. Ibid., 76–77; emphasis supplied.

25. What follows (here and in Appendix 2) is by no means meant to be exhaustive, but these scholars explicitly label Peter's confession (or another closely related pericope) the turning point of the Gospel: Stock, *Call to Discipleship*, 133; Hurtado, *Mark*, 136; Boers, "Reflections on the Gospel of Mark," 259; Guelich, *Mark 1:1—8:26*, xxxvi; Dewey, "Mark as Interwoven Tapestry," 230; Cook, *Structure and Persuasive Power of Mark*, 295; Tolbert, *Sowing the Gospel*, 114; Painter, *Mark's Gospel*, 124; Johnson, *Writings of the New Testament*, 164; Evans, *Mark 8:27—16:20*, 19; Witherington III, *Gospel of Mark*, 38; Moloney, *Storyteller, Interpreter, Evangelist*, 83. Others use synonyms such as "watershed" (see Hare, *Mark*, 97; Edwards, *Gospel according to Mark*, 233; France, *Gospel of Mark*, 327; and Moloney, *Gospel of Mark*, 21n72), "pivot" (see Lane, *Gospel of Mark*, 288; Hooker, *Gospel According to St. Mark*, 200; Smith, "A Divine Tragedy," 246; and Guttenberger, "Why Caesarea Philippi of All Sites?," 119), or "high point" (Focant, *Gospel according to Mark*, 331). See also, Baarlink, *Anfängliches Evangelium*, 92, who himself calls 8:27 the

## Conclusion

As can be seen from this analysis, the early commentators on the issue of turning point can be relegated into two camps—those addressing the issue from a *historical* perspective and those addressing turning point from a *literary* perspective.[26] Bultmann stands out as the sole commentator that addresses turning point from the perspective of the reader. As I mentioned in the first chapter, this study purports to analyze the turning point of *Mark's narrative*. I am interested in historical questions, especially questions related to the historical Jesus, and while I would not dispute that Peter's confession (or even another event "on the way" to Jerusalem) was a decisive moment in Jesus' life, I am not prepared to argue for a turning point from a historical perspective. On the other hand, Mark's Gospel—in its final form—may offer clues to what could constitute a narrative turning point, the kind of turning point that Aristotle (and others) speaks of in terms of plot development. In setting forth my proposal for such a turning point, I will argue that there are indeed such clues in the way in which Mark crafts his story. Thus, the focus of my work is on the literary turning point of the Gospel of Mark.

The above historical survey has shown that the vast majority of scholars recognize a literary turning point *somewhere* in Mark's central section. The majority holds the key scene to be Peter's confession. That declaration is an important pericope in the Gospel and should certainly be considered a possible turning point. However, before addressing it and other potential candidates for the *Wendepunkt* in the Gospel, let us look at Mark's central section in more detail.

## OVERVIEW OF MARK'S CENTRAL SECTION

## Defining the Limits of the Central Section

Before offering an overview of Mark's central section, it is important to determine the limits of Mark's "central section." As the discussion of outlines in

---

"central point" (*Mittelpunkt*).

26. This sentiment is summed up by Blatherwick ("The Markan Silhouette?," 190): "It is generally assumed that Peter's profession of faith was the turning-point of Jesus' life, and it has been accepted by Wrede and Lightfoot and more modern students of the Gospel that it was also the decisive moment for Mark's presentation."

chapter 1 made apparent, scholars have analyzed the structure of the Gospel in a number of ways. In many respects, Mark's so-called "middle section" follows the broad manner in which the Gospel as a whole is outlined: topographically, thematically, literarily, or topically. There is no need to readdress each of these in this context. The main issue confronting us at this point relates to its limits. Where does the "middle section" begin and end?

I will begin with the culmination of the middle section—it is the easier of the two to determine. Almost all scholars recognize the important scene shift that occurs in the narrative at 11:1, beginning a section that has been dubbed "the triumphal entry" by many.[27] Here the pace of the narrative slows as the narrator shows the movement of Jesus and his followers as they approach Jerusalem from the east via the Jericho road--first Bethpage, then Bethany, finally the Mount of Olives (11:1). Jesus enters Jerusalem in 11:11 and from there until the end of the Gospel (16:8), there is no significant change in scenery—Jesus resides outside Jerusalem in Mark's Gospel, but regularly enters the holy city with his disciples (11:15, 27, 14:17). Based on 11:1, then, the ending of Mark's middle section must be 10:52, the verse that immediately precedes Jesus' drawing near to Jerusalem. Most scholars concur with this observation. Vincent Taylor, for example, follows the physical movement of Jesus—a ministry that begins in Galilee (1:14), moves "beyond Galilee" (5:1), includes the journey to Jerusalem (8:27–10:52), and culminates in Jerusalem with the Passion and Resurrection narrative (11:1–16:8).[28] Attention to these geographical movements causes Taylor to see the "middle section" beginning in 8:27 since Jesus and his followers on "on the way" (ἐν τῇ ὁδῷ) to Jerusalem, a significant change from the ministry in and around Galilee (1:14–8:26). This type of analysis is not reserved only for those who divide the material based on topography. Dennis Nineham, who outlines Mark's Gospel based on a combination of geographical and topical concerns, defends 8:27–10:52 as the central section since a major disclosure occurs "on the way" from Galilee to Jerusalem: Jesus discloses

---

27. At least one scholar, Kelber (*Kingdom in Mark*, 92–93), challenges the "triumphal" nature of Jesus' entrance into Jerusalem: "[T]he acclamation [11:9b–10] is schemed in such a way that it does in fact not concur with the entry into the city. Mark, and Mark alone, has Jesus' companions cut leafy branches 'from the fields' (11:8b), which adverts to a rural location. It is only *after* Jesus has been hailed that he enters city and temple, by himself (11:11a: *eisēlthen*), unobserved and unapplauded" (emphasis original). See also, Lohmeyer, *Das Evangelium des Markus*, 233.

28. Taylor, *Gospel According to St. Mark*, 107–10.

the character of his messiahship.²⁹ This disclosure, Nineham observes, dominates the narrative until Jesus' entry into Jerusalem (11:1–11).³⁰ If the end then is secure, what about the beginning of Mark's central section? Where in the narrative does the middle section commence?

According to Taylor and Nineham, the middle section of Mark's Gospel begins at 8:27. They reach their respective conclusions due mainly to their recognition of the fact that Jesus is "on the way" to Jerusalem (8:27). Indeed, prior to this notation, Jesus' travel has been in or around Galilee and the reference to "on the way" does successfully depict a change in location.³¹ However, to be precise, the pericope immediately prior to 8:27 (Jesus healing a blind man [8:22–26]) occurs in Bethsaida, a city on the northeastern shore of the Sea of Galilee and therefore technically outside the territory of Galilee.³² Jesus' arrival into Bethsaida (8:22) comes as the final boat trip on or across the Sea of Galilee (see also, 4:35–5:1; 5:21; 6:32–34 [not an actual crossing]; 6:45–53; and 8:10 [not an actual crossing]).³³ So, what should be the determining factor with respect to the limits of the middle section—the fact that 8:22–26 is the conclusion of the "boat cycle," or the fact that Bethsaida is beyond the boundary of Galilee?

When 8:22–26 is considered, a different geographical phenomenon emerges: as Jesus crosses the Sea of Galilee for the last time, a new set of regional information is provided that, in my judgment, provides a helpful marker of the central section. To many, this data tracks the movement of Jesus once he arrives on the eastern shore and in so doing offers evidence of

---

29. Nineham, *Gospel of St. Mark*, 223–86.

30. Ibid., 227.

31. Some scholars place a great deal of significance on the ὁδός motif. See esp., Swartley, "The Structural Function of the Term 'Way' (Hodos) in Mark's Gospel," 73–86; Marcus, *The Way of the Lord*, 12–47; and Watts, *Isaiah's New Exodus*, 123–36.

32. On Bethsaida, see Arav and Freund, eds., *Bethsaida*; and Strickert, *Bethsaida*. On the significance of Bethsaida being on Gentile soil, see esp. Kelber, *Kingdom in Mark*, 57–62; and Malbon, *Narrative Space and Mythic Meaning*, 15–49.

33. For a discussion of the boat journeys, see Kelber, *Mark's Story of Jesus*, 30–42. Petersen ("The Composition of Mark 4:1—8:26," 194) observes that the boat is actually first mentioned in 3:9 as a contingency for Jesus against the burgeoning crowd. Jesus first puts the boat into use in 4:1 as he sits in it as he teaches alongside the sea. "Prior to 4:1, Jesus had been beside the sea on three occasions (1:16; 2:13; 3:7), but never on it, let alone across it. Yet, in 4:1—8:26 he is repeatedly on the sea and crossing it. Moreover, with the completion in 8:22 of a sea crossing begun in 8:13, both the boat and the sea case to play a role in the narrative." For a useful discussion on the boat motif in Mark, see Fowler, *Loaves and Fishes*, 57–68.

the beginning of the middle section. This regional information can visualized as follows:³⁴

1. 8:22—Bethsaida

2. 8:27—Caesarea Philippi

3. 9:30—Galilee (9:33 Capernaum)

4. 10:1—Judea and beyond Jordan

5. 10:32—On the way to Jerusalem

6. 10:46—Jericho

All the geographic references highlighted above are spots "along the way" of Jesus' journey toward Jerusalem.³⁵ True, the first reference to ὁδός is 8:27, but the shift away from Galilee as the center of Jesus' work to the travel journey "on the way" begins in 8:22. In addition, Norman Perrin observes that the first and last of these movements involve stories about people being given their sight—the blind man at Bethsaida (8:22–26) and a second blind man, named Bartimaeus (10:46–52).³⁶ These two "blind miracles" frame the material in between or, as Perrin states, transitional stories that go along with Mark's summary reports (*Sammelberichte*), which have previously divided major sections of the Gospel (1:14–15; 3:7–12; 6:6b).³⁷ The motif of seeing is indeed important to the discussion and, in fact, serves as another confirming piece of evidence for determining the limits of the central section.

In the narrative, the disciples have become increasingly blind to the true identity of Jesus and the significance of that reality. They were

---

34. Perrin, "Toward an Interpretation of the Gospel of Mark," 7.

35. Why Mark narrates a northward movement from Bethsaida to Caesarea Philippi when Jesus' ultimate destination is Jerusalem (to the south) is unclear. Best (*Gospel as Story*, 44–45) suggests that Caesarea Philippi represents the furthest point from Jerusalem in the Gospel and may thus be a symbolic place marking Peter's great confession (see also Kelber, *Kingdom in Mark*, 69–70; Gould, *Gospel According to St. Mark*, 151). The references to Galilee in 9:30 and Capernaum in 9:33 are either re-entry points along the way (see Moloney, *Gospel of Mark*, 187) or represent redactional elements inserted into the story (Kelber, *Kingdom in Mark*, 69).

36. Perrin and Duling, *New Testament*, 233–61, esp. 239. This material in the revised edition can be found at Duling and Perrin, *New Testament*, 295–327, esp. 304–5. The fourth edition of this work has now been published as Duling, *New Testament: History, Literature, and Social Context*.

37. Ibid., 239. See also my representation of this in Appendix 1.

astonished at his calming of the sea in 4:35–41 and even asked: "who then is this that even the wind and the sea obey him?" In 6:45–52, they witnessed Jesus walking toward them on the Sea of Galilee as they struggled against the wind and were astonished when he stilled the wind. Mark highlights their increasing fear (4:40–41; 5:15; 6:50), failure to understand (4:13; 6:52; 8:17, 21) and hardness of heart (6:52). In 8:22–10:52, Jesus attempts to make these hard-hearted and blind disciples "see" his true nature. But what is Jesus' true nature according to Mark?

Three times in the middle section—once in Caesarea Philippi, once in unidentified Galilee, and once on the ὁδός to Jerusalem—Jesus predicts the suffering (in the case of the first prediction), death, and resurrection of the Son of Man. However the disciples have understood Jesus, they have not understood him in the way in which Jesus himself desires to be understood. This middle section—with its emphasis on the necessity of suffering/death and the significance of that for discipleship—focuses the reader on the true nature of who Jesus is and what that means for discipleship.

Thus, I maintain that there are three significant reasons for seeing the beginning of the central section at 8:22 rather than 8:27: (1) new geographic references, marking Jesus' non-Galilean journey; (2) the "blind miracles" serving as frames or bookends; and (3) the content of Jesus' teaching about himself (i.e., passion predictions) and the significance of that for a proper understanding of discipleship. The substance of the material in this section—in between the transitional frames of 8:22–26 and 10:46–52—can be summarized into four subjects: (1) Peter's confession and Jesus' teaching on discipleship (which contains the first passion prediction); (2) the Transfiguration; (3) Jesus healing a possessed boy; and (4) Jesus' teaching on a variety of subjects related to discipleship. This fourth section is flanked on both sides by the second and final passion predictions. A simplistic outline of the central section that follows the geographic markers referred to above and the content of the section can therefore be shown as follows:[38]

[A]  Blind man (8:22–26)—Bethsaida

[1]  Peter's confession and discipleship material (8:27—9:1)
     —Caesarea Philippi

[P1]  *Passion Prediction* (8:31)

---

38. I acknowledge that my outline here significantly compresses much of the material in 9:30—10:45. As I will discuss below, the second and third passion predictions frame a larger body of material that depicts Jesus' instructions to disciples.

[2] Transfiguration (9:2–13)

[3] Healing of a possessed boy (9:14–29)

[P2] *Passion Prediction* (9:30–32)—Galilee

[4] Jesus' teaching on various aspects of discipleship (9:33–10:45)—Judea

[P3] *Passion Prediction* (10:32–34)—On the way to Jerusalem

[A] Blind Bartimaeus (10:46–52)—Jericho

## Brief Overview of the Central Section

With the above structure of the central section in place, let me briefly summarize this section of Mark's narrative.

### *Blind Man at Bethsaida*

The first pericope in the central section (8:22–26) sees Jesus landing on the northeastern shore of the Sea of Galilee—in Bethsaida—after completing what would be his last trip on or across the Sea. At Bethsaida, "some people" bring Jesus an unidentified blind man and ask him to touch him.[39] Jesus takes the man outside the village, places saliva on his eyes, places his hands on him (thus literally fulfilling the people's request), and asks the man, "Do you see anything?" (εἴ τι βλέπεις;). The man responds that he does, in fact, see human beings, but they look as if they are trees walking about (βλέπω τοὺς ἀνθρώπους ὅτι ὡς δένδρα ὁρῶ περιπατοῦντας). After this, Jesus places both hands on the man's eyes (ἐπὶ τοὺς ὀφθαλμούς), looks intently at him, and his sight was restored. After this "second touch," the man is able to see clearly (ἐνέβλεπεν τηλαυγῶς ἅπαντα) and Jesus sends him away instructing him not to enter into the village (κώμη).

---

39. While the RSV depicts that "some people" brought Jesus this man, the Greek is simply καὶ φέρουσιν αὐτῷ τυφλόν ("they brought [historical present] to him a blind man"). The precise identity of the persons bringing Jesus the blind man is not clear nor is the manner in which they heard of Jesus' presence in Bethsaida. The important feature is that he cannot move without help.

## Peter's Confession and Teaching on Discipleship

The narrative continues with Jesus and his disciples going on to the villages (κῶμαι) Caesarea Philippi (8:27–9:1), a journey northward of some 40 kilometers. On the way to Caesarea Philippi, Jesus asks the disciples "who do men say that I am?" *They* respond (εἶπαν) by saying some believe him to be John the Baptist, while others hold him to be Elijah or one of the prophets. But pointedly (the syntax here is reminiscent of 4:12 in the so-called "parable theory") Jesus asks *them* this question: ὑμεῖς δέ τίνα με λέγετε εἶναι. *Peter* responds with the declaration σὺ εἶ ὁ χριστός. While Jesus does not expressly acquiesce or deny this recognition, he does warn or rebuke (ἐπετίμησεν) the disciples not to tell anyone this and then goes on to predict his eventual suffering and death (8:31). After this prediction, Peter takes Jesus aside and rebukes (ἐπιτιμᾶν) him for such talk. Jesus turns to the *disciples* and harshly rebukes (ἐπετίμησεν) *Peter*, calling him Satan (8:32–33). After this stinging word to Peter, Jesus calls the crowd (ὄχλος) together with the disciples and offers them instruction about what it means to be a disciple, namely, that it involves denial, cross-bearing, and following (8:34). This type of discipleship carries with it much responsibility (8:35–37) and much reward (8:38–9:1). Ironically, it is in this middle section that the Peter and the disciples show the increasing tendency to misunderstand these demands, ultimately failing to comprehend the reality of Jesus and the significance of that reality to their lives (Peter: 8:30–33; 9:5–6, 10; 10:28; Disciples: 9:18; 10:32, 34; James/John: 10:35–40).

As observed above, this scene contains the first of the three passion predictions. After Jesus warns Peter and the others not to tell anyone about his true identity as Messiah/Christ, he begins to teach them that the *Son of Man* must suffer many things, including rejection, and be killed. But, there is hope, because three days after his death, Jesus tells these followers he will rise again (ἀναστῆναι). This is not the place to review in detail the particulars of the passion predictions, but at a minimum several items should be noted. First, in this prediction (as in all three), Jesus refers to himself in the third person as "Son of Man." By using the indirect reference of Son of Man, Jesus is supplementing Peter's confession of him as Christ. Like the blind man who saw things blurry, so too has Peter "seen" a fuzzy picture of Jesus. Though I would not go so far as to say that Jesus' response is corrective, simply seeing Jesus as Messiah (and not Son of Man or Son of God) is incomplete.⁴⁰ Second, there is a discussion of some form of suffering and/or rejection at the hands of others. Whatever type of Messiah first-century people (especially first-century Jews) were expecting, they were not expecting one who would *suffer*.⁴¹ And finally, after the prediction of death, there is the announcement by Jesus that he will not remain dead, but will rise in three days. The subsequent predictions, while varying slightly, contain these essential elements.

## *Transfiguration of Jesus*

The second substantive scene after the opening transition deals with the transfiguration of Jesus. Mark connects this scene with the previous one through the use of the temporal marker "after six days" (καὶ μετὰ ἡμέρας ἕξ).⁴² Jesus leads Peter, James, and John, his inner circle of disciples up to a high mountain where his garments become thoroughly white and he becomes changed or transfigured (μετεμορφώθη). Appearing with Jesus in this state of transformation are two prophets of old: Elijah *with* Moses.⁴³ Peter's voice is the first heard after this surprising sight (9:5). Not knowing what to say (the narrator relates—9:6), Peter asks Jesus for permission to set up three shelters or booths—one for Jesus, one for Moses, and one for Elijah—for he has decided that it is good for them to be there.⁴⁴ Peter has not

---

40. On corrective Christology, see esp. Kingsbury, *Christology of Mark's Gospel*, 25–45.

41. The precise expectations concerning Messiah are difficult to determine. For discussions on these matters see, Neusner, Green, and Frerichs, eds., *Judaisms and their Messiahs*; Charlesworth, *The Messiah*; Collins, *Scepter and the Star*; and Fitzmyer, *One Who Is to Come*.

42. The "six days" reference has been the focus of much discussion. Some interpreters see dependence on Exod 24:15b–18 (Beare, *Earliest Records of Jesus*, 142–43); others hold it to be evidence of an actual experience of Jesus and the disciples (Taylor, *Gospel According to St. Mark*, 388); still others see cultic or fasting connections (Thrall, "The Transfiguration," 311). For a helpful summary of these issues, see McCurley, "'And After Six Days,'" 67–81.

43. The fact that Elijah's name appears first troubles many interpreters. Since Moses is considered the greatest of the prophets, his name should be primary. Moses is mentioned first in Matt 17:3 and Luke 9:30. However, Mark is careful to note that Elijah was "with" (σύν) Moses. According to Heil ("A Note on 'Elijah with Moses' in Mark 9, 4," 115), in all the instances where Mark uses the preposition σύν, the object of the preposition represents the more notable party.

44. The notion of "being there," that is, in the presence of the transfigured Christ is a crucial element in the spirituality of Mark's Gospel. On the spirituality of the Gospel in general, see Minor, *Spirituality of Mark*.

*Surveying the Possible Turning Points*

fully comprehended what is happening and responds in fear (ἔκφοβοι γὰρ ἐγένοντο). As soon as Peter says this, a cloud envelops them after which they hear a voice from heaven summoning them to listen to Jesus. Hearers or readers will recognize the content of this declaration since it resembles the voice heard (by Jesus) at his baptism (1:11). As soon as Peter and the others looked around, Moses and Elijah had disappeared leaving only Jesus (9:8). As they were leaving the mountain, Jesus instructed them (διεστείλατο) not to tell anyone what they had seen on the mountain—that is, until they see the *Son of Man* rising from the dead (9:9). Confused, the three disciples keep the matter to themselves but wonder among themselves what "rising from the dead" means.

## Exorcism of a Mute Spirit

The third pericope in this middle section relates the final exorcism in the Gospel—an exorcism of a mute spirit who has taken up in a boy. The setting of this story is also linked with the previous one in that after Jesus, Peter, James, and John are coming down from mountain, they (eventually) come to the other disciples, who are in the center of a great crowd arguing with the Scribes.[45] As the crowd sees Jesus, they were amazed (had he some remaining effect of the transfiguration?) and ran to greet him (9:16). He asks the crowd what they had been discussing with the others and one from the crowd answers that he tried bringing his possessed son to him and when he asked the disciples to cast it out, they were unable to do so. Jesus' response to the man is perplexing: "O faithless generation, how long am I to be with you? How long am I to bear with you? Bring [the boy] to me" (RSV). Members from the crowd bring the boy to Jesus and when the mute spirit (πνεῦμα) saw Jesus, it immediately threw the boy into a convulsion. This type of convulsion was customary for the boy, who had been stricken with this demonic spirit since childhood. As the convulsion continues, the father pleads with Jesus, "If you are able to do anything, assist us by having compassion on us." Jesus replies, "If I am able? All things are possible to the

---

45. It the Greek, it is unclear whether the scribes are arguing with the crowd (ὄχλος) or with the disciples (μαθηταί). The antecedent of the pronoun αὐτός could be either one since both nouns are masculine in gender. The nearer referent would be ὄχλος, but one would think that the Scribes would be arguing with Jesus' disciples. However, in another equally ambiguous verse (9:17), Jesus asked *them* (the disciples?) what are you discussing with *them* (the Scribes?). Oddly, one of the ὄχλος (rather than one of the disciples) answers Jesus.

one who believes." The father desperately seeks Jesus' help by claiming "I believe; help my unbelief!" In response to the man's expression of faith, as the crowd comes running, Jesus commands the unclean spirit to come out of the boy, which it does after crying out and convulsing violently. The boy's body is left on the ground appearing lifeless. But Jesus takes the boy by the hand and lifts him to his feet and the text claims "he arose" (καὶ ἀνέστη). After moving indoors (to an unnamed house), Jesus' disciples asked Jesus privately (similar to the parable theory; 4:10–12) why they were unable to exorcise the demon from the boy. Jesus cryptically replies, "This type [of exorcism] is not able to come out except in prayer" (τοῦτο τὸ γένος ἐν οὐδενὶ δύναται ἐξελθεῖν εἰ μὴ ἐν προσευχῇ).[46]

## *Teaching to Disciples (and Others)*

The fourth section of this middle section (9:30—10:45) is really a collection of stories that at first appear to be disconnected to one another. However, upon a closer look, each of these stories deals with the notion of discipleship—either as direct teaching by Jesus or his responses to the questions or action of the disciples (or others). Anchoring, as it were, on the front end of this final section is the second passion prediction (9:30–32). The final prediction (10:32–34) falls near the conclusion of the section and serves to balance out this section of the narrative.

The teaching about discipleship, which forms the heart of this section, highlights the motif of seeing and misunderstanding. The disciples have been with Jesus (see 3:14), following him along his journey, and have been privy to miraculous healings/exorcisms and authoritative teaching. Yet, they still do not seem to grasp who he is, what his ministry is all about, or how they fit into it. In this section, the disciples' failure to understand or properly "see" Jesus and the primary focus of his ministry takes center stage.[47] The manner in which this occurs is primarily through an interchange between Jesus and the disciples and between the disciples (or others) and Jesus. The form of this section (after the passion prediction of 9:30–32) alternates in an A:B pattern depending on who takes the

---

46. A few MSS add "and fasting." The textual evidence for omitting the latter phrase is strong (Codex Siniaticus and Codex Vaticanus do not include καί νηστείᾳ) and it is easy to understand that a scribe may have added the phrase in an effort to conform the text to the practice of the early church. On this, see Metzger, *Textual Commentary*, 85.

47. Kingsbury, *Conflict in Mark*, 103.

*Surveying the Possible Turning Points*

initiative—"A" representing Jesus taking the initiative, "B" representing the opposite, where others initiate a discussion with Jesus. The questioning (or sometimes explicit teaching and even rebuke) leads to a significant piece of instruction on the nature of discipleship. This back-and-forth presentation produces the following structure:

| Pattern | Person Taking Initiative | Teaching Focus |
|---|---|---|
| [Frame] | Passion Prediction—Galilee (9:30–32) | |
| A | *Jesus* questions the disciples about what they were discussing (9:33–37) | Receptivity of Jesus (and God) like a child |
| B | *Disciples* question Jesus about another man casting out demons (9:38–41) | Bearing the name of Jesus |
| A | *Jesus* teaching the disciples (9:42–50) | Temptation and sin |
| B | *Pharisees* question Jesus (10:1–12) | Divorce |
| A | *Jesus* rebukes disciples (10:13–16) | Receptivity of the Kingdom of God |
| B | *Rich Man* questions Jesus (10:17–22) | Possessions |
| A | *Jesus* teaches disciples (10:23–31) | Entrance into the Kingdom of God |
| [Frame] | Passion Prediction—on the way to Jerusalem (10:32–34) | |
| B | *James and John* request to sit at either side of Jesus (10:35–45) | Servanthood |

*Table 1*

In the above analysis, note three key features. First, the structure of the section—in an alternating pattern—stresses Jesus as the master teacher and underscores his method, a method characterized by questions and responses to questions, peppered with direct didactic discourse. The second feature relates to the content of the teaching. The sole focus of this section, in one way or another, is on discipleship and (or perhaps better "in") the Kingdom of God. The Kingdom has been the centerpiece of Jesus' ministry from the beginning (1:14–15) and now he spends considerable time and energy working through two main obstacles: (1) the disciples' misunderstanding of its nature and (2) others' (namely the Pharisees' and the rich man's) misconception of it. The final observation is that these interchanges are all set in the context of the final two passion predictions—as shown above, they flank this section. Teaching about discipleship, however abstract it may seem to those listening, is inextricably linked with Jesus' death and resurrection. But as the last pericope of this section highlights, Jesus' death is not something that will be imposed on him against his will.[48] Rather, he will give it away (δοῦναι) as a ransom for many (λύτρον ἀντὶ πολλῶν). It should not be missed that Jesus again speaks in the third person (i.e., the Son of Man) in this statement. The Kingdom cannot and will not come in power (9:1) until its Messiah and King is put to death—a death that is for many—so that he might rise again.

## *Blind Bartimaeus at Jericho*

The final section in the middle section is the story of Jesus movement to Jericho and his restoring the sight of a man named Bartimaeus (10:46–52). This "blind miracle" mirrors the previous healing of a blind man that begins the central section (8:22–26). There are, however, some important differences. In this event, there is no need for a second touch. As we saw above,

---

48. As seen in the above presentation, the last pericope—the request of James and John (10:35–45)—falls outside the framing device of the passion prediction. This request is self-seeking, a characteristic unbecoming in the kingdom of God. James and John's response is a completely inappropriate response to Jesus' prophecy about his impending suffering, death, and resurrection. This pattern of inappropriate response followed by Jesus' "corrective" instruction on proper behavior of a disciple (in this case servanthood) is also present in the previous two predictions (8:34—9:1; 9:35). For a discussion of this pattern (prediction, misunderstanding, failure), see Perrin, "The Christology of Mark," 130. For an analysis of this pattern with respect to this pericope, see Reardon, "The Cross, Sacraments and Martyrdom," 105–6.

Jesus' additional touch of the unnamed blind man serves a key purpose in the narrative—it helps to interpret Peter's confession of Jesus as Christ and Jesus' subsequent "correction" of that confession. Here, Bartimaeus cries out to Jesus using a different title—Son of David (10:47). Though the title reappears later in the narrative (12:35), Mark seems to have little interest in it.[49] The more important issue is that this blind man has understood—by faith based on mercy—who Jesus is and in accordance with that understanding believes Jesus can restore his sight. Unlike the disciples in the previous section, Bartimaeus understands precisely the essence of Jesus' identity and ministry. As Jesus calls for him to come near, the man does and again Jesus initiates a discussion through questioning: "what do you wish (that) I do for you?" (τί σοι θέλεις ποιήσω;). Bartimaeus replies with another title of importance—"Teacher (ῥαββουνί), let [my eyesight] be restored."[50] Jesus response brings into clear view now the key issue at stake, faith. He responds: "Go, your faith has saved/healed you" (ὕπαγε, ἡ πίστις σου σέσωκέν σε), language virtually identical to the healing that the hemorrhaging woman experienced in 5:34. The voice of the narrator concludes the middle section by completing the story for us. Immediately (εὐθύς), Bartimaeus received his sight and followed him "on the way" (ἐν τῇ ὁδῷ).[51] Bartimaeus, who has not been seen in the narrative heretofore and will not be seen again, is the *ideal* disciple—recognizing Jesus' identity and

---

49. Moloney, *Gospel of Mark*, 209. Matera ("Transcending Messianic Expectations," 203, 213) argues that Jesus' criticism of the scribal claim in 12:35 that the Messiah is the son of David indicates "that the category of Davidic messiahship must be transcended since even David calls the Messiah his Lord. The sonship of the Messiah, therefore, must be rooted elsewhere (Mark 12:37)."

50. The title "Rabbi" links the previous material, which showed Jesus as the teacher *par excellence*, with this story. Jesus here questions Bartimaeus just as he had done the other blind man ("Do you see anything?" in 8:23) in the opening frame and the others in the penultimate section (9:33; 10:36).

51. Some interpreters see the concluding reference of "on the way" as an *inclusio*, marking off the central section as 8:27—10:52. Such a device is found in Mark (e.g., for example 1:1/1:14-15 with εὐαγγελίον; 1:10/15:38 with σχίζω). Achtemeier ("And He Followed Him," 132) argues that the two blind miracles are *inclusiones*. Marcus (*Mark 1–8*, 534) defines the term inclusion as "the framing of a literary unit by the usage of the same or similar words at its beginning and end." I see *inclusio* as a more narrow term than frame or bookend. *Inclusiones* deal mostly with literary similarities. The latter is not limited to literary connections, but can be thematic in nature. Here there are both literary (ἐν τῇ ὁδῷ) and thematic (blind/sight) connections. The advice of Moloney (*Gospel of Mark*, 19) is helpful: "Narrative units are not separated by brick walls. One flows into the other, looks back to issues already mentioned, and hints at themes yet to come."

The Turning Point in the Gospel of Mark

the power associated with that, responding in faith to the inquiries of this "Rabbi," and following him on his way.[52]

## POSSIBLE TURNING POINTS

In what follows, I will discuss what I believe are the *possible* turning points from the perspective of the Markan narrative. In analyzing the Markan material, it is best to address the possible turning points using three categories. The first option has to do with total rejection of the notion of turning point. As will be shown, a few scholars hold that there is no such thing as "a" or "the" turning point in the Gospel. The second and most common option suggests that the Markan narrative contains a single turning point located within a single pericope. I will address five possible turning points in this section—8:21; 8:29; 8:30; 8:31; and 9:7—and reasons why it could be the decisive pivot in the narrative. Finally, it is possible that the so-called turning point of the narrative is not limited to single pericopae, but is found in one or more pericopae (usually in the central section).

## No Single Turning Point

Two commentators argue against any form of climatic turning point in the Gospel. As we have already seen, Paul J. Achtemeier is hesitant to declare any outline of Mark sufficient.[53] One reason for this, he believes, is the insufficient attention to the narrative that Markan scholars give. He also holds that it is possible that Mark himself did not shape his Gospel with "any such central point" in mind—he simply arranged the material chronologically as best he could.[54] Regarding the confession of Peter, Achtemeier employs even stronger language against the notion of turning point: "In short, there

---

52. Bartimaeus is a "minor character" in the narrative. See Malbon, *In the Company of Jesus*, 210–13. Yet he exhibits the kind of faith that Jesus requires, including leaving all (i.e., his garment) to follow Jesus. I agree with Culpepper (*Mark*, 351–55, esp. 355): "The garment, therefore, may represent that which the disciple leaves behind to follow Jesus." See also Culpepper, "Why Mention the Garment?"

53. Achtemeier, *Mark*, 40. According to Achtemeier, "a satisfactory solution to the problem of the outline of Mark thus remains to be found."

54. Ibid.

*Surveying the Possible Turning Points*

is little if any literary evidence to justify the contention that 8:27–30 represents a turning point in Mark's portrayal of the career of Jesus."[55]

"Mark presents a collage, not a diptych or a triptych or any other carefully segmented portrayal of Jesus," according to Robert H. Gundry.[56] The absence of structure in the Gospel correlates with absence of any *intended* turning point in the narrative. To Gundry, Mark is simply a "loose disposition of materials" governed primarily by the traditions associated with John the Baptist, Jesus' ministry in and around Galilee, and the passion of Jesus in Jerusalem.[57] Not even the "widely accepted break between 8:26 and 8:27" qualifies as a significant transition for Gundry. He offers three reasons why one should see no major break (and consequently no turning point—though he does not use that phrase). First, though the text (in 8:27) indicates that he is "on the way" to Jerusalem (for the passion and resurrection), Gundry observes that "neither the forensic victories nor his magnetism nor the miraculous element ceases or even wanes" in the middle section.[58] Second, Jesus does not focus his attention solely on the disciples, but upon making his first prediction of his upcoming passion, he summons the crowd and the disciples to take up their cross and following him (8:34–38). In fact, Jesus' speaking patterns—publicly to crowds and privately to disciples—does not cease while "on the way."[59] Finally, Peter's confession of Jesus represents no fundamental break in the identification of Jesus. Had the demons ceased calling him "Son of God" right up until Peter's confession, such a fundamental break may have been in view. But the demons cease to calls Jesus by this title in 5:7. Besides, according to Gundry, Peter's confession of Jesus as Christ does not equate with the demons' declaration of Jesus as Son of God. Similarly, Mark's audience knows already (since 1:1) that Jesus is Messiah/Christ—this is certainly no surprise for the hearer/reader. With respect to the suffering that is predicted immediately following the confession, Jesus has already experienced rejection (3:20–21, 31–35; 5:18–20; 6:1-6a) and opposition (2:1–3:6, 22–30; 7:1–13; 8:11–13).

---

55. Ibid., 37.

56. Gundry, *Mark*, 1049.

57. Ibid., 1048. The basis of Gundry's contention lies in the testimony of Papias. Pointedly, he asks, "who is correct, then—these scholars [who believe Mark used an outline or who imitated ancient Greek drama] or Papias' elder?" (quote at p. 1046).

58. Ibid., 1048.

59. Ibid.

The Turning Point in the Gospel of Mark

Thus, such a declaration as Peter's should not signal such a discontinuity in the narrative as to "signal a bifurcation of the gospel."[60]

So, these two scholars argue based on structural and exegetical grounds that no real turning point exists in the narrative. Their reasoning is based either on Papias' testimony or upon the fact that it is difficult to determine whether Mark consciously saw Peter's confession (or some other point in the middle section) as the climatic mid-point in the Gospel.

## One Single Turning Point

The purpose of this section is to survey the possible *single* turning points within the middle section of Mark's Gospel. By "single" turning point, I mean that the περιπέτεια is identified with one statement (usually one verse) within a defined pericope. Below are five possibilities, each labeled by the verse in which may be held as the significant indicator.

### Mark 8:21—"Do you not yet understand"

In 8:13, Jesus leaves the Pharisees, gets into a boat and goes to the other side of the Sea of Galilee. The narrator is quick to point out that "they" (i.e., the disciples) had forgotten to take bread with them (ἐπελάθοντο λαβεῖν ἄρτους)—that is except for one loaf, which was with them in the boat. During the boat trip, Jesus—reflecting on the previous confrontation with the Pharisees (8:11–13)—instructs the disciples to "watch out, beware" (ὁρᾶτε, βλέπετε) of the yeast of the Pharisees and the yeast of Herod. The mention of yeast (ζύμης) prompts a discussion about the lack of bread on board (8:16). Upon learning of the disciples' discussion, Jesus asks them why they are arguing about having no bread. Pointedly, he states, "do you still not understand or perceive? Have your hearts been hardened?" (οὔπω νοεῖτε οὐδὲ συνίετε; πεπωρωμένην ἔχετε τὴν καρδίαν ὑμῶν;). Jesus reinforces this indictment by using Jeremiah 5:21, which is latent with images of unseeing eyes and unhearing ears (8:18). To these two preeminent body parts, he adds a third, the mind—"Do you not remember?" (καὶ οὐ μνημονεύετε). Jesus must remind the disciples of the feeding miracles they had previously witnessed—one on Jewish soil where Jesus fed five thousand men (6:30–44) and one on Gentile soil where he fed four thousand (8:1–10). Again, Jesus

60. Ibid.

## Surveying the Possible Turning Points

asks the disciples about each feeding and how many baskets full of leftovers they retrieved. Their mouths utter the correct words ("twelve" and "seven"; 8:19–20), but it is obvious that their minds have not comprehended the significance of the two events. With a concluding question Jesus asks, "Do you not yet understand?" (οὔπω συνίετε).[61]

This penetrating question of Jesus to the disciples to some serves as the "climactic word not only of this unit but of the entire first half of Mark (the Galilean ministry)."[62] In light of all that the disciples have witnessed—miraculous deeds, healings, exorcisms, extraordinary teaching—the question highlights the misunderstandings of the disciples, and in a much more subtle way the Pharisees and even Herod. In light of this brief summary of the context of 8:14–21, the reasons for seeing this pericope—especially its culminating question—as the turning point of the Gospel can be summarized based on formal/structural, literary, and exegetical reasons.

### Formal/Structural Reasons

Within the Markan narrative, there are formal or structural reasons why the turning point of the Gospel might be Jesus' question in 8:21, οὔπω συνίετε.[63] These formal identifications can be broken down further in terms of what *ceases* in this pericope and what *begins* in this pericope. In terms of what ceases in this pericope, remember that five previous times in the narrative, Jesus boards a boat and "crosses" the Sea of Galilee (4:35–41; 5:21; 6:45–52; 8:10; 8:14–21).[64] The importance of the sea cannot go understated.

---

61. Quesnell (*The Mind of Mark*, 104) has argued that 8:17b, 17c, 18, and 21 could all be either statements or questions. In the context, it is best to see them as questions and not direct statements. In support of this, see Fowler, *Let the Reader Understand*, 145.

62. Williamson, *Mark*, 146. For others who see 8:21 as a key moment in the narrative, see deSilva, *Introduction to the New Testament*, 198–201; LaVerdiere, *Beginning of the Gospel*, 2.1–3; Marcus, *Mark 1–8*, 62–64, 506–15; Myers, *Binding the Strong Man*, 390–91; and Senior and Stuhlmueller, *Biblical Foundations for Mission*, 211–32, esp. 215, 226.

63. A few MSS [B Γ 28 579 700 2427$^{vid}$ 2542 and a large number of other 𝔐 texts] replace οὔπω with πῶς οὐ ("how not so") while others [A D N W Θ ($f^{13}$) 33 565 *pm* lat sy$^{p.h}$] insert πῶς before οὔπω. The MSS supporting the NA$^{27}$ are ℵ C K L Δ $f^1$ 892 1241 1424 and some that differ from the Majority text. Though this presents the text critic with the situation where Codex Sinaiticus, Codex Alexandrinus, and Codex Vaticanus disagree with one another, the fact that οὔπω is unambiguously found in 8:17 lends support to the fact that the text represents the more reliable reading. That οὔπω is a Markan word, see also 4:40; 11:2; and 13:7.

64. Kelber (*Mark's Story of Jesus*, 30–42, esp. 35) cites six boat trips. Kelber's third

The Turning Point in the Gospel of Mark

In Mark's Gospel, the Sea of Galilee represents a boundary marker—on the western side is Jewish land, the eastern side Gentile. Almost without exception, the ministry Jesus undertakes in Jewish land is complemented with similar ministry in Gentile territory.[65] The kingdom of God (which was announced in 1:14–15) is meant to extend beyond ethnic and religious tradition to include others. Not only can this extension be seen in terms of ethnicity (e.g., Jew/Gentile) and religious tradition (e.g., Israel cult/pagan), but also in terms of gender. After one of these boat trips (6:45–52), Jesus proceeds into the region Tyre (Gentile territory) where a Syrophoenician woman seeks Jesus out so that he might cast out a demon that had possessed her daughter (7:24–29). After an interesting interchange, the woman's faithful persistence prompts Jesus to exorcise the demon from afar. The kingdom that Jesus proclaims and exhibits is hardly able to be contained by the expected means of race, ethnicity, gender, and religious persuasion. All this "expansion" language, as it relates to the kingdom, is tied together with the sea crossings. The final boat trip to "the other side" (8:13) is the site of the exchange between Jesus and the disciples about the yeast of the Pharisees and Herod. After 8:21, Jesus does not enter a boat again in the Markan narrative. Given the importance of the inclusive mission of Jesus, to many this fact alone might be enough to suggest that 8:21 marks a turning point in the Gospel. But, there is another possible structural clue in the narrative—one that has been discussed previously and only needs brief mention here.

As the above summary analysis of Mark's central section (8:22–10:52) showed, this section of narrative is marked off by two blind miracles—one of an unnamed man in Bethsaida (8:22–26) and the other about Bartimaeus (10:46–52). These two "bookends" allow the central section of the Gospel to remain intact and could be a formal distinction by Mark to designate as such. But the lines here are not hard and fast. As will be noted below, the first blind miracle serves as a transition or hinge passage—looking back to

---

trip (6:32) is not included in the above listing since Jesus and his disciples simply went away by themselves in the boat and, as such, did not "cross" the sea. Kelber admits this: "This third voyage [6:32] is therefore not a crossing of the lake but a change of place on its Jewish shoreline." Furthermore, in what is referred to above as the third of these (6:45–53), the term "crossing" is really a misnomer (though the text uses διαπεράσαντες; 6:53). According to v. 53, they land not what one might think of as "across the sea," but in Gennesaret, a fertile plain on the Western side of the Sea of Galilee just south of Capernaum. For an explanation of the reasons for this failure to make it to Gentile land, see Malbon, *Narrative Space and Mythic Meaning*, 26–30.

65. Kelber, *Mark's Story of Jesus*, 33–42.

*Surveying the Possible Turning Points*

previous material and forward to subsequent material. Nevertheless, the clear lines of the central section do serve in an important way to set off the next major section of the Gospel, leaving 8:21 as the climactic moment in the first half of the narrative.

## Literary Reasons

A primary literary reason why some see this section as the turning point of the narrative is due to the significant series of questions in 8:14–21, which culminates with the final "do you not yet understand" (8:21). This series of questions can be visualized in this manner:

1. τί διαλογίζεσθε ὅτι ἄρτους οὐκ ἔχετε; (8:17a)
   (Why are you discussing not having bread?)

2. οὔπω νοεῖτε οὐδὲ συνίετε; (8:17b)
   (Do you not yet understand or perceive?)

3. πεπωρωμένην ἔχετε τὴν καρδίαν ὑμῶν; (8:17c)
   (Have your hearts been hardened?)

4. ὀφθαλμοὺς ἔχοντες οὐ βλέπετε καὶ ὦτα ἔχοντες οὐκ ἀκούετε; (8:18ab [Jer 5:21])
   (Though having eyes, do you not see and though having ears do you not hear?)

5. καὶ οὐ μνημονεύετε, (8:18c)
   (Do you not remember?)

6. πόσους κοφίνους κλασμάτων πλήρεις ἤρατε (8:19b)
   (How many baskets full of fragments [from the 5,000] did you take up?)

7. πόσων σπυρίδων πληρώματα κλασμάτων ἤρατε (8:20b)
   (How many large baskets full of fragments [from the 4,000] did you take up?)

8. οὔπω συνίετε; (8:21)
   (Do you not yet understand?)

65

## The Turning Point in the Gospel of Mark

As can be seen from this presentation, the questions of Jesus continue to press upon the disciples their lack of understanding and perception about who he is and what the kingdom of God is about. The questions of Jesus do not cease (see for example 8:23), but here reach climactic proportion as they are directed at the disciples.

In addition to these formal elements that may convince some that 8:21 is the turning point in Mark, there is one addition potential literary reason. As mentioned in chapter 1, a common literary device employed by Mark is sandwiching or intercalation.[66] The intercalation is a literary technique that one story interrupts another and usually the "inner" story aids in interpreting the flanking narratives. Tom Shepherd identifies the following six Markan sandwiches:[67]

1. Jesus' relatives and the Beelzebul controversy (3:20–35)
2. Jairus and the woman with a hemorrhage (5:21–43)
3. The mission of the Twelve and John the Baptist (6:7–32)
4. The Cursing of the Fig Tree and Cleansing of Temple (11:12–25)
5. The Passion Plot and Anointing at Bethany (14:1–11)
6. Peter's Denial and Jesus' Trial (14:53–72)

Three (four if one follows Edwards) intercalations are found in the first six chapters of Mark—*before* the so-called middle section. The remaining three (or five according to Edwards) occur once Jesus has arrived in Jerusalem. Thus, there are no sandwich stories in the central section of 8:22–10:52. If intercalation was used consciously by Mark as a literary device, the concentration of these stories in the opening chapters and the closing chapters may be tangential evidence that the central section is "marked off" by other features. To some, the absence of sandwich stories may be another reason why 8:21 closes the first major section of the Gospel and 8:22 opens the all-important middle section.[68]

---

66. On this, see Edwards, "Markan Sandwiches," 193–216; and Shepherd, *Markan Sandwich Stories*.

67. Shepherd, *Markan Sandwich Stories*, 388–92. Edward ("Markan Sandwiches," 197–215) includes three other sandwiches in addition to these: 4:1–20; 14:17–31; 15:40—16:8.

68. LaVerdiere (*Beginning of the Gospel*, 2, 5–6) seems to hint at this as he examines the literary characteristics of the Gospel. There is no doubt that he sees 8:21 as the close of the first major section.

*Surveying the Possible Turning Points*

Exegetical Reasons

As alluded to earlier, 8:14–21 serves as a hinge passage.[69] The mention of bread looks backwards to the two feeding miracles (6:30–34; 8:1–10) and indicates that the disciples have completely missed (or at best misunderstood) the identity of Jesus and the nature of his ministry.[70] The use of ἀρτός (bread) is consistently used in each of these stories and the addition of ζύμη (yeast or leaven) in 8:15 (the only occurrence of the word in Mark) connects the previous material. Similarly, the feeding miracles are seen by many interpreters to possess Eucharistic dimensions. Norman A. Beck, for example, argues that the dominant theme in 6:30–8:21 is the sufficiency of "one loaf," which includes Jewish followers and non-Jewish followers. He structures the section of the Gospel that he labels "eucharistic teachings" as follows:[71]

1. 6:30–44: Feeding the 5,000 (a Jewish feeding)
2. 6:52: Lack of understanding about the loaves
3. 7:2–5, 15–19: Food going in; words coming out
4. 7:27–28: Crumbs for the Syrophoenician woman
5. 8:1–10: Feeding the 4,000 (a Gentile feeding)
6. 8:14–21: Lack of understanding about the loves and the one loaf

Within this section of the narrative (which Beck accepts as either Markan or pre-Markan) 8:14–22 is the climax.[72]

Another exegetical decision involves the incomprehension of the disciples, which seems to reach a climax in this scene. Jesus' use of images of hard hearts and seeing/understanding is reminiscent of Mark 4, the so-called parable chapter. There Mark presents the key or secret (μυστήριον) of the kingdom of God to the Twelve: *to them* the mystery of the kingdom has already been given (δέδοται) presented, but to "those on the outside" (ἐκείνοις δὲ τοῖς ἔξω) everything is presented in parables with the express purpose being (ἵνα) that they may see but not perceive and hear but not understand (4:11). In 8:14–21, the "insider" group (i.e., disciples) are being

69. Stock, "Hinge Transitions in Mark," 29.

70. However, Mark's use of Jer 5:21 in 8:18 with the motif of seeing/understanding looks forward to the following story of a blind man gaining sight.

71. Beck, "Reclaiming a Biblical Text," 52.

72. Ibid., 53.

presented as "outsiders." This is clear from Jesus' use of "seeing," "understanding," "eyes/ears," and "hard hearts" (8:17–18, 21). As Kingsbury notes:

> This third boat scene is climactic in emphasizing the incomprehension of the disciples. By citing the feeding miracles and addressing such matters as lack of perception, hardened heart, and the failure to remember, Jesus' words recapitulate the substance of the three boat scenes and the two feeding miracles. Despite auspicious beginnings, the disciples, by the end of this series of scenes and miracles, show themselves to be like "outsiders." Like "outsiders," they "think the things not of God, but of humans" and regard reality from a this-worldly point of view. Of course, unlike "outsiders," the disciples follow Jesus and are "with him" in commitment to his cause. Accordingly, incomprehension on the one hand and commitment on the other are hallmark traits of the disciples. Jesus' struggle with them is to lead them to overcome their incomprehension lest it undermine their commitment to him. This is the central issue in Jesus' relationship with the disciples, and this third boat scene highlights it vividly.[73]

So, structural clues point to the *possibility* that 8:21 is the interim climax of the narrative. Some may argue that the interruption in intercalations and the crescendo effect of Jesus' questions are literary reasons supporting such a proposal. Finally, to many the exegetical issues involved in such a study—primarily the function of 8:14–21 as a hinge passage and the misunderstandings of the disciples—support this verse as constituting the turning point. No one would doubt the dramatic effect 8:21 might have on an audience or on a reader.

## Mark 8:29—"You are the Messiah"

As the listing in Appendix 2 demonstrates, the majority of commentators consider Peter's confession of Jesus as the Messiah/Christ (8:29) as the key moment in the narrative and thus the phrase σύ εἶ ὁ χριστός has enjoyed

---

73. Kingsbury, *Conflict in Mark*, 101–2. On the incomprehension of the disciples, see also Matera, "The Incomprehension of the Disciples, 153–72. Petersen ("The Composition of Mark 4:1—8:26"), like Kingsbury, reaches back to the parable chapter to argue that 4:1—8:26 is a single compositional unit in Mark's Gospel. The features that mark this unit are topographical and repeated content (i.e., boat miracles). Though Petersen's "compositional unit" ends at 8:26, he refers to 8:21 as the "thematic climax to 4:1—8:26" (209).

many labels: the "decisive turning point in Mark's Gospel,"[74] "the great transitional scene,"[75] a "pivotal point,"[76] a "high point, or more exactly a first point of arrival,"[77] a "major break,"[78] the "beginning of a new epoch for the reader,"[79] the "midpoint of the Gospel."[80] One scholar even likens it to the "continental divide."[81] Indeed, this confession represents a climatic moment between Jesus and the disciples due to one of three emphases: (1) compositional; (2) thematic; (3) aural.

## Compositional Reasons

The first perspective by which we might examine the pericope of Peter's confession is compositional. Bultmann, working within the constraints of form criticism, sees 8:27 as a structural break in the Gospel.[82] This is the point in the Markan narrative where Jesus abandons his Galilean ministry (except for a brief reference in 9:30 to Jesus "passing through Galilee" [παρεπορεύοντο διὰ τῆς Γαλιλαίας]) and proceeds "on the way" to Jerusalem. As the above overview of the "central section" drew attention to, many exegetes (especially those placing special significance in the geographic movement in the Gospel) see this scene change as a significant dividing mark for the Gospel.[83] Jesus' ministry is transitioning from Galilee (ulti-

---

74. Stock, *Call to Discipleship*, 133.

75. Juel, *Master of Surprise*, 73.

76. Witherington III, *Gospel of Mark*, 239.

77. Focant, *Gospel according to Mark*, 331.

78. Vielhauer, *Geschichte der urchristlichen Literatur*, 331.

79. Bultmann, *History of the Synoptic Tradition*, 350.

80. France, *Gospel of Mark*, 327.

81. Edwards, *Gospel according to Mark*, 233.

82. Bultmann, *History of the Synoptic Tradition*, 350. The full quote demonstrates vividly Bultmann's view of Markan authorship and use of traditional material: "Mark is not sufficiently master of his material to be able to venture on a systematic construction himself. The one actual section—apart from the preface and the period in Jerusalem—is the confession of Peter in 8$^{27ff}$."

83. Of course, such an analysis is not limited to interpreters who argue for a structure based on geography. The text-linguist, Cook (*Structure and Persuasive Power of Mark*, 295–97), argues that "the branch of linguistics that uses the theory of action to analyze and structure texts" supports the notion that this is a major turning point in the Gospel. "No matter how one approaches 8:27ff., it is a major text in the Gospel's structure." Cook also places confidence in what he calls the spatial marker of ὁδός. See also, Lührmann, *Das Markus-evangelium*, 151–54.

mately) to Jerusalem. What happens on the road/way to Jerusalem is significant not only for Jesus and the disciples, but also for the reader/hearer of the Gospel narrative.

Robert M. Fowler approaches Mark's Gospel from the perspective of the reader.[84] He observes that in this midpoint scene of the Gospel (8:27—9:1), a "pivotal development" between Jesus and the disciples occurs. But since this development includes disciples in the narrative, the scene is also important to readers. Its importance lies in the fact that with Jesus' question in 8:27, the reader is identified with the disciples and must (eventually) make a choice about Jesus. Will the reader side with the other disciples who think Jesus is Elijah or one of the prophets (8:28); or with Peter who claims Jesus is the Christ, "but apparently he does not share Jesus' understanding of what that means;" or with Jesus who speaks of the suffering and death of the Son of Man?[85] By the time the narrator reaches 8:33 ("Get behind me Satan"), it become evident, according to Fowler, that the author wants the reader to side with Jesus.[86]

Though not specifically related to the structure of the Markan narrative, closely related is the notion of narrative movement. Mary Ann Tolbert, for example, suggests that in 8:27–30 there is a change in momentum: "If Mark 8:27–30 marks the *peripeteia* of the Gospel, it is not the surprising shift in fortune characteristic of tragedy but rather a change in momentum. From the apparent random journeying of the early chapters, Jesus and the disciples now have a definite, announced, and anticipated goal."[87] James R. Edwards concurs with this momentum shift, especially as it is contrasted between the aimless wandering of Jesus and his disciples in the first half of the Gospel to the resolute direction as he is "on the way" to Jerusalem.[88] The deliberation of Jesus after the confession compared to his seemingly erratic portrayal prior to it is stark, suggesting that Peter's confession and the dialogue around it represents of significant change in the momentum of the narrative.

---

84. Fowler, *Let the Reader Understand*.

85. Ibid., 71.

86. One here is reminded of the historical sketch of how the notion of "turning point" has been used by scholars through the years. It was Bultmann who suggested that the story of Peter's confession was a turning point for the reader.

87. Tolbert, *Sowing the Gospel*, 114n52.

88. Edwards, *Gospel according to Mark*, 233.

*Surveying the Possible Turning Points*

THEMATIC

Peter's confession of Jesus as Messiah/Christ is seen by many as the climax in the Markan narrative for two related reasons. First, this is the first time in the narrative that a character in the story has confessed Jesus as the Messiah/Christ. The readers of the story have been privy to this information since the opening line (1:1), but with Peter's declaration a new theme—Jesus the Messiah—emerges from the perspective of the disciples.[89] But as the narrative continues, this notion of messiah is of a different kind—a suffering messiah (8:31; 9:30–32; 10:32–34).[90] As Hooker has demonstrated, the notion of suffering messiah and crucifixion become the inextricably linked in this pericope: "the moment of recognition at Caesarea Philippi introduces a new theme which dominates the second half of the Gospel: the inevitability of the cross."[91] This recognition serves as the beginning point for much of what will follow in the narrative, especially the instructional material Jesus presents to his disciples. The focus of this teaching (along with the confession itself) is designed to explain not just that Jesus is the Messiah, but what kind of Messiah (namely, a suffering one).[92]

Another way of focusing on Peter's confession as a "new theme" in the Gospel has been suggested by Vernon Robbins.[93] Robbins sees a three-step progression in the formal structure of the Gospel. In the middle section, then, the first unit of progression is 8:27–30, which introduces the term ὁ χριστός into narrative, a title he notes has not been used since 1:1. Peter's answer to Jesus' question is thus "a restatement of a feature of Mark 1:1 in a setting that gathers together the thought and action from the intervening scenes and asks the disciples to relate that thought and action to their understanding of the identity of Jesus."[94] The second unit of progression

89. On the privileged position of the readers, see Matera, "The Prologue as the Interpretive Key to Mark's Gospel." See also, Dowd, *Reading Mark*, 85.

90. Veilhauer (*Geschichte der urchristlichen Literatur*, 331) calls Peter's confession a "major break" because a new theme of the passion is introduced. Hare (*Mark*, 97–98) holds that the "Gospel has from the very beginning *implicitly* presented Jesus as the Messiah who must die. Now the implicit will be rendered *explicit*" (emphasis supplied). From the perspective of the plot, I cannot agree with Hare. There is, in my judgment, an element of surprise present in the confession and the attendant dialogue. On the notion of surprise, see Juel, *Master of Surprise*, 3–10.

91. Hooker, *Beginnings*, 5.

92. Donahue and Harrington, *Gospel of Mark*, 265.

93. Robbins, *Jesus the Teacher*.

94. Ibid., 39.

(8:31–33) features Jesus teaching the disciples of his necessary suffering, rejection, and death. "At this point the identity of Jesus becomes an item of instruction in Jesus' program of teaching."[95] This is the first time in the story, Robbins argues, where the disciples are asked to embrace an element of Jesus' identity based on *future* events rather than on events that have already occurred. The final unit of progression (8:34–9:1) contains Jesus' summons to the crowd and the disciples, which requires a disciples/reader to reflect on the identity of Jesus and respond accordingly.[96] This "three-step progression" model builds on each other so that the notion of Jesus' identity has a corresponding call for action.

The lens through which I have been addressing this "new theme" has been, of course, on Jesus; the recognition of his *true* identity. But 8:29 may also be considered as "the" turning point of the Gospel when one changes perspective away from Jesus and focuses on the scene from the perspective of Peter and the disciples. The theme of their incomprehension, which reached a climax in 8:26 as was discussed above, has now reversed—a *disciple* grasps "who Jesus is" (see 4:41).[97] Elias Bickermann rightly refers to the material of 8:27–30 as a "recognition scene," for in it someone other than God (1:11) and representatives of the spirit-world (1:24; 3:12) comprehends who he is.[98] Borrowing terminology from Aristotle's *Poetics* (1452), Bickermann describes Peter's confession as a μετάβασις μετά ἀναγνωρισμοῦ (transition with recognition).[99] It is indeed a transition (in that the focus of the narrative changes) that comprises a recognition (Jesus as the anointed one). This judgment is shared by others, especially those who argue that the genre of the Gospel resembles Greek tragedy.[100] Marie-Joseph Lagrange, for example, suggests that 8:27 (or more accurately 8:29) is the turning point (*péripétie*) that divides the narrative into two major sections for prior to this recognition (1:1–8:26), Jesus preaches the gospel to the disciples and

---

95. Ibid.

96. Ibid., 40.

97. Painter (*Mark's Gospel*, 124) concurs and goes so far as to call this a "turning point *for the disciples*" (emphasis original).

98. Bickermann, "Das Messiasgeheimnis und die Komposition des Markusevangeliums," 132. See also, Edwards, *Gospel according to Mark*, 249.

99. Bickermann, "Das Messiasgeheimnis und die Komposition des Markusevangeliums," 132.

100. See esp. Bilezikian, *Liberated Gospel*, 79–106; Standaert, *L'Évangile selon Marc*, 298–325; and Smith, "A Divine Tragedy," 226.

others; after Peter's recognition and throughout the second section (8:27—16:8), Jesus becomes the object of the gospel.[101]

Thus, for structural reasons and thematic reasons Peter's confession at 8:29 may well be considered—at a minimum—as a possible περιπέτεια in the Gospel of Mark. Before settling the matter, however, we must address Jesus' reaction to this confession, a reaction that many hold is more important to the narrative than Peter's declaration.

## Mark 8:30—"And he charged them to tell no one"

The majority of commentators who acquiesce to a turning point in the central section of the Gospel hold it to be Peter's confession at 8:29; however, a few note that Jesus' surprising reaction to Peter's statement may indicate otherwise. According to the narrator, Jesus' response to Peter and the other disciples was a command to silence: καὶ ἐπετίμησεν αὐτοῖς ἵνα μηδενὶ λέγωσιν περὶ αὐτοῦ. What is a reader to make of this warning toward silence?[102] Is Jesus rebuking Peter for his declaration and thereby dismissing the title Christ? Or is Jesus neither acquiescing to the title nor denying it? The vagueness of the verb becomes an interpretive issue and depending on how one chooses to translate it, could affect where the perceived turning point is located. Those who see no rebuke intended may continue to see Peter's confession as the climactic moment and the language of 8:30 (which is from the narrator) is a wrap-up verse to the pericope or another instance of Jesus' insistence on maintaining secrecy over his messianic identity (see 1:25, 34, 44; 3:11–12; 5:43; 7:36; 8:26).[103] If one interprets the verb in a stricter manner, then the climactic moment of the Gospel may have been shifted away from the declaration of Peter and to Jesus' stern rebuke. In

---

101. Lagrange, *Évangile selon Saint Marc*, lxiv.

102. The verse is usually translated "and he charged [or warned] them that they should not tell anyone about him. The word for "charged" or "warned" is ἐπιτιμάω can carry more severe tones, such as "rebuke" or "reprove." See BDAG, 384, s.v., ἐπιτιμάω.

103. Hooker (*Gospel according to Mark*, 203) observes that ἐπιτιμάω was also used in 1:25 and 3:12 in the silencing of unclean spirits. This command (in 8:30) should not be understood as a denial of messiahship (on the part of Jesus—or even Mark), but rather as part of the "messianic secret." Quoting Hooker: "If Jesus commands secrecy, this is because the truth about his identity can be grasped only by those who are his disciples." Moloney (*Gospel of Mark*, 167) suggests that Peter is correct in what he confesses, but he is only partially correct. Like the blind man in 8:22–26 who saw hazily at first, so Peter *sees* Jesus' true identity but does not fully comprehend what that might mean.

the latter case, though Peter may be saying the "right words," Jesus may be attempting to "correct" what could only be labeled a misunderstanding by Peter and the disciples.[104] Thus, Jesus' "gag order" could be the pivot of the narrative.[105]

Another way of looking at the interplay between 8:29 and 8:30 is to view things from the perspective of first-century oral performance.[106] Whitney Shiner in *Proclaiming the Gospel* has addressed the issue of oral performance in the first-century, in general, and the Gospel of Mark, in particular. Shiner argues that first-century performances—like that of the Gospel of Mark—were done "in character" by the performer and would have involved much physical movement, such as gestures and voice inflection. A performer's delivery would have likely not been recited *verbatim*, but would have been memorized in "blocks," around a series of episodes.[107] The reactions of the audience were extremely important to a first-century performer. The performer would be very interested in "feedback" from the audience *during the performance*. Accordingly, an actor would allow for "applause lines" in the narrative. Listeners would have applauded for (1) the substance of a speech or discourse; (2) the style of the speech; or (3) the delivery of the speech.[108]

After the above discussion of 8:27–30, one might expect the audience to break out into applause at the confession of Peter—after all, a disciple *finally* gets who Jesus is. But Shiner argues that though applause might have been expected in 8:29, the declaration of Peter does not carry the usual markings of an applause line.[109] The command to silence in 8:30 serves to

---

104. This is certainly the understanding of Lane (*Gospel of Mark*, 291–92): "The disciples as yet had no way of knowing what conception Jesus had of his messianic vocation and it was imperative that they should not be allowed to fill the content of the term with their own dreams. Peter's words were correct in themselves, but his conception was wrong, and Jesus sternly charged them to tell no one about him, precisely as he had done earlier when the demons identified him (Ch. 1:25; 3:12)."

105. France (*Gospel of Mark*, 327) refers to 8:30 as the "gagging order."

106. On Mark and orality, see esp. Dewey, "Oral Methods of Structuring Narrative in Mark"; Dewey, "Mark as Aural Narrative"; Dewey, "The Gospel of Mark as an Oral-Aural Event"; Kelber, *Oral and Written Gospel*; Shiner, *Proclaiming the Gospel*; and Horsley, Draper, and Foley, eds., *Performing the Gospel*.

107. For the structure of these "blocks," which are delineated as four "triplets" (1:16—3:35; 4:35—8:21; 8:31—10:52; and 11:1—12:44), see Shiner, *Proclaiming the Gospel*, 115–16.

108. Ibid., 154.

109. Applause lines are often introduced ("and Jesus said") or come at the conclusion

*Surveying the Possible Turning Points*

squelch any applause that an audience member might want to cast after the confession.[110] Shiner argues that as with the miracle stories, which also included commands to silence, the commands are used to control applause.[111] "By undercutting applause for the confession, however, Mark subordinates the confession to the following material about the death of Jesus and the impending death (or threat of death) of his followers."[112] Thus, if Shiner's observations are valid, Peter's confession is not a break in the narrative (because no applause line is offered). Rather, the corresponding command to silence—as the final one in the narrative—forms a fitting conclusion to the first half of the narrative.

## Mark 8:31 — "And he began to teach them"

After the above discussed, it should not come as a surprise that a few interpreters see Jesus' words (not the narrator's) as the decisive point of change in the Gospel. The narrator's introduction even points toward such a change; καὶ ἤρξατο διδάσκειν αὐτούς (and *he began* to teach them; emphasis supplied).[113] Eduard Schweizer calls 8:31 "the center of the Gospel."[114] It is here that Jesus "corrects" Peter's understanding of messiah to note that *the Son of Man* must suffer many things, be rejected by the Jewish leaders, and be put to death.[115] This first passion prediction is just cause, according to some, for seeing the turning point—the orientation of the entire Gospel shifts now to the fulfillment of this (and subsequent) prediction. John Painter is one who holds 8:31 to be the turning point in the Gospel:

---

of a major speech by a character in the story or some other natural pause in the narrative. Peter's declaration is short (four words in Greek) and is "given no verbal embellishment" and the following passage is a command to silence. See Shiner, *Proclaiming the Gospel*, 164–68. One could certainly see that a place where a hearer/reader would not want to offer applause is where Jesus is commanding silence.

110. Dowd, *Reading Mark*, 85.

111. Ibid., 167.

112. Ibid., 168.

113. Hare (*Mark*, 7) refers to 8:29 as the turning point, but notes: "Its narrative importance is accented by the verb 'began' in Mark 8:31."

114. Schweizer, *Good News According to Mark*, 183.

115. Son of Man (ὁ υἱὸς τοῦ ἀνθρώπου) occurs twelve times in the Markan narrative (2:10, 28; 8:31; 9:9, 12, 31; 10:33, 45; 13:26; 14:21 [*bis*], 62). A discussion of its meaning and significance in Mark is premature at this point (see chapter 5).

75

> The new episode can be understood as a correction story. Having silenced the disciples, Jesus now *began* to teach them. But this is not just the beginning of another teaching session. It is a turning point, the beginning of a new phase of teaching, a new theme, a new teaching. The focus is on the Son of Man, which is a change from Peter's confession of the Christ. Jesus had spoken of the Son of Man before (2.10, 28), so that it is not the new element. Nor does the Markan Jesus simply replace 'Christ' with 'Son of Man'. Rather 'Christ' is being redefined by what the Markan Jesus says *about* the Son of Man. This constitutes the new teaching correcting Peter's confession.[116]

To Painter, the content of Jesus' prediction (the suffering of Messiah Jesus) is sufficient to be considered the turning point of the Gospel. A narrative's turning point is often a conclusion of a scene (like those who view 8:30 as the turning point) or the beginning of something new (hence 8:31).

## *Mark 9:7—"And a voice came from heaven"*

The following pericope in Mark's middle section is the scene commonly called the Transfiguration. As discussed earlier in this chapter, in this scene, Jesus is transformed on a mountain in the presence of three disciples—Peter, James, and John. With Jesus appear Moses and Elijah. As Peter stumbles over how to respond to this phenomenal sight, a voice from heaven declares οὗτός ἐστιν ὁ υἱός μου ὁ ἀγαπητός, ἀκούετε αὐτοῦ. That God speaks in the main body of the narrative (a similar divine voice occurred in the Prologue at 1:11) is evidence enough that such a declaration should be considered the turning point of the narrative. Luke Timothy Johnson writes: "It has often been observed that a critical turning point in Mark's story occurs when Peter declares Jesus to be the Messiah (8:27–30). . . . The transfiguration account is an essential part of this turning point in the story. When Jesus is shown to his closest followers as glorified, the voice from heaven identifies him, 'This is my beloved son; listen to him' (9:7). The command 'Listen' sets up the instructions on discipleship that follow (chaps. 9–10)."[117]

The voice declares Jesus to be "the beloved Son"—indeed a key christological concept for the Gospel of Mark (see 1:1, 2:10; 14:61–62; 15:39) especially in light of the fact that Jesus' message is about the Kingdom of

---

116. Painter, *Mark's Gospel*, 124–25; emphasis original.
117. Johnson, *Writings of the New Testament*, 164.

*Surveying the Possible Turning Points*

God (1:14–15). Jesus' kingship and his relationship to God as beloved Son are linked in Mark's Gospel. Hooker sees this link in that references to ἡ βασιλεία τοῦ θεοῦ (kingdom of God) occur at three strategic places in the narrative—the beginning (1:15), the middle (9:1), and the end (14:25).[118] These three references to the coming kingdom of God also occur in close proximity to disclosures of Jesus being Son of God (1:11; 9:7; 15:39)—designations also occurring at the beginning, middle, and end of the narrative. Hooker's conclusion is that the kingdom of God and Jesus' identity as Son of God go together:

> It has often been pointed out that these three declarations of Jesus as "Son of God" occur at three strategic points in the narrative—that is, at the very beginning (1:1), at the *turning-point* of the Gospel (9:7), and at the moment of Jesus' death (15:39). I am intrigued to discover that the three references to the future coming of the kingdom should also occur in very similar places: as Jesus' first words in the Gospel (1:15), at its *turning point* (9:1), and as his final words at the Last Supper (14:25). I suggest, therefore, that for the evangelist Mark there is a very close connection between the coming of the kingdom and Jesus' identity as Son of God. And like the parables, these crucial references to the kingdom focus our attention on the person of Jesus, who proclaims and embodies its coming.[119]

Hooker's referred to Mark's so-called turning point twice, providing two different references—9:7 and 9:1 for support. With Johnson, Hooker finds it difficult to separate the declaration of Jesus as God's Son from the previous pericope. Her multiple references to turning point (9:1, 7) bring us to the last of the possibilities regarding a Markan turning point. This option, contrary to those we have been addressing in this section, sees not a single turning point (like 8:21, 29, 30, 31 or 9:7), but *multiple* turning points.

## More Than One Turning Point

Howard Clark Kee is skeptical of strict divisions in the Gospel of Mark. Like Joanna Dewey, he thinks the structure of Mark is similar a fugue—repetitive elements interwoven throughout the story.[120] In analyzing one out-

---

118. Hooker, "Mark's Parables of the Kingdom," 82.
119. Ibid.; emphasis supplied.
120. Kee, *Community of the New Age*, 75. See also Dewey, "Mark as Interwoven

line proposal (that of Ernst Lohmeyer), Kee states that Lohmeyer "rightly marks out as important turning points in the Markan story the confession of Peter (8:27–30) and the entry into Jerusalem (11:1ff.)."[121] The notion of Peter's confession as a turning point has been amply discussed. But why would Kee refer to 11:1 as a second turning point in Mark's Gospel? Two possible reasons exist. The first is that 11:1–11 narrates Jesus' entry into Jerusalem—thus marking the conclusion to his journey "on the road" (which began at 8:27). Jerusalem is indeed an intriguing location in the Markan narrative. It is the City of David and Jesus is referred to as David's son four times in Mark 10–12 (10:47, 48; 11:10; 12:35), once in the entry story. Yet, Mark shows Jesus as disinterested in Jerusalem—he does not even sleep there, choosing instead to stay in Bethany. So, what could be the reason for Kee including the entry as a turning point?

The text indicates that Jesus was riding into Jerusalem *on an ass* (11:7), which Kee sees as an allusion to Zech 9:9. To him, this links the Markan narrative (and the Markan community) with the eschatological happening described in Zech 9–11, which offer images of a smitten shepherd "whose rejection by the covenant people brings down God's judgment, but who becomes the central focus of God's compassion and the nation's penitence (12:10) and thus leads to the restoration of the people of God (10:6–12) and eventually to all nations' joining in the worship of the God of Israel (14:61ff.)."[122] Kee makes these connections in an effort to establish the identity of the community to which Mark was writing. However, this identification of multiple turning points highlights the significance of Jesus' identity—he is the shepherd-king. The purpose of this chapter is not to provide a detailed critique of Kee's work, but rather to note that at least one scholar identifies multiple turning points in the Markan narrative. Is there a way forward in this discussion of narrative turning points?

---

Tapestry," 221–36.

121. Kee, *Community of the New Age*, 62. Lohmeyer's (*Das Evangelium des Markus*, 29) outline is (1) 1:1—3:6, The Beginnings; (2) 3:7—6:16, By the Lake of Gennesareth / 6:17—29, John the Baptist; (3) 6:30—8:26, The Miracle of the Bread; (4) 8:27—10:52, The Road to Suffering; (5) 11:1—13:37, Jesus' Message to Jerusalem; and (6) 14:1—16:8, The Passion.

122. Kee, *Community of the New Age*, 110–11.

## CONCLUSION

In this chapter, I have tried to accomplish three things: to present the history behind the notion of turning point in Mark's Gospel; to provide a general discussion of Mark's central section; and (most importantly) to discuss the possible turning points in the Markan narrative. This final section has highlighted a significant feature of the Gospel of Mark: while there are certainly key scenes in the central section, it is difficult to arrive at a consensus as to what pericope (or what statement) is *the* turning point in the narrative. Hooker, it may be remembered, labels three different verses the turning point (8:29; 9:1; 9:7). As the above analysis demonstrated, two key sections are critical: the declaration of Peter (8:27–9:1) and the declaration by God (9:2–13). These pericopae are important because of their explicit christology—they narrate the true identity of Jesus—He is the Christ, the Son of Man, and the Son of God. The focus on these two pericopae forces another question: is there another way to look at the turning point in the Gospel that takes into account these two critical pericopae and that holds in tension the christological declarations of 8:29, 31, and 9:7? I believe the answer to that question is yes and the following chapter will outline another approach to the problem of Mark's so-called turning point.

# 3
# A Look at Another Approach

## INTRODUCTION

THE PREVIOUS CHAPTER SURVEYED the various possible turning points in the Markan narrative. That analysis showed that though most exegetes choose a single pericope in which to locate the pivot, at least two scholars—Howard Clark Kee and Morna D. Hooker—hold (intentionally or unintentionally) that the turning point is located in more than one pericope. Kee argued that there were two turning points in the Gospel and located them at Peter's confession (8:27–30) and Jesus' entrance into Jerusalem (11:1–11). Hooker, in separate publications, offers three different turning points—the confession of Peter (8:29), the future coming of the kingdom (9:1), and the divine voice (9:7). Her analysis not only notes the difficulty inherent in choosing a single turning point but weds inextricably two important pericopae in Mark's presentation of Jesus—the declaration by Peter and the Transfiguration. My own presentation of the turning point in Mark's Gospel, which is outlined below, builds on the work of Hooker (and others) and suggests that these two pericopae *together* function as the turning point of the narrative.

As was presented in chapter 2, the final pericope of Mark 8 narrates Peter's response to Jesus' question, "Who do people say that I am?" Peter's response ("You are the Messiah/Christ") is followed by Jesus' warning (rebuke?) not to tell anyone about himself (8:30) and further statements about the cost of discipleship (8:34–38). The first pericope of Mark 9 narrates the Transfiguration of Jesus (9:2–13). In the Transfiguration scene, there is likewise a charge by Jesus not to tell anyone about himself (9:9). Located strategically between Peter's declaration in 8:29 and the declaration of God in 9:7 is another reference to discipleship—not to its cost (as above), but to its benefits: καὶ ἔλεγεν αὐτοῖς· ἀμὴν λέγω ὑμῖν ὅτι εἰσίν τινες ὧδε τῶν ἑστηκότων οἵτινες οὐ μὴ γεύσωνται θανάτου ἕως ἂν ἴδωσιν τὴν βασιλείαν τοῦ θεοῦ ἐληλυθυῖαν ἐν δυνάμει (9:1). With 9:1 serving as a hinge, the twin pericopae of Peter's confession (8:27–38) and the transfiguration of Jesus (9:2–13) serve in a Janus-like manner enabling the reader to see Mark's true intention: the identity of Jesus as Messiah/Christ, Son of Man, and Son of God—and the significance of that reality to his disciples. A critical question is whether these two pericopae should be read together. If not, then, one is less likely to be able to prove sufficient evidence for the "Janus" argument. Yet I suggest there is, in fact, sufficient evidence to make this assertion. I will argue based on linguistic and thematic grounds that these two scenes are meant to be read together and that Mark has crafted this part of the story (within the larger context of the center section) to point to other key events in the life of Jesus and the disciples, which reiterate and develop Mark's overall plot. A second important element will be to determine if (or how) this presentation of Jesus converges with the other aspects of Mark's complex and often confusing presentation of Jesus. In other words, if this Janus-like portrayal of Jesus as Messiah/Christ and Son of God is primary, then to what extent do other images and themes about Jesus (especially the self-identification of ὁ υἱός τοῦ ἀνθρώπου; see for example 8:31) corroborate or detract from this presentation. The assumption is: the greater the convergence, the stronger the thesis.[1]

In this chapter, I will present an overview of the arguments for this "Janus approach." Subsequent chapters will supply the details of the argument including how this treatment of the turning point impacts Mark's presentation of Jesus (i.e., Markan Christology). The first section will look at the Janus idea and how it can be helpful in addressing the turning point of the Gospel. The next section will present in summary fashion the evidence for reading these two pericopae together. The final section in this chapter discusses in what ways this dual turning point affects Mark's presentation of Jesus.

---

1. Johnson ("The Christology of Luke-Acts," 49–65, esp. 59) asks a similar question of his understanding of Luke's Christology, namely his portrayal of Jesus as prophet.

The Turning Point in the Gospel of Mark

## FACING JANUS IN THE MARKAN NARRATIVE[2]

Janus is known as the Roman mythological character that had two faces—that is he was able to look in two directions at one time. More precisely, he was the god of door and gate at Rome and thus, like a door, faced both ways. Oxford historian Nicholas Purcell writes: "More generally he controlled beginnings, most notably as the eponym of the month January ... and was linked with the symbolism of the gate at the beginning and end of military campaigns."[3] As one might imagine given the cultural context, he was considered a god of considerable importance.[4]

Applying this image to the two Markan pericopae under discussion, then, illustrates the function I suggest is present in this central section of the Gospel. The two "faces"—Peter's confession of Jesus as ὁ χριστός and the divine declaration of Jesus as ὁ υἱός μου ὁ ἀγαπητός—stand, as it were, back-to-back and look out over the narrative, one backward, the other forward.[5] Peter's confession of Jesus as "the anointed one" looks backward to the opening line of the Prologue (1:1): Ἀρχὴ τοῦ εὐαγγελίου Ἰησοῦ Χριστοῦ [υἱοῦ θεοῦ]. This opening verse sets the agenda for the Markan narrative—it shall present Jesus as the Christ, the Son of God—and why his life (and ultimate death) should be considered "good news." Peter's unprecedented confession faces backward toward the Prologue and functions as a sort of mid-course conclusion to the narrative, reminding readers (and hearers) of what they have heard about Jesus and (like Janus) propelling them forward in the narrative. The declaration by God on the mountain faces forward and

---

2. The image of Janus (and more particularly "facing Janus") came to me by way of Kraftchick in his essay "Facing Janus." After commencing my research on this topic with the Janus motif in mind, I came across another Janus reference with respect to the Gospel of Mark. Meier (*A Marginal Jew*, 2:691) sees the blind miracle of 8:22–26 as having "a Janus-like quality."

3. Purcell, *Oxford Classical Dictionary*, 793.

4. Ibid.

5. Boers ("Reflections on the Gospel of Mark," 258–59) sees something similar going on in this section; however, his reference points are different than mine: "As the statement of the peoples' speculation about the identity of Jesus in verse 29 looks back to the first part of the gospel, so Jesus' prediction his passion, death and resurrection looks forward to the second part. At the center is Peter's confession that Jesus is the messiah. It is the turning point of the gospel. On the one hand it points back to the earlier part of the gospel by contrasting the speculation of the people with the correct identification of Jesus as the messiah. Because of its ambiguity, however, it also points forward through Jesus' interpretation in terms of his passion to the second part of the gospel which further discloses that meaning."

serves to introduce or foreshadow the "end-course" conclusion, that is, the centurion's climatic utterance from the shadow of the cross: ἀληθῶς οὗτος ὁ ἄνθρωπος υἱὸς θεοῦ ἦν.⁶ Jesus three times in the central section predicts his passion (8:31; 9:30–32; 10:32–34), using each time the reference of Son of Man. Christologically, in these twin pericopae, the images of Jesus as Messiah/Christ (Peter's confession), Son of God (Transfiguration) and Son of Man (Passion Prediction) converge and present Jesus, the crucified, as king, ushering in the kingdom of God in power (9:1). When one is confronted with this Jesus, the only wise decision—according to the Markan story—is to calculate the costs and follow Jesus in discipleship (8:34–38). Let us now turn to the question of whether these two pericopae really are "twins."

## READING PETER'S CONFESSION AND THE TRANSFIGURATION TOGETHER

I am using the Janus image heuristically, that is as a device to stimulate interest and as a means of furthering investigation into Mark's purpose in writing. If this device is to be successful, there must be some thoughtful connection between the two stories *by Mark*. In this section, I propose that there are strong links between the two scenes—first in the use of similar vocabulary and syntactical constructions, and second in thematic parallels.⁷

---

6. An argument could be made that there is really a "double Janus" effect in this passage: Peter's confession of Jesus as "the Christ" not only looks backward to 1:1, but forward to 14:61–62 where the high priest asks Jesus if he is the Christ, the son of the blessed one (σὺ εἶ ὁ χριστὸς ὁ υἱὸς τοῦ εὐλογητοῦ;), to which Jesus responds in the affirmative (ἐγώ εἰμι). Likewise, the divine voice in 9:7 echoes the narrator in 1:1 (Ἀρχὴ τοῦ εὐαγγελίου Ἰησοῦ Χριστοῦ [υἱοῦ θεοῦ]) and the voice from heaven in 1:11 (σὺ εἶ ὁ υἱός μου ὁ ἀγαπητός), while foreshadowing the centurion's statement in 15:39 (ἀληθῶς οὗτος ὁ ἄνθρωπος υἱὸς θεοῦ ἦν). The convergence of christological statements, especially the references in 14:61–62 will be discussed in chapter 5.

7. Perhaps here it is helpful to remember Dewey's ("Mark as Interwoven Tapestry," 221–36, esp. 224) image of Mark's structure as "interwoven tapestry," that is, a "structure made up of multiple overlapping structures and sequences, forecasts of what is to come and echoes of what has already been said." She offers several ways in which scenes/stories are interconnected: "theme, manifest content, particular aspects of content such as setting, geography, or characters, form-critical type, and rhetorical devices such as key and hook words, inclusios, intercalation and frames, parallel and chiastic repetitions." In what follows, I am paying especially close attention to what she labels (1) theme and (2) key or hook words.

The Turning Point in the Gospel of Mark

## Shared Vocabulary and Syntactical Construction

Appendix 3 provides a chart of the Greek of Mark 8:27–9:13 so the reader may perhaps better visualize the shared vocabulary and syntactical constructions.[8] One immediately recognizes the abundance of shared or similar vocabulary, though a few are common expressions (e.g., εἶναι, λέγω ὑμῖν), especially in narratives. Ignoring for the moment the shared proper names (Ἰησοῦς, Ἠλίας, and Πέτρος), there are at least thirteen words or phrases that appear in both stories (as summarized below):

| Word or Phrase | Confession 8:27–9:1 | Transfiguration 9:2–13 |
|---|---|---|
| ἐπερωτάω (+ λέγω) | vv. 27, 29 | v. 11 |
| εἶναι | vv. 27, 29 | v. 5 |
| ἀποκριθείς | v. 29 | v. 5 |
| αὐτοῖς ἵνα μηδενί | v. 30 | v. 9 |
| ὁ υἱὸς τοῦ ἀνθρώπου | vv. 31, 38 | v. 9 |
| πολλὰ παθεῖν | v. 31 | v. 12 |
| ἀναστῆναι | v. 31 | v. 10 |
| τὸν λόγον | v. 32 | v. 10 |
| θέλω | vv. 34, 35 | v. 13 |
| ἔρχομαι | v. 38; 9:1 | vv. 11, 12, 13 |

---

8. I do not discuss recurring Markan features, such as parataxis, the frequent verbs such as λέγω (except its syntactical use), or the use of the historical present. For discussion on these topics, see Fowler, *Let the Reader Understand*, 81–154; and Rhoads, Dewey, and Michie, *Mark as Story*, 39–62.

| Word or Phrase | Confession 8:27–9:1 | Transfiguration 9:2–13 |
|---|---|---|
| λέγω ὑμῖν | 9:1 | 9:13 |
| ὧδε | 9:1 | 9:5 |
| ὁράω | 9:1 | 9:4, 8, 9 |

*Table 2*

One might argue that the vocabulary choices of an author alone do not provide sufficient evidence for maintaining an intentional linkage.[9] I agree. However, there are a number of syntactical similarities to note: (1) once in each pericope ἐπερώταω and some form of the verb λέγω is used (8:27; 9:11); (2) a personal pronoun is used in conjunction with the infinitive εἶναι in each pericope (8:27; 9:5);[10] (3) the pleonastic participle ἀποκριθεὶς is used in conjunction with the λέγω (historical present) in 8:29 and 9:5; (4) the command to secrecy in each of the two pericopae (8:30; 9:9) have similar constructions (αὐτοῖς ἵνα μηδενὶ) though different main verbs (ἐπιτιμάω in 8:30; διαστέλλομαι in 9:9); and (5) the emphatic λέγω ὑμῖν occurs in 9:1, 13—the first instance being joined with the veritable ἀμήν (one of its fourteen uses in the Gospel).

## Thematic Similarities

These similarities are striking, but every author tends to rely on an established set of vocabulary, not to mention employing a comfortable writing style. What is more impressive in terms of connection between these two

---

9. At this point, a detailed analysis of Mark's use of traditional material is premature. The purpose of this chapter is to set forth my argument. Mark as a redactor and the use of traditional material will be discussed in chapter 4.

10. In the first instance (8:27), syntax is confusing. The interrogative pronoun τίνα in the accusative is used in conjunction with the personal pronoun μέ also in the accusative. In such an instance, the interrogatory pronoun serves as the predicate term, since lexically it fills the slot of the unknown, while the personal pronoun serves as the object of the predicate. In the second situation (9:5), the grammatical construction is that of a substantival infinitive. See Wallace, *Exegetical Syntax*, 195n71; 600.

The Turning Point in the Gospel of Mark

pericopae are the thematic links. First of all, in each of the two scenes, Peter is a main character (8:29, 32; 9:2, 5–6). On the way to Caesarea Philippi, Jesus asks the disciples "who do people say that I am?" *They* respond (εἶπαν) by saying some believe him to be John the Baptist, while others hold him to be Elijah or one of the prophets. But pointedly (the syntax here is reminiscent of 4:12 in the so-called "parable theory") Jesus asks *them* this question: ὑμεῖς δὲ τίνα με λέγετε εἶναι. *Peter* responds with declaration σὺ εἶ ὁ χριστός. While Jesus does not expressly acquiesce or deny this recognition, he does command (ἐπετίμησεν) the disciples not to tell anyone this and then goes on to predict his eventual suffering and death (8:31).[11] After this prediction, Peter takes Jesus aside and rebukes (ἐπιτιμᾶν) him for such talk. Jesus turns to the *disciples* and rebukes (ἐπετίμησεν) *Peter*, calling him Satan (8:32–33). Peter, while the focal point of Jesus' words, is not the only one who is supposed to understand the message—the disciples also are meant to grasp this rebuke. In the next scene, Jesus takes (παραλαμβάνει) Peter to a high mountain, along with fellow-disciples James and John (9:2). Here Jesus is transformed before their eyes and appears with Moses and Elijah. In the Markan narrative, the first voice after this surprising sight is Peter's (9:5). Not knowing what to say (the narrator relates—9:6), he asks Jesus for permission to set up three shelters or booths—one for Jesus, one for Moses, and one for Elijah—for he has decided that it is good for them to be there! Peter clearly has not fully comprehended what is going on and responds in fear (ἔκφοβοι γὰρ ἐγένοντο). As soon as Peter says this, a cloud envelops them after which they hear the Divine voice summoning them to listen to Jesus. Peter is clearly a major character in both these stories.

Second, as alluded to above, Peter was not the only disciple present in each of the two scenes—other disciples were present also. We have already seen the disciples when Jesus looks at them to rebuke Peter and the presence of James and John accompanying Peter on the mountain of transfiguration. At the beginning of the first scene, these "other disciples" were with Jesus on the way (ἐν τῇ ὁδῷ) to Caesarea (and eventually Jerusalem). While on the way, Jesus questions them (8:27), teaches them about himself and what he must face (8:31), and instructs them what it means to be one of his followers (8:34–38). The fact that Jesus called the crowd (τὸν ὄχλον) along with

---

11. The word used here for "command" is ἐπιτιμάω, which could mean command, order, rebuke, or scold (see BDAG, 384, s.v. ἐπιτιμάω). While I have interpreted it here as "command," the stronger "scold" or "rebuke" could be in view especially in light of 8:32–33. If the latter is in view, then Jesus may in fact be denying (albeit implicitly) Peter's confession. See the discussion in chapter 4.

his disciples in 8:34 strengthens this theme of disciples being present. The "inside" group (the Twelve; see 4:10–13) and those who perhaps desire to be on the inside (the crowd) are both present to hear the teaching of Jesus.

Third, when Jesus asks the disciples "who do people say that I am," they respond with "John the Baptist, Elijah, or one of the prophets" (8:28). While the Baptist certainly has a role in Mark's Gospel (1:4–8; 6:14–29), it is Elijah and Moses who appear with Jesus on the mountain. While Elijah and Moses' presence in the transfiguration is curious indeed, my purpose in alerting readers to this at this point is to highlight their presence in both pericopae. To reiterate, the primary names in both stories are similar: Jesus, Peter, other disciples, Elijah, and Moses. The concentration of these main characters does not happen in any other place in the narrative.

Fourth, each story includes a secrecy motif (8:30; 9:9). The first command to silence occurs immediately following Peter's confession of Jesus as the Christ: καὶ ἐπετίμησεν αὐτοῖς ἵνα μηδενὶ λέγωσιν περὶ αὐτοῦ. While the theme of secrecy has been prominent throughout the narrative thus far (1:25, 34, 44; 3:11–12; 5:43; 7:36; 8:26), this is the only place in the Gospel where a specifically *messianic* secret is mentioned.[12] In 9:9 a similar command (καὶ καταβαινόντων αὐτῶν ἐκ τοῦ ὄρους διεστείλατο αὐτοῖς ἵνα μηδενὶ ἃ εἶδον διηγήσωνται) is given to Peter, James, and John as they are descending from the mountain after having heard a voice from heaven declare Jesus to be ὁ υἱός μου ὁ ἀγαπητός (9:7). In both cases, the command to silence appears on the heels of a revelation about Jesus' true identity (8:29; 9:7).[13]

The next major theme shared by these two passages is that of Jesus' instructions to disciples. After predicting his suffering and death in 8:30 to his disciples, which itself can be considered discipleship material, he calls the crowd who were with the disciples (Καὶ προσκαλεσάμενος τὸν ὄχλον σὺν τοῖς μαθηταῖς αὐτοῦ εἶπεν αὐτοῖς) and warns them about the cost of being a disciple. A person, if he or she really wants to be a follower of Christ, must deny oneself (ἀπαρνησάσθω ἑαυτόν), take up one's cross (ἀράτω τὸν σταυρόν) and follow him (8:34). Similarly, whoever desires to save his own life will lose it; but whoever loses his/her life for Jesus' sake (and the gospel's) will save (σώσει) it (8:35). For, according to Jesus, what

---

12. France, *Gospel of Mark*, 330. On the so-called messianic secret, see Wrede, *Messianic Secret*; Tuckett, ed., *Messianic Secret*; Räisänen, *"Messianic Secret" in Mark*; and Telford, *Theology of the Gospel of Mark*, 41–54.

13. The previous commands to silence were in response to Jesus' deeds or actions (i.e., healing, miracle). In 9:9, the command is in response to words from God about Jesus.

is most important is a person's ψυχή (8:37). Discipleship language of this nature has not been seen heretofore in the narrative, presumably because it is only here (8:31) where "the Son of Man's" destiny has been disclosed to the disciples. In 9:1, Jesus offers additional commentary for disciples (and perhaps would-be disciples), introduced by the familiar ἀμὴν (see also 8:12; 9:41; 10:15, 29; 11:23; 12:43; 13:30; 14:9, 18, 25, 30). This notoriously difficult verse (see below) appears out of place, but as the grammatical analysis shows (Appendix 3), there are verbal links; and I would add that this statement is meant to speak not of the *cost* of discipleship, but of the *benefits* associated with being a disciple. In a way, it functions as a bridge between the pericopae because of the content of the instruction. The benefit of being Jesus' disciple means that *some* (τινες) will not taste death before they see that the kingdom of God has come (ἐληλυθυῖαν). Mark, I believe, is discreetly presenting a cost/benefit paradigm of what it means to follow Jesus—the Christ, Son of Man, and Son of God.

Another theme that is present is that of Jesus' passion/resurrection. Mark presents the first of three "passion predictions" at 8:31 (the others being 9:30–32 and 10:32–34). In this prediction Jesus teaches four things: (1) that ὁ υἱὸν τοῦ ἀνθρώπου must (δεῖ) suffer many things, (2) be rejected by the Jewish authorities, (3) be killed, and (4) rise again (ἀναστῆναι) after three days.[14] Passing over the difficult "Son of Man" label for the moment, the notions of suffering, death, and resurrection appear again in 9:9, 10, and 12. Is this convergence of themes a coincidence?

The final joint theme almost needs no introduction: revelation of Jesus' true identity. Peter boldly declared Jesus as ὁ χριστός (8:29). For the *characters in the story*, this is the first notion of Jesus as the anointed one of God.[15] *Readers*, however, have read the Prologue, especially the opening line (1:1) and the declaratory voice of God (1:11), and therefore know that Mark is presenting Jesus as the Christ, the Son of God. In this case, this is the first time in the narrative proper that the reader is reminded of Jesus' identity.[16] This declaration is precisely the point where many interpreters

---

14. On the Markan passion predictions, see Strecker, "Passion- and Resurrection Predictions."

15. It is important to keep in mind that the characters in the story do not have "access" to the Markan Prologue (1:1–13). This revelation, therefore, should be viewed from two perspectives: that of the participants in the drama and that of the readers (or hearers) of Mark's Gospel. On this see Matera, "The Prologue as the Interpretive Key"; and Moloney, *Gospel of Mark*, 27–41.

16. Moloney (*Gospel of Mark*, 165) observes that there has been a "glimmer of

## A Look at Another Approach

inject the phrase "turning point." This confession is of great importance to the plot of the narrative and to the theological purposes of its author. Yet it is not the only christological revelation present in this central section.

The twin pericope of 9:2–13 sees the ominous voice from a cloud declare: οὗτός ἐστιν ὁ υἱός μου ὁ ἀγαπητός, ἀκούετε αὐτοῦ (v. 7). Similar to Peter's confession, something significant is going on regarding this declaration. Unlike the Messianic revelation uttered by Peter, this revelation has occurred previously in the narrative. In 3:7–12, Jesus withdraws with his disciples to the seaside. A great crowd (πολὺ πλῆθος) from Galilee and the surrounding area follows. In what Schmidt called a *Sammelbericht*, the narrator indicates that Jesus healed many and whenever the unclean spirits beheld him, they fell face-down and cried out: σὺ εἶ ὁ υἱὸς τοῦ θεοῦ (3:11). Jesus orders them not to reveal his identity (καὶ πολλὰ ἐπετίμα αὐτοῖς ἵνα μὴ αὐτὸν φανερὸν ποιήσωσιν) (3:12). Should the disciples be expected to believe the insights of unclean spirits?

Readers, on the other hand, have been privy to this insight since (again) the Prologue—Jesus' baptism by John (1:11). In that scene, as Jesus was coming up out of the water, the Spirit descended upon him like a dove and a voice came from heaven and said: σὺ εἶ ὁ υἱός μου ὁ ἀγαπητός, ἐν σοὶ εὐδόκησα. Several features should be noticed when comparing 1:11 and 9:7. First, the syntax of the announcement is identical: ὁ υἱός μου ὁ ἀγαπητός. Second, the voice from heaven addresses Jesus (and only Jesus) in 1:11—"*you* are my beloved son, in *you* I am well-pleased," while in 9:7, the address is toward the disciples present: "*This* is my beloved son; (*you* [pl.]) listen to him." Finally, and perhaps most important, this presentation of Jesus as God's Son looks *forward* to a climatic moment in the narrative— the crucifixion (15:33–39). After Jesus lets out two loud cries and dies, a centurion standing near the cross remarks: ἀληθῶς οὗτος ὁ ἄνθρωπος υἱὸς θεοῦ ἦν (15:39).[17] Thus, the true (but not complete) identity of Jesus is revealed in both the confession on the way from Caesarea Philippi and on the mountain of transfiguration.

With 9:1 acting as an appropriate swivel or hinge passage, the thematic links between the two pericopae can be summarized as follows:[18]

---

recognition" by the use of Isa 35 in 7:37. While he is technically correct, 8:29 is nevertheless the first *explicit* reference in the narrative.

17. Much has been made of the anarthrous designation (ἄνθρωπος υἱὸς θεοῦ) in 15:39. For a helpful discussion of this, see Brown, *Death of the Messiah*, 2:1146–52.

18. Donahue and Harrington (*Gospel of Mark*, 273) note that 9:1 "serves as a bridge from the final (eschatological) saying on discipleship in 8:38 to the story of the

The Turning Point in the Gospel of Mark

| 8:27–38<br>Peter's Confession at Caesarea | 9:1<br>Swivel | 9:2–13<br>The Mountain of Transfiguration |
|---|---|---|
| Peter as a main character (8:29, 32) | | Peter as a main character (9:2, 5–6) |
| Other disciples present (8:27, 33–34) | | Other disciples present (9:2) |
| Reference of Elijah/Prophet (8:28) | Transition: Seeing the Kingdom of God coming in power | Presence of Elijah/Moses (9:4) |
| Charge to secrecy (8:30) | | Charge to secrecy (9:9) |
| Instruction to disciples (8:31–38; 9:1) | | Instruction to disciples (9:11–13) |
| Cost of discipleship (8:34–38) | | Benefits of discipleship (9:2–3) |
| Passion/Resurrection (8:31) | | Passion/Resurrection (9:9, 10, 12) |
| Revelation of Jesus' Identity (Peter) (8:29)<br>CHRIST | | Revelation of Jesus' Identity (God) (9:7)<br>SON OF GOD |

*Table 3*

---

transfiguration in 9:2–8. By placing it just before the transfiguration Mark has given an interpretation to both the saying and the narrative." Although I prefer the term "swivel" or "hinge," I see no major distinction between either and "bridge."

*A Look at Another Approach*

It is worth noting that Matthew and Luke retain the essential elements of these two pericopae *in this order*.[19] In other words, whatever redactional freedom the other evangelists felt, they did not alter the compositional sequence of these two stories. I. Howard Marshall, in commenting on the Lukan Transfiguration account (Luke 9:28–36), notes: "The story of the transfiguration is so closely coupled to the preceding scene that we are justified in seeking some intimate relationship between them in the mind of the Evangelists."[20] Mark may have spliced together these stories from other, non-related sources, but if he did the authors of the other Gospel accounts were unwilling to tinker with that arrangement.

## THE TWIN PERICOPAE AND MARKAN CHRISTOLOGY

As has already been shown, the context of the twin pericopae of 8:27–9:1/9:2–13 is the passion predictions of Jesus—where Jesus instructs his disciples that the Son of Man must suffer, die, and be raised on the third day. Let us return, then, to the narrative and focus specifically on the christological designations of ὁ χριστὸς, ὁ υἱὸς τοῦ θεοῦ, and ὁ υἱὸς τοῦ ἀνθρώπου and identify preliminary issues surrounding the identity of Jesus.

Both the Hebrew root משח and the Greek χριστός mean "anointed" or when applied to a person, "anointed one."[21] Because of the placement of the word in the Prologue (1:1), it must hold some priority for Mark.[22] Precisely how those in the first century world (particularly the first century *Jewish* world) conceived of messiah or a messianic figure is a thorny issue. First century Jews most likely expected some sort of royal figure who would be appointed by God as a political and religious leader of the people (Exod 29:7, 21; 1 Sam 10:1, 6; 16:13; 1 Kgs 19:16; Ps 105:15; Isa 61:1–4). This Messiah, it is generally believed, would come from the house of David (2 Sam

---

For a discussion of hinge transitions in Mark, see Stock, "Hinge Transitions in Mark's Gospel," 27–31. Stock does not consider 9:1 a hinge passage, but rather maintains that 8:22–26 is Mark's second major "hinge transition" (cf., 1:14–15; 10:46–52; 15:40–41). I will discuss 9:1 in context in greater detail in chapter 4.

19. See Matthew 16:13–28/17:1–9 and Luke 9:18–27/9:28–36. This, of course, assumes Markan priority.

20. Marshall, *Commentary on Luke*, 380.

21. BDB, 602–3, s.v. משח; BDAG, 1091, s.v. χριστός.

22. Other instances of the term in Mark include 9:41; 12:35; 13:21–22; 14:61; 15:32.

7:14–16; Ps 2:7; Isa 55:3–5; Jer 23:5–6).[23] Early Christians believed that Jesus was this long awaited Messiah of God and that his life and ministry was effective for not only Jews, but Gentiles as well (cf., Rom 1:16–17; 3:27–31; Gal 3:23–29). Recent discoveries in the Judean desert (Dead Sea Scrolls) now offer additional evidence as to what those in the first century may have thought concerning a coming Messiah. The *Messianic Apocalypse* found in Cave 4 (4Q521) notes that "[heav]ens and the earth will listen to his anointed one" (למשיחו) and that "he will honour the pious upon the throne of an eternal kingdom, freeing prisoners, giving sight to the blind, straightening out the twis[ted]. . . And the Lord (אדני) will perform marvelous (*sic*) acts such as have not existed, just as he sa[id]."[24] If this interpretation of Messiah is representative of a commonly held first century viewpoint, then is it any wonder that Mark appropriates this term χριστός in reference to Jesus, given the manner in which he narrates the life and ministry of Jesus?[25]

However, a puzzling feature of the use of the term in 8:29 is Jesus' response to Peter's declaration. There is no "blessed are you, Simon" language in Mark (Matthew alone inserts that into his narrative; 16:17). The Markan Jesus does not affirm or deny Peter's use of the title.[26] What he *does* do, how-

---

23. On the many views of Messiah in the first century, see esp. Neusner, Green, and Frerichs, eds., *Judaisms and Their Messiahs*; Charlesworth, ed., *The Messiah*; Evans and Flint, eds., *Eschatology, Messianism, and the Dead Sea Scrolls*; Hess and Carroll R., eds., *Israel's Messiah*; and Fitzmyer, *One Who Is to Come*.

24. Martínez and Tigchelaar, *Dead Sea Scrolls Study Edition*, 1045. For a discussion on the concept of messiah in the scrolls of the Judean desert, see esp. Collins, *Scepter and the Star*. On 4Q521, see Puech, "Une apocalypse messianique," 475–522.

25. On the eternal kingdom, see 1:14–15; on the setting free prisoners, see 5:1–20 (?); on the giving sight to the blind, see 8:22–26 and 10:46–52; on the straightening out the twisted, see 3:1–6; on the marvelous acts, see (among many) 5:21–43. In October 1987, Princeton Theological Seminary hosted an international symposium on Judaism and Christian Origins. The symposium focused on Jewish, Christian, and other interpretations of Messiah. On the last day of the conference, a vote was taken of those present to determine if a consensus could be reached on certain issues. One issue where there was considerable agreement was the fact that there was "no single, discernable role description for 'Messiah' into which a historical figure like Jesus could be fit. Rather, each group (of scholars) which entertained a messianic hope interpreted 'Messiah' in light of its historical experiences and *reinterpreted* Scripture accordingly" (emphasis supplied). The papers presented at this symposium are published in Charlesworth, *The Messiah* (quote on xv).

26. Matera ("Transcending Messianic Expectations," 212) suggests that Peter and the readers of the Gospel must "go beyond" this confession. Mark, in his judgment, presents the need to transcend messianic expectations. See also Matera's essay "The Incomprehension of the Disciples and Peter's Confession," 165–172.

ever, is immediately instruct them not to tell anyone this. Why would Jesus command this (and why would Mark choose to include this "messianic secret" language here)? If Peter's confession of Jesus as the Christ carried with it the overtones mentioned above (4Q521), then Mark's placement of Jesus' command to silence *at this juncture* might be intended to heighten a reader's awareness of who Jesus is and what his mission on earth is really about.[27] That interpretation approaches the matter from a compositional or literary level—on the historical level, such a charge would hush a crowd.[28]

Immediately following this charge to silence, Jesus explains his forthcoming suffering, death, and resurrection by indicating that the Son of Man must undergo these things. Some have suggested that Jesus' response to Peter in 8:31 is meant as a corrective measure—Jesus is correcting Peter's misunderstanding of the term ὁ χριστός.[29] Perhaps. But I rather think that Jesus affirms Peter's confession, but just like the blind man in the previous pericope (8:22–26) gains partial sight, so too Peter (and the disciples) possess only partial sight into Jesus' true identity. The deeper reality is that Jesus will not be a political revolutionary or even an exalted religious leader, but rather he will be a messiah who suffers, is rejected by the masses, betrayed by his allies, and eventually put to death.[30] Why, then, does Jesus employ this cryptic term ὁ υἱὸς τοῦ ἀνθρώπου—a term that is used in all three passion predictions?[31]

"Son of Man" could be simply a modest way for Jesus to talk about himself. One can easily substitute the first person pronoun into any sentence containing the phrase and the sentence will work grammatically and syntactically. Of course, a popular notion of the phrase is to look at Daniel 7 and interpret the phrase in an eschatological/apocalyptic sense with Jesus being the fulfillment of the eschatological "son of man." Yet in Daniel 7,

27. Evans, *Mark 8:27—16:20*, 15–16.

28. The language is stern: Jesus ἐπετίμησεν (rebuked, reproved, censured, warned) them not to tell anyone about him. See BDAG, 384, s.v. ἐπιτιμάω.

29. Some scholars argue that by not explicitly condemning Peter's action, Jesus accepts the confession and simply begins to explain/teach another aspect of his messiahship, namely that of suffering (see Donahue and Harrington, *Gospel of Mark*, 261). Others take a more tempered view (as do I); see Moloney, *Gospel of Mark*, 166–67; France, *Gospel of Mark*, 330.

30. Moloney, *Gospel of Mark*, 167.

31. A detailed discussion on the Markan conception of "Son of Man" at this point is premature. See Hooker, *Son of Man in Mark*; Schweizer, *Mark*, 166–71; and Burkett, *Son of Man Debate*. A more substantive look at Son of Man in Mark and how it converges with other christological titles will be discussed in chapter 5.

the eschatological figure is presented as (ultimately) victorious, not as a figure who suffers.[32] According to Moloney, Jesus used the phrase to speak of the *need* to experience suffering, but those who are faithful in the midst of affliction will be vindicated by God (like the original context of Daniel 7).[33] If that is true, then Jesus' expression of the need for suffering is critical in terms of interpreting the twin pericopae. As France observes, this is a powerful new theme in the Markan narrative: death as the fulfillment of God's purpose.[34] "If the Gospel had stopped at 8:26, Jesus would be a great prophet, teacher, healer, but he would not have been the crucified Messiah."[35] So Jesus modifies Peter's confession in terms of Son of Man in order to describe more accurately his true identity.[36]

The most difficult verse to interpret within these two pericopae is, in my judgment, 9:1. Though the above analysis suggests that it fits nicely within the Markan narrative, its *meaning* in the context is highly debated. Two items should be noted that bear upon the convergence of themes in Mark's christology. First, the verse should be considered a bridge or hinge passage. By that I mean that it serves a *transitioning* function within the narrative. This transition I suggested above is in the arena of discipleship. Where Jesus previously spoke of the "cost" of discipleship (8:33–38), 9:1 speaks of the "benefits" of being a disciple. The benefit of being a disciple of Jesus is that *at some point* one will see the kingdom of God and thus be privy to Jesus in all his glory. Peter, James, and John got a glimpse of this glory on the mountain of transfiguration. Other disciples "saw" such glory (paradoxically) as Jesus was crucified and later resurrected. Still others must await the *Parousia* in order to enjoy the fulfillment of the promise of 9:1. Interpreters throughout the ages have insisted on choosing a horizon for which this verse must be fulfilled—the immediate context (transfiguration), the resurrection, or an eschatological fulfillment. Is it not possible, especially in light of the narrative strategies Mark employs to his immediate readers (and by extension

---

32. France, *Gospel of Mark*, 334; Donahue and Harrington, *Gospel of Mark*, 261.
33. Moloney, *Gospel of Mark*, 212–13.
34. France, *Gospel of Mark*, 332–33.
35. Larsen, "'Do You See Anything?,'" 6.
36. Painter (*Mark's Gospel*, 130) understands "corrective Christology" at work in 8:29, 31, and 9:7. Peter's confession of Jesus as Messiah is "corrected" by Jesus; God then "corrects" Jesus' statement by the Son of God reference. While I do not agree with the overall tenor of "corrective Christology," I do see a neatly packaged "modification" going on here. All three suggest something about the identity of Jesus that I believe strengthens the Janus motif.

*A Look at Another Approach*

beyond the immediate community) that *multiple horizons* are in view here? Mark wants "his" community to grasp the significance of Jesus' true identity—exalted Christ, suffering Son of Man, beloved Son of God—and the *benefits* of following him regardless of the cost, so he whets the appetites of the community with the transfiguration narrative, which as I have argued points beyond itself to the cross. Once at the cross, the narrative does not end, but closes enigmatically with the women standing in fear because Jesus' body has disappeared. The women and the Markan community hope they will soon see Jesus. The extended Markan community, that is, the second and subsequent generations of readers/hearers share in the hope of seeing Jesus also, indeed, the glory of the Christ *when he comes* in (eschatological) power. In this way, 9:1 is the quintessential elastic verse—it stretches across horizons fulfilling *precisely* its intended purpose.

Second, the reference to ἡ βασιλεία τοῦ θεοῦ in 9:1 should not go unnoticed. The kingdom of God is mentioned fourteen times in Mark's Gospel (1:15; 4:11, 26, 30; 9:1, 47; 10:14–15 [twice], 23–25 [three times]; 12:34; 14:25; and 15:43). The first reference to kingdom of God occurs in 1:15, where Jesus declares his message: πεπλήρωται ὁ καιρὸς καὶ ἤγγικεν ἡ βασιλεία τοῦ θεοῦ· μετανοεῖτε καὶ πιστεύετε ἐν τῷ εὐαγγελίῳ. The "insider group" (i.e., disciples) are given the mystery of the kingdom in 4:11 though their hearts become hardened (8:17). The other references in Mark 4 are in the context of parables about the kingdom ("the kingdom is like . . ."). Several of the references (9:47; 10:14–15, 23–25; 12:34; 15:43) refer to either entering the kingdom or to being near or far from it. The penultimate reference (14:25—"I will never drink of the fruit of the vine until the day when I drink it anew in the kingdom") seems to be referring to his death and, more importantly, that his death is necessary for the kingdom to arrive. With those references in mind, it will be remembered that Morna Hooker has argued persuasively that references to ἡ βασιλεία τοῦ θεοῦ occur at three strategic places in the narrative—the beginning (1:15), the middle (9:1), and the end (14:25). These three references to the coming kingdom of God also occur in close proximity to disclosures of Jesus being as ὁ υἱὸς τοῦ θεοῦ (1:11; 9:7; 14:61–62; 15:39). Hooker's conclusion is that the kingdom of God and Jesus' identity as Son of God go together. As was demonstrated in chapter 2, in presenting this conclusion, Hooker refers to Mark's so-called turning point twice, providing two *different* references—9:1 and 9:7.[37] In her commentary, she notes that "the story

---

37. Hooker, "Mark's Parables of the Kingdom," 82.

of Caesarea Philippi is aptly called a 'watershed', for it is an important *pivot* in Mark's narrative, belonging closely to the preceding paragraph [8:22–26] as to the one that follows [8:31–33], and we might well have made it the *climax* to the last division, rather than the opening of a new one…so at this half-way point in the story, we have a reiteration of the truth about Jesus' identity."[38] Thus, the notion of turning point is used of three passages in Hooker's analysis: 8:27–30 (Peter's confession); 9:1 (the kingdom of God); and 9:7 (the declaration of Jesus as Son of God). Her presentation has highlighted the complexity and importance of these two pericopae in Mark's central section and has, in my opinion, corroborated my thesis for a new approach to the turning point: the twin pericopae of 8:27–9:1/9:2–13 do indeed go together and, as such, affirm Mark's fundamental purpose in writing—the identity of Jesus. The heuristic device of "Janus" illustrates this point precisely. From the very outset (1:1), Mark has his eye on presenting Jesus as both Christ and Son of God.[39] In this crucial middle section, Peter's declaration and the divine voice face in opposite directions in the narrative, affirming and foreshadowing this overarching Christological presentation. The Son of Man language in 8:31 introduces how this Christ/Son of God will bring "good news"—by his suffering, death, and resurrection. The suffering and death of Jesus, however, has a teleological goal: that a person will hear this news, wisely calculate the costs, and choose to follow (ἀκολουθέω) him. In Mark's Gospel, discipleship and Christology are two sides of the same coin.

## CONCLUSION

The purpose of this chapter was to present an overview of my argument for a new approach to the so-called turning point in the Gospel. I have argued, based on the support of other exegetes (especially Hooker) that there is not one single pericope that hints at the turning point. Rather, I have presented preliminary linguistic and thematic evidence that suggests that Mark intended these two stories to be read together. Due to the similar vocabulary and themes—especially the christological designations—these two stories function for Mark in a critical manner. They help present the identity of

---

38. Hooker, *Gospel According to Saint Mark*, 200–201; emphasis and parenthetical material supplied.

39. Because of 1:11, the reference to Son of God is still appropriate, regardless of how one decides the textual issue in 1:1.

*A Look at Another Approach*

Jesus and they do so in a unique manner, by looking backward over the first half of the narrative (in the case of Peter's confession) and forward over the final half (in the case of the divine voice) affirming Jesus' true identity. However, the whole story is not told with those two declarations, there is a need to "go beyond"—to transcend normal understandings of these titles. In the form of predictions, Jesus completes the picture by referring to himself as a suffering Son of Man—one who will usher in the kingdom of God in power (9:1). Here, in the middle of the Gospel, are three primary designations—Messiah/Christ, Son of God, and Son of Man. As Aristotle taught, every narrative has a beginning, middle, and end with the ever-crucial περιπέτεια occurring in the middle (*Poet.* 7.3–7). Mark not only follows this pattern with respect to the turning point or "great reversal," but also in that these three christological statements are found in each section: beginning (Mark 1–2), middle (Mark 8–9), and end (Mark 14–15). Before discussing the convergence of these christological sayings, let us now turn to a more substantive look at the linguistic and thematic links that enable one to read the twin pericopae together.

# 4
# Reading Peter's Confession and the Transfiguration Together

## INTRODUCTION

IN THE PREVIOUS CHAPTER, I suggested that the turning point of Mark's narrative rests not in a single episode or a lone verse, as some interpreters have suggested, but rather in two pericopae: Peter's confession of Jesus as Messiah (8:27—9:1) and the Transfiguration (9:2–13). There I suggested that these two pericopae were linked by virtue of their shared vocabulary and similar grammatical constructions and furthermore that this linkage was a conscious attempt on behalf of its author. This intentionality appears to be corroborated when one observes the thematic parallels between the two passages. In addition, upon examining the other Synoptic Gospels it becomes evident that tradition preserved the two stories in succession.

The primary purpose of this chapter is to develop the grammatical, thematic, and traditional links in greater detail with the intent to show that these two scenes should be read together. In the earlier chapter I also introduced the image of the Roman deity Janus as a heuristic device that offers at least one way in which to read this part of the narrative. In what follows, I will use this image to articulate what I believe the linking of the two episodes produces: the revelation of the identity of Jesus and the significance of that reality for disciples. Interestingly, the identity of Jesus is clustered in three sections—beginning, middle, and end—a phenomenon the Janus image evokes and one that other scholars have observed. But before tackling these issues, an approach (i.e., method) from which to study the twin pericopae in question must be established.

## METHODOLOGICAL MATTERS

Of primary concern in a study of this nature is how to study the text at hand or what exegetical and/or interpretive method should one employ in order to arrive at a text's meaning? The reading enterprise is notoriously complex and a detailed analysis of it is beyond the scope of this work.[1] Suffice it to say, however, that interpretation of any text, especially one like the Gospel of Mark, is the negotiation of the inherently complex tension present between author, text, and reader.[2] Readers of a biblical text in the twenty-first century have many methods from which to choose. There are those that focus on the diachronic nature of the biblical text, that is, the issues and questions that arise when focusing on matters behind the text. These generally concern the raw material of the writing—the stories, folktales, source documents, perhaps even stage performances that gave rise to the written account. If diachronic issues are of paramount concern, the historical-critical method of study with source, form, and redaction criticism as its pillars would be the logical choice of an exegete. If one wishes to focus more at the text itself (as it has been received in its final form), then a method of study known as narrative or compositional criticism would be the preferred method, with its focal point on the plot, storyline, or "narrative flow" of the Gospel. Similarly, one interested in the author's expression of ideas might wish to focus on the language and/or style of an author or the evangelist's use of persuasion in an attempt to articulate the purpose of the work. In such a case, rhetorical criticism or discourse analysis (sometimes broadly labeled "text linguistics") could be employed. These latter, synchronic methods are less concerned with the historical antecedents of

---

1. For a good basic work on New Testament hermeneutics, see Green, ed., *Hearing the New Testament*. For a more philosophical approach to the issue of biblical interpretation, see the three works by Thiselton (*Two Horizons*; *New Horizons in Hermeneutics*; and *Thiselton on Hermeneutics*). See also the introductory work by Morgan (*Biblical Interpretation*) and the more advanced work of Vanhoozer (*Is There a Meaning in This Text?*).

2. In discussing the parables, Perrin ("The Modern Interpretation of the Parables"; repr., *Parable and Gospel*, 35–50, esp. 49) discusses this tension: "But this point of dynamic interaction between text and interpreter is the heart of the hermeneutical enterprise and worth our every effort to understand. In a sense, everything else we have discussed comes into play here: the questions of historical intent and purpose, of the vision of the author, of the literary and linguistic form of the text. All this can and must help us come to the text of a parable with the kind of openness the parable itself demand, or as Bultmann would put it, with the kind of questions the parable intends to answer." This sense of letting the text itself direct the inquiry is the driving factor of the current study.

the text (whether events or sources) and more focused on the time period of the writing.[3] Finally, some more recent interpreters, especially those embracing a postmodern epistemology, argue that a text is not really a text unless or until it is *read*.[4] That is, the reading enterprise itself remains incomplete until someone reads what is written. In such a case, unlike the historical method and narrative/rhetorical methods, attention is devoted to the reader who becomes paramount in the reading enterprise. Such is often the case in the so-called "new criticisms" of the twentieth century: reader-response criticism, deconstructive criticism, feminist criticism, social-scientific criticism, liberation criticism, postmodern criticism, and psychological criticism. The number of "criticisms" in this category seems to be dependent solely on the number and kind of readers. Many of these newer models of interpretation have found their way into Markan studies.[5]

What, then, is a suitable manner in which to approach the central section of Mark's Gospel knowing, as I have proposed, that there are considerable links between the two passages? Is searching for a single method advisable? To answer that question, let me restate my primary purpose in investigating this matter. The purpose of this monograph is threefold: first, to survey the various analyses of the turning point of Mark's Gospel; second, to offer another approach in search of an interim climax in the Markan narrative; and finally to assess this approach's impact on Markan christology. The second of these goals, namely, my offering of another approach in seeing the interim climax of the narrative, weds together two important issues that are connected in Mark's Gospel: the nature of the turning point (i.e., what it is) and its importance in the Markan story (i.e., what it does).

---

3. For a useful discussion of diachronic and synchronic methods of interpretation, see Moloney, "Narrative Criticism of the Gospels." For two thought-provoking essays on "behind" and "in front of" language regarding biblical texts, see Thiselton, "'Behind' and 'In Front Of' the Text"; and Healy, "Behind, in Front of . . . or Through the Text?"

4. The literary critic Stanley Fish opens his work, *Is There a Text in This Class?*, vii, by answering the title's question this way: "The answer this book gives to its title question is 'there is and there isn't.' There isn't a text in this or any other class if one means by text what Hirsch and others mean by it, 'an entity which always remains the same from one moment to the next' (*Validity in Interpretation*, 46); but there is a text in this and every class if one means by text the structure of meaning that is obvious and inescapable from the perspective of whatever interpretive assumptions happen to be in force." For a discussion of this notion in the theological realm, see Vanhoozer, *Is There a Meaning in This Text?* 103–13.

5. For example, in *Mark & Method*, the following methods are applied to Mark's Gospel: narrative criticism; reader-response criticism; deconstructive criticism; feminist criticism; and social criticism (what some call social-scientific).

In other words, I am investigating not only the nature of the narrative's turning point but also its function.[6] Those two issues are interrelated and it is possible that the employment of different methodologies may aid in the investigation of each. Restricting oneself to a single methodology may actually result in less clarity, not greater. What methodologies, therefore, should we consider?

Earlier, I commented that I was interested in searching for the turning point of the narrative of Mark's Gospel and admitted that such a statement might lead many to assume that I would be approaching the text in question (8:27–9:13) solely from a narrative-critical perspective. Narrative criticism is indeed a fruitful method of biblical study and serves a critical purpose in the enterprise of determining the nature of Mark's περιπέτεια.[7] However, I also suggested that Mark's Gospel is not merely a narrative but a narrative about "theologically significant historical events" (borrowing the phrase from Peter Bolt).[8] With the mention of history and theology, we enter into perhaps the more difficult realm of authorial purpose or, to be more precise, the function or purpose (as opposed to nature) of the turning point in the Markan narrative.

Investigating historical concerns along with theological concerns is not a new phenomenon in biblical studies. It has been going on for quite some time. Albert Schweitzer, for example, attempted to determine the issues inherent in a study of the historical Jesus.[9] Similarly, scholars have attempted to "get behind" Mark's Gospel to either an *Ur-Markus* (proto- or secret Mark) or to the source stories used to compile the Gospel.[10] Redactional critics like Willi Marxsen, Quentin Quesnell, Paul J. Achtemeier, and Leander Keck (among others) have analyzed the Markan material in search for redactional elements that would provide hints to Mark's theological purpose in writing.[11] To be fair, redaction criticism in the study of Mark's

---

6. I discussed the nature of the narrative's turning point (8:27—9:13) in the previous chapters. I now move to the function of the turning point in this and the subsequent chapter.

7. See, for example, Rhoads, Dewey, and Michie, *Mark as Story*; and the commentaries by France (*Gospel of Mark*) and Moloney (*Gospel of Mark*).

8. Bolt, "Mark's Gospel," 409.

9. Schweitzer, *Quest of the Historical Jesus*.

10. For elaborate treatments of "proto-Mark," see esp. Koester, "History and Development of Mark's Gospel," 35–57; and Crossan, *Four Other Gospels*, 91–121.

11. Marxsen, *Mark the Evangelist*; Quesnell, *Mind of Mark*; Achtemeier, "'He Taught Them Many Things'; and Keck, "Mark 3:7–12 and Mark's Christology."

Gospel is more difficult than redactional study of Matthew or Luke's Gospel, assuming Markan priority.[12] Despite that caveat, redaction criticism has proved a fruitful method of exegesis of the Markan text, especially when focusing on the theological concerns of its author.

C. Clifton Black outlines the contributions of redaction criticism to Markan studies in an article published in *The Journal for the Study of the New Testament*.[13] He points out that redaction criticism has helped readers in three respects: first, through redaction criticism the evangelists are seen as authors in their own right rather than as mere editors of someone else's material; second, redaction criticism brings out the theological nature of the evangelist's intentions; and third, *Redaktionsgeschichte* "secures the multiple concerns for the history, tradition, theology, and literary character of the Gospels."[14] Black's views are helpful in identifying the positive aspects of redactional criticism, especially as it grew out of the earlier source- and form-critical methods of engagement. However, Black also points out the limitations in such a method (for no single method can address every concern). Regarding authorial intention, Black observes that the intentions of an author no longer alive are unverifiable. "[B]y locating the author at the centre of critical attention, Markan redaction criticism has raised fundamental questions that it cannot answer, at least with any reasonable degree of confidence."[15] Similarly, since redaction criticism often focuses on theological themes in the text in attempts to ascertain the evangelist's theological position, such a study usually involves literary-critical assessment rather than purely redactional assessment. These concerns lead Black to consider that redaction criticism is one useful method among many. "The way forward," Black contends, "lies in the exploration and interrelation of the historical, social, theological, and literary contexts to which *Redaktionsgeschichte* has directed us, and in the clarification and refinement of the critical disciplines germane to those interpretive contexts."[16]

---

12. Strecker ("The Passion- and Resurrection Predictions," 422) concurs: "The task of identifying genuine redactional statement in the Gospel of Mark is much more complicated than it is in the case of the parallel Synoptic Gospels, since in Mark, in distinction from Matthew and Luke, there are no sources existing which were used by the redactor and which might be compared in order to show the redactor's own work."

13. Black, "The Quest for the Markan Redactor."

14. Ibid., 29.

15. Ibid., 31.

16. Ibid., 33.

## Reading Peter's Confession and the Transfiguration Together

Black's caution over a purely redactional analysis of a Gospel text and my concern for treating Mark as a narrative about theologically significant historical events force one to look beyond one single method in order to arrive at a text's meaning (or, as I have packaged it here, the turning point's function in the Markan text). Before suggesting the methods that I will employ, some readers may argue that there is no way for a biblical scholar to deal with all three concerns: historical, literary, and theological. Some may insist that an exegete must choose one method and stick with it throughout her or his reading of the text. Such thinking has sometimes prevailed in scholarly circles.[17] Yet there are commentators who wish to employ more than one methodology (or one primary one) to study a text.[18] The Gospel of Mark, because of its very nature as a narrative about theologically significant historical events, demands a fusion in methodology. This commingling of historical, theological, and literary concerns led Martin Hengel to conclude:

> It is clear from what has been said so far that the extremely different assessments of the Second Gospel by scholars rest on the fact that this work—probably more than any other New Testament writing, at least for the modern reader—is concerned with a *coincidentia oppositorum* which combines what German theological scholarship for a long time saw as an irreconcilable opposition: on the one hand narrative with dramatic tension, a clear theological and kerygmatic profile worked out with great literary skill, and on the other what for the circumstances of antiquity was a very respectable fidelity to tradition and history.[19]

To bring this methodological discussion to a conclusion, there are three interrelated methods that will be used in the study of the twin pericopae of Mark 8:27–9:1/9:2–13. Narrative criticism—already a method

---

17. A few examples may suffice: in historical-critical studies Taylor (*Gospel According to St. Mark*; in socio-rhetorical criticism, Witherington III (*Gospel of Mark*); in reader-response criticism, van Iersel (*Mark*); and in feminist studies, Levine, ed. (*Feminist Companion to St. Mark*).

18. Recent examples of those doing this are France (*Gospel of Mark*) and Moloney (*Gospel of Mark*), who both employ narrative-critical methods primarily but also address historical/redactional concerns. The same could be said for Marcus (*Mark 1–8* and *Mark 8–16*) along with Donahue and Harrington (*Gospel of Mark*). An interesting application of this intentional fusion of methods to the teaching of Scripture can be found in Montague's presidential address at the 1978 annual meeting of the Catholic Biblical Association ("Hermeneutics and the Teaching of Scripture," esp. 14).

19. Hengel, "Literary, Theological and Historical Problems," 39.

employed above to address the nature of the Markan turning point—and rhetorical criticism, its cousin, also can be useful in addressing the function of the turning point, especially in its grammatical links.[20] Redactional analysis, while capable of helping a reader see the traditional material Mark employed, will enable us not only to address grammatical links but also to identify the theological presuppositions of Mark, thus teasing out certain thematic links. None of these methods should, I contend, be applied rigidly. Rather, in fusing them together, a certain amount of flexibility must be maintained. As Joel Green has put it: "Today, no one interpretive method can claim to provide the one authentic understanding of any given text."[21] Thus, in what follows, there will be a conscious effort made to weave together narrative, rhetorical, and redactional methods in order to link the nature with the function of the Markan turning point.

## AN ARGUMENT BASED ON GRAMMATICAL LINKS

It is probable that the Gospel of Mark was first presented orally to a listening audience.[22] It later became a written document and circulated among Christians seeking to learn more about Jesus.[23] If that is the case, then various parts of the narrative would be tied together in various ways, all in an attempt to communicate to the listening/reading audience. This could be done in a number of ways, employing a number of devices. Joanna Dewey has suggested a number that form the basic assumption in this chapter. She states:

---

20. Stamps ("Rhetorical and Narratological Criticism," following quote on p. 220) has an excellent essay on these two related methodologies' theoretical and interpretive issues and their relevance for exegesis. In general, "rhetorical criticism is concerned with how the arrangement of the components of argumentation work towards proof or persuasion. Narratological criticism examines the way the narrative components work to create a story. This concern for the effects of textual strategies can, in both cases, be called a rhetorical concern." For another discussion of rhetorical and narrative criticism, see Powell, *What is Narrative Criticism?*, 14–21, and his more recent discussion of it in Iverson and Skinner, ed., *Mark as Story: Retrospect and Prospect* ("Narrative Criticism: The Emergence of a Prominent Reading Strategy," 19–43).

21. Green, "The Challenge of Hearing the New Testament," 9.

22. Shiner, *Proclaiming the Gospel*, 1. See also, Dewey, "The Gospel of Mark as an Oral-Aural Event"; Dewey, "Oral Methods in Structuring Narrative in Mark"; Dewey, "The Survival of Mark's Gospel"; and Kelber, *Oral and Written Gospel*.

23. Bauckham, "For Whom Were the Gospels Written?," 9–13.

Interconnections, or repetitions and anticipations, are anything and everything that remind a hearer of other parts of the narrative. A list of the ways episodes or series of episodes can be interconnected would include theme, manifest content, particular aspects of content such as setting, geography, or characters, form-critical type, and rhetorical devices such as key and hook words, inclusios, intercalations and frames, parallel and chiastic repetitions. These means may be used to structure a single episode, to interrelate a few episodes, or to interconnect an entire narrative.[24]

Apart from proper nouns, there are thirteen grammatical connections in the twin pericopae of 8:27–9:1/9:2–13 (see Appendix 3).[25] While many of these grammatical, syntactical, or vocabulary links are found in other parts of the Markan narrative, there is no part of the Markan narrative where all thirteen of these occur within the same pericope (or adjacent pericopae). These grammatical connections, when taken together, offer compelling evidence that Mark intended these two pericopae to be read together. Let me begin by elaborating on these connections in greater detail. At the conclusion of this section, I will also present other intratextual links; that is, links within one of the single pericope that share similarities with the twin pericopae.[26]

## Grammatical Link 1: ἐπερωτάω + λέγω (8:27/9:11)

Our first link is a difficult one from which to draw any conclusions since the verb is typically employed in narrative, especially a narrative that purports to be dialogue. The verb ἐπερωτάω (to ask) is found twenty-five times in Mark's Gospel (5:9; 7:5, 17; 8:23, 27, 29; 9:11, 16, 21, 28, 32, 33; 10:2, 10, 17; 11:29; 12:18, 28, 34; 13:3; 14:60, 61; 15:2, 4, 44). In the majority of these instances (15 times), the verb is in the imperfect tense, which has long been

---

24. Dewey, "Mark as Interwoven Tapestry," 225.

25. The proper nouns in these two pericopae include: ὁ Ἰησοῦς (8:27/9:2, 4, 5, 8); ἡ Καισάρεια (8:27); ὁ Φίλιππος (8:27); ὁ Ἰωάννης (the Baptist, 8:28; the Apostle, 9:2); ὁ Ἡλίας (8:28/9:4, 5, 11, 12, 13); ὁ Πέτρος (8:29, 32, 33/9:2, 5); ὁ Ἰάκωβος (9:2); and ὁ Μωϋσῆς (9:4, 5). As indicated by the parallel notations in the above parenthesis (and in Appendix 3), the nouns in both pericopae are the proper names of Jesus, Elijah, and Peter.

26. The focus of this section is grammatical and/or syntactical. I will not discuss other matters, such as theology, themes, or motifs. Those issues will be dealt with in later sections of this chapter.

## The Turning Point in the Gospel of Mark

observed as a peculiarity of Mark's style.[27] The mention of questioning occurs both from the perspective of Jesus asking others questions and others interrogating Jesus.[28]

In the first half of Mark, Jesus asks questions of three groups: (1) certain individuals (5:9; 8:23; 9:21); (2) the crowd (9:16); and (3) the disciples (8:27, 29; 9:33). In the latter half of the Gospel, Jesus asks no questions of the disciples (which one might expect given the increasing tendency of the disciples to fail Jesus) but instead makes inquiries of the Pharisee (11:29) and of the high priest (14:61). The verb is also used when others ask questions of Jesus: Pharisees (7:5; 10:2); disciples (7:17; 9:11, 28, 32; 10:10—Peter, James, John, and Andrew in 13:3); a rich man (10:17); Sadducees (12:18); scribes (12:28); the high priest (14:60); and Pilate (15:2, 4, 44). At first sight, the concentration of a verb of request simply reflects the discourse nature of narrative. However, in only six instances is the attendant verb λέγω used (8:27, 29; 9:11; 12:18; 14:61; and 15:4), each time in the present tense (four participles and two indicatives). Since λέγω, especially in its participle form, is often pleonastic, one may be tempted to discard this observation as being of no value to seeing these pericopae together—simply a quirk in Mark's style.[29] Yet, like many of the following links, it could set in motion a manner of reading that might alert a sensitive reader to something ahead.[30]

---

27. Elliott, *Language and Style*, 232.

28. In one instance, the narrator simply indicates that "no one dared ask him any questions" (12:34).

29. BDF §484. On the nature of pleonastic participles, see Wallace, *Exegetical Syntax*, 649–50.

30. Turner ("Marcan Usage," 136), in speaking about the absence of λέγων after verbs introducing a statement or a questions observes: "Perhaps no very striking results emerge. Nearly half the instances cited are in connexion with a single verb ἐπερωτάω (ἐρωτάω), and here we may safely say that Mark uses it without λέγω, the other two tend either to add λέγω (so Luke 4/6) or to substitute it (so Matt. 7/9) . . . And just as with Mark's ἐπερωτάω, so with the other verbs [of saying], Matthew prefers the substitution of λέγω, Luke the addition. Mark's omission of λέγω is no Latinism, but is probably just colloquial rather than literary language. But it accounts for some half-dozen of these agreements between Matthew and Luke [the so-called minor agreements] against Mark which have disturbed the judgement of so many critics."

## Grammatical Link 2:
## εἶναι + a verb of perception/communication (8:27, 29/9:5)

The present infinitive εἶναι occurs seven times in the Markan narrative, primarily in connection with a verb of perception or communication (8:27, 29; 9:5, 35; 10:44; 12:18; 14:64).[31] The use of this construction is common in the Greek New Testament, but relatively rare in Markan syntax.[32] The fact that it is seen only seven times in the Gospel supports such a conclusion. What is interesting, however, is that of its seven occurrences, three of them (43%) occur in the twin pericopae of 8:27–9:1/9:2–13. In addition, all but two constructions (12:18; 14:64) occur in Mark's so-called central section. Perhaps the most striking issue is that the construction is first found in 8:27, followed by another usage twenty-eight words later (v. 29), and then again at 9:5. This unusual Markan construction should give an exegete or a reader pause and consider that something might be going on (three uses in seventeen verses).

## Grammatical Link 3:
## The Participle ἀποκριθείς (8:29/9:5)

As in the discussion above of ἐπερωτάω, one might expect dozens of uses of words of communication, especially in texts involving direct and indirect discourse. Such is the case with the pleonastic participle ἀποκριθείς. In the Gospel, ἀποκριθείς occurs fourteen times, always with some form of λέγω (3:33; 6:37; 8:29; 9:5, 19; 10:3, 24, 51; 11:14, 22; 12:35; 14:48; 15:2, 12).[33] Some hold that it resembles a Semitic idiom.[34] Similar to the previous grammatical link, of the fourteen uses of this idiom in Mark, only three times is it found in the same pericope: 8:29/9:5 (Peter's confession/

---

31. Wallace (*Exegetical Syntax*, 603) includes this in his discussion of indirect discourse.

32. Boyer, "Classification of Infinitives," 8.

33. In addition to the participial use of this verb, in the pericopae in question, the aorist passive subjunctive (ἀποκριθῇ) is found at 9:6; the aorist passive indicative (ἀπεκρίθησαν) in MSS A f¹ 𝔐 and syʰ at 8:28; and the aorist passive indicative (with αὐτῷ λέγων) in MSS D (W) Θ 0143 f¹³ 28 (33) 565 *pc* and lat at 8:28. On whether the aorist passive is "good Greek," see Elliott, "The Middle of ἀποκρίνομαι."

34. Wallace, *Exegetical Syntax*, 650.

transfiguration); 11:14/22 (cursing and lesson of the fig tree); and 15:2/12 (Jesus before Pilate). The remaining uses are scattered throughout the narrative. If the purpose of a narrative critic is to "read the text as the implied reader," could Mark be placing these redundancies and grammatical links to prepare the reader for a significant element of the narrative?[35]

## Grammatical Link 4: αὐτοῖς ἵνα μηδενί + subjunctive mood verb (8:30/9:9)

Twice in the twin pericopae of 8:27–9:13, we find the following grammatical construction:

1. Main verb (generally a verb of command or warning; ἐπετίμησεν in 8:30, διεστείλατο in 9:9)

2. A genitive plural pronoun (αὐτοῖς)

3. ἵνα μηδενί and a verb in the subjunctive mood.[36]

Use of ἵνα with a subjunctive mood verb is standard Greek grammar, but seldom in the NT is it interrupted by the use of the negative pronoun μηδείς (here in the dative case).[37] In fact, of its four uses in the NT, three are in Mark's Gospel (7:36; 8:30; 9:9) and one in Matthew (16:20, the parallel passage to Mark 8:30). While ἵνα normally indicates purpose (or rarely result), C. H. Turner has argued convincingly that Mark frequently employs ἵνα in a nonpurpose manner. After cataloging each of the uses of these nonpurpose uses of ἵνα, he concludes that Mark has a "fondness for ἵνα after verbs like παρακαλεῖν διαστέλλεσθαι παραγγέλλειν ἐπιτιμᾶν ἐντέλλεσθαι." Turner suggests that this fondness is due to the Latin influence on Mark's Greek.[38] Perhaps he is correct. But what is of interest to me in the analysis of this section is to observe that here Mark employs an unusual construction

---

35. On the purpose of the narrative critic, see Powell, *What is Narrative Criticism?*, 20.

36. In 8:30 the sentence reads: καὶ ἐπετίμησεν αὐτοῖς ἵνα μηδενὶ λέγωσιν περὶ αὐτοῦ. Similarly, in 9:9, the construction is: καὶ καταβαινόντων αὐτῶν ἐκ τοῦ ὄρους διεστείλατο αὐτοῖς ἵνα μηδενὶ ἃ εἶδον διηγήσωνται, εἰ μὴ ὅταν ὁ υἱὸς τοῦ ἀνθρώπου ἐκ νεκρῶν ἀναστῇ. In 9:9, the negative particle and the subjunctive mood verb is interrupted by the relative clause ἃ εἶδον.

37. See BDF §369.

38. Turner, "Marcan Usage," in Elliott, *Language and Style*, 132.

within a few sentences of each other to convey the notion of secrecy, a key theme throughout Mark but of special significance in these twin episodes.

## Grammatical Link 5: ὁ υἱὸς τοῦ ἀνθρώπου (8:31, 38/9:9, 12)

The phrase ὁ υἱὸς τοῦ ἀνθρώπου is found fourteen times in Mark's Gospel, in each instance in arthrous form (2:10, 28; 8:31, 38; 9:9, 12, 31; 10:33, 45; 13:26; 14:21 [bis], 41, 62).[39] As is widely known, the term is used only by Jesus in the Synoptic Gospels. Joseph A. Fitzmyer observes that the phrase is applied to Jesus in three ways: (1) in his earthly ministry (2:10, 28; 10:45); (2) in his suffering (8:31; 9:12, 31; 10:33; 14:21 [bis], 41); and (3) in his exalted state, sometimes as judge (8:38 possibly in reference to another person; 9:9; 13:26; 14:62).[40] Based on Fitzmyer's analysis, categories 2 and 3 are represented in the twin pericopae of 8:27–9:1/9:2–13—in reference to Jesus' suffering (8:31 and 9:12) and in reference to his exalted state (8:38 and 9:9).

That the Greek expression carries Semitic undertones has been well documented.[41] Yet as Fitzmyer has shown, there is no example in Aramaic material prior to the NT where the phrase is used either as a form of address, a title for an apocalyptic figure, or as a circumlocution for the first person pronoun. "When one views the NT Greek phrase ὁ υἱὸς τοῦ ἀνθρώπου over against this background, one sees that the NT usage is special. As it now appears in the Gospels, the arthrous form must be understood as a title for Jesus. Whether it stems from an Aramaic phrase that he himself used, either of himself or of someone else, may be and will continue to be debated, because it is a question to which in the long run only a speculative

---

39. The phrase is normally in the nominative case. It is in the accusative case in 8:31; 9:12; 13:26; and 14:62. Cranfield (*Gospel According to Saint Mark*, 272) notes that the phrase occurs eighty-four times in the singular in the NT (thirty-one in Matt; fourteen in Mark; twenty-six in Luke; twelve in John; once in Acts); in each case both nouns contain the articles. The anarthrous υἱὸς ἀνθρώπου occurs only four times in the NT (once in John; once in Hebrews; and twice in Revelation). Cranfield goes on to note the usages and parallels in Hebrew, Aramaic, and the LXX. For the best background study to the phrase, see Hooker, *Son of Man in Mark*.

40. Fitzmyer, "'Son of Man' Philologically Considered," 144.

41. Sjöberg, "בן אדם und בר אנש im Hebräischen und Aramäischen"; Black, "The Son of Man Problem"; Vermes, "The Use of בר נש/בר נשא in Jewish Aramaic"; and Fitzmyer, "'Son of Man' Philologically Considered."

answer can be given."[42] Thus, while a theological or christological interpretation of the phrase in Mark's Gospel will be discussed in chapter 5, that it is a title can be determined based on the evidence. Similarly, the fact that this title and its use (whether in reference to his suffering to Jesus' exalted state) occurs four times in the twin pericopae out of fourteen occurrences in Mark (or 28%) warrants serious consideration as a "link" between the two episodes.

## Grammatical Link 6: πολλὰ παθεῖν (8:31/9:12)

The adverb πολλά occurs twenty one times in Mark, but only three times with the verb πάσχω (5:26; 8:31; 9:12).[43] The first instance (5:26) refers to the sufferings of the hemorrhaging woman. In the latter two instances, clearly the reference is to ὁ υἱὸς τοῦ ἀνθρώπου as discussed above. George D. Kilpatrick, in discussing the peculiarities of Markan syntax and grammar, observes that πολλά normally follows its main verb (1:45; 4:2, 10, 23, 38, 43; 6:23, 34; 15:3) except at 3:12 (with the verb ἐπιτιμάω) and the three instances of πολλὰ πάσχω. Since these are the only instances of πάσχω in Mark and because this syntactical irregularity is often "fixed" by Matthew (16:21, the parallel to 8:31) and Luke (9:22, also the parallel to 8:31), the phrase in Mark is a "stereotyped phrase."[44] While this alone is sufficient to make my point about the two stories being read together, additional support for this position can be found in the note of urgency found in the use of δεῖ in 8:31 and what I take to be a telic use of ἵνα in 9:12.[45]

## Grammatical Link 7: ἀναστῆναι (8:31/9:10)

Just as with the reference to πολλά and some form of πάσχω (suffering), now there is the employment of (ἀν)ίστημι (rise). This should be expected, given that 8:31 is the first of three predictions the Markan Jesus makes

---

42. Fitzmyer, "'Son of Man' Philologically Considered," 154.

43. In 5:26, the verb is in a participial form; in 8:31 it is an infinitive, while in 9:12 the verb is in the subjunctive mood.

44. Kilpatrick, "Some Notes on Marcan Usage," in Elliott, *Language and Style*, 170–71.

45. On the telic or purpose use of ἵνα, see Wallace, *Exegetical Syntax*, 472.

of his impending passion (9:30–32; 10:33–34). In both these verses (8:31 and 9:10), the third aorist infinitive active (the intransitive) is used despite the fact that the word is on the lips of different characters (Jesus in 8:31; the narrator in 9:10). That passion/resurrection is at the core of the two pericopae is apparent from a thematic perspective; however, grammatical evidence here provides another connection.

## Grammatical Link 8: τὸν λόγον (8:32/9:10 [λογούς, 8:38])

Of all the grammatical links surveyed in this study, this one occurs most frequently in Mark's Gospel.[46] As commentators point out, Mark's vocabulary is limited (1,270 words, excluding proper nouns, according to Swete) and is considered by some to be unsophisticated.[47] Λόγος would no doubt be a common word to use. That Mark used this particular word is not at all peculiar. What is striking, however, is Mark's manner of use of the noun λόγος in 8:27–9:13. First, it is striking because many of the English translations of these verses offer a more idiomatic rendering of λόγος. For example, the *RSV* translates 8:32 as: "And he said this plainly."[48] Perhaps a more literal translation would be "and he spoke the word with frankness."[49] What "word" is it that was spoken? In context, the "word" is the "prediction" that Jesus made in 8:31 regarding his impending suffering, death, and resurrection. The *RSV* similarly translates 9:10 as: "So they kept the matter to themselves, questioning what the rising from the dead meant."[50] This translation is acceptable since the semantic range of λόγος includes "thing or matter," much like the Hebrew דבר.[51] But translating λόγος as "the matter" in this verse misses an important nuance that provides the second notable

---

46. The noun λόγος occurs twenty-two [twenty-three] times in the Gospel: (1) nominative: 13:31; (2) dative: 10:22, 24; 12:13; and (3) accusative: 1:45; 2:2; 4:14, 15, 16, 17, 18, 19, 20, 33; 5:36; 7:13, 29; 8:32, 38; 9:10; 11:29; 14:39 [16:20].

47. See Swete, *Gospel According to St. Mark*, xliv–l. See also, Taylor, *Gospel According to St. Mark*, 44–54. Reference has already been made to the fine collection in Elliott, *Language and Style*. See esp. Turner's work entitled "The Style of Mark."

48. The editors of the *RSV* have translated τὸν λόγον as either "this" (8:32) or "the matter" (9:10). The Greek of 8:32 is καὶ παρρησίᾳ τὸν λόγον ἐλάλει.

49. Or "And he spoke the word with openness." See BDAG, 781, s.v. παρρησία.

50. The Greek of 9:10 is: καὶ τὸν λόγον ἐκράτησαν πρὸς ἑαυτοὺς, συζητοῦντες τί ἐστιν τὸ ἐκ νεκρῶν ἀναστῆναι.

51. See BDAG, 598–601, s.v. λόγος.

feature of Mark's use of λόγος. In 9:7, after the gathered disciples (Peter, James, John) heard the divine voice declare Jesus as "the beloved Son," they are commanded to listen to Jesus. In 9:9—two verses later—the narrator tells the reader that Jesus instructs "them" (i.e., Peter, James, John) not to tell anyone what they had seen until the Son of Man rises from the dead (καὶ καταβαινόντων αὐτῶν ἐκ τοῦ ὄρους διεστείλατο αὐτοῖς ἵνα μηδενὶ ἃ εἶδον διηγήσωνται, εἰ μὴ ὅταν ὁ υἱὸς τοῦ ἀνθρώπου ἐκ νεκρῶν ἀναστῇ). It is this λόγος, that is, Jesus' word about the Son of Man rising that is in focus in 9:10. As the previous discussion demonstrated, this reference to suffering/death and resurrection is no insignificant issue to Mark and the narrative.

In 8:38, it is not the singular accusative τὸν λόγον that is found, but rather the plural accusative λόγους (if anyone is ashamed of me and my words ... ).[52] It is generally held that 8:38 is a Markan rewrite of previous traditional material.[53] If that is the case, then what words (plural) in the context of the narratives does Mark intend by this rewrite? Commentators are, by and large, silent on this issue. Some equate the "words" with the Gospel message that is mentioned in 8:35.[54] Indeed, the syntax of the two verses resembles one another. The "good news" has been in the forefront of the Gospel since 1:1 and much of Jesus' teaching could be summarized under it. However, in the context of this passage, I think that the "words" Mark puts on the lips of Jesus at the point refer to the passion prediction of 8:31. The suffering nature of Jesus' life, which would be a surprise to the reader/hearer, might cause some to be ashamed. Mark attempts to subvert this possibility by linking the λόγους of 8:38 with the τὸν λόγον of 8:32 (which points back to 8:31) and later to 9:10.

## Grammatical Link 9: The verb θέλω (8:34, 35/9:13)

Certain words are unavoidable when writing narrative. The verb θέλω was unavoidable by the author of Mark's Gospel. In its verbal form, the word occurs twenty-five times in Mark alone (compared to thirty-nine times in

---

52. The following MSS omit λόγους: P45[vid] W k sa. This is likely due to homoioteleuton. See Metzger, *Textual Commentary*, 84.

53. Lambrecht, "A Note on Mark 8.38," 122.

54. Edwards, *Gospel According to Mark*, 258–59n57. See also, Donahue and Harrington, *Gospel of Mark*, 264.

Matthew's Gospel and twenty-eight in Luke's account). In the two pericopae under discussion, the verb is found twice in the present tense/indicative mood in 8:34–35 and once in the imperfect tense/indicative mood in 9:13.[55] That three of its twenty-five instances are found within a span of twenty-five verses (488 Greek words) should not in itself cause anyone to believe the two were meant to be read together. In fact, C. H. Turner argues persuasively that for Mark the verb θέλω should be viewed more as an auxiliary verb, similar to Mark's use of δύναμαι, rather than the standard definition of "wish," "will," or "desire." Regarding the verses under examination here, Turner adds: "No instances could show more clearly that θέλω is *practically* an auxiliary verb, and nothing else."[56]

## Grammatical Link 10: The verb ἔρχομαι—including compounds (8:27, [34], 38; 9:1/9:11, 12, 13)

The verb ἔρχομαι is a common verb used in narrative, especially when a major character in the story is traveling like the Markan Jesus.[57] Thus, on the surface, it might be difficult to include such a word in our study of grammatical links between 8:27–9:1 and 9:2–13. However, a closer inspection of the various forms of the verb in the Gospel reveals that only twice does this verb occur in its simple (second) perfect stem (ἐληλυθ-), both times in this passage (as a participle in 9:1; and as an indicative in 9:13). The fact that the perfect tense (carrying the notion of a completed action with continuing significance) is relevant, but so is the context. In each case, the verse begins with an introductory phrase (λέγω ὑμῖν—to be discussed

---

55. Of the twenty-five occurrences, eighteen uses are in the present tense, six in the imperfect, and one in the aorist. We have already observed the Markan tendency to use the imperfect (see Turner, "Marcan Usage," 90; and Turner, "The Style of Mark," 232, both in Elliott, *Language and Style*).

56. Turner, "Marcan Uses," in Elliott, *Language and Style*, 98; emphasis original.

57. With cognates and compounds, I found more than 120 occurrences of the verb: thirty-six in the present stem ἐρχ-; twenty-two in the second aorist stem ἠλθ-; thirty-seven times with a compound preposition [ἀπ- = seventeen times; εἰσ- = five times; ἐκ- = seventeen times; and πρόσ- = one time]; six in the future stem ἐλευσ-; four in the perfect stem ἐληλυθ- [two of which were with the compound preposition ἐκ-]; and sixteen times with the stem ἐλθ-. For a helpful discussion of this verb and its Greek root(s), see Mounce, *Morphology of Biblical Greek*, 260nn5–8, 319. Similarly, for a discussion of this verb in Mark (along with πορεύομαι), see Kilpatrick, "Πορεύεσθαι and its Compounds," 157–58.

next) and discusses a significant event in the Markan story—the (future) coming of the kingdom of God in 9:1 and the (prior?) coming of Elijah in 9:13. The presence of the verb on the one hand should signify the conclusion to a pericope and, on the other hand, link the two pericopae together. These two verses will be interpreted in context below.

## Grammatical Link 11: λέγω ὑμῖν ὅτι (9:1/9:13)

The phrase λέγω ὑμῖν ὅτι has been observed by many to be a redactional phrase.[58] The phrase occurs twelve times with the opening refrain ἀμήν. E. J. Pryke has proposed five categories of redactional usage of this construction: (1) summaries of what has been said over and over again (1:15; 3:11 [bis]); (2) direct speech overcoming indirect speech (1:40; 2:12 3:22; 10:32; 13:6; 14:58 [bis]); (3) impersonals (3:21; 5:35; 6:14, 15, 16; 8:28 [bis]); (4) explanatory parenthesis (3:21; 5:28 6:14–16 [3 times]); and (5) introduction to sayings, classified as either (a) emphatic (3:28; 9:1, 13, 41; 11:23; 12:43; 13:30; 14:18); (b) unemphatic (4:21; 9:1, 31); or (c) miscellaneous (2:17; 7:20; 14:27).[59] Pryke considers the two instances in our pericopae part of the "emphatic" category.[60] Here it is sufficient to note that the grammatical construction is present in both pericopae and that each instance comes as a concluding remark make by Jesus.

## Grammatical Link 12: ὧδε (9:1/9:5)

The adverb ὧδε occurs sixty-one times in the Greek New Testament. Of these sixty-one instances, ten are found in the Gospel of Mark (6:3; 8:4; 9:1, 5; 11:3; 13:2, 21; 14:32, 34; 16:6). The narrator usually places this word on the lips of Jesus (six times) though it is also found coming from others, namely, "many" from the crowd (πολλοί, 6:3); the disciples (collectively in 8:4; Peter in 9:5);

---

58. Pryke, *Redactional Style*, 73–79.

59. Ibid., 74.

60. Ibid., 77. This is interesting since the usage in 9:13 does not include the formulaic introduction ἀμήν like 9:1, yet Pryke considers it emphatic (perhaps because of the ἀλλά) and includes it with the other ἀμὴν λέγω ὑμῖν statement. To Pryke, these eight emphatic formulae "might well be crucial texts for an understanding of the redactional theology of the evangelist."

the "young man" (νεανίσκος) at the tomb (16:6). In our case, the fact that these two uses occur within a few verses from each another (86 words) can be paralleled only in two other places: the set-up to and the speech of the so-called Olivet Discourse (13:2, 21) and Jesus in the Gethsemane (14:32, 34). In the latter two instances, like this one, the linkage or play on words is striking (i.e., the use in 14:32/14:34 [sit *here* while I pray/remain *here* and watch] has a similar echo to 9:1/9:5 [some standing *here*/it is good for us to be *here*]). It seems as though this author has employed this adverb in a paired fashion constructing the scene in such a way that the emphasis would be noticeable by the hearing (or reading) audience.

## Grammatical Link 13: The verb ὁράω (8:33; 9:1/9:4, 8, 9)

The importance of this verb in this passage may be obscured by its lexical and morphological difficulties.[61] Indeed, verbs of seeing are common in narrative, especially in this Gospel, and the theological motif is as important here as it is in other gospel narratives.[62] In the twin pericopae in question, the verb occurs in the aorist system (though in different moods) so that its usage could be easily identifiable phonetically to the hearing audience and linguistically to the reading audience. As discussed at the outset of this section and was seen with other grammatical links, the use of this recurring word is not special in and of itself, but its phonetic component (i.e., the successive aspirates) adds another interesting element to an otherwise "eye-oriented" discussion.[63]

---

61. Mounce (*Morphology of Biblical Greek*, 270) suggests that ὁράω (whose root originally probably included an initial digamma) was in the process of being replaced by βλέπω, θεωρέω, and ὀπτάομαι in first-century Greek. The morphological difficulties are discussed in Mounce. See also Smyth, *Greek Grammar*, §431.

62. To support the assertion that "seeing" is an important Markan feature, see the essay by Kilpatrick, "Verbs of Seeing," 179–80. On "seeing" as a Markan theme, see Griffin, "Seeing and Perceiving." For a work that uses the concept of "seeing" (and especially the verb βλέπω) as a key element in a study of Markan sources, see Vasiliadis, "Behind Mark."

63. Dewey, "Mark as Interwoven Tapestry," 224. See also Lee, "Some Features of the Speech of Jesus," 23; and Robbins, "Orality, Literacy, Memory, and Mark."

## The Turning Point in the Gospel of Mark

### Other Common Factors

From a redactional/traditional point of view, Frans Neirynck has demonstrated that Mark's Gospel is full of dual expressions.[64] Duality for Neirynck, are places in the narrative where the Evangelist apparently inserted a word or phrase to express a particular point where his word or phrase is redundant and to many unnecessary.[65] While the redaction critic focuses on the seams between Mark's use of sources verbatim and his own editorial craftsmanship, I am interested in this work in the Gospel of Mark in its final form. Employing redactional analysis does not mean that one must apply that method strictly.[66] Nevertheless, Neirynck has outlined several "dual" expressions in Mark that can be mentioned in support of my thesis. These are listed in summary fashion with the specific reference in the twin pericopae noted.

Multiplication of Cognate Verbs:

- 8:34: ἀκολουθεῖν ... ἀκολουθείτω
- 9:6–7: ἐγένοντο ... ἐγένετο ... ἐγένετο
- 9:8–9: περιβλεψάμενοι ... εἶδον ... εἶδον
  [see also 9:1 ... ἴδωσιν]

Analogous Non-Verbal Repetitions:

- 8:34, 35, 36, 37:
  ἑαυτὸν ... τὴν ψυχὴν αὐτοῦ ... αὐτήν ... τὴν ψυχὴν αὐτοῦ ... αὐτήν ... τὴν ψυχὴν αὐτοῦ ... τῆς ψυχῆς αὐτοῦ
- 8:35, 36, 37, 38: γὰρ ... γὰρ ... γὰρ ... γὰρ
- 9:6: γὰρ ... γὰρ

Repetition of the Antecedent:

- 8:27b: τοὺς μαθητὰς αὐτοῦ (Antecedent: 8:27a)
- 8:35b: τὴν ψυχὴν αὐτοῦ (Antecedent: 8:35a; see also 8:36, 37)
- 8:37: τῆς ψυχῆς αὐτοῦ (Antecedent: 8:36)
- 9:3c: οὕτως (Antecedent: 9:3b—οἷα)

---

64. Neirynck, *Duality in Mark*, 37–44.

65. Ibid., 13.

66. This point seems to be inferred in the intriguing essay by Petersen, "'Literarkritik', the New Literary Criticism and the Gospel according to Mark."

Synonymous Expression:
- 8:31: πολλὰ παθεῖν ... καί ἀποδοκιμασθῆναι
- 9:12: πολλὰ πάθῃ ... καί ἐξουδενηθῇ

Series of Three:
- 8:28: οἱ δὲ εἶπαν αὐτῷ λέγοντες ὅτι Ἰωάννην τὸν βαπτιστήν καὶ ἄλλοι Ἠλίαν   ἄλλοι δὲ ὅτι εἷς τῶν προφητῶν
- 8:31: ὑπὸ τῶν πρεσβυτέρων καὶ τῶν ἀρχιερέων καὶ τῶν γραμματέων
- 9:2: τὸν Πέτρον καὶ τὸν Ἰάκωβον καὶ τὸν Ἰωάννην
- 9:5: τρεῖς σκηνάς, σοι μίαν καὶ Μωϋσεῖ μίαν καὶ Ἠλίᾳ μίαν

Direct Discourse Preceded by Qualifying Verb:
- 8:27: ἐπηρώτα τοὺς μαθητὰς αὐτοῦ λέγων αὐτοῖς· τίνα με λέγουσιν
- 8:33: ἐπετίμησεν Πέτρῳ καὶ λέγει· ὕπαγε ὀπίσω μου
- 9:11: καί ἐπηρώτων αὐτὸν λέγοντες· ὅτι λέγουσιν οἱ γραμματεῖς ὅτι

Neirynck's analysis covers the entirety of Mark's Gospel, and simply identifying the dual expressions in the twin pericopae itself does not support my thesis. However, it does provide intratextual evidence that the two pericopae in question share elements that cause them to be read together. These duplicate expressions, while not limited to the twin pericopae, do support the linking together of these two episodes. Mark's use of the tradition, along with his creative employment of dual expressions, help explain one of the narrative's curious features—in this case, the curious feature of linking pericopae together.

# Conclusion

At this point, I have attempted to identify thirteen grammatical links that are found in the twin pericopae of Mark 8:27—9:13. Some of the links indicate nothing in and of themselves. Authors write (consciously or unconsciously) in a particular style, generally using a limited collection of words. In this analysis, several of the grammatical links fall into this recurring pattern (e.g., links 1, 3, 7, 9, 10, 12, and 13). A few of the links, while using recurring vocabulary, employ unusual forms or constructions in the twin pericopae (as noted above, links 8 and 10). Five of the links are rare or special to Mark or to the twin pericopae and signal a stronger linkage (links 2, 4, 5, 6, and 11). As we have seen, while this shared vocabulary and similar grammatical constructions are found in various places in the Markan narrative, there is no part of the Gospel where all thirteen of these links occur within the same (or adjacent) pericopae. Thus, when taken together, these recurring, extra recurring, and intratextual connections provide sufficient reason to consider that the author of the Gospel of Mark placed these two episodes side by side for a reason. The next section suggests that in addition to grammatical links there are attendant themes or motifs that also tie these two stories together.

## AN ARGUMENT BASED ON THEMATIC LINKS

As impressive as the above grammatical links are, in my opinion, in linking Peter's confession (8:27–9:1) and the Transfiguration (9:2–13), an argument could be made that every author writes with a particular style and has a limited vocabulary range.[67] Grammatical links alone are not sufficient evidence to conclude that the two pericopae should be read together. However, when shared themes are analyzed, one begins to see additional evidence for the interconnectivity of these two scenes.[68] For the sake of clarity, we can take the eight thematic links outlined in the previous chapter and classify them into three categories: (1) the characters (other than Jesus); (2) Jesus as a main character; and (3) discipleship.

## The Characters (Other Than Jesus)

Other than Jesus, there are three main characters or references to characters present in both pericopae: (1) Simon Peter; (2) other disciples (James and John are named in 9:2); and (3) Elijah and a prophet (of which the greatest prophet, Moses, appears in the Transfiguration, 9:2).

---

67. A recent article on Mark's style is Evans, "How Mark Writes."

68. It is possible that one reason why scholars have lacked consensus regarding *the* turning point of the Markan narrative is that too many attempt to locate it in a single phrase (e.g., "You are the Messiah") or a single pericope (e.g., 8:27—9:1). The narrative itself, because of these grammatical and thematic similarities, resists this single identification.

## Peter

Understanding Peter as a major character in the Gospel takes little effort. His presence is noticeable throughout the narrative (1:16, 29, 30, 36; 3:16; 5:37; 8:29, 32, 33; 9:2, 5; 10:28; 11:21; 13:3; 14:29, 37) and others have written about his role in the Markan story.[69] This is not the place for another full-scale analysis of Peter in the Gospel, but rather a time to begin to develop a thread that ties together the beginning, middle, and end of the narrative—a thread that, as mentioned previously, has not gone unnoticed by commentators (e.g., Hooker among many).

Peter's presence in the narrative is widespread, but a close inspection reveals a concentration of his involvement in the narrative at three distinct places: the calling of the disciples and subsequent events (1:16–34); the twin pericopae of Peter's Confession/Transfiguration (8:27–9:13); and the Passion Narrative, or more precisely Peter's denial and the events of the cross/resurrection (14:27–16:8).[70] Peter is mentioned five times outside these three sections and three of the five are simply listings of him either with the Twelve (3:16) or with the "inner circle" that included James/John (5:37), and Andrew (13:3). The other two instances find Peter making a single statement to Jesus that leads to respond with a "truly, I say to you" (ἀμὴν λέγω ὑμῖν [ὅτι]) statement.[71] While my goal has been to point out the shared themes between the twin pericopae of Peter's confession and the Transfiguration, in both of which Peter is found as a main character, an ancillary result has been to uncover yet another way in which the narrative ties together its beginning, middle, and conclusion.

---

69. Peter is mentioned both first (1:16) and last (16:7) in the narrative. Regarding Peter in Mark's Gospel, see esp. Best, "Peter in the Gospel According to Mark"; Boomershine, "Peter's Denial as Polemic or Confession"; Vorster, "The Characterization of Peter in the Gospel of Mark"; Wiarda, "Peter as Peter in the Gospel of Mark"; and Whitaker, "Rebuke or Recall?" Concerning Peter's relationship to the author of the Gospel, see esp. Black, *Mark*, 201–9. For a fuller treatment of Peter in the New Testament, see Brown, Donfried, and Reumann, eds., *Peter in the New Testament*; and Cullman, *Peter: Disciple, Apostle, Martyr*.

70. For a study of Mark's account of Peter's denial, see Borrell, *The Good News of Peter's Denial*; Herron, *Mark's Account of Peter's Denial*; and Pesch, "Die Verleugnung des Petrus."

71. The first instance (10:28) is in the context of Jesus and the Rich Man (10:17–31) and the second (11:21) is in the concluding "sandwich" of the so-called lesson of the fig tree (11:20–26).

# The Turning Point in the Gospel of Mark

## *The Disciples*

The second major character group in 8:27–9:13 can be studied more briefly and simply referred to as "the disciples." Of course, the disciples collectively represent a major character in the Markan narrative and studies of the disciples in Mark's Gospel are not in short supply.[72] In our pericopae, two salient features must be noted. First, the scene that is so often labeled "Peter's confession" begins not with Peter but with the disciples. On the way to Caesarea Philippi, Jesus asks the disciples, "who do men say that I am?" They respond (εἶπαν) by saying some believe him to be John the Baptist, while others Elijah or one of the prophets. Jesus responds to their answer by asking them (αὐτοῖς) the question (in the plural)—but who do you say that I am? (ὑμεῖς δὲ τίνα με λέγετε εἶναι;). Peter becomes the spokesperson of the disciples at this point. While the confession is Peter's, the question that prompted this declaration was to the disciples as a group. In the following pericope, a small delegation of the disciples—Peter, James, and John—are found going with Jesus up to a mountain of Transfiguration six days later (καὶ μετὰ ἡμέρας ἕξ, 9:2).[73]

The second notable feature regarding the disciples is that the instruction on discipleship that Jesus offers both in response to Peter's confession (8:31-38; 9:1) and the events of the Transfiguration (9:9, 11, 13) are aimed at the disciples as a whole or their representative delegation:

8:31: καὶ ἤρξατο διδάσκειν αὐτούς (and he began to teach them)

8:33: ὁ δὲ ἐπιστραφεὶς καὶ ἰδὼν τοὺς μαθητὰς αὐτοῦ ἐπετίμησεν Πέτρῳ καὶ λέγει

(and turning and seeing *his disciples* he rebuked Peter and said)

---

72. On the disciples in Mark, see esp. Tannehill, "The Disciples in Mark"; Best, *Following Jesus*; Best, *Disciples and Discipleship*; Kingsbury, *Conflict in Mark*, 89–117; Malbon, "Text and Context," 81–102 (repr., *In the Company of Jesus*, 100–130); Shiner, *Follow Me!*; and Rhoads, Dewey, and Michie, *Mark as Story*, 122–29.

73. As discussed in the section on Peter, this "inner circle" is found in four pericopae in Mark: Jesus and Jairus (5:37); here (9:2); with Andrew at the Mount of Olives (13:3); and at the Garden of Gethsemane (14:33). The temporal reference of "six days" is often seen as another link between the passages (see Evans, *Mark 8:27—16:20*, 29). On the importance of "six days," see Abrahams, "After Six Days"; and McCurley, "'And After Six Days'".

8:34: καὶ προσκαλεσάμενος τὸν ὄχλον σὺν τοῖς μαθηταῖς αὐτοῦ εἶπεν αὐτοῖς
(and calling the crowd with his *disciples*, he said *to them*)

9:1: καὶ ἔλεγεν αὐτοῖς (and he said *to them*)

9:9: καὶ καταβαινόντων αὐτῶν ἐκ τοῦ ὄρους διεστείλατο αὐτοῖς
(and as *they* were coming down from the mountain, he charged *them*)

9:11: καὶ ἐπηρώτων αὐτὸν λέγοντες
(and *they* were asking him, saying)

9:12: ὁ δὲ ἔφη αὐτοῖς (and he said *to them*)

9:13: ἀλλὰ λέγω ὑμῖν (but I say *to you* [plural])

In this section, Jesus' teaching is clearly meant for the disciples as a whole, whether represented en masse or with a smaller group of designees.

## John the Baptist, Elijah, and a Prophet (Moses)

The final character or set of characters that are found in this passage involves John the Baptist, Elijah, and a prophet (unnamed in Peter's confession; Moses in the Transfiguration).

John the Baptist is, of course, a prominent figure in the early part of Mark's narrative, especially the Prologue (1:4–11).[74] There, with the opening (loose) quotations from the OT (1:2–3), John is identified as the messenger crying in the wilderness preparing the way for the Lord.[75] His ministry is set in the wilderness—a key theme in the Prologue—and involves the preaching of a baptism of repentance for the forgiveness of sins (1:4).[76] John's dress, as described in the Prologue, is reminiscent of Elijah's in 2 Kgs 1:8 and of an eschatological prophet in Zech 13:4.[77] His diet, while

---

74. Explicit references to John are found in 1:4, 6, 14; 6:14, 16; and 8:28. An implicit reference (as will be discussed below) is found in 9:11–13.

75. For a useful look at this introductory citation, see Watts, *Isaiah's New Exodus*, 53–90.

76. On the wilderness theme, see Mauser, *Christ in the Wilderness*.

77. Donahue and Harrington, *Gospel of Mark*, 63. See also Guelich, *Mark 1:1—8:26*, 21.

seemingly an odd comment for the opening paragraph of such a narrative, further depicts him as a "man of the wilderness." His message, bound with the statement ἔρχεται ὁ ἰσχυρότερός μου ὀπίσω μου ("the one stronger than I [is] coming after me"), serves the purpose of making clear the subject matter of the entire narrative. It is not John who will be the focus of Mark's story but rather the one who comes after John. John baptizes with water, the narrator continues, but this later character (Jesus) will baptize you with the Holy Spirit (1:8).[78] As the Prologue winds to a conclusion, John is the one who baptizes Jesus (1:9) in the Jordan River and then in an almost cursory manner, the narrator speaks of John's arrest (1:14). From that point, John drops out of the narrative until Mark 6.

In Mark 6:14-29, John the Baptist, though dead, reappears in the narrative in between Jesus' sending out of the Twelve for ministry (6:7-13) and their return (6:30). Mark's placement of John the Baptist at this point in the story is curious and we might do well to simply note that his reappearance is connected with the question of Jesus ("Who is this" of 4:41) and the ultimate fate of Jesus (i.e., his death).[79]

In the central section, the name of John the Baptist is suggested as one possible answer to Jesus' question of the disciples "Who do people say I am?" (8:28). The answer, "John" (along with Elijah and one of the prophets), recounts the same threesome of 6:14-16. "Since Jesus received John's baptism (Mark 1:9) and at some point was attached to John's movement and shared at least some of John's expectations about the coming kingdom of God, it is not surprising that Jesus should be identified as John returned to life."[80] And while his name is not explicitly mentioned in the narration of the Transfiguration, Jesus implicitly speaks of him in connection with Elijah (9:11-13).[81] Thus, as we saw from the Prologue (especially 1:6), John the Baptist and Elijah are connected for they share the role of prophet/spokesperson and eschatological forerunner; and while no further mention of John occurs in the narrative after the Transfiguration, his role has set the stage for the completion of the ministry of Jesus, in particular his looming fate.

---

78. As some have observed, the presence of the Holy Spirit is limited or veiled in Mark. For a helpful work on the Spirit in Mark, see Mansfield, *"Spirit and Gospel" in Mark*.

79. For a brief, but helpful discussion of this, see Moloney, *Gospel of Mark*, 125-26.

80. Donahue and Harrington, *Gospel of Mark*, 260.

81. See esp. France, *Gospel of Mark*, 253.

Elijah or his memory is explicitly evoked in three scenes in the Gospel: the death of John the Baptist (6:14–29), Peter's confession and the Transfiguration (8:27–9:13), and the crucifixion of Jesus (15:33–39), and is alluded to in one scene—the Prologue, as mentioned above (1:1–13).[82] The majority of references to Elijah in the Gospel are concentrated in the twin pericopae of 8:27–9:1/9:2–13. In this middle section, as in the reference to John, Elijah is one of the "answers" the disciples give to Jesus in response to his question about his identity. As Donahue and Harrington have observed, "The traditions about Elijah's mysterious departure (2 Kgs 2:1–12) and his role as precursor of 'the great and terrible day of the Lord' (Mal 4:5) probably led to speculation about Jesus, as the prophet of God's kingdom, being Elijah (but see 9:11–13). Certainly it was natural that Jesus, who claimed to speak for God about the coming kingdom of God, should be regarded as a prophet."[83] No doubt, the Jewish followers of Jesus would have known of Elijah's departure "in a whirlwind" and his expected role in the "end times" and even his stature as prophet par excellence. Thus, linking Jesus with Elijah is not out of character for either Jesus or Elijah.

Yet, several things related to Mark's treatment of Elijah deserve attention. As David M. Hoffeditz observes, the Markan narrative refers to Elijah more frequently than to any other character from the OT.[84] Hoffeditz argues that Elijah's presence serves three primary purposes in the Gospel: first, as a bridge between the OT, especially the prophet Malachi, and the Gospel; second, as the messianic identifier, by serving as a template to Messiah's coming and suffering; and third, as an indicator of the coming kingdom.[85] A brief review of Hoffeditz's thesis in general, and these three roles in particular, will serve our purpose of not only showing the links between the two pericopae in question but also offer another reason to see the golden thread that ties together the three distinct phases of the narrative.

Hoffeditz's work is based on the conceptual framework of the Isaianic New Exodus, that is, the notion that the "long-awaited coming of YHWH as king and warrior has begun."[86] The basis for this presupposition is the

---

82. Actual reference to Elijah is found at 6:15; 8:28; 9:4, 5, 11, 12, 13; 15:35, 36. For an analysis of Elijah in Mark's Gospel, see esp. Dautzenberg, "Elija im Markusevangelium."

83. Donahue and Harrington, *Gospel of Mark*, 260.

84. Hoffeditz, "Portrayal of Elijah," 1. See also Hoffeditz, "A Prophet, a Kingdom, and a Messiah," 26–33.

85. Hoffeditz, "The Portrayal of Elijah," 1–32, esp. 1, 32.

86. Ibid., 3. On Isaiah's "new exodus" theme in Mark, see Watts, *Isaiah's New Exodus*, 134–36.

## The Turning Point in the Gospel of Mark

beginning (conflated) quotation from Exod 23:20, Mal 3:1, and Isa 40:3. Though Elijah is never explicitly mentioned in the Prologue, Hoffeditz argues that both the context of vv. 2–3 and his "indirect presentation" through John the Baptist as the eschatological prophet suggests Elijah's presence.[87]

Elijah is referred to directly in the story of the death of John the Baptist (6:14–29). The correlation of the Baptist to Elijah is striking for two reasons. "First, the account foreshadows Jesus' suffering. . . . Second, the pericope strengthens the ties between John the Baptist and the predicted Elijah by providing yet further correspondence between the two characters, and thus, bridging the testaments."[88] This evidence leads Hoffeditz to conclude that Mark portrays John the Baptist as the eschatological Elijah of Malachi 3. For our purposes, it is important to observe that Elijah's first role—that of intertestamental bridge—occurs primarily at the beginning of the narrative in the Prologue. Hoffeditz's other two roles for Elijah in Mark occur at similar significant locations in the Gospel—the middle and the end, respectively.

Hoffeditz's second role for Elijah in the Markan narrative is that of messianic identifier. This occurs both in terms of Elijah as the identifier of the Messiah's coming in addition to the identification of the Messiah's suffering. The former is validated in the "forerunner" motif applied to John (who is, as noted in the above section, identified with Elijah). The forerunner or eschatological prophet (i.e., John in the Gospel of Mark) is to "prepare the way of the Lord" and does so through a message of repentance. "This forerunner motif is most obvious from the selected OT citations in 1:2–3, the connection of John's arrest with the beginning of Jesus' ministry (1.14), and the comments of Jesus in 9.11–13."[89] The latter role (identification of messiah's sufferings) is observed by Hoffeditz in the account of the Transfiguration (especially 9:11–13). As the disciples descend from the mountain, they are confused about the meaning of the Son of Man rising from the dead (9:9). Hoffeditz argues that the Peter, James, and John did indeed understand the resurrection phenomenon since Jesus had just spoken of it (8:31). The confusion was not over the issue of resurrection

---

87. The evidence for this "indirect" presentation involves similarities with John the Baptist in speech (calls for repentance), environment (wilderness), clothing (leather girdle and camel hair garment), and diet (locusts and honey). See Hoffeditz, "The Portrayal of Elijah," 4–6.

88. Ibid., 7. Hoffeditz ("*Femme Fatale* Redux") correctly sees a striking similarity between John and Herodias and that of Elijah and Jezebel.

89. Ibid., 9–10, esp. 9.

but rather over the presence of the kingdom and the reasons why the Son of Man must die. Regarding the necessity of the death of the Son of Man, he states, "The disciples could not harmonize Jesus' words with Elijah's presence (9.11). Peter, James, and John thought they had just witnessed the coming of Elijah as foretold by the scribes. Jesus does not deny this scribal teaching but corrects the disciples by stating that Elijah will restore all things. . . Hence, Jesus reminds the disciples that the mere presence of Elijah is not sufficient."[90] Thus, in the all-important middle section of the narrative, the Elijah figure testifies to the coming Messiah, who as Son of Man (as Hoffeditz maintains) must suffer.

Finally, Hoffeditz presents Elijah as an indicator of the coming kingdom. His defense of this position is nuanced and need not be outlined in detail here. It is noteworthy, however, to point out that the basis of this role was "seen in the association of the OT prophet with the voice of God at Jesus' baptism, the transfiguration, and the crucifixion. The main reason Mark's Elijah failed to accomplish his anticipated mission was that, according to Mark, the kingdom was not fulfilled. News that the kingdom is yet to be fulfilled serves as an encouragement to the readers who are suffering persecution."[91] The comment concerning the purpose of the Gospel to its original readers is not the point of this discussion. The pertinent information concerns the connection between the Elijah reference to the coming kingdom and their occurrence at the beginning (i.e., Jesus' baptism), the middle (i.e., the Transfiguration), and the end (i.e., the crucifixion). The previous two roles occurred at the beginning and the middle of the narrative, respectively. This final role for Elijah, as indicator of the kingdom, occurs at all three places—the beginning (voice at the baptism), middle (the Transfiguration), and the end (the crucifixion). This key character, while not always an explicit character shows up at three strategic places in the narrative, which echoes the Aristotelian rhythm presented in chapter 1.

The final character in this section is Moses. The name μωϋσῆς occurs eight times in the narrative (1:44; 7:10; 9:4, 5, 10:3, 4; 12:19, 26), primarily in the passing reference to "the book of Moses" (12:19, 26) or "as Moses commanded/said" (1:44; 7:10; 10:3, 4). Only in the Transfiguration (9:4, 5) does Moses the prophet appear and even in apparent subordination to Elijah ("Elijah *with* Moses").[92] In one sense, Moses' presence at the Trans-

90. Ibid., 11–12.
91. Ibid., 31–32.
92. This apparent subordination is addressed in Heil, "A Note on 'Elijah with Moses.'"

figuration may indicate that Jesus (in his transfigured state) must be the fulfillment of the Law (i.e., Moses) and the Prophets (i.e., Elijah). Many have put this forth.[93] However, as Margaret Thrall argues, allowing Elijah to stand as a writing prophet is at a minimum curious and, if the fulfillment of the Law and Prophets motif was intentional, why not list Moses first?[94]

Moses' role in the Transfiguration account, while by no means agreed upon by all, is nevertheless important in linking these two scenes together. Morna D. Hooker has suggested that Moses' presence in the Transfiguration reminds readers of the incident at Sinai, where the glory of Yhwh was seen in Moses. In the Markan narrative, Hooker observes two things. First, Jesus' glory at the Transfiguration not only reminds readers of Moses' glory (heightened because of Moses' presence on the mountain) but also transcends it: "The echoes of the story of Moses on Sinai remind us that the glory of Jesus is even greater than the glory of Moses."[95] Second, "the story of the Transfiguration spells out the truths of the preceding paragraphs, 8:27–9:1. Jesus is not John, nor Elijah, nor one of the prophets, but a much greater figure—the Christ (or Son of God, cf. Mark 14:61); his destiny is suffering and death, and those who wish to follow him must expect to share his fate; but his final destiny is glory—a glory which he will share with those who are loyal to him."[96] This quotation illustrates precisely the linkage present between these two pericope. The ambiguous reference to "one of the prophets" on the lips of the disciples in 8:28 is now visibly seen in the presence of Moses and Elijah. The superiority of Jesus to Elijah and Moses is illustrated by Peter whose naïve reaction of building three shelters (implying that Jesus, Moses, and Elijah are equals) is quickly corrected by the cloud that overshadowed them, the divine voice's response to listen to him (Jesus, not them, Elijah and Moses), and by the two prophet's hasty disappearance, leaving only Jesus alone (9:5–8). Thrall states it well, "He [Jesus] is not simply one amongst other inhabitants of heaven: he is the messianic Son of God himself."[97]

Therefore, the characters present in these two scenes wed together this portion of the narrative. While the disciples and Peter have major roles in

115.

    93. See, for example, Nineham, *Gospel of St. Mark*, 234–35.
    94. Thrall, "Elijah and Moses," 308.
    95. Hooker, "'What doest thou here, Elijah,'" 70.
    96. Ibid.
    97. Thrall, "Elijah and Moses," 30.

other sections of the Gospel, the others seem to be concentrated in the middle section, especially in what we are calling the twin pericopae. A familiar pattern emerges—a concentration of key persons in the beginning, middle, and end of the narrative. This pattern continues and will play an even more significant role in our discussion of the christology of Mark.

## Jesus as a Main Character

### Identity of Jesus

The intent of this section is not to present a fully developed christology that emerges from these two pericopae. I will address the christological implications of reading these two pericopae together in the subsequent chapter. For now, I will simply show that a shared theme present in both the account of Peter's confession and the mountain of Transfiguration is that of Jesus' identity—or perhaps better, the revelation of Jesus' identity.[98]

Peter's confession is the first time in the narrative where a character in the story confesses what the readers have known since the Prologue (1:1)—Jesus is the "anointed one" of God, the Messiah/Christ. That Jesus does not formally embrace or accept the title without reservation has already been noted. Rather, Jesus rebuked (ἐπετίμησεν) the disciples (αὐτοῖς) for this statement so that (ἵνα) they would not tell anyone about him. As in the previous pericope (8:22–26) where the blind man gained sight, but only partial sight, so now Peter has offered insight into the identity of Jesus, but it is inadequate.[99]

Peter's insight is inadequate because it is not the full story regarding Jesus' identity. The sternness of Jesus' reply to the disciples (8:30) and later to Peter individually (8:33) suggests that this is true. Jesus begins to teach the disciples about the Son of Man and how the Son of Man must suffer and die only to be raised later (8:31; see also 9:30–32; 10:32–34). Rather

---

98. Some may be uncomfortable with the notion of "revelation." What I mean by this term, as applied to the narrative of Mark, is simply that "who Jesus is" (the question asked of the disciples in 4:41) is answered or partially answered by those in the story or by the narrator.

99. Matera (*New Testament Christology*, 17) says it this way: "For a *brief* moment, Peter and the disciples see everything clearly, for their eyes have been opened. They finally understand what the reader already knows: that Jesus is the Shepherd-Messiah. But it will soon become apparent that even though Peter's confession is formally correct, it is inadequate."

than a correction of Peter's confession, as many have proposed, I believe what Jesus' response dictates is another revelation of the person of Jesus.[100] As I will discuss in chapter 5, "Son of Man" is not a confessional title in Mark's Gospel; no character in the story addresses or confesses Jesus in this manner.[101] Rather, in the Gospel the reference is used of Jesus only by Jesus. Yet, in Jesus' use of the phrase for himself, there is a certain privileged disclosure that goes with it. Like the "second touch" caused the blind man in 8:22–26 to see more clearly, so the "second designation" of Jesus as Son of Man should enable the reader to see Jesus' identity more clearly. The disciples in the story had a hard time understanding its meaning. Mark, however, wants the reader to see that this "anointed one" is not to be thought of solely in royal terms but in light of the suffering Son of Man. The first of two pericopae has "revealed" two insights into the identity of Jesus: he is Messiah/Christ, the anointed of God; and he is the Son of Man, who must suffer and die before rising.

The Transfiguration (9:2–13) offers another significant insight into the identity of Jesus. In 9:7, the voice from the cloud declares: οὗτός ἐστιν ὁ υἱός μου ὁ ἀγαπητός, ἀκούετε αὐτοῦ ("This is my beloved son; listen to him"). This language is, of course, similar to the opening line of the Gospel (1:1) and to the voice that Jesus heard at his baptism (in Mark's words): σὺ εἶ ὁ υἱός μου ὁ ἀγαπητός, ἐν σοὶ εὐδόκησα ("You are my beloved son, in you I am pleased"). Yet, those actors in the story do not know the opening line and the declaration at the baptism. The Prologue, as has been demonstrated, is reserved for readers—providing as it were privileged information, the likes of which (it becomes apparent) the characters in the story know nothing of. In 9:7, however, the characters present (Peter, James, and John) hear this news, *this one* is my son; and with this understanding comes an injunction, listen to him. While Peter uttered the confession ὁ χριστός in 8:29 and Jesus responded (in Mark's presentation) by calling himself ὁ

---

100. As Kingsbury (*Christology of Mark's Gospel*, 25) explains the central thesis of the so-called corrective christologies: "The second evangelist, for one or more reasons, regarded the title 'Son of God' (with which 'Messiah,' too, is aligned) as defective for conveying the true meaning of the person of Jesus. As a result, a major part of the program the evangelist set for himself in writing his Gospel was to 'correct' the title Son of God. This he did, through his espousal of a theology of the cross and the use he made of the title 'Son of Man.'" While I agree with Kingsbury that corrective Christology is not what Mark has in view, the notion that Son of God alone is insufficient for conveying Mark's true meaning of Jesus is correct. See Kingsbury's more recent work, "The Christology of Mark and the Son of Man."

101. Matera, *New Testament Christology*, 26.

υἱὸς τοῦ ἀνθρώπου in 8:31, in 9:7 a voice "happened" (ἐγένετο) from the cloud, declaring Jesus as ὁ υἱός μου ὁ ἀγαπητός. The repetition of these three titles of Jesus occurs here and in other strategic places in the narrative as we shall see.

## Charge to Secrecy

As I alluded in chapter 3, the theme of secrecy is a prominent theme in the first half of Mark's Gospel. The significance of the theme can be traced back to Wrede, who in 1901 penned the influential *Das Messiasgeheimnis in den Evangelien*.[102] In this work, Wrede argued that the commands to silence and the so-called parable theory of Mark 4:10–12 should be understood as a single, unified theme. Jesus, from a historian's perspective, made no explicit (or implicit) messianic claims. The commands to silence, which Wrede entitled "the messianic secret," were devices used by the Markan community (and put to writing by the evangelist) for evangelistic and apologetic reasons.[103] The criticism of Wrede's thesis was vigorous, but it nonetheless introduced and highlighted a major issue in Markan studies that continues in contemporary scholarship.[104]

In the Gospel, the commands to silence can be viewed by looking at the recipients of the commands: demons (or "supernatural beings"); human beings who have been healed or cured by Jesus; and the disciples (either en masse or a selection of disciples) and, how they occur after significant events in the presentation of Jesus. The pattern can be viewed in the following manner:

1. Demons (1:25, 34; 3:11–12)—command to silence occurs after exorcisms

2. Humans (1:44; 5:43; 7:36; 8:26)—command to silence occurs after healings[105]

---

102. Wrede, *Das Messiasgeheimnis* (ET: *Messianic Secret*).

103. Räisänen, *"Messianic Secret" in Mark*, 47–48; Aune, "The Problem of the Messianic Secret," 2.

104. For a helpful general critique of Wrede's hypothesis, see Aune, "The Problem of the Messianic Secret," 2–8. For contemporary works on the "messianic secret," see esp. Hengel, *Studies in the Gospel of Mark*, 41–45; Tuckett, ed., *Messianic Secret*; Räisänen, *"Messianic Secret" in Mark*; and Telford, *Theology of the Gospel of Mark*, 41–54. For a comparison of Wrede's secrecy motif and that of Homer, see MacDonald, "Secrecy and Recognitions in the *Odyssey* and Mark," 139–53.

105. See Telford, *Theology*, 41. Hay ("Mark's Use of the Messianic Secret," 20) does

3. Disciples (8:30; 9:9)—command to silence occurs after revelation[106]

This categorization is helpful to understanding the Markan motif and especially in seeing that, for this evangelist, the commands to disciples' are seen back to back in the twin pericopae. In their narrative expressions, the first two categories (the commands to silence to demons and human beings) occur after some sort of mighty deed by Jesus. In the case of the demons, each command is in response to the demon's correct identification of Jesus (the Holy One of God, 1:25; the Son of God, 3:11) or the narrator's summary of the demon's reaction ("they knew him," 1:34). The demons' identification of Jesus is correct to a point and occurs before the characters in the story come to that conclusion (especially the disciples).

Similarly, the second category—the healing of various diseased/sick individuals—sees each command given after a particular healing had occurred. These commands to silence are presented with mixed results. A leper who is made well does not heed Jesus' command to silence and the result is that Jesus could no longer enter a town openly because of the crowds (1:44–45). Similarly, in 7:36, after Jesus heals a deaf and mute man, the crowds zealously proclaimed the work they witnessed. Yet, in two examples, Jairus (5:43) and the unnamed blind man of Mark 8 were instructed to keep silent (8:26) and the narrative does not indicate that they disobeyed the command. Thus, if the purpose of the command to silence was to either hush the spirit-world until the time was right (in the case of the demons) or not to frustrate the travel plans of Jesus (in the case of the diseased), then what is the purpose of the commands to silence of the disciples?

These two commands are interesting, for they are both wrapped up with christological significance. Telford notes that the command to silence is given to Jesus' inner circle "after revelation."[107] What does this mean? It is true that the grammar of 8:30 suggests that the disciples are instructed to remain quiet *concerning him* (περὶ αὐτοῦ), a statement that comes on the heels of Peter's declaration of Jesus as Messiah. This appears to be a "revelatory" statement. However, in 9:9, the language related to the command to silence is directed not directly toward "who he is" but rather toward what the inner group of disciples saw (ἃ εἶδον), the transfiguration of Jesus and the appearance of Moses and Elijah. Strictly speaking, there is a difference

not include 8:26 and adds 7:24.

106. Telford, *Theology*, 41. Hay ("Mark's Use of the Messianic Secret," 21) includes both of these references and adds 9:30–31, esp. 9:30 (καὶ οὐκ ἤθελεν ἵνα τις γνοῖ).

107. Telford, *Theology of the Gospel of Mark*, 41.

in these two commands.[108] However, with Räisänen, I think that these two commands are indeed related and do occur in response to a narrative description/revelation of Jesus' identity.[109] In 8:30, Mark has Jesus instruct the disciples to remain silent because there is more to Peter's confession, namely, the first passion prediction, a prediction that will speak of a suffering Messiah, indeed the Son of Man. The only other command to the disciples in the Gospel (9:9) comes as a result of seeing a foreshadowing of the glory that is to be revealed and hearing this Jesus identified as the Son of God (9:7). If those two christological referents were not enough, the command to silence in 9:9 includes an atypical qualification—that they should remain silent until the time in which the Son of Man rises from the dead (εἰ μὴ ὅταν ὁ υἱὸς τοῦ ἀνθρώπου ἐκ νεκρῶν ἀναστῇ).

There is no doubt that questions remain regarding the messianic secret. Is it a unified prohibition? Should it be connected to the parable theory in the Gospel?[110] What is the purpose of secret in each of the above-mentioned categories? For our purposes, it is sufficient to note that the only command to silence that is directed to Jesus' disciples occurs in the twin pericopae of 8:27–9:1/9:2–13. In addition (and this point will be addressed more fully in the next chapter), the secrecy motif and Jesus' identity are interwoven. It is no accident that 8:30 instructs the disciples to remain quiet περὶ αὐτοῦ (about Jesus, whom Peter identified as Messiah) while 9:9 instructs a delegation of disciples to keep silent about the Son of God until the Son of Man rises from the dead.

There is something interesting here structurally. We have observed the tripartite nature of the Markan narrative—in Aristotelian terms how there is a discernable beginning, middle, and end. With the secrecy motif and the passion predictions, something of a bipartite structure emerges.[111] The secrecy motif is present only in the first half of the narrative; the last occurrence occurs in 9:9. Yet it is in the middle section of 8:27–9:13 that the passion (and resurrection) predictions begin, which overshadow the latter

---

108. Luz ("The Secrecy Motif and the Marcan Christology") argues that Mark 9:9 does not contradict 8:30 but rather interprets it. (Luz's essay was reprinted in the collection of essays edited by Tuckett, *Messianic Secret*, 75–96, esp. 86. My reference is to the later reprint.)

109. Räisänen, *"Messianic Secret" in Mark*, 192–95.

110. Räisänen (*'Messianic Secret' in Mark*, viii; 76–143) suggests it should be connected.

111. Evans ("How Mark Writes," 145–47) also observes a bipartite structure to the Gospel.

half of the narrative. The middle section functions as a fulcrum with respect to these two themes. Just as Mark "finishes" one, the other "begins."[112] Perhaps a clue lies in the fact that Jesus speaks this word (the first passion prediction) with παρρησία (frankness, openness) (8:32). This serves as a signal to the reader that the manner in which Jesus speaks of himself is going in a new direction. What may have been presented in mystery earlier is now being spoken of with uncharacteristic clarity. Unfortunately for the disciples, this "plain speaking" does not bring them, especially Peter, any closer to grasping Jesus' true identity as the narrative of 8:32b-33 indicates.

## *Passion/Resurrection*

If the first half of Mark's narrative has been dominated by the theme of secrecy, which is curiously absent from the second half, then the second half of the narrative (beginning at 8:31) is dominated by the passion/death and resurrection of Jesus—a theme that is only hinted at in the first half of the narrative (2:19–20).[113] Indeed, after Peter's confession of Jesus as Messiah and Jesus' rebuke of Peter and command to silence, Jesus began to teach (ἤρξατο διδάσκειν) the disciples about his impending death and resurrection (8:31).[114]

A detailed study of the passion/resurrection predictions of 8:31; 9:30–32; and 10:33–34 is beyond the scope of this chapter. Fuller treatment can be found elsewhere.[115] Below is a table of the three predictions:

---

112. Dewey ("Mark as Interwoven Tapestry," 224) similarly observes this type of phenomenon and Kee (*Community of the New Age*, 64, 75) analogously calls the Gospel of Mark a fugue. This blending of grammar, themes, and theology is why I consider both pericopae to be the turning point in the Gospel.

113. Wright (*Resurrection of the Son of God*, 620n15) suggests that the parable of the seed growing secretly (4:26–29) contains a hint of death and resurrection (the sower "goes to sleep and arises"). But such a connection seems stretched.

114. Donahue and Harrington (*Gospel of Mark*, 262) observe: "While it is customary to describe Mark 8:31; 9:31; and 10:33–34 as Passion predictions, they each reach their climax by referring to Jesus' resurrection." See also, Bolt, *Cross from a Distance*, 48n2.

115. See esp. Taylor, "The Origin of Mark's Passion Sayings"; Strecker, "Passion Predictions in Mark's Gospel"; Reedy, "Mk 8:31—11:10 and the Gospel Ending"; McKinnis, "An Analysis of Mark X 32–34"; Culpepper, "Passion and Resurrection in Mark"; and Schaberg, "Daniel 7, 12 and the New Testament Passion-Resurrection Predictions."

## Reading Peter's Confession and the Transfiguration Together

| Mark 8:31 | Mark 9:30-32 | Mark 10:32b-34 |
|---|---|---|
| ³¹ καὶ ἤρξατο διδάσκειν αὐτοὺς ὅτι δεῖ τὸν υἱὸν τοῦ ἀνθρώπου πολλὰ παθεῖν καὶ ἀποδοκιμασθῆναι ὑπὸ τῶν πρεσβυτέρων καὶ τῶν ἀρχιερέων καὶ τῶν γραμματέων καὶ ἀποκτανθῆναι καὶ μετὰ τρεῖς ἡμέρας ἀναστῆναι· | ³⁰ κἀκεῖθεν ἐξελθόντες παρεπορεύοντο διὰ τῆς Γαλιλαίας, καὶ οὐκ ἤθελεν ἵνα τις γνοῖ· ³¹ ἐδίδασκεν γὰρ τοὺς μαθητὰς αὐτοῦ καὶ ἔλεγεν αὐτοῖς ὅτι ὁ υἱὸς τοῦ ἀνθρώπου παραδίδοται εἰς χεῖρας ἀνθρώπων, καὶ ἀποκτενοῦσιν αὐτόν, καὶ ἀποκτανθεὶς μετὰ τρεῖς ἡμέρας ἀναστήσεται. ³² οἱ δὲ ἠγνόουν τὸ ῥῆμα, καὶ ἐφοβοῦντο αὐτὸν ἐπερωτῆσαι. | ³²ᵇ καὶ παραλαβὼν πάλιν τοὺς δώδεκα ἤρξατο αὐτοῖς λέγειν τὰ μέλλοντα αὐτῷ συμβαίνειν ³³ ὅτι ἰδοὺ ἀναβαίνομεν εἰς Ἱεροσόλυμα, καὶ ὁ υἱὸς τοῦ ἀνθρώπου παραδοθήσεται τοῖς ἀρχιερεῦσιν καὶ τοῖς γραμματεῦσιν, καὶ κατακρινοῦσιν αὐτὸν θανάτῳ καὶ παραδώσουσιν αὐτὸν τοῖς ἔθνεσιν ³⁴ καὶ ἐμπαίξουσιν αὐτῷ καὶ ἐμπτύσουσιν αὐτῷ καὶ μαστιγώσουσιν αὐτὸν καὶ ἀποκτενοῦσιν, καὶ μετὰ τρεῖς ἡμέρας ἀναστήσεται. |

*Table 4*

The three predictions contain several common features: (1) the Son of Man (2) will be killed and (3) after three days (4) will rise again.[116] In addition to these features shared by all three predictions, the first two contain an additional similarity: this statement by Jesus is part of his teaching ministry to the disciples (i.e., the presence of διδάσκω in 8:31 and 9:31).[117] However,

---

116. Strecker, "The Passion- and Resurrection Predictions," 424. See also Bolt, *Cross from a Distance*, 48.

117. To Luz ("Das Geheimnismotiv und die markinische Christologie," 21–22n60), the presence of ἤρξατο διδάσκειν signals the beginning of a new pericope or a new, originally separate tradition. Gundry (*Mark*, 445) argues that 8:31 does not signal a new pericope since there is no mention of a topographical change, a feature that is subsidiary

there are several notable differences between these predictions. While the first prediction speaks of Jesus' suffering, the second and third do not; they employ the rather cryptic "will be delivered up." Further, the description of the Jewish authorities differs among the three accounts—"elders, chief priests, and scribes" in 8:31, "chief priests and scribes" in 10:33, while 9:31 contains the more general "into the hands of men." Only 8:31 speaks of the Son of Man being "rejected," and 10:33–34 include a great deal more detail concerning Jesus' passion than the other two accounts.[118]

An earlier generation of NT scholars were interested in the tradition history of these predictions and, in particular, Mark's redaction of this received tradition.[119] Strecker was one of these. However, Strecker observes another feature that, from a literary-critical perspective, is very useful in seeing how this theme of passion/resurrection is interwoven into the Markan story. He suggests that "the passion- and resurrection predictions, like the unifying theory of the messianic secret, fit into the total framework of the Gospel."[120] The basic elements of the messianic secret motif, he argues, are the notions of revelation, secrecy, and misunderstanding. "It is no accident," he claims, "that these exact motifs can be detected in the passion- and resurrection predictions."[121] His suggestion can be viewed by the following table:

---

to topographical notations. My contention is that the presence of ἤρξατο διδάσκειν does not signal the beginning of a new pericope precisely because of the many linguistic and thematic links present in the sections.

118. Strecker, "The Passion- and Resurrection Predictions," 424.

119. See, for example, the essays by Strecker and Reedy mentioned above as well as the works of Lohmeyer (*Das Evangelium des Markus*, 1:165); Tödt, *Son of Man*; and Pesch, *Das Markusevangelium*, 2:48–56.

120. Strecker, "The Passion- and Resurrection Predictions, 441. See also his essay entitled "Zur Messiasgeheimnistheorie im Markusevangelium."

121. Ibid., 440–41.

|  | Secret | Prediction 1 | Prediction 2 | Prediction 3 |
|---|---|---|---|---|
| **Revelation** | "You are the Messiah" (8:29) | "The Son of Man must suffer" (8:31) | "The Son of Man is to be handed over" (9:31) | "The Son of Man will be handed over" (10:33) |
| **Secrecy (Hiddenness)** | Command to silence (8:30) | Peter rebukes Jesus (8:32)[122] | "And he did not want anyone to know" (9:30) | Jesus separates himself from the Twelve (10:32) |
| **Misunderstanding** | Jesus rebukes Peter (8:30) | Peter rebukes Jesus (8:32) | Disciples misunderstand (9:32) | James and John's ensuing request (10:35) |

*Table 5*

There is no need to give a detailed critique of Strecker's analysis of the secret and the passion predictions, but a few comments may be made. First, the overall, threefold pattern of the secrecy motif is correct. There is indeed a revelation of the identity of Jesus that occurs prior to the actual "messianic secret," as was seen in the previous section. Indeed, misunderstanding on the part of the disciples is a general feature of 8:30 (and I would add 9:9 as discussed above also). However, the idea of hiddenness or secrecy in the passion predictions is not clear. Strecker's belief that the motif of hiddenness is "expressed in the form of Peter's misunderstanding" (p. 441) in 8:32 is not supported by the Markan narrative. While I cannot agree with Strecker on the precise details of this "unifying" framework of the Gospel, I do think that he is correct about what Mark intended to be heard, namely, that there is a correspondence between the so-called messianic secret and the passion/

---

122. Strecker indicates that the motif of hiddenness or secrecy is expressed in the form of Peter's misunderstanding.

## The Turning Point in the Gospel of Mark

resurrection predictions. They do share a certain overarching form with each other, even if this form does not match precisely as Strecker suggests. Where the secrecy motif ends, the passion/resurrection theme begins.

Jesus' impending death is not only brought to the attention of Mark's readers' in the three so-called predictions, but it is either hinted at or explicitly mentioned several other times subsequent to the three predictions.[123] In 10:45, a verse that is most important for the understanding of Mark's view of atonement, the Son of Man is "to give his life as a ransom for many" (καὶ δοῦναι τὴν ψυχὴν αὐτοῦ λύτρον ἀντὶ πολλῶν). Similarly, in the parable of the wicked tenants (12:1–12), the son of the vineyard owner is taken and killed (ἀπόκτεινω), a parable that has been called "the plot of the Gospel of Mark in a nutshell."[124] On both sides of the "little apocalypse" of Mark 13, women foreshadow the death of Jesus—the widow in 12:44 is said to give her whole life (ἔβαλεν ὅλον τὸν βίον αὐτῆς) into the treasury, and in 14:3–8 a woman anoints Jesus' body with expensive ointment just as one would do after death. Naturally, the Passion Narrative proper (14:1–15:47) contains language of the plot to kill Jesus (14:1–2), Jesus' betrayal by Judas (14:10–12), Jesus' instruction at the last supper, which speaks of his blood of the new covenant being poured out (14:22–25), the Gethsemane prayer (14:32–42), and the final crucifixion itself. The death of Jesus, culminating on a Roman cross, is a key motif in the Gospel, perhaps the key motif. But in the Gospel the mention of the cross or death must be coupled with the notion of hope and resurrection. This is true in all three passion predictions and is confirmed by the Transfiguration narrative of 9:2–13.

The focus of the above paragraphs has been primarily on the first passion prediction of 8:31, a verse that is closely related—not only in proximity—to the initial secrecy command to disciples (8:30). The subsequent predictions, along with the rest of the Markan narrative, speak of the importance of the death and resurrection of Jesus. However, there is another pericope that must be addressed, the "twin" pericope of 9:2–13, the Transfiguration. It is this narrated story, when juxtaposed to the first passion prediction that causes one to believe that the two pericopae are meant

---

123. Wright (*Resurrection of the Son of God*, 620) observes this fact also: "These predictions shape and punctuate the narrative of the second half of the gospel, and belong closely with Mark's telling us that Jesus really is Israel's Messiah (8.29; 14.61–2). Mark's gospel has a stark and simple structure: chapters 1–8 build up to the recognition of Jesus' Messiahship, and chapters 9–15 build up to his death. But always, in looking ahead to his death, they look ahead as well to his resurrection."

124. Van Eck and van Aarde, "A Narratological Analysis of Mark 12:1–12," 778.

## Reading Peter's Confession and the Transfiguration Together

to be read together. Let us examine briefly the death and resurrection ideas present in the Transfiguration.

We begin with 9:9, a verse that has already been reviewed in connection with the familiar secrecy motif. Here, Jesus, as he is coming down from the mountain of the Transfiguration, instructs the inner circle of disciples (αὐτοῖς, see 9:9) not to tell anyone what they had seen until the time in which the Son of Man should rise from the dead (εἰ μὴ ὅταν ὁ υἱὸς τοῦ ἀνθρώπου ἐκ νεκρῶν ἀναστῇ). The characteristics of the passion predictions (and 8:31 in particular) are that they consisted of four features—Son of Man; suffering/being killed; rising; after three days. Therefore, just as with the first passion prediction, 9:9 includes (at least implicitly) all of the common features, except the reference to "after three days."[125] Based on the evidence of 9:10, the inner circle appear to obey Jesus' command to silence but kept discussing what "rising from the dead" meant.[126]

So what are we to make of this key theme of Jesus' death and resurrection? First, it is intriguing to note that this theme is coupled with Jesus' instructions to his disciples (whether the Twelve or the inner three) to remain silent. Second, from a structural standpoint, no substantive mention of Jesus' death and resurrection has occurred in the narrative until the first passion prediction (and then in the Transfiguration narrative and in the subsequent predictions). Once Jesus' suffering and death is predicted in 8:31, however, the remainder of the narrative concerns the passion of Jesus (in one form or another). In that sense, Martin Kähler's famous footnote (concerning all the Gospels) is appropriate for Mark: "To state the matter somewhat provocatively, one could call the Gospels passion narratives with extended introductions."[127] Just the reverse is true of the secrecy motif. It has been a prominent motif since the beginning of the narrative (1:25, 34, 44; 3:11; 5:43; 7:36; 8:26) and has—strictly speaking—been seen in its truest sense in the twin pericopae (8:30; 9:9). After 9:9, however, the command to silence is not maintained. If the first half of the narrative contained

---

125. A perhaps veiled reference to the suffering/death of the Son of Man is mentioned in connection with the Elijah discussion (from Malachi 3) in 9:12 (καὶ πῶς γέγραπται ἐπὶ τὸν υἱὸν τοῦ ἀνθρώπου ἵνα πολλὰ πάθῃ καὶ ἐξουδενηθῇ).

126. The Greek of 9:10 is difficult—especially the first part (καὶ τὸν λόγον ἐκράτησαν πρὸς ἑαυτούς). It is not clear whether τὸν λόγον refers to the entire transfiguration event (which might be translated "the matter"), the command to silence in 9:9 (which would be rendered "the word"), or the divine word they heard from the cloud (9:7, which again would be translated "the word"). See Donahue and Harrington, *Gospel of Mark*, 271.

127. Kähler, *So-called Historical Jesus*, 80, n.11.

little or no references to Jesus' impending death and resurrection, then the latter half contains little or no references to the messianic secret. The key shift or turning point in these interconnected narrative/motifs is the twin pericopae of Peter's confession and the Transfiguration. Finally, the christological designation associated with death and resurrection—in both pericopae (not to mention all three predictions)—is "the Son of Man." As we will see in the next chapter, this key christological disclosure is strategically employed in order to focus the reader's attention on the proper identity and destiny of Jesus—the Messiah, the Son of God (1:1).

## Discipleship

### Instruction to Disciples: The Cost (and Benefits) of Following Jesus

As we have seen, Mark's narrative is not solely a story that concerns the proper identification of "who Jesus is" (4:35–41). It is also an interwoven story of "what that means" for the readers/listeners of the story. One of the ways that Mark draws the reader into this complex combination of christology and discipleship is to have them respond in a particular way to the characters in the story along with the message(s) the characters present.[128] Larry W. Hurtado suggests that Mark presents two types of material in the narrative that relate to the issue of discipleship or following Jesus: (1) teaching on discipleship that is directed to the disciples/readers; and (2) the portrayal of the Twelve, which seems to have a strong didactic purpose in mind.[129] Since we have previously dealt with the disciples' place in the twin pericopae, this section focuses on the actual instructions given (usually by Jesus in the narrative) on what it means to follow Jesus.

As others have observed, the entire middle section of Mark's Gospel (8:22—10:52) is concerned with discipleship.[130] Much of the discussion surrounding the middle section involves the three passion predictions, as discussed above. Norman Perrin was one of the first to recognize that the three predictions are closely related and each involves the notion of discipleship. The pattern includes: (1) geographical reference; (2) prediction; (3) misunderstanding by the disciples; and (4) teaching by Jesus

---

128. Tannehill, "Reading It Whole," 75.
129. Hurtado, "Following Jesus in the Gospel of Mark," 9.
130. Ibid., 14. See also Best, *Following Jesus*, 15–145, esp. 15–65 and 134–45.

## Reading Peter's Confession and the Transfiguration Together

concerning discipleship.[131] Applying this analysis to the first prediction, the one contained in the first pericope under examination, yields the following, according to Perrin:

1. Geographical reference: 8:27
2. Prediction: 8:31
3. Misunderstanding: 8:32–33
4. Instruction on Discipleship: 8:34–9:1

While Perrin's structural observations are sound, one should not infer from this that the sole instructional material on discipleship is limited to 8:34–9:1. Quite the contrary, the material of 8:31 includes a significant teaching component about what it means to be a disciple of Jesus, namely, that disciples must understand properly the destiny of Jesus—it is a way of suffering, rejection, and vindication (through resurrection). While some have called this element of the teaching "corrective christology," it nevertheless is an indispensable element of Jesus' guidance of "followship."[132]

An often-overlooked issue of discipleship arises in 8.32; it is that Mark emphasizes that Jesus spoke this prediction "clearly" (παρρησίᾳ). Up to Peter's confession, much of Jesus' teaching had been anything but clear, the parables being a prime example. Yet, with the indication of suffering, death, and resurrection, the language of Jesus becomes plain.

Similarly, in 8:33, Peter appears to interrupt Jesus and begins to rebuke him for such talk. Then Jesus, looking at his disciples, rebukes Peter (the play on ἐπιτιμάω is intentional where it occurs in 8:30, 32, and 33), calling him Satan, but more importantly telling him to get behind Jesus. The image that a reader gets is that Peter has stepped in front of Jesus as he is "on the way" to Jerusalem, rebuking him for speaking such nonsense about suffering, rejection, and death. Yet Jesus would have nothing of this kind of impediment. He teaches Peter a dramatic lesson not only by rebuking him and calling him Satan but by replacing him in the proper position behind Jesus. In Mark's Gospel, as the ensuing narrative will show, discipleship is about following Jesus and Jesus makes that point to Peter first as he

---

131. Perrin, *Proclamation and Parenesis, Myth and History*, 155.

132. Narratively speaking, this point seems to be confirmed by the fact that it occurs three times in the narrative. For the importance of "threes" in the Gospel, see Tannehill, "Reading It Whole," 72. For a brief discussion on "corrective christology" in the Gospel, see Kingsbury, *Christology of Mark's Gospel*, 25–45.

took him aside (8:32) and subsequently while looking at and addressing the larger group of disciples (8:33). As Perrin would say, Peter has misunderstood the nature of the prediction indeed.

The material contained in 8:34–9:1 is very much concerned with discipleship. The text presents an ever-widening circle of followers (from Peter, to the disciples on the way, to the crowd with his disciples, 8:34) whom Jesus now instructs regarding the nature of proper followship. The instruction involves three key elements: (1) denying self; (2) taking up one's cross; and (3) following Jesus. The last element has been spoken about and is essentially the gist of discipleship in the Gospel. "Both the Passion announcement in 8:31 and the call to follow by taking up one's cross in 8:34–35 point forward to the Passion story."[133] The first element, that of denying self, is elaborated on in the following verses (8:35–38).

Robert C. Tannehill observes several key features of this passage, 8:34–35 in particular.[134] First, both 8:34 and 8:35 begin in the same way, employing the indefinite pronoun (τις) or the relative pronoun (ὅς) plus the infinitive. Second, 8:34 reiterates the notion of following Jesus as the central requirement for discipleship.[135] Finally, "the saying about saving and destroying one's life is constructed from contrasting words combined in paradoxical fashion. This paradox is repeated in both halves of the sentence: the attempt to save one's life will destroy it; destroying one's life will save it."[136] This form of speech of brief, pointed statements that make sharp, paradoxical contrasts he calls "antithetical aphorisms."[137] These statements are presenting in the narrative to show the extent of true discipleship—following Jesus is likely going to lead to suffering and death, the same fate as Jesus'.[138] There is indeed a cost associated with discipleship. But will following Jesus also lead to resurrection or vindication as the first passion

---

133. Tannehill, "Reading It Whole," 73–74. See also, Meyer, "Taking Up the Cross."

134. Ibid., 68–69.

135. The verb ἀκολουθέω occurs some twenty times in the Markan narrative (1:18; 2:14 [bis]; 2:15; 3:7; 5:24, 37; 6:1; 8:34 [bis]; 9:38; 10:21, 28, 32, 52; 11:9; 14:13; 14:51, 54; 15:41. Best (*Following Jesus*, 37) suggests that Mark's use of the word came from the tradition and was used by Mark in relation to discipleship: "Mark understood its significance [in the tradition] and extended its use."

136. Tannehill, "Reading It Whole," 68. Tannehill consistently translates ἀπόλλυμι as "destroy" (see p. 77n2).

137. Ibid. See also Tannehill, *Sword of His Mouth*, 88–101.

138. Tannehill ("Reading It Whole," 69) calls this "corrective teaching," which for him applies to all three passion predictions in a manner not unlike Perrin's.

prediction indicates for Jesus (and which is confirmed by the other two predictions)?

The answer to this perplexing question seems to be yes in the Markan narrative. The answer is found in 9:1, a verse that has been given many labels such as "enigmatic saying," "remarkable statement," "puzzling statement," and "a *crux interpretum* for Markan studies."[139] Morna Hooker argues that "this is one of the most discussed verses in the whole of Mark's Gospel."[140] A review of the literature associated with this verse corroborates Hooker's thesis.[141] Ironically, a few commentators hardly mention 9:1 in their exegesis or interpretation of the Gospel, which goes against Hooker's labeling of it being one of "the most discussed verses in Mark." For example, Ched Myers devotes a mere 59 words to it in his discussion on 8:34—9:1 (he includes a passing reference to 9:1 in his discussion on the crucifixion).[142] Francis J. Moloney, while offering a more substantive comment on the verse and its interpretation in context, speaks of 9:1 only in a portion of one paragraph (147 words) with an attendant footnote (77 words).[143] Elizabeth Struthers Malbon's work, *Hearing Mark: A Listener's Guide*—though not a commentary in the typical sense—refers to the verse in her section dealing with 8:34–9:1 in 43 words.[144]

For me, 9:1 is the quintessential hinge or swivel verse. By "hinge," I mean that it serves a transitioning function within the narrative.[145] This

---

139. France (*Gospel of Mark*, 343) calls it enigmatic; Evans (*Mark 8:27—16:20*, 28) considers it remarkable; Edwards (*Gospel According to Mark*, 259) observes that it is a puzzling statement; and the logion is Bird's ("Crucifixion of Jesus as the Fulfillment of Mark 9:1," 24) *crux interpretum* in the Gospel.

140. Hooker, *Gospel According to St. Mark*, 211. This is also observed by Hurtado (*Mark*, 139).

141. An examination of journal articles that have appeared in the last forty years corroborates this statement. For example, see Öhler, "Die Verklärung (Mk 9:1–8)"; Wenham and Moses, "'There Are Some Standing Here . . .'"; Trimaille, "Le Récit de la Transfiguration"; McDermott, "Gegenwärtiges und kommendes Reich Gottes"; Smith, "Wounded Lion"; Auer, "Die Bedeutung"; Kilgallen, "Mk 9:1—the Conclusion of a Pericope"; Crawford, "Near Expectation"; Lambrecht, "Q-Influence on Mark 8:34; 9:1"; Nardoni, "A Redactional Interpretation of Mark 9:1"; Brower, "Seeing the Kingdom in Power"; Chilton, "Dominical Assurance and Apostolic Vision"; Greeven, "Nochmals Mk 9:1 in Codex Bezae"; and Perrin, "Composition of Mark 9:1."

142. Myers, *Binding the Strong Man*, 248, 391.

143. Moloney, *Gospel of Mark*, 177.

144. Malbon, *Hearing Mark*, 57–58.

145. Donahue and Harrington (*Gospel of Mark*, 273) note that 9:1 "serves as a bridge from the final (eschatological) saying on discipleship in 8:38 to the story of the

transition is in the arena of discipleship. Where Jesus spoke of the cost of discipleship in 8:33–38, in 9:1 he speaks of the benefits of being a disciple. A significant benefit of being a disciple of Jesus is that at some point one will enter the kingdom of God and thus be with Jesus in all his glory.[146] Peter, James, and John got a glimpse of this glory on the mountain of Transfiguration. Other disciples saw such glory (paradoxically) as Jesus was crucified and later resurrected. Still others must await the *parousia* in order to enjoy the fulfillment of the promise of 9:1. Interpreters throughout the ages have insisted on choosing a horizon for which this verse must be fulfilled—the immediate context (Transfiguration), the crucifixion, Jesus' resurrection, or an eschatological fulfillment. Is it not possible, especially in light of the narrative strategies Mark employs for his immediate readers (and by extension beyond the immediate community) that multiple horizons are in view here? Mark wants his community to grasp the significance of Jesus' true identity—exalted Messiah, suffering Son of Man, beloved Son of God—and the benefits of following him regardless of the cost, so he whets the appetites of the community with the Transfiguration narrative, which points beyond itself to the cross. Once past the cross, the narrative does not end but closes enigmatically with the women fleeing in fear because Jesus' body has disappeared. The women and the Markan community hope they will soon see Jesus. The extended Markan community, that is, the second and subsequent generations of readers/hearers share in the hope of seeing Jesus also, indeed, the glory of the Christ *when he comes* in (eschatological) power. In this way, 9:1 is the quintessential bridge verse—it stretches across horizons fulfilling precisely its intended purpose.

So, whether one reads 9:1 as the conclusion to a pericope or the beginning of a new one or (as I have) a swivel point between two, the focus is that Jesus instructs his disciples on matters of discipleship. Significant teaching occurs in 8:31–33 and again in 8:34–38 and in the all-important hinge verse of 9:1. But, the Transfiguration pericope is not void of discipleship material. Seeing Jesus' teaching on discipleship in the Transfiguration narrative

---

transfiguration in 9:2–8. By placing it just before the transfiguration Mark has given an interpretation to both the saying and the narrative." Although I prefer the term "hinge," I see no major distinction between the two terms. On this point see Stock, "Hinge Transitions in Mark's Gospel." Stock considers 8:22–26 a second major "hinge transition" (cf. 1:14–15; 10:46–52; 15:40–41) and makes no reference to 9:1 as a hinge passage.

146. Kingsbury (*Conflict in Mark*, 106) sees the coming in the near future: "What is more, disciples can also rest assured that they can anticipate seeing in the near future the rule of God come in power and splendor (9:1)."

supports the assertion that this key theme crosses over both pericopae in question.

One of the most significant elements of the teaching that occurs in the Transfiguration scene occurs first not on the lips of Jesus to the gathered small group of disciples (Peter, James, and John), but through the voice heard from a cloud and by those present with Jesus in his transfigured state. The voice declares the all-important content concerning Jesus' identity. The presence of Elijah and Moses help the disciples see that Jesus stands in the trajectory of these two great prophets. As Jesus' subsequent teaching will support, Elijah was to precede the long-awaited Messiah of Israel (Mal 3:23–24). On the one hand Elijah's presence on the mountain fulfills this prophecy, but on the other hand foreshadows how Jesus will connect Elijah and John the Baptist in 9:11–13. Moses, the prophet par excellence and giver of the Law of God, "appears as the representative of the old covenant and the promise, now shortly to be fulfilled in the death of Jesus."[147] As William L. Lane notes, "The presence of Elijah with Moses thus has eschatological significance in the specific sense that they proclaim the coming of the end."[148] This cognitive component (versus the character component; 8:34–38) of the instructions to disciples is continued by Jesus as he instructs them not to tell anyone what they had seen (and presumably heard) on the mountain *until* the Son of Man has been raised from the dead (9:9). Emboldened by what they had seen on the mountain, the three disciples decide to ask Jesus about Elijah (9:11). If Elijah's and Moses' presence on the mountain suggests that the end is near, does not Elijah have to come first in order to prepare the people for the eschatological judgment to come (Mal 3:11; 4:5; Sir 48:10)?[149] Jesus responds to their question by indicating that Elijah has already come in the form of John the Baptist (9:13), whose presence and death in the narrative has been strategic (1:2–8; 6:14–29). Coupled with this message is yet another reference to the Son of Man and the impending suffering and contempt he must endure (9:12).

To sum up, discipleship is a major theme in the middle section of Mark's Gospel. Jesus' teaching on discipleship includes carefully considering the cost of being a disciple—it will indeed cost one his or her life, but paradoxically that is how one saves his/her own life. But there are also benefits associated with discipleship. As the hinge passage of 9:1 indicates, at

---

147. Lane, *Gospel According to Mark*, 319.
148. Ibid.
149. Ibid., 324.

some point, followers of Jesus will see the Kingdom of God come in power. Similarly, disciples—through the testimony of James, John, and Peter—will *know* the true identity of Jesus, the one who is Messiah (8:29), Son of Man (8:31; 9:9), and Son of God (9:7). The instructions on the costs and benefits of being a disciple of Jesus form the true corrective teaching on the nature of discipleship.[150] These two pericopae provide that corrective.

## AN ARGUMENT BASED ON SYNOPTIC STUDIES

The final argument for reading these two pericopae together is grounded in a study of the synoptic relationship between the first three Gospels. As a close study of the first and third Gospel reveals, neither Matthew nor Luke tinkered with the order of presentation in these two scenes (this, of course, assumes Markan priority).[151] In fact, while Matthew and Luke edited Mark's material for their own purposes, "each narrates essentially

---

150. In saying "corrective," I am not saying that the form of the teaching on discipleship in the Transfiguration scene is that of Tannehill's "antithetical aphorism." However, it is interesting to observe that the sayings of 9:11–13 do involve "sayings which make a strong, unqualified statement containing a sharp contrast" (Tannehill's definition of antithetical aphorism), but they are not of the brief and sharp nature that Tannehill had in mind (and they do not begin with the indefinite pronoun or equivalent). So, while the form is not the same, the essential substance is similar.

151. In assuming rather than arguing for Markan priority, I realize that for some people I may be stepping into a hornet's nest. No doubt, the so-called synoptic problem is a complex and demanding issue. While there are those who oppose seeing Mark's Gospel as the earliest written gospel, most contemporary New Testament scholars favor the priority of Mark's Gospel and the so-called "Two-Source Hypothesis" (Mark's Gospel and the hypothetical "Q," a nonextant sayings document). One of the earliest proponents of the "Two-Source Hypothesis" was Holtzmann, *Die synoptischen Evangelien*. Neirynck (see esp. "Introduction: The Two-Source Hypothesis," in *The Interrelations of the Gospels*) and his students spent the last quarter of the twentieth century systematically defending the Two-Source Hypothesis. For more recent advocates of Markan priority, see esp. Kloppenborg (*Q and the Earliest Gospel*, 1–40), Marcus (*Mark 1–8*, 40–45, esp. 41), and France (*Gospel of Mark*, 41–45, esp. 45). The major opposing view to Markan priority is the so-called "Two-Gospel Hypothesis," first proposed by Griesbach in *Synopsis Evangeliorum Matthaei Marci et Lucae una cum iis Joannis pericopis quae omnino cum caeterorum evangelistarum narrationibus conferendae sunt*, which has been translated into English and published as "A Demonstration That Mark Was Written after Matthew and Luke," in *J. J. Griesbach: Synoptic and Text-critical Studies 1776-1976*. Farmer (*The Synoptic Problem*) continues to keep Griesbach's proposal alive. On the development of the synoptic problem, see esp. Dungan, *History of the Synoptic Problem*. For a recent discussion of "Q" and Markan Priority, see Goodacre, *The Case against Q*, 19–45.

the same sequence of literary motifs for its respective Gospel audience."[152] Given the nature of the material, one might expect Matthew and Luke to veer from the sequence when it comes to Mark's Transfiguration account.[153] While it does not serve our purposes to engage in a detailed analysis of the Matthean and Lukan accounts of the twin pericopae, a brief overview outlining this similar sequence is necessary.[154]

## Similarities in the Three Synoptic Accounts

As a cursory analysis at Kurt Aland's *Synopsis Quattuor Evangeliorum* shows, the stories of Peter's Confession (No. 158), Jesus Foretells His Passion (No. 159) "If Any Man would Come After Me . . ." (No. 160), and The Transfiguration (No. 161) all fall in succession in the three Synoptic Gospels.[155] The common features regarding the Transfiguration are as follows.[156] First, Jesus takes the "inner circle" of disciples (Peter, James, and John) up a mountain (Mark 9:2a; Matt 17:1; Luke 9:28). Second, Jesus is transfigured on the mountain before the three disciples (Mark 9:2b-3; Matt 17:2; Luke 9:29). Third, Moses and Elijah appear and speak with the transfigured Jesus (Mark 9:4; Matt 17:3; Luke 9:30-32). Fourth, Peter offers to build three tents, one for Jesus, one for Moses, and one for Elijah (Mark 9:5-6; Matt 17:4; Luke 9:33). Fifth, a cloud overshadows presumably the entire party (Mark 9:7a; Matt 17:5a; Luke 9:34).[157] Sixth, a voice from the cloud instructs them to "listen to him"

---

152. Heil, *Transfiguration of Jesus*, 33.

153. This is due to the curious nature of the Transfiguration account, especially its literary genre. The genre labels given to the Transfiguration are numerous: "misplaced resurrection story," "misplaced ascension story," "pronouncement story," "magical story," "darashic scenification," "theophany," "apocalyptic vision," and "epiphany" (to mention a few). For the bibliography associated with each, see Heil, *Transfiguration of Jesus*, 23, nn.6–11.

154. Heil's monograph is the only significant work I am aware of that looks at all three Synoptic accounts from a narrative-critical perspective (and some might argue that his perspective is more audience-critical). The literature on the Transfiguration in each respective Gospel is vast. For a helpful overview of the state of research into the Synoptic relationship of the Transfiguration, see Heil, *Transfiguration of Jesus*, 21–22, esp. nn.1–3.

155. Aland, *Synopsis Quattuor Evangeliorum*, 577.

156. For a helpful discussion of the similarities of each account, see Heil, *Transfiguration of Jesus*, 24–31.

157. In each account, the cloud overshadows them. The Markan account has the participle ἐπισκιάζουσα, with the plural pronoun in the dative case (αὐτοῖς). The Matthean and Lukan accounts employ finite verbs (though in different tenses) with the plural

## The Turning Point in the Gospel of Mark

(Mark 9:7b; Matt 17:5b-7; Luke 9:35). Finally, Moses and Elijah disappear and Jesus is alone with the three disciples (Mark 9:8; Matt 17:8; Luke 9:36). Thus, the overarching structure of the Transfiguration account in Matthew and Luke matches or tracks the Markan account quite closely. Thus, the evidence suggests that neither Matthew nor Luke felt comfortable divorcing the Transfiguration narrative from the narrative of Peter's confession.

## Differences in Matthew's Transfiguration Story

There are, however, differences between the accounts and these differences should not be ignored. However, I believe that a brief examination of the differences in Matthew's and Luke's Transfiguration account will prove that they each followed Mark's account, but for their own reasons, redacted or edited matters in order to tell their own story.[158] This is further confirmation that the tradition held these stories together and that the two subsequent evangelists amended the Markan version in order to construct their own narrative, but did not separate the two accounts.

Matthew's most substantive additions to the Markan story include (1) the addition of καὶ ἔλαμψεν τὸ πρόσωπον αὐτοῦ ὡς ὁ ἥλιος in 17:2 (cf. Mark 9:2), and (2) the addition of vv. 6–7 in their entirety (a passage that concerns the fate of the disciples, curiously placed after the cloud and divine voice). As Donald A. Hagner observes, "In the first instance, we probably have a tradition other than Mark—one reflected also in Luke; in the second, we have perhaps Matthean elaboration of the reference to fear in Mark 9:6 (omitted by Matthew from what would have been its place following v 4)."[159] Only in Matthew's version does Jesus speak (17:7).[160] The point of this addition is to

---

accusative αὐτούς.

158. There are places in which the Matthean and Lukan accounts appear to resemble each other. These relatively minor points of resemblance have been dubbed "minor agreements." On the minor agreements in the Transfiguration narrative, see esp. Neirynck, "Minor Agreements Matthew-Luke in the Transfiguration Story," 797–810. As Davies and Allison (*Matthew*, 2:684–85) point out, "such agreements have been understood to imply (i) that something is wrong with the theory of Markan priority, (ii) that Matthew and Luke were, in telling the story of the transfiguration, influenced by a source other than Mk 9.2–8, or (iii) that Luke knew and used Matthew." Davies and Allison were not inclined to accept any of these options. Neither am I.

159. Hagner, *Matthew 14–28*, 490. For a more detailed analysis of the differences in Matthew's Transfiguration narrative, see Davies and Allison, *Matthew*, 2:685–93.

160. Heil, *Transfiguration of Jesus*, 32.

highlight Matthew's own sensitivity to christological concerns, christological concerns that are nevertheless different than Mark's (focusing on Jesus as the new Moses).[161] Another significant omission by Matthew is understandable in light of the narrative purposes of his Gospel: the incomprehension of the disciples, a major Markan theme perhaps illustrated in Mark 9:10, is absent in the Matthean Transfiguration account. Matthew's purposes for his disciples were vastly different from Mark's.[162]

## Differences in Luke's Transfiguration Story

Joseph A. Fitzmyer concurs with many Lukan scholars in seeing Luke 9:28–36 as a redaction of the Markan narrative.[163] He attributes the differences either to Lukan redaction or to Lukan composition. In the former category, Fitzmyer includes the following: "about eight days" (9:28) instead of Mark's "six days later"; the καὶ ἐγένετο constructions (9:28, 29, 30); the ἐν τῷ + infinitive construction (9:29, 33, 34, 36); the use of καὶ ἰδού (9:30), καὶ αὐτοί (9:36), and εἶπεν πρός (9:33).[164] The material on prayer is likewise redaction according to Fitzmyer (9:28, 29), as is the substitution of "Master" for "Rabbi" in 9:35 (cf. Mark 9:5).[165] To Lukan composition Fitzmyer attributes 9:30–33, 34b, 36bc.[166]

This latter reference to what Fitzmyer calls "Lucan composition," includes several interesting features of comparison. One difference relates to christological concerns. In Luke 9:35, the voice from the cloud indicates that Jesus is "my chosen son." The Markan and Matthean accounts simply refer to Jesus as the beloved Son. The focus on "chosen" rather than "beloved" may emphasize the theme of selection, which has already been introduced in the narrative at 6:13.[167] In addition, as Luke Timothy Johnson

---

161. Davies and Allison, *Matthew*, 2:705. See also, Schnackenburg, *Gospel of Matthew*, 164.

162. Indeed, Luz (*Matthew 8–20*, 395; emphasis original) observes that "Matthew has significantly changed the *conversation with the disciples*." The reason for this change, Luz notes, is so that "the somewhat chaotic conversation in Mark [can be] much clearer in the Matthean version." As we will see with Luke's version, Matthew does not seem to want to project Jesus' disciples as unable to comprehend the gravity of the situation.

163. Fitzmyer, *Luke (I–IX)*, 790.

164. Ibid., 792.

165. Ibid.

166. Ibid.

167. On this point, see Johnson, *Gospel of Luke*, 154. For another view, see Fitzmyer,

has observed, Luke's composition deliberately "excises" Mark 6:45–8:26, a series of repetitive pericopae in which Mark develops the theme of the incomprehension of the disciples. "Luke does not like this theme repetition, and has quite a different understanding of the disciples to develop. He connects the sequence here directly to the sending of the Twelve and the multiplication of the loaves, thereby compressing the narrative and fixing its focus on the Twelve as the new leaders of restored Israel."[168] It is agreed that Luke (and Matthew) take their narratives in different ways, at times choosing to ignore various pericopae in order to tell their own stories: Luke does not do it with Peter's confession and the Transfiguration.

## Conclusion

Matthew and Luke redacted the material that was common to them in various ways and included in their respective narratives details not in Mark. That point is assumed in Synoptic Gospel studies. The more important point is that though Matthew and Luke amended the Markan material in minor ways, the structure of the two accounts (Peter's confession; Transfiguration) was unaltered. Modern commentators have observed this feature also. For example, I. Howard Marshall states: "The story of the transfiguration is so closely coupled to the preceding scene that we are justified in seeking some intimate relationship between them in the minds of the Evangelists."[169] W. D. Davies and Dale C. Allison similarly observe, "If one accepts the priority of Mark it is natural to see Mt. 17.1–8 as a reworking of Mk 9.2–8."[170] Donald A. Hagner writes, "All three Synoptic Gospels preserve the sequence of (1) the confession at Caesarea Philippi, (2) the announcement of Jesus' suffering and death (together with the subsequent saying about true discipleship), and (3) the transfiguration."[171] And finally Heil, "Each version, then, presents a unified, consistent narrative that is of the same basic literary genre, evoking in general the same basic responses from their respective implied Gospel audiences familiar with the genre."[172] The confession of Peter with its ensuing teaching to the disciples and the

---

*Luke (I-IX)*, 793–95.
- 168. Johnson, *Gospel of Luke*, 154.
- 169. Marshall, *Gospel of Luke*, 380.
- 170. Davies and Allison, *Matthew*, 2:684.
- 171. Hagner, *Matthew 14–28*, 489.
- 172. Heil, *Transfiguration of Jesus*, 33.

Transfiguration of Jesus on a mountain came to Mark together in the tradition: he preserved the two by linking them grammatically and thematically, and the subsequent evangelists (for whatever reason) did not attempt to alter this cohesion.

## THE JANUS IMAGE AND MARK'S PURPOSE

To this point in the chapter, I have tried to argue that the turning point of the Markan narratives lies in the twin pericopae of 8:27–38/9:2–13 with 9:1 serving as a link or hinge between the two. The argument so presented has three features that support this conclusion. First, grammatical or linguistic links tie the two pericopae together. Second, common themes reach across both stories. Finally, Matthew and Luke kept these two stories together, choosing not to insert their own special material in between, something they felt free to do in other places. The evidence so presented leads one to ask why is Mark so concerned that a reader (or hearer) read these two stories together. What is the author's purpose in the narrative as a whole? My conclusion is that he is attempting to present the true identity of Jesus as Messiah, Son of God, and Son of Man. As discussed above, these three christological images are found not only in this middle section, but also in the Gospel's beginning material and later in the Passion Narrative. In fact, it is not just the christological material that is present in the beginning, middle, and end of the Markan narrative. Other thematic features are present as well (i.e., key characters such as Peter and the tandem of messianic secret/passion predictions). This narrative is cleverly crafted—beginning, middle, and end all seem to go together (and at times not go together, for a reason). Mark as a storyteller has developed a narrative that he hoped would compel readers to deal with the person of Jesus. This he does, in my opinion, with these three christological images—Messiah, Son of God, and Son of Man—the three images that function in a Janus-like manner (i.e., looking back and forward).

The Janus image, as a heuristic device, is meant to aid a reader in discovering Mark's purpose in his narrative. Before settling on what the Janus motif offers in terms of the study of the Markan text, let us first look at four recent works that also found significance in the tripartite structure of the narrative, albeit for different reasons. A critical reading of the works of John Paul Heil, Dorothy Lee, C. Clifton Black, and Marie Noonan Sabin should provide corroborating evidence that Mark's beginning, middle, and end do contain the "key" to understanding the purpose and message of the Gospel.

## Four Significant Works

### John Paul Heil's *The Transfiguration of Jesus*

Heil argues that the genre of the transfiguration account is not a settled issue. Transfiguration narratives have been labeled "misplaced resurrection [or ascension] narratives," "pronouncement stories," "magical stories," darashic scenifications," theophanies, apocalyptic visions, and epiphanies.[173] He dismisses the earlier ones and focuses in on the last three—theophanies, visions, and epiphanies—and distinguishes the last from the first two. In so doing, he argues that the Transfiguration account in Mark is a special type of epiphany, one in which he calls a "pivotal mandatory epiphany."[174] A mandatory epiphany is "any epiphany whose whole orientation and final focus centers upon a specific mandate, a *climactic command*, of an epiphanic being or voice to the recipient(s) of the epiphanic activity."[175] Such a command is, of course, present in Mark's transfiguration account (9:7). "Because the command . . . occurs at a pivotal point in the overall narrative, with significant contextual relations both prior and subsequent to the command," he labels the account a pivotal mandatory epiphany.[176]

Heil's work is the only work that treats the three synoptic accounts of the Transfiguration from a narrative-critical perspective. His attention to the genre of the Markan transfiguration account is significant and his articulation of the "pivotal mandatory epiphany" is persuasive. The outstanding feature relates to the notion of pivot and, in particular, how he suggests that the nature of the Transfiguration has contextual "relations both prior to and subsequent" to the command of 9:7.[177] This resembles my argument of Janus with a backward-looking and forward-looking component. The feature Heil calls "backward looking" focuses primarily on the previous scene (8:31–9:1) and enables "the disciples and the audience to grasp the more profound identity of the transfigured Jesus as God's beloved Son in

---

173. For works associated with each genre, see ibid., 22–23nn6–11.
174. Ibid., 51.
175. Ibid.; emphasis original.
176. Ibid.
177. Ibid.

## Reading Peter's Confession and the Transfiguration Together

contrast to the heavenly figures of Moses and Elijah."[178] Similarly, since the divine voice instructs those present to "listen to Jesus," Heil sees that Mark is trying to convey to his readers "that they must follow Jesus on his way of suffering and death."[179] This is the only way they will be able to join him in the "ultimate and permanent heavenly glory that his transfiguration prefigures."[180] However, Heil also sees other prior teaching that the command "pivots" the readers' attention to:[181]

> 4:2–3: He said to them in his teaching, "Listen (ἀκούετε)!"
>
> 4:9: "Whoever has ears to listen, let him listen (ἀκούειν ἀκουέτω)!"
>
> 4:23: "If anyone has ears to listen, let him listen (ἀκούειν ἀκουέτω)!"
>
> 4:24: "Attend to what you are listening (ἀκούετε)!"
>
> 7:14: "Listen (ἀκούσατε) to me, all of you, and understand!"
>
> 8:18: "Having ears do you not listen (ἀκούετε)?"
>
> 9:7: "Listen (ἀκούετε) to him!"

This backward look is joined by a forward look to what is ahead in the narrative. To use Heil's own words: "It [the command of 9:7] has also pivoted them forward to the subsequent predictions of the necessity for him (9:12, 31–32; 10:32–34; 12:1–12; 14:8, 22–25, 27–31, 32–42) as well as them (10:35–45) to give their lives in humble, suffering service for others with the assurance of being raised from the dead (9:9; 12:18–27; 16:5–8) and seeing his final coming in the heavenly glory (13:26; 14:62) prefigured by his transfiguration."[182] This pattern, a pivot as Heil calls it or Janus as I suggest, ties together the narrative and gives it "significant theological ramifications."[183]

---

178. Ibid., 167.
179. Ibid.
180. Ibid.
181. Ibid., 166.
182. Ibid., 199.
183. Ibid., 319.

# The Turning Point in the Gospel of Mark

## *Dorothy Lee's Transfiguration*

Another recent interpreter has observed a similar phenomenon with respect to the twin pericopae of the central section. Dorothy Lee, in writing about the Transfiguration in Mark, presents a similar image to mine regarding the central section. She suggests that the Transfiguration occupies a strategic position in the Markan narrative. In fact, she describes the "heart of the Markan narrative," 8:27–9:13 (what I am calling the "twin pericopae"), as a "diptych."[184] Lee's diptych is represented by two major "panels" with an introduction (8:27–30) preceding the first panel (8:31–38) and a conclusion (9:10–13) following the second panel (9:2–9). Connecting the two panels is a "transitional" scene or verse—9:1.[185]

We have already addressed the content of these pericopae in an earlier chapter. However, below is an illustration of Lee's diptych approach:

| Introduction | PANEL 1 (Suffering) Location: "On the way" | Transition | PANEL 2 (Glory) Location: Mountain | Conclusion |
|---|---|---|---|---|
| Secrecy of revelation | Revelation of Jesus to disciples as suffering Son of Man, who will rise from the dead and return in glory (8:31–38) | Seeing God's reign come in power (9:1) | Revelation of Jesus to three disciples as beloved Son, transfigured in radiance and light (9:2–9) | Secrecy of revelation |
| Role of Elijah and John the Baptist | | | | Role of Elijah and John the Baptist |
| Disciples' lack of understanding (8:27–30) | | | | Disciples' lack of understanding (9:10–13) |

*Table 6*

---

184. Lee, *Transfiguration*, 10.

185. There are indeed many similarities of her diptych image and my Janus image. I will articulate below why I prefer the Janus image.

## Reading Peter's Confession and the Transfiguration Together

There are several noteworthy strengths in Lee's presentation. First, she has identified many of the same shared themes of the two pericopae: secrecy; the role of Elijah/John the Baptist; presence of disciples; christological revelations (Son of Man/Beloved Son). Second, each of her panels focuses on a different aspect of Jesus' life and ministry, namely, his suffering (Panel 1) and glory (Panel 2). To her, these are integral concepts since each is incomplete without the offer. As she puts it: "Suffering *and* glory stand together at the heart of Mark's Gospel.[186] These two notions are important in the exegesis of the passage. Third, she rightly observes that Jesus' identity is both revealed and concealed. "The theme of the Markan diptych is primarily Jesus' identity, which is both manifest and secret at the same time. Throughout, there is a procession of voices that addresses the question of Jesus' identity, each moving closer to the innermost circle: other people (8:27), the disciples ('you', 8:29), Jesus himself ('the Son of Man', 8:31, 39), and finally the voice of God from the cloud (9:7)."[187] Paradoxically, Jesus' identity is made manifest in the two confessions (by Peter and God) and Jesus self-revelation but also hushed and shrouded in mystery. Fourth, she rightly recognizes the transitional role of 9:1 in the diptych.[188] Finally, though not precisely depicted in the illustration, she acknowledges (and embraces) the apocalyptic and epiphanic nature of the Transfiguration, a tension that we will see is often debated.

As helpful as Lee's illustration is, there are several features that she does not consider. First, there are other thematic links than the ones she has identified. As we have previously noted, in each pericope there is:[189]

1. Peter as the main character: 8:29, 32/9:2, 5–6

2. *Other disciples present:* 8:27, 33–34/9:2

---

186. Lee, *Transfiguration*, 12; emphasis in original.

187. Ibid., 11.

188. Some people prefer to call this verse a "bridge" between the two pericopae (Lee uses this language; see also Donahue and Harrington, *Gospel of Mark*, 273). As observed above, I prefer to call it a "hinge" or "swivel" passage in that the verse not only concludes the first pericopae but also introduces or propels one into the second. On this, see Kilgallen ("Mk 9, 1—the Conclusion of a Pericope," 82): "It [9:1] is a fitting ending to a unit and a good basis from which to launch the next unit, the transfiguration story, another form of encouragement to those whose fate includes self-renunciation and the cross."

189. Those presented in *italics* are the themes that she notes in her illustration. Regarding the disciples, she observes their lack of understanding, but not Jesus' specific instructions concerning the cost/benefit of discipleship.

The Turning Point in the Gospel of Mark

> 3. *Reference to Elijah/Prophet:* 8:30/9:4
>
> 4. *Charge to secrecy:* 8:30/9:9
>
> 5. *Instructions to disciples:* 8:31–38; 9:1/9:11–13
>
> 6. *Cost/benefit of discipleship:* 8:34–38/9:1
>
> 7. *Passion/Resurrection:* 8:31/9:9, 10, 12
>
> 8. *Revelation of Jesus' Identity:* 8:29, 31/9:7

These themes, when taken together with the grammatical and syntactical links, would add further support to her diptych presentation. Second, while I affirm that the climactic theme is the revelation of Jesus' identity, she holds that the first panel of the diptych (8:31–38) reveals Jesus as the suffering Son of Man. She says nothing about Peter's confession of Jesus as the Messiah (8:29). Her reasoning is that Jesus rebuke/sternly warns Peter immediately after his confession (8:30).[190] She does not mention the incident in 8:22–26 between Jesus and the blind man, who when Jesus touches him the first time sees "dimly," but later (upon a second touch) sees clearly. As I argued in chapters 2 and 3, there is a parallel to that incident and Peter's confession. While Jesus indeed rebukes him (ἐπιτίμησεν) this is not a denial of Peter's declaration. Rather, there is an immediate teaching session whereby Jesus predicts the passion/resurrection of the Son of Man. Peter's "blurry" vision of Jesus is made clearer with Jesus' own teaching. As I have argued (and will develop further in chapter 5), Peter's declaration of Jesus as Messiah is an important and integral element of the narrative.

My final criticism of Lee's diptych is that it does not go far enough. She has all the rudiments of my "Janus" presentation, yet she fails to connect the entire diptych with the beginning and end of Mark's narrative.[191] Lee does acknowledge the Transfiguration's shared characteristics (including helpful comments regarding the opposition and parallelism with certain shared symbols) with Jesus' baptism (at the beginning) and the passion narrative (at the end), but she does not link the two pericopae together as I suggest the narrative deserves.[192]

---

190. Lee (*Transfiguration*, 13–14) hints at this: "Peter's confession at Caesarea Philippi receives not commendation (as in Matthew's Gospel), but a stern command to secrecy, and Peter's subsequent reaction to the first passion and resurrection prediction confirms the limited nature of his understanding (8:29–33)."

191. Compare this to Black, "The Face Is Familiar," 33–49, esp. 35–36.

192. Lee, *Transfiguration*, 25–32.

## C. Clifton Black's "The Face is Familiar—I Just Can't Place It"

In a festschrift in memory of Donald H. Juel, C. Clifton Black, whose essay on redaction criticism in Mark's Gospel we examined previously, suggests that Mark's Gospel presents an ever-near but elusive God who in Christ gives readers glimpses of the divine and the kingdom but never a complete picture (as the title to his essay suggests).[193] The gist of the essay is set out in three major sections. The first acknowledges the work of Norman Perrin and his threefold pattern of the passion predictions noted above. "There is, however, another tripartite structure within Mark," Black suggests, "the triptych composed of Jesus' baptism (1:9–11), transfiguration (9:2–8), and death (15:33–41)."[194] He argues that these three episodes "beg joint consideration as mutually interpretive" because: (1) their location is critical—"the transfiguration story lies in almost the dead center of the Second Gospel, whose bookends are the baptism and death of Jesus; (2) "All three anecdotes are drenched in imagery that is apocalyptic or revelatory"; (3) Mark's intervening narrative shows how these three episodes are interconnected; (4) the central thrust of all three is Jesus as God's son, a claim that Black calls "comparatively rare" in the Gospel; and (5) these three episodes, while normally construed to be of *christological* import, are also "no less significant for construing Mark's presentation of *God*."[195]

In the second major section of his essay, Black examines the "face" motif in general, and the first bookend of Jesus' baptism in particular.[196] Black focuses on the divine voice's revelation of Jesus; a revelation that he suggests is contained in a poetic stich:

---

193. Black, "The Face is Familiar," 34, 46. The reference to "elusive presence" is acknowledged by Black to be an echo of Terrin's seminal work in OT theology (*Elusive Presence*).

194. Ibid., 35.

195. Ibid. In the last sentence, the italicized christological is supplied; the italicized God is original.

196. Ibid., 36–38. The "face" motif draws upon three verses from each of the three major episodes and focuses on the preposition of each. Relating to the baptism of Jesus, Black highlights 1:2a: Behold, I send my messenger *before your face*, who will prepare your way (Black's translation; emphasis mine in each). In the second section—the transfiguration—he points to 9:2c: . . . and he was transformed *in front of them*. In the final section, he quotes 15:39: . . . *facing him*, he beheld that thus he had expired. The play on "face" and elusive presence is, in my opinion, a helpful image to understand not only Black's argument but also the Gospel *in toto*.

## The Turning Point in the Gospel of Mark

> A: "You are my Son,
>
> B: the beloved,
>
> C: in whom I am well pleased."

According to Black, the stage is set in 1:1–11 for how Jesus will demonstrate "the habits acquired by living in the divine presence: God will be God, binding himself, intractably anointing and eventually sacrificing his own beloved Son, in the face of unrepentant humanity's efforts to fabricate a god in human image."[197]

The transfiguration account is, for Black, "this puzzling Gospel's most enigmatic passage," especially in terms of its function within the narrative as a whole.[198] "Christologically considered, the primary burdens of Mark 9:2–8 are to coordinate and to counterbalance at least three kinds of claims made by the material that frames the passage: the relationship between Jesus and his Israelite precursors, the distinctive identity of Jesus with respect to God, and the point at which such things may be properly declared."[199] Like the baptism narrative, the motifs of apocalyptic vision, divine declaration, and scriptural foreshadowing are present in the transfiguration.[200] The poetic stich, while differing in the final element, is quite similar to its counterpart in 1:11:

> A: "This is my Son,
>
> B: the beloved:
>
> C: Listen to him."

Having addressed the baptism and the transfiguration, Black moves to the passion narrative, namely the crucifixion scene (15:33–41). For Black, there are three critical moments in the episode. The first is 15:34, Jesus' so-called cry of dereliction. Here Jesus stares back at God—"into God's unveiled face which now resembles an abyss"—and asks why God has abandoned him. "Not only that: Jesus hurls back to the absent God the comparably intense, personal address that the voice from heaven has twice used for the beloved Jesus: *ho huios mou* (Mark 1:11; 9:7). It is as none other than the beloved Son, going faithfully as it is written of him (14:21), that

---

197. Ibid., 38.
198. Ibid.
199. Ibid., 39–40.
200. Ibid., 40.

the crucified Jesus prays to the God who is absent in his hidden presence."[201] The second critical moment is 15:38, which Black calls a "revelatory sign," a sign because "by God's deliberate intervention, there is no longer any shield between the holy presence and the world around it."[202] The final critical moment in this key episode is 15:39, the centurion's declaration of Jesus. Here, although the syntactical elements are rearranged, the familiar poetic stich is found:

A: "Truly,

B: this man,

C: was God's son."

As is well known, here "for the first and only time in the Gospel, the voice acknowledging Jesus as God's son belongs to a human character."[203] And this character, a Roman soldier no less, declares this as he "faces him" (or is opposite him).

Black's essay is thought provoking and, to some, might be considered brilliant. He is a very keen and insightful reader of the text. Several features I wish to highlight that corroborate the issues I have raised in this chapter (or in previous chapters). The first relates to structure. Black correctly sees a tripartite structure in the Gospel of Mark—not the tripartite structure of the passion predictions only (as Perrin observed), but an overarching structure that focuses on three episodes whose "verbal and conceptual similarities may not be quite so obvious as those of the passion predictions" but nonetheless is central.[204] This sounds tantalizingly close to the tripartite structure of Aristotelian fame—beginning, middle, and end. Second, Black notices the apocalyptic or revelatory features of these three key episodes. He suggests that it is Jesus' sonship that is revealed and that in doing so, God's (elusive) presence is also revealed. I agree that God is often the neglected factor in the study of Mark's Gospel, but generally the content of the revelation of God in Mark's Gospel is through Jesus.[205] Thus, christology and

201. Ibid., 43.
202. Ibid., 43–44.
203. Ibid., 44.
204. Ibid., 35.
205. On the neglect of theological issues in Mark and/or NT theology, see esp. Dahl, "A Neglected Factor in New Testament Theology"; Donahue, "A Neglected Factor in the Theology of Mark"; Kingsbury, "'God' within the Narrative World of Mark"; and Driggers, *Following God through Mark*.

theology are inextricably interwoven in the Gospel. I have concentrated on the christological concerns while Black focuses on the theological ones. While some readers might object to Black's use of the word "apocalyptic" in tandem with "revelation," I am happy to concede the use of both in this context. In the narrative, Mark is trying to bring out what is hidden (God, Jesus' identity, the kingdom, etc.) and this occurs in many different ways (i.e., parables, christological "confessions," narratives with christological content). Finally, I am drawn to Black's use of "face" as a heuristic device in reading Mark's Gospel. I am doing the same with my image of Janus. Black arranges the face motif in ways not dissimilar to mine: at the baptism, the messenger of God is sent before your face; Jesus was transfigured in front of them; the centurion declares Jesus' sonship facing or opposite him.

My principal criticisms of Black's essay are that (1) he does not address christological concerns sufficiently and (2) his tripartite structure does not go far enough. As I have argued, the structure of Mark's Gospel is threefold. The twin pericopae of the middle section, for reasons that I have outlined above, appear to go together in the mind of the author. It is therefore central, both in terms of location in the narrative and in terms of revelatory content. While Black focuses on the revelation of Jesus as God's Son, he does not note that (especially in the central section) the Son of God image is joined with two other repeated images of Jesus (Messiah; Son of Man) and that these three images collectively appear at three strategic places in the narrative (prescinding from the text-critical issue of 1:1 for the moment):

Beginning
- Messiah (1:1)
- Son of God (1:1, 11)
- Son of Man (2:10) [206]

Middle
- Messiah (8:29)
- Son of God (9:7)
- Son of Man (8:31, 38; 9:9, 12)

---

206. Some may object to the reference to Son of Man in 2:10 as being part of the so-called beginning section. While it occurs near the beginning of the narrative, it is not part of the same unit as Messiah and Son of God, both of which belong to the Prologue. This issue will be addressed in more detail in the subsequent chapter.

End
- Messiah (14:61–62)
- Son of God (or son of the Blessed One, 14:61–62; 15:39)
- Son of Man (14:62)

Black is focusing on the elusive divine presence in Mark's Gospel, which may explain the focus on Son of God in 1:11, 9:7, and 15:39. Yet, a holistic reading of the narrative suggests these additional images, which brings into account messianic and eschatological issues that also are theological in nature.

## Marie Noonan Sabin's *The Gospel According to Mark*

In her commentary on Mark's Gospel, Marie Sabin depicts the narrative in this way: "Rich in Scripture, theological in purpose, and brilliant in design, Mark's Gospel invites its readers to become followers of Jesus' transfiguring wisdom."[207] The final two words, "transfiguring wisdom," are not simply theological terminology, but are the heart of what Sabin understands about the Gospel's structure and its main character, respectively. Regarding the structure of the Gospel, Sabin picks up on the fact that the Transfiguration scene stands "exactly in the middle of the Gospel (9:2)."[208] To her, "the transfiguration is Mark's way of imagining [Jesus'] resurrection."[209] Structurally, Sabin sees the whole of Mark arranged in triad form.[210] The triads are built on the three "beginnings" in the Gospel. The first is 1:1, "suggesting the very opening of Genesis and the idea of God creating 'in wisdom.'"[211] The second beginning is the ἀπὸ δὲ ἀρχῆς κτίσεως in 10:6, which for Sabin

---

207. Sabin, *Mark*, 14.

208. Ibid.

209. Ibid. Presumably, the reference to imagining is in response to the fact that the Markan Jesus does not appear after his resurrection. The resurrected Jesus is spoken about by the young man at the empty tomb (16:1–5), but no character in the story sees the resurrected Jesus nor does the hearer of the story (assuming a 16:8 end for the narrative).

210. Ibid., 159. Sabin also offers a reading of the Gospel by examining the "doublets" of the narrative. However, because her main thesis about Mark's Gospel centers on the transfiguring wisdom presented by the narrative, the triad form—with the Transfiguration as its midpoint—appears to be the driving force of her structure.

211. Ibid. This is also an important feature of her previous work, *Reopening the Word*, 34–39.

### The Turning Point in the Gospel of Mark

"follows upon the transfiguration and introduces Jesus' radical teachings on poverty, powerlessness, and childlikeness."[212] The final "beginning" of this triadic structure is "in chapter 16 with its images of a new day and its message of Jesus' return, at what looks like the end, to the beginning of his ministry in Galilee."[213] In addition, structurally speaking, there are three sections that each end in a scene of resurrection: the raising of Jairus's daughter (5:43), the transfiguration (9:8), and the scene at the empty tomb where the women learn that Jesus has been raised (16:6). In both of these configurations, "the re-creative, transfiguring power of God's wisdom is at the center."[214]

However, structure—with its emphasis on triads and the Transfiguration at the center—is not the only distinguishing feature of the Gospel. It also involves wisdom. As the previous quotation suggests, Sabin notes that God's wisdom is central in that it is the creative power behind Transfiguration, both Jesus' Transfiguration on the mountain and the disciples' following of Wisdom's transfiguring call (i.e., Prov 1:22).[215] However, it is not only God's wisdom that is on display in the Gospel but also Jesus as Wisdom personified. "God's Wisdom is imagined as a maternal figure—life-giving, nurturing and healing, restorative and transfiguring. When Mark wanted to communicate the significance of Jesus, it was quite natural for him to present him as God's Wisdom made flesh."[216]

Scholars may differ on the finer points of Sabin's proposal that Mark intentionally presented Jesus as God's Wisdom personified. For our purposes in this chapter, the more intriguing proposal concerns her structural presentation of the Transfiguration as the center (similar to Dorothy Lee's work) and the triadic nature of the Gospel. She sees something that I have argued is present in the Gospel, namely, a discernable beginning, middle, and end of the narrative. I disagree with her analysis of the structure. First, her observation about the three "beginnings" (ἀρχή in Greek) is questionable since the final beginning (16:1–8) does not actually use the word ἀρχή. Similarly, Sabin does not mention two additional instances of ἀρχή, both in Mark 13. Not including these two beginnings is understandable since they both come as speech from Jesus and in reference to end time events

---

212. Sabin, *Mark*, 159.
213. Ibid.
214. Ibid., 160.
215. Ibid., 9, 20.
216. Ibid., 9. See also her *Reopening the Word*, 148–70.

(i.e., the "beginning of the birth pangs" in 13:8 and "such tribulation has not been from the beginning of the creation which God created until now in 13:19"). More persuasive is her observation that there are three "resurrections", one in each of the three triads (5:43, 9:8, 16:6). The debatable feature, as we have seen above, relates to the question as to the function of the Transfiguration account in the Markan narrative.[217]

## The Nature of a Heuristic Device

What the analysis of the works by Heil, Lee, Black, and Sabin confirms is that there seems to be three discernable sections to the Markan narrative. The movement of Mark's plot resembles the pattern observed by Aristotle centuries before Mark wrote. The crucial question this chapter has addressed is how the twin pericopae of Peter's confession and the Transfiguration are joined together and what does this mean for Mark's purpose? The common factor in these two pericopae is the identity of Jesus and what his identity means for disciples. I have suggested that the twin pericopae function in a Janus-like manner. In so stating this, I have tried to make the point that I am using the Janus image heuristically, that is, as a discovery tool. Before briefly applying this image to the question of christology and discipleship, a brief word on the image of Janus and its use as a heuristic device is necessary.

Janus was the Roman god of the gate or entryway. As such, the "face" of Janus looked two ways at the same time. Interestingly, Janus as an exegetical (heuristic) device has been used in biblical studies (especially in Hebrew Bible studies) since 1978. In an article in the *Bulletin of the American Society of Papyrologists*, Cyrus H. Gordon first observed a phenomenon in Cant 2:12, which he called "Janus parallelism."[218] Janus parallelism, Gordon noted, is a kind parallelism that "hinges on the use of a single word with two entirely different meanings: one meaning paralleling what precedes, and the other meaning, what follows."[219] This literary technique (a form of paronomasia, one author suggests) has been examined in many passages in

---

217. On this, see esp. Stein, "Is the Transfiguration (Mark 9:2–8) a Misplaced Resurrection-Account?"

218. Gordon, "New Directions," 59–60.

219. Ibid., 59.

the Hebrew Bible and has even been the subject of a monograph in connection with the book of Job.[220]

I am not suggesting that Mark knew of the literary technique "Janus parallelism," or even was conscious of the notion of paronomasia. However, if Mark knew his Bible (what we would call the LXX)—and the evidence is that he did employ it quite strategically—then, it is possible that he has made use of something that he would not have been able to identify as such. Often writers employ certain types of plots though they may have never taken a course on plot development or even are aware of the differing types of plot. The same may be true of Mark. He may have never been conscious of one word or one scene looking in both directions, but employed it because it made for a good story. Just as scholars have gained insight examining texts from the Hebrew Bible with this technique in mind, so also I suggest we can learn a great deal from the Markan text examining it with the same motives—heuristically—seeking to discover what the texts means in light of the technique employed.

## The "Janus" Application to Mark

What are we to discover about Mark's Gospel using the image of Janus? First, we have to see the importance of the middle section in the Gospel (8:27–9:13). This middle section is linked together in various ways, primarily through grammatical and thematic links (as argued above). Similarly, this linkage was so strong and the tradition that gave birth to it so solid that subsequent Gospel authors chose not to change the order of events. Second, two other larger sections—a discernable beginning and a discernable ending, flank the middle section. This is the pattern Aristotle observed in *Poetics* and contemporary NT scholars have confirmed, whether implicitly or explicitly. Finally, the purpose of the Janus image is found in the substance of the pericopae. This substance is the identity of Jesus and what that means for his disciples (and would-be disciples). Jesus' identity is summarized in the three christological images or titles that are found in the twin pericopae—Messiah, Son of God, and Son of Man. It is of great importance that

---

220. Noegel, *Janus Parallelism in the Book of Job*; Noegel, "Janus Parallelism in Job"; Tsumura, "Janus Parallelism in Nah 1:8"; Tsumura, "Janus Parallelism in Hab. III 4"; Ceresko, "Janus Parallelism in Amos's 'Oracles Against the Nations'"; Kselman, "Janus Parallelism in Psalm 75:2"; Malul, "Janus Parallelism in Biblical Hebrew"; Christensen, "Janus Parallelism in Genesis 6:3"; and Rendsburg, "Janus Parallelism in Gen 49:26".

these three titles—and only these three—appear in the beginning, middle, and end of the Gospel. Other images or titles are used for Jesus (Shepherd, 6:34; Son of David, 12:35–37; King of Israel, 15:31–32), but none is used repeatedly as these three. Mark is urging his readers to see Jesus as he really is—the long-awaited Messiah, God's own Son, whose future resembles that of the eschatological Son of Man. When readers observe this, after counting the cost, the only wise conclusion to draw is to follow this man—to be "with him" (3:14) wherever he goes, even if that path involves suffering, humiliation, and death.

## CONCLUSION

In this chapter, I set out to do four things: to articulate in detail the grammatical links between Peter's confession (8:27–9:1) and the Transfiguration (9:2–13), to articulate the thematic links between the two pericopae, to articulate why the pericopae are also linked in the other Synoptic Gospels, and to articulate why the Janus image is helpful in determining Mark's overall purpose in writing his Gospel.

As noted above, thirteen grammatical links join the two stories. Some of the grammatical links are not determinative in and of themselves. Every author writes in a particular style, often using an established vocabulary. Similarly, Mark likely drew from traditional material where they may have been words and constructions that were not Markan but that nevertheless could be compared with other passages. So, grammatical links alone might not make the case I am trying to make that the two pericopae should be read together. However, when one observes the eight thematic links the evidence mounts that these two stories are inextricably interwoven, each in a way contributing to the interpretation of the other. Then, when one observes that neither Matthew nor Luke separated these two accounts but instead reworked them in ways to tell their own stories, a reader is faced with the conclusion that maybe Mark intended that these two pericopae be read together in order to tell his story of Jesus and the implications of that story on the lives of the hearers/readers.

The Janus image is indeed a helpful tool because if these two pericopae are linked, then the purpose of their linking is of primary importance to an interpreter. Since the three major sections of the Gospel include the same christological images (Messiah, Son of God, Son of Man), one begins to sense that this was what Mark wanted to highlight. In true dramatic form, Peter's confession of Christ in 8:29 "looks backward" to the Prologue (1:1) or "beginning" and serves as a midpoint climax. Is it a coincidence that the other two christological images are present also (Son of God in 1:1, 11; Son of Man in 2:10)? Likewise, in 9:7 the divine voice speaks from the cloud that Jesus is God's beloved Son. Such a declaration faces forward to the "end," especially the trial (14:61–62) and crucifixion, which reaches a climax when a Roman (Gentile) soldier declares Jesus as Son of God (15:39). In between these two faces—the backward one pointing to the Prologue and the forward one pointing to the crucifixion—stands Jesus' own prediction of his passion/resurrection, referring to himself as the Son of Man. This image is present in 2:10 (the beginning third of the narrative) and is also present in 14:61–62 (the ending section of the narrative). In this way, Son of Man joins or converges with Messiah and Son of God to provide the hermeneutical key in understanding Mark's overall purpose in writing—the identity of Jesus and the corresponding decision that disciples face when that true identity is revealed.

Thus far the meaning of these christological disclosures has not been explored in detail. In the next chapter, Jesus as Messiah and Son of God, as understood by Mark, will be examined first. These two titles go together naturally since they are both confessional titles, that is, titles used by characters in the narrative that Mark uses to reveal Jesus and his message. The final title, Son of Man, is different. It is not confessional in nature but is rather used only by Jesus in a self-declaring manner. The meaning of Son of Man in Mark, as it converges with the other two dominant titles, will conclude the discussion of Mark's christology.

# 5
# Converging Lines in Markan Christology

## INTRODUCTION

In the previous chapters, I set out to examine the so-called turning point of Mark's story of Jesus. A close examination of 8:27–9:13 reveals that Mark intended that the story of Peter's confession and the Transfiguration be read together. When read together, Mark's purpose in writing the Gospel comes into clearer focus: to persuade his readers to see Jesus in a particular way (as Messiah, Son of God, and Son of Man) and in seeing him in this manner to better understand his life and ministry, especially his death and resurrection. Seeing Jesus "as he was" (4:36) would present the reader or hearer with a choice. Would a reader "see and understand" (8:17, 21, 23) and "follow" Jesus (8:34)—even if the end result was the same, suffering and death—or would the reader abandon Jesus because his "way" (8:27) is too difficult. In the narrative, readers see examples of both: several people exhibit faith and follow Jesus regardless of the cost (e.g., the hemorrhaging woman, Bartimaeus, other "minor characters"). Others, especially the disciples, fail to understand and even abandon Jesus (14:50) in his moment of greatest need.

As I have suggested, in Mark's Gospel matters of christology (who is Jesus?) can never be divorced from discipleship (what does this mean?). They function as two sides of the same coin.[1] However, in saying that christology and discipleship belong together, there is an inherent priority of one

---

1. This dimension is captured nicely in the title of the work by Henderson (*Christology and Discipleship in the Gospel of Mark*).

in Mark's mind, namely, christology. If there is an ordering of sorts present in the Gospel, it is that Mark intends the christological question be dealt with prior to the discipleship one. The content of Jesus' own preaching corroborates this: the kingdom of God is near in Christ (1:14–15). Attempts to perceive matters concerning the kingdom, particularly how to become affiliated with such a kingdom, is thwarted unless one first embraces the one whom God anointed (ὁ χριστός); he is the one who will usher in God's kingdom with power (9:1). Even in the flow of the narrative itself, the contemplative christological question in 4:41, τίς ἄρα οὗτός ἐστιν; (Who then is this?) precedes the volitional inquiry of the Gerasene Demoniac in 5:7, τί ἐμοὶ καὶ σοί, Ἰησοῦ υἱὲ τοῦ θεοῦ τοῦ ὑψίστου; (What have you to do with me, Jesus, son of the most high God?). In other words, before asking oneself "what must I do?" in light of this story, a reader must decide "who is Jesus?"

As I have noted previously, three christological images dominate the Markan narrative: (1) Messiah, (2) Son of God, and (3) Son of Man. These three designations set forth Mark's particular understanding of Jesus.[2] The history of interpretation of Mark's Gospel confirms that I am not alone in stressing the importance of these three images or titles in Mark's presentation of Jesus. Yet often, many interpreters adopt one of these images as the primary or dominant understanding of Jesus in the Gospel to the exclusion or minimization of the other two. Similarly, a few interpreters have chosen to look beyond these three designations in search of the key to Mark's christology. For example, some have focused on other titles used for Jesus in the Gospel (i.e., Son of David). However, even when agreeing on an overarching title (like Son of God), they differ as to the meaning of the title (e.g., divine man versus royal figure). Still others focus on other images the narrative evokes (i.e., prophet, teacher, shepherd).

In this chapter, I have two objectives. First, I will present a brief survey of scholarship of Mark's christology since 1900. Analyzing the study of Markan christology over the past one hundred years should enable certain aspects of Mark's christology to come into sharper focus, especially the three key terms of Messiah, Son of God, and Son of Man. As we have seen in previous chapters, narrative criticism on Mark's Gospel has concentrated on the plot of the Gospel and, in so doing, has steered the discussion away

---

2. Moloney (*Storyteller, Interpreter, Evangelist*, 125) expresses this sentiment: "Mark's Gospel indicates his [Mark's] desire to communicate a *particular* understanding of Jesus of Nazareth" (emphasis supplied). I will argue that this particular understanding includes Messiah, Son of God, and Son of Man with equal weight being attached to each.

from solely historical questions to a blend of historical and theological. Second, since my work attempts to fit squarely within a narrative-critical perspective, I will follow the survey of Markan christological scholarship with an examination of the terms Messiah, Son of God, and Son of Man as it develops using my understanding of Mark's narrative flow. Mark centers his christology on these three terms precisely because they converge at the beginning of the narrative, in the middle at the so-called turning point, and at the end, specifically the Passion Narrative.

## OVERVIEW OF MARKAN CHRISTOLOGY SINCE 1900

Since the Gospel of Mark is a "narrative about theologically significant historical events," it behooves a reader to consider precisely those things "theologically significant" in the narrative.[3] I maintain that Mark is primarily interested in crafting a narrative that addresses the true nature of Jesus with all the complexities and multidimensional facets that such involves. Thus, to use a label from systematic theology, what is the christology of Mark's Gospel?[4]

When addressing matters of theology and/or christology, it is helpful to review the state of scholarship on the subject. Doing so is certainly not an easy task and simply seeing where emphasis has been placed in the past does not make those judgments and conclusions any more correct than the conclusions we may draw. Surveying the scholarship on Markan christology would be quite an undertaking and here we can only consider the highpoints.[5] Jacob C. Naluparayil has discussed the present state of

---

3. Bolt, "Mark's Gospel," 409.

4. I am hesitant to employ the term "Mark's Christology," since we can only discern the nature and extent of Mark's written understanding of Jesus. Said differently, what the author thought of Jesus and/or Christology (to the extent Mark would use such a term) cannot be known with certainty. However, we can seek to determine his understanding of Jesus from what is written. Thus, I favor "Markan Christology," a phrase that (to me) addresses the nuance that it is Mark's Christology as expressed in the narrative. Some prefer to call this type of examination a study in the "Markan Jesus." As Jacobs ("Mark's Jesus," 53) observes, biblical scholars have not come to a consensus regarding a definition of Christology.

5. For helpful surveys of Markan Christology, see Naluparayil, *Identity of Jesus*, 5–42; Jacobs, "Mark's Jesus," 53–85; Matera, *What Are They Saying About Mark?*, 18–37; and Martin, *Evangelist and Theologian*, 84–139.

research on what he calls "the identity question" in Mark's Gospel and divided his analysis into seven categories.[6] Altering his typology slightly, I will briefly survey the scholarship on Markan christology since 1900 under the following topics: (1) Messiah and messianic secret; (2) Divine Man (θεῖος ἀνήρ); (3) Son of God; (4) Son of Man; (5) Christologies based on Structure; (6) Prophet/Teacher; and (7) Other Markan Christologies. As I shall demonstrate, these seven "christologies" are primarily redactional in terms of methodology.[7] Thus, after a brief interlude describing the shift from redaction-critical methods of study to literary methods, I will add an eighth category, which I call "Narrative Christologies."

## Messiah and Messianic Secret

There is a reason to begin this discussion of Markan christology in the first decade of the twentieth century. It was in 1906 that William Wrede published his influential work *Das Messiasgeheimnis in den Evangelien: Zugleich ein Beitrag zum Verständnis des Markusevangeliums* (English translation: *The Messianic Secret*).[8] Prior to that work, there had been, of course, scholarly work on the life of Jesus—from a historical perspective—and the life of Jesus as presented in the canonical Gospels.[9] But, with Wrede's book the field of study changed radically.

Much of the academic study of Jesus in the late eighteen and nineteenth centuries focused on historical questions (i.e., Jesus' actual words; whether he believed himself to be the Jewish Messiah, etc.) and scientific matters (i.e., the role of the supernatural/miracles, etc.). Wrede challenged the so-called "liberal lives of Jesus" school, especially those who worked

---

6. Naluparayil, *Identity of Jesus*, 5–42. Naluparayil's seven categories are: (1) messianic secret of Wrede; (2) the divine man / θεῖος ἀνήρ Christology and corrective Christology; (3) Son of God Christologies; (4) Son of Man Christologies; (5) polar Christologies; (6) Jesus as the Teacher/Prophet-Teacher; and (7) narrative method and the integrative Christology. I am indebted to Naluparayil for his survey and for several of his observations. Jacobs ("Mark's Jesus," 55–80) presents his survey in five categories: (1) William Wrede and the Messianic Secret; (2) Mark's Jesus as ΘΕΙΟΣ' ΑΝΗΡ, under which Son of Man is subsumed; (3) Jesus as Teacher in Mark's Gospel; (4) Mark's Jesus as the Son of God; and (5) The Jesus of Mark's Narrative.

7. This point is conceded by Naluparayil (*Identity of Jesus*, 40).

8. Wrede, *Das Messiasgeheimnis*; ET, *Messianic Secret*.

9. The major works include Reimarus, *Fragments*; Strauss, *Life of Jesus*; Renan, *Life of Jesus*; and Weiss, *Life of Jesus*.

## Converging Lines in Markan Christology

and wrote within the psychological milieu of messianic consciousness.[10] His challenge came primarily from his reading of the Gospel of Mark with its recurring references to secrecy or silence (1:25, 34, 44; 3:11–12; 5:43; 7:36; 8:26, 30; 9:9). Wrede referred to this phenomenon as *Messiasgeheimnis* (usually translated "messianic secret").[11]

The question Wrede was attempting to address was whether Jesus himself concealed his messianic status to those around him or whether his messianic status was something he was not aware of or concerned about (but rather came after the resurrection). If the answer was the latter, then how does one explain the many references in Mark's Gospel to the secret? Wrede concluded that it was Mark's creative use of the tradition that gave rise to the secrecy notion, not something that the historical Jesus experienced.[12] Thus, Wrede "understood the 'messianic secret' (which for him combined several features, e.g., the disciples' incomprehension and esoteric teachings by Jesus, into one motif already existent in the oral tradition), not as actual events in the life of Jesus, but as a theological construct used by Mark to reconcile the primitive view of Jesus as human with the messianic view of Jesus' life and person after the resurrection."[13]

On the same day that Wrede's work was published, Albert Schweitzer's book appeared in print.[14] Schweitzer's work, translated into English as *Mystery of the Kingdom of God: The Secret of Jesus' Messiahship and Passion*, resembled Wrede's in more than just title.[15] The two works match in "their agreement in the criticism of the modern historical conceptions of the life of Jesus," which sometimes extends to the very phraseology, and "yet they are written from quite different standpoints, one from the point of view of literary criticism [Wrede], the other from that of the historical

---

10. Rollmann, "Wrede," 659–61.

11. Tuckett ("Problem of Messianic Secret," 22n1) notes that the semantic range of the German *Geheimnis* includes "mystery" as well as "secret," making the notion of "messianic secret" sometimes misleading.

12. Wrede (*Messianic Secret*, 230) concludes his work: "If my deductions are correct, then they are significant for the assessment of Jesus' historical life itself. If our view could only arise where nothing is known of an open messianic claim on Jesus' part, then we would seem to have in it *a positive historical testimony for the idea that Jesus actually did not give himself out as messiah*" (emphasis in original). See also, Naluparayil, *Identity of Jesus*, 9–10.

13. Rollmann, "Wrede," 660.

14. Schweitzer, *Das Messianitäts- und Leidensgeheimnis*.

15. Schweitzer, *Mystery of the Kingdom of God*.

recognition of eschatology [Schweitzer]."[16] In one sense, Schweitzer's work and Wrede's work collectively dealt the death blow to those interested in creating a portrait of Jesus' life, including what he did and did not know regarding himself and his destiny. Yet, in another way, Schweitzer distanced himself from what he called the "literary solution" of Wrede and opted for an eschatological solution (what he called "thoroughgoing eschatology").[17] "Thoroughgoing eschatology" maintains that Jesus expected the end of the world to come during his time on earth and that he (Jesus) was an instrument for bringing about this end.[18] Jesus, thus, becomes somewhat of an eschatological prophet bringing about a significant theological message.

The impact of Wrede's and Schweitzer's work on the study of the NT cannot be overestimated.[19] In one sense, they both stand as giant bridges between two worlds, the world of historical investigation into first-century Christianity or what some call primitive Christianity (*Religionsgeschichte*) and the world of theological investigation of texts of religious significance. While neither Wrede's nor Schweitzer's proposal was accepted uncritically, both shaped (and continue to shape) biblical scholarship. Wrede's attention to the "literary solution" sparked what ultimately became form criticism and later redaction criticism.[20] Schweitzer's view on eschatology and mysticism (from the perspective of both Jesus and Paul) continues to creep into modern scholarship.[21]

The reaction to Wrede and Schweitzer's critique of Wrede ran the gamut. There were those that reacted positively to Wrede's proposal that the secrecy motif was a Markan invention.[22] Other works criticized Wrede's

---

16. Schweitzer, *Quest*, 296.

17. Ibid., 302.

18. Borg, "An Appreciation for Albert Schweitzer," vii–xi.

19. For a helpful essay dealing with the aftermath of Wrede and Schweitzer (among other things), see Aune, "The Problem of the Messianic Secret."

20. Rollmann ("Wrede," 660) notes this: "He drew attention to the need to understand the traditions in the Gospels primarily as theological products of the community's faith and with his tradition-historical inquiry prepared the way for subsequent approaches, notably form criticism and redaction criticism."

21. A notable example of Schweitzer's influence is seen in contemporary Pauline scholarship and the stress on Paul's apocalyptic and mysticism. See esp. Schweitzer, *Mysticism of Paul*; Beker, *Paul the Apostle*, 3–22; Becker, "Schweitzer's Quest for Jesus and Paul"; and Westerholm, *Perspectives Old and New*, 101–16.

22. For helpful surveys of the reactions to Wrede, see esp. Tuckett's introductory essay in *Messianic Secret*, 1–28; Naluparayil, *Identity of Jesus*, 8–13; and Collins's Excursus in *Mark*, 170–72. Those that reacted positively to Wrede's proposal include Dibelius

reading of Mark, choosing instead to posit their own readings of Mark's christology.[23] The most lasting of Wrede's critics knew that Wrede had hit upon an important aspect of Markan (and indeed Gospel) scholarship, but added their own "corrections" or interpretations of Mark's presentation of Jesus. Two such critics were Ulrich Luz and Heikki Räisänen.[24]

Luz began his essay entitled "The Secrecy Motif and the Marcan Christology" with this: "the 'messianic secret' is still a mystery."[25] By beginning his essay with what some might call a rather sensational statement, he neither accepted totally the theory of Wrede nor did he attempt to disprove it on its merits. Instead, he offered two distinguishing features before drawing conclusions regarding the secret. First, he separated the messianic secret into two phenomena, the "messianic secret" (proper) and the "miracle secret," both of which are the product of tradition rather than of the historical Jesus.[26] Then, he argued that the former, which is given to demons and to the disciples, is capable of being obeyed while the latter cannot be kept and as such should be distinguished from the former.[27] The second distinguishing feature of Luz's proposal was that he then appropriated the two secrets (messianic vs. miracle) to the christological concerns of the Gospel. "There is, however, a fundamental theological difference [between the two secrets], because regardless of all kinds of converging motifs, the secrecy

---

(*From Tradition to Gospel*), Bultmann (*History of the Synoptic Tradition*), Ebeling (*Das Messiasgeheimnis*), and Strecker ("Zur Messiasgeheimnistheorie;" repr., "The Theory of the Messianic Secret in Mark's Gospel").

23. Naluparayil, *Identity of Jesus*, 8-13, esp. 10-11. Sanday ("Injunctions to Silence in the Gospels") focused more on the contention that the resurrection was inadequate to explain the belief that Jesus was the Messiah. Lohmeyer (*Das Evangelium nach Markus*, 2:25-41) sided with Schweitzer, seeing the secrecy motif as originating with Jesus and not a Markan convention. Sjöberg (*Der verborgene Menschensohn*, 48-90) argued that the genesis of the secrecy motif lies in the Son of Man title, and therefore the motif originated with the historical Jesus.

24. Kingsbury (*Christology of Mark's Gospel*, 1-45) discusses Wrede and his critics in the opening two chapters of his narrative-critical work on Mark's Christology. Since his latter chapters are more constructive, I will mention his work below in the section dealing with narrative attempts at Mark's Christology.

25. Luz, "The Secrecy Motif," 75. Luz's essay was first published in German in *ZNW* 56 (1965) 9-30 and translated into English (for the above monograph) by Morgan. References are to the English translation. Matera (*What Are They Saying About Mark?*, 22) labels Luz's work "an important essay . . . [that] made an important contribution to the discussion."

26. Ibid., 86-87.

27. Ibid. See also, Naluparayil, *Identity of Jesus*, 10-11.

motif embraces different contents and indicates theologically two different things; the miracle secret points to the power of Jesus' miracles which cannot remain hidden because it is the sign of the messianic age; the messianic secret qualifies the nature of Jesus' messiahship which must be understood kerygmatically, i.e., from the perspective of the cross and resurrection, if it is to be really understood."[28] Luz neither embraced Wrede's secret uncritically, nor did he push the notion of secrecy back to the historical Jesus (as Schweitzer did); rather, he distinguished the secrecy motif and, in so doing, kept alive the tendency to look at historical issues and redactional concerns together. From a christological perspective, Luz's work narrowed the focus of the identity question to Mark's conception of sonship. To quote Luz: "Jesus' messiahship, or as Mark would say in his own terms, Jesus' divine sonship, which remains hidden from the world and is known only to demons—due to their supernatural knowledge—and since Caesarea Philippi to the disciples—through the miracles of Jesus' authority which they repeatedly experienced."[29]

Räisänen, on the other hand, focused on the following main problems associated with Wrede's presentation of the messianic secret. The first question related to the origin of the secret, whether it is a theological construct of Mark or is it already a traditional viewpoint as Wrede suggested? Second, should the secret be understood as a unitary concept or broken down into one or more subcategories?[30]

On the latter question, Räisänen concluded that there was not a single, overarching secrecy motif in the Gospel of Mark. Rather, the "silencing commands addressed to the demons and those addressed to the disciples" belong together and thus make up the messianic secret proper.[31] Then, the motif of the lack of understanding among the disciples in the Gospel (which he labeled the "incomprehension of the disciples") has a "clear point of contact" with the messianic secret since they both involve proper identification of Jesus, but the two are not the same thing.[32] In addition, Jesus' secret healings should be distinguished from the messianic secret since

---

28. Luz, "The Secrecy Motif," 87.
29. Ibid., 85.
30. Räisänen, *"Messianic Secret" in Mark*, 75.
31. Ibid., 242.
32. Ibid.

Jesus most often instructs those who have been healed not to say anything (which is usually disobeyed).[33]

Räisänen's answer to the first question, regarding the origins of the secrecy theme, ran counter to Wrede's conclusion. Rather than seeing Mark as a creative user of traditional material, Räisänen argued that Mark was the creator of the secrecy motif.[34] Therefore, the so-called messianic secret was a theological construct of the author of the Gospel whose aim was primarily apologetic and revelatory in nature.[35]

So, the early history of Markan scholarship (as it relates to christology) is centered mostly on Wrede and his insistence on the messianic secret. Curiously, over the course of the next one hundred years, there has been very little discussion of Jesus' identity as Messiah from the perspective of Markan christology.[36] It seems that the secrecy motif is given ample attention but a definitive treatment of the depiction of Jesus as ὁ χριστός is lacking.

---

33. Ibid., 242–43.

34. Ibid., 248. The quote is: "According to Wrede, the messianic secret was not an idea which was first created by Mark. This view has not been supported by our analysis."

35. Ibid., 247.

36. The significant exception to this is the essay by Juel ("Origin of Mark's Christology," 450) who states that "the fundamental category in Mark's view of Jesus is that of Messiah (Gk. 'Christ'), a conception that has roots in the Jewish Bible but that had a history in post biblical circles prior to its use by Jesus' followers." Juel (ibid., 452) makes clear that he believes Mark sees "the Christ" as a royal figure. This notion draws on his previous work, *Messiah and Temple*. Hooker ("Christology of Mark's Gospel," 81) observes that "the fact that Mark describes Jesus as 'Christ' (*Christos*) in 1:1 is highly significant, even though Jesus is not openly proclaimed as "the Christ" (*ho Christos*) during his ministry (cf. 8:29–30)." She even claims that Jesus' recognition as "the Messiah" is "an essential part of the Gospel." However, she then goes on to discuss Son of God, the Kingdom, the meaning of discipleship, even the messianic secret, but never really the notion of Messiah *in Mark*. Similarly, Matera (*New Testament Christology*, 24) offers that the title "Christ" plays a "central role" in Mark's Christology, but discusses it in a mere two paragraphs with no attendant footnotes of voices in support of it as the overarching Markan christological motif. However, see his earlier work, *Kingship of Jesus*. For others who see "Christ" as the central christological account in the Gospel, see two essays by Burger, "Zum Problem der Messianität Jesu" and "Die Königlichen Messiastraditionen des Neuen Testaments."

The Turning Point in the Gospel of Mark

## Divine Man (θεῖος ἀνήρ)

The history-of-religions school (*Religionsgeschichtliche Schule*) produced another idea, Divine Man or Θεῖος ἀνήρ, which dominated Markan christology for a number of years (and remnants of which can still be seen in contemporary Markan scholarship). The notion of the Divine Man originated in Hellenistic circles and "describes the exceptionally gifted and extraordinary individual whose command of a higher, revelational wisdom and of divine power displays that the tension experienced by other men has been resolved by the increasing dominance of the divine aspect of human nature. Consequently, his humanity becomes an epiphany of the divine nature."[37] In short, advocates of this analytical approach see in the Markan Jesus a synthesis of the so-called Hellenized Divine Man.[38] Most scholars observe that scholarship on θεῖος ἀνήρ, at least as it has been appropriated in the study of Mark's Gospel, occurred in two phases, the first a positive construal of the concept while the second, the "corrective phase," was generally less positive.[39]

The dominant voice in the first phase was Rudolf Bultmann.[40] Bultmann believed the Hellenistic influence over all the Gospels, even the Gospel of Mark, was quite strong and dominated Mark's view of Jesus.[41] Based on the preponderance of miracles in the Gospel, Bultmann concluded: "In Mark [Jesus] is a Θεῖος ἄνθρωπος, indeed more; he is the very Son of God

---

37. Lane, "*THEIOS ANĒR* Christology," 145–46. For another helpful definition, see Betz, "Jesus as Divine Man," 114–33, esp. 116: "He [the Divine Man] is exceptionally gifted and extraordinary in every respect. He is in command both of a higher, revelational wisdom and of divine power (*dynamis*) to do miracles. Yet he is not identical with deity, but can be called a mixture of the human and the divine." For an early (and flawed) but exhaustive study on the divine man of Hellenistic literature, see Bieler, *Theios Anēr*.

38. Blackburn, "Divine Man," 190. For additional helpful overviews of Divine Man Christology in Mark's Gospel, see Naluparayil, *Identity of Jesus*, 13–20; Jacobs, "Mark's Jesus," 57–62; Kingsbury, "The 'Divine Man' as the Key to Mark's Christology"; and Kingsbury, *Christology of Mark's Gospel*, 25–46.

39. Naluparayil, *Identity of Jesus*, 13–14. Jacobs ("Mark's Jesus," 61) calls it the "corrective phase."

40. While Bultmann's name is associated with the early phase of this concept, the groundwork was laid by Reitzenstein (*Hellenistische Wundererzählungen*) and Wetter ("*Der Sohn Gottes*"). For additional background information, see Naluparayil, *Identity of Jesus*, 14–15; Jacobs, "Mark's Jesus," 58–59; and Lane, "*THEIOS ANĒR* Christology," 147–48.

41. Lane, "*THEIOS ANĒR* Christology," 148. On Bultmann's understanding of Hellenistic influences, see esp. his *Primitive Christianity*, 135–74.

walking the earth. This mythological light in which Jesus is set by Mark is there for the most part on the author's own account but also in part on account of his material, and especially of the miracle stories. . . . In Mark and most of all in his miracle stories, Hellenism has made a vital contribution."[42]

Especially important to this study is Bultmann's insistence that Jesus is presented as Divine Man and, on top of that, "the very Son of God walking the earth."[43] This "positive notion" of θεῖος ἀνήρ, insofar as it presented a useful portrait of Mark's Jesus, was challenged by a number of scholars and decisively put to rest by the trio of P. Wülfing von Martitz, David L. Tiede, and Carl H. Holladay.[44] Von Martitz, an accomplished philologist, surveyed the use of θεῖος ἀνήρ in conjunction with the Son of God in Hellenistic literature in the early Christian period and concluded that the phrase was rare in occurrence with no fixed or universally determined meaning.[45] Tiede concurred with von Martitz by arguing that up until the second century there were two types of divine men, one who is divine based on his extraordinary wisdom, the other by his ability to perform miraculous feats.[46] Holladay's focus was neither on the use of the phrase in Hellenistic literature exclusively (e.g., von Martitz) nor upon the types of heroes in the literature (e.g., Tiede), but upon the employment of the phrase in Jewish-Hellenistic literature of the first century, especially in the works of Philo, Josephus, and Artapanus. In these Jewish authors, Holladay found that there was no agreement on the use of the phrase "Divine Man" and consequently it is improper to speak of *a* divine man in Hellenistic Judaism in the first century.[47] As Kingsbury asks regarding this important period of study: "Do the results of Holladay's investigation support the thesis that behind the title 'Son of God' in the Gospel of Mark there stands a concept of 'divine man' as mediated by Hellenistic Judaism? The answer is negative."[48] Thus,

---

42. Bultmann, *History of the Synoptic Tradition*, 241. Bultmann developed this notion further in his influential *Theology of the New Testament*, 1:130.

43. Bultmann, *History of the Synoptic Tradition*, 241.

44. Von Martitz, "υἱός υἱοθεσία," 335-40; Tiede, *Charismatic Figure*; and Holladay, *Theios Aner in Hellenistic Judaism*.

45. Von Martitz, "υἱός," 339. His actual quote is: "As regards the question whether divine sonship is connected with the Hellenistic idea of the θεῖος ἀνήρ it is thus to be noted that θεῖος ἀνήρ is by no means a fixed expression at least in the pre-Christian era." See also Naluparayil, *Identity of Jesus*, 15; and Kingsbury, *Christology of Mark's Gospel*, 33-34.

46. Tiede, *Charismatic Figure*, 289-91.

47. Holladay, *Theios Aner*, 236-41, esp. 239; emphasis supplied.

48. Kingsbury, *Christology of Mark's Gospel*, 35.

the work of von Martitz, Tiede, and Holladay effectively put an end to the so-called "positive phase" of Divine Man theories.

The second phase of development in the Divine Man christologies came from Theodore J. Weeden and Norman Perrin, both of whom were less positive about the divine man concept as an acceptable category for Mark's presentation of Jesus.[49] In fact, their view has been reduced to the phrase "corrective christology," though the content of the correction is different for each. Rather than seeing θεῖος ἀνήρ as contributing positively to Mark's picture of Jesus, Weeden argued that Mark attempted to correct or improve inaccurate views of Jesus among members of the Markan community, namely those associating Jesus with a theology of glory.[50] The corrective to this *theologia gloriae* is in Mark's concentration on the "theology of the cross," especially the notion of Jesus' suffering as depicted in the passions predictions of Mark 8, 9, and 10.

Weeden's proposal enjoyed success, especially in North America. One of those indebted to his analysis was Norman Perrin. Perrin agreed with Weeden that the evangelist set out to "correct" an improper view of Jesus that had prevailed. To Perrin, Mark's correction lay not in correcting inaccurate views of *theologia gloriae* among Mark's readers but how, in the narrative, Son of Man seemed to correct a less than satisfactory Son of God description. Perrin, straddling the worlds of redaction criticism and literary criticism, saw Mark as a creative writer who used the accepted titles of Messiah and Son of God to "establish rapport with his readers and then deliberately reinterprets and gives conceptual content to these titles by a use of 'Son of Man,' a designation that is not, properly speaking, a christological title but which to all intents and purposes becomes one as Mark uses it."[51]

---

49. Weeden, *Traditions in Conflict*; Perrin, *Modern Pilgrimage*. Weeden's work stemmed from his 1964 doctoral dissertation, the nucleus of which was published as "The Heresy That Necessitated Mark's Gospel." Perrin's work first appeared as "The Christology of Mark: A Study in Methodology" (which was reprinted in the *Modern Pilgrimage* and in slightly revised form in *The Interpretation of Mark* (ed. William Telford). This essay, along with several other essays by Perrin, has been reproduced in *Parable and Gospel*, ed. Hanson.

50. Weeden, *Traditions in Conflict*, 159–68; Weeden, "The Heresy," 147–49.

51. Perrin, *Modern Pilgrimage*, 121.

## Son of God

"Divine Man" christology dominated the scene for a number of years. Yet, like many previous ideas (i.e., the messianic secret), it would eventually lose favor among scholars as the primary depiction of Mark's christology.[52] Kingsbury suggested the reasons for its demise were twofold: one related to methodological matters, the other related to the questionable assumptions on which the concept was built.[53] Methodologically, θεῖος ἀνήρ christology was built on what most would call redactional-critical techniques. That is, Mark sought to take what was known (i.e., the Hellenistic "Divine Man" concept) and edit it or construct his own version of it into the Gospel he was writing.[54] Similarly, redaction criticism seemed focused on isolating the pre-Markan material (such as miracle stories) from Mark's self-consciously constructed material (hence the work of Keck and Achtemeier). Redaction critics were determined to look for seams in the Gospel that might uncover the theological purposes of the author, especially as it relates to his community and its *Sitz im Leben*.

By the 1980s, when Kingsbury's essay was published, redactional analysis was giving way to narrative or compositional criticism. In fact, after critiquing the Divine Man concept, Kingsbury turned his attention to the Gospel itself and offered a preliminary look at Mark's christology not in terms "a reconstruction of the pre-Marcan tradition or of the alleged heresy of Mark's church, but [of] the contours of Mark's story."[55]

The second reason for the dismissal of Divine Man christology was that it rested on the assumption that there was a fixed concept of Divine Man in the first-century Hellenistic world. Kingsbury drew on the work of Tiede and Holladay and suggested that the proper backdrop was the

---

52. Kingsbury ("'The Divine Man' as a Key to Mark's Christology," 243) begins his influential essay with this statement: "There are indications that a notable era in the study of Marcan Christology is fast drawing to a close."

53. Ibid., 247–52. Kingsbury identified four "problem areas": (1) the term θεῖος ἀνήρ itself; (2) the scholarly probe into pre-Markan material; (3) the scholarly inclination to find the "key" to Mark's christology outside his Gospel; and (4) the viability of the contention that Mark employed one single Christology. I have combined his four concerns into two—methodological and assumptions—since his first problem area deals with matters of the Hellenistic origin of the term and the other three (in some way) deal with redactional/traditional issues.

54. This can be seen in the so-called first phase or positive phase of Bultmann.

55. Kingsbury, "The End of an Era?," 252. This constructive analysis of the Markan narrative was later put into monograph form in *Christology of Mark's Gospel*, 47–180.

OT, particularly the royal passages found in 2 Samuel 7 and Psalm 2.[56] His argument depended largely on discoveries from Qumran that seemed to indicate that Son of God and Messiah belonged together in pre-Christian Judaism.[57] Thus, the assumption that θεῖος ἀνήρ was an exclusively Greek notion was being chipped away and the door was now open for examining Divine Man as it may have existed in Judaism of the pre-Christian era and, specifically, how Son of God (which was not developed in Holladay's critique) and Messiah may have related to each other.[58]

## Hellenistic vs. Jewish Theories of Son of God

Christologies built around the notion of Son of God are of course inevitable, given its strategic placement and prominence in the Gospel of Mark (1:1, 11; 9:7; 14:61; 15:39). It has been called "an important title, and even ... the key to the Gospel."[59] While the Divine Man concept was dying out, others (taking a cue from Kingsbury) began looking at the antecedent background to the Son of God description from the OT. Scholars began to focus on 1:11, where the divine voice declares "you are my beloved Son, with you I am well-pleased." The declaration evokes two passages from the Hebrew Scriptures, Ps 2:7, in which the king is reported to be called "God's son," and Isa 42:1, in which God says, "Behold my servant, whom I uphold, my chosen, in whom my soul delights."[60] Adela Yarbro Collins has argued that to the Jewish reader of the Gospel these allusions (along with evidence from the DSS, especially 4Q246) would be interpreted as the joining of messianic notions with the depiction as Son of God. When coupled with the royal images that are presented in the Passion Narrative, namely with its allusions to

56. Kingsbury, "The End of an Era?," 249–50.

57. Ibid.

58. For some, this also is connected with the study of the messianic secret, specifically whether the "messianic secret" is really a "Son of God secret." On this, see Matera, *New Testament Christology*, 25; Telford, *Theology of the Gospel of Mark*, 52; and Kingsbury, *Christology of Mark's Gospel*, 21.

59. Jacobs, "Mark's Jesus," 69. A selection of those christologies that put primacy on Son of God include (but is not limited to) Vielhauer, "Erwägungen zur Christologies des Markusevangeliums"; Kazmierski, *Jesus, the Son of God*; Juel, *Messiah and Temple*; Blank, "Die Sendung des Sohnes"; Hengel, *Son of God*; Steichele, *Der leidende Sohn Gottes*; Kingsbury, *Christology of Mark's Gospel*; Matera, *Kingship of Jesus*; and Black, "The Face Is Familiar." For helpful surveys, see Matera, *What Are They Saying About Mark?*, 29–36 and Naluparayil, *Identity of Jesus*, 20–30.

60. On this, see Marcus, *Way of the Lord*, 48–79.

Daniel 7 and Psalm 110, Collins concludes that "the picture of the messiah that emerges is a cosmic ruler, a heavenly being who mediates the blessing and rule of God to all creation."[61]

In a subsequent essay, Collins turns to Greek and Roman readers and asks how they would respond to a presentation of Jesus as Son of God, especially as it is presented in the baptism narrative of Mark's Gospel (1:9–11).[62] After surveying relevant Greek and Roman literature, primarily those works rendering Greek mythological figures, Collins turns to Mark's narrative and recounts the primary depiction of Jesus in the Gospel. To her, "the nature of Jesus in the Gospel of Mark is ambiguous."[63] The account of the transfiguration (9:2–8) could have given rise to some seeing Jesus as a preexistent heavenly being, but she discounts this since there is no explicit mention of such in the narrative and no mention is made of any kind of virginal conception in the Gospel.[64] She concludes that Jesus is depicted as the Son of God narratively by recounting his mighty deeds, his authoritative teaching, his prophecy, and his death for the sake of others.[65] "The members of the audience educated in Greek and Roman traditions would associate the elements of this portrayal with their traditions regarding divine men: workers of miracles, philosophers and other wise men, inspired diviners, and benefactors, especially Heracles, who labored for the benefit of humankind and died a noble death."[66] Though the title Son of God had Jewish roots and would carry messianic notions, Gentile Christians in Asia Minor, Rome, and Alexandria would have understood Son of God from

---

61. Collins, "The Son of God among Jews," 408. Collins's interpretation of the evidence from Qumran is subject to debate. For a critical view on the early understanding of Son of God at Qumran, see Fitzmyer, "4Q246: The 'Son of God' Document from Qumran," 170–74. Similarly, Fitzmyer (*One Who Is to Come*, 45, 56–59) objects to a messianic reading of Daniel 7 and Psalm 110 in his most recent work. For a more positive understanding of its connection with Jewish messianic ideals, see Horbury, *Jewish Messianism and the Cult of Christ*; and Horbury, "Jewish Messianism and Early Christology," 17–23.

62. Collins, "The Son of God among Greeks and Romans."

63. Ibid., 100. In her 2007 commentary (*Mark*, 44), Collins eschews the notion of a "Christology" of Mark's Gospel and opts rather for the "interpretation of Jesus." She believes that the Gospel's author employs traditions that already carried implicit interpretations about the person and activity of Jesus, which make for a presentation of Jesus that is "complex, multifaceted, and somewhat ambiguous."

64. Ibid.
65. Ibid.
66. Ibid.

the perspective of their own culture and in light of their own divine men traditions.

## *Son of God as Royal Messiah*[67]

As the previous discussion indicates, the Gospel seems to bring together the notions of Jewish Messiah and Son of God. This is seen primarily in the Prologue (1:1–13, esp. 9–11), which alludes to Ps 2:7 and Isa 42:1 in the same verse. Thus, 1:11 brings together the image of sonship with the image of the Isaianic servant. This has caused many scholars to focus on one image to the exclusion of the other. For example, Philipp Vielhauer made a distinction between the θεῖος ἀνήρ concept, which he saw displayed in the Markan miracles, and the royal Messiah connotations, which are found in the Son of God passages.[68] For Vielhauer, along with others as we shall see, the latter was given prominence and the former simply subsumed under it. He insisted that Son of God was the dominant image since the Son of God declarations functioned as notices of (1) adoption in 1:11; (2) proclamation in 9:7; and (3) acclamation in 15:39 and appeared at strategic places in the narrative.[69] This threefold movement, he suggested, had its origins in the royal enthronement ceremonies in Egyptian literature.[70]

Hans Steichele examined the Gospel in a manner similar to Vielhauer, especially in addressing the notion of royal enthronement.[71] But rather than seeing the background of this in terms of Egyptian enthronement narratives, Steichele argued that is OT narratives about Elijah that give rise to Mark's inclusion of this idea.[72] Both divine declarations (1:11 and 9:7) should be read in reference to Psalm 2; however, the declaration of the centurion in 15:39 is a Markan redaction according to Steichele.[73] The background of this declaration is not Psalm 2 but Psalm 22, a psalm where

---

67. In addition to the works mentioned below, Kingsbury also addresses the topic of messianic Son of God in his work, *Christology of Mark's Gospel*.

68. Vielhauer, "Erwägungen," 165.

69. Ibid., 166–67. See also Jacobs, "Mark's Jesus," 70.

70. Vielhauer, "Erwägungen," 166–67. For a useful summary on this point, see Naluparayil, *Identity of Jesus*, 22.

71. Steichele, *Leidende Sohn*.

72. Ibid., 107–8.

73. Ibid., 208.

the suffering one is vindicated in the end.⁷⁴ This use of Psalm 22 in light of the earlier image of Psalm 2 (in Mark 1:11 and 9:7) is used by Mark to show that Jesus is a righteous sufferer who upon death was vindicated as messianic king.⁷⁵ "Jesus is the Son of God," thus, "in the royal messianic sense in his suffering and death."⁷⁶

Donald H. Juel focused on the trial scene of 14:61–62 instead of the three christological declarations of 1:11, 9:7, and 15:39.⁷⁷ To him, the Passion Narrative supports the view that the Son of God designations have royal connotations. The focus was the parallel between the epithets in the question of the high priest, are you the Messiah, the Son of the Blessed (One)?" Messiah and Son of the Blessed (i.e., Son of God) must be held on the same par with each other, Juel argued.⁷⁸ This dual title carries a royal (Davidic) distinction since royal imagery pervades the whole of Mark 15 (e.g., Jesus is called king in 15:2, 9, 12, 18, 26, and 32). Jesus' response in 14:62 does not "trump" this royal distinction nor does it "correct" an incorrect Son of God understanding; rather, "the Son of Man saying points to the final vindication of 'the gospel of Jesus Christ, the Son of God.'"⁷⁹

Mark 15 is examined in the early work of Frank Matera.⁸⁰ Matera looks at Mark 15 in particular because it is essentially structured around the theme of kingship, the title King of the Jews is mentioned six times in Mark 15 and the mocking of Jesus ironically highlights his kingship.⁸¹ If that were not enough, Jesus presentation as king in Mark 15 is brought to an emotional climax in 15:39 with the use of Son of God, making the latter a royal title.⁸² But there is more. For Matera, the central question is how should this royal kingship be understood? Jesus' kingship can only be understood in light of the Son of Man passages. What links together the Son of Man passages with the Son of God passages is Psalm 118, which is

74. Ibid., 238–51.

75. Ibid., 258–73; see also Matera, *What Are They Saying About Mark?*, 33.

76. Naluparayil, *Identity of Jesus*, 23.

77. Juel, *Messiah and Temple*, 77–125.

78. Ibid., 77–79.

79. Ibid., 92.

80. Matera, *Kingship of Jesus*. Much of Matera's subsequent work is taken with the notion of Christology, including Markan Christology. Those works, which will be discussed below, include *New Testament Christology*, 5–24, and "Transcending Messianic Expectations," 201–16.

81. Ibid., 60–63.

82. Ibid., 62.

alluded to in Mark 12:1–12, the so-called parable of the wicked tenants.[83] To Matera, "Jesus is the King of the Jews and the King of Israel because, as the centurion correctly confessed, he is the royal Son of the Baptism, the Transfiguration, and the parable of the vineyard. Thus, the royal theme may be the thread which runs through the titles of Mark's Gospel."[84]

Others have also noted the connections between royal Messiah and Son of God.[85] It has also had its critics. One critic in particular has been Joel Marcus, who challenged the reading of Juel in particular, with his emphasis on a Davidic messianic notation.[86] For Marcus, when the high priest asks Jesus whether or not he is "the Messiah the Son of God" (14:61), he is not using the two terms as synonyms but rather in what Marcus calls "restrictive apposition."[87] The effect of this apposition is that the emphasis is on the latter, not the former. To use Marcus's own words: "It [the appositional statement of 14:61] indicates which messianic figure Jesus is being interrogated about; the high priest is not asking him whether or not he is the royal Messiah, the Messiah-Son-of-David, but whether or not he is the Messiah-Son-of-*God*."[88]

## *Son of God as Suffering Servant*

Just as the Psalm 2 allusion ("You are my beloved Son") in 1:11 has garnered the attention of many scholars, so has the Isaiah 42 reference ("in whom I am well pleased"). The context of the Isaiah passage is one of the prophet's so-called "Servant Songs." One scholar who addressed the Isaianic background of 1:11 as it relates to Markan christology was Carl Kazmierski.[89] In Mark 1:9–11, Jesus' mission is laid out by the evangelist, who brought together "the apocalyptic presentation of the anointing of Jesus as the Beloved Servant of God."[90] In this key baptismal scene, the images of Psalm 2, Isaiah 42, and Genesis 22 are all brought together and expanded through

---

83. On Mark's use of psalms, see Rowe, *God's Kingdom and God's Son*.

84. Ibid., 147–50, esp. 150.

85. See, for example, Breytenbach, "Grundzüge markinischer Gottessohn-Christologie," 169–84.

86. Marcus, "Mark 14:61: 'Are You the Messiah-Son-of-God?'"

87. Ibid., 138.

88. Ibid.; emphasis in original.

89. Kazmierski, *Jesus, the Son of God*.

90. Ibid., 71.

the addition of the temptation narrative.[91] The effect is that Mark has depicted Jesus who can be described "in terms reminiscent of an anointed Servant of God, one whose mission as Beloved Son is already linked with death."[92] While Kazmierski focused primarily on the baptismal scene to bring together the Isaiah 42 reference, others expanded it to include other key passages such as 9:7 and 15:39.[93]

## Son of God as Eschatological Prophet

As Matera observed, the royal Son of God image resembles the image presented in the parable of the vineyard/wicked tenants (12:1–12).[94] Josef Blank held that Mark 12 was the key christological passage in the Gospel since it focused on the final eschatological messenger, the beloved son (12:6).[95] The image finds prominence not just in the parable but also because (as mentioned above) it is central in the baptismal scene as the veiled reference to Genesis 22. The eschatological prophet motif is underscored for Blank in the transfiguration scene (9:2–8) where the heavenly son, Jesus, meets two eschatological prophets (Elijah and Moses).[96]

## Concluding Thoughts on Son of God

Naturally, those who focus on the overarching christology of Mark's Gospel in terms of Son of God hold this view because of the prominence of that title in key places in the Gospel. Greek and Roman readers may have been influenced by the "Divine Man" antecedents of Hellenistic culture and thus may have read Mark's Gospel as an attempt to go beyond such a presentation. Jewish readers would likely have seen the Hebrew Scriptures as the necessary background for such a presentation. As the key passages are "confessional" (two by God; one by the centurion), the dominant backdrop to the confession is disputed. Some tend to lean toward the royal sonship motif associated with the Psalms, particularly Psalm 2. Others focus on the

---

91. Ibid.

92. Ibid. See also Naluparayil, *Identity of Jesus*, 27–28.

93. Lührmann (*Das Markusevangelium*, 37–39, 154–56) holds that the suffering servant motif underlies all three key Son of God sections—1:11; 9:7; and 15:39.

94. Matera, *Kingship of Jesus*, 78, 82–83.

95. Blank, *Der Jesus des Evangeliums*, 145–46.

96. Ibid., 147–48.

The Turning Point in the Gospel of Mark

Isaianic reference to (suffering) servant. Still others see the binding of Isaac in Genesis 22 as the focus. Regardless, Mark's Gospel does indeed make acute the notion of Jesus as God's Son.

## Son of Man

In the last one hundred years, there has been no lack of interest in the Son of Man in the Gospels in general, or in the Gospel of Mark in particular.[97] It is often confusing how scholars look at Son of Man in the Gospel of Mark. Many address the phrase by attempting to ascertain its meaning in the Gospel. Primary among those scholars would be the work of Morna Hooker in a monograph entitled *The Son of Man in Mark*.[98] Others, without denying the need to look for the function of Son of Man in the Gospel, see it as the crowning achievement in Mark's presentation of Jesus. We might call this latter group those arguing for Son of Man as the dominant christological theme in the narrative, while the former could be put under the label of works addressing the interpretation of Son of Man in Mark. Our attention in this section is to look at a few scholars who see Son of Man as the dominant christological theme in Mark's Gospel.

The "corrective christology" of Perrin has already been noted above in the section dealing with Divine Man.[99] As was stated there, Perrin understood Mark's use of Son of Man as correcting a misunderstanding among those in the Markan community regarding Son of God. Two scenes in the Gospel were crucial for Perrin's interpretation of Mark's christology—the trial scene (14:53-71) and Peter's confession at Caesarea Philippi

---

97. The literature on this subject is vast. The following is a sample of Mark's view: Hooker, *Son of Man in Mark*; Perrin, "Creative Use of the Son of Man Traditions"; Tuckett, "The Present Son of Man"; Malbon, "Narrative Christology and the Son of Man"; Danove, "Rhetoric of the Characterization of Jesus"; Gathercole, "Son of Man in Mark's Gospel"; Adams, "The Coming Son of Man"; Chronis, "To Reveal and to Conceal"; and Broadhead, "Reconfiguring Jesus"; and Kingsbury, "The Christology of Mark and the Son of Man."

For general works on Son of Man in the NT, see the following: Tödt, *Son of Man in the Synoptic Tradition*; Borsch, *Son of Man in Myth and History*; Casey, *Son of Man*; Vermes, *Jesus the Jew*; Kim, *Son of Man as the Son of God*; Lindars, *Jesus Son of Man*; Caragounis, *Son of Man*; Hooker, "The Son of Man and the Synoptic Problem"; Chilton, "The Son of Man: Human and Heavenly"; and Hurtado, *Lord Jesus Christ*, 290-306.

98. Hooker, *Son of Man in Mark*.

99. A collection of his works on Christology was published as *Modern Pilgrimage*. The following references are to that version.

*Converging Lines in Markan Christology*

(8:27–9:1).[100] In 14:61, Jesus is addressed as Messiah and Son of the Blessed (which for Perrin is Son of God) by the high priest. For Perrin, the crucial fact is found in 14:62 where Mark has Jesus accepting those two titles and "immediately interprets them by means of the use of Son of Man."[101] A similar thing happens in Peter's confession: Peter confesses Jesus as Messiah; Jesus accepts this declaration and immediately "goes on to interpret the designation in terms of the Son of Man."[102] These literary features (i.e., two key scenes in the narrative) lead Perrin to look at Mark's purposes for the acceptance/interpretation pattern; his answer is the corrective feature noted above. Though Perrin is remembered primarily in relation to "corrective" christology, he could easily also be remembered for his attention to Son of Man as the key christological concept in the Gospel of Mark.

One of Perrin's students, John R. Donahue, followed his teacher by focusing on the trial scene as a central text in the Gospel.[103] Donahue argued that the convergence of the three titles in 14:61–62 (i.e., Messiah, Son of Blessed [God]; Son of Man) was the result of Markan redaction. In other words, Mark "brought together all the major titles used of Jesus in his gospel in a context which shows he is about to give a definitive meaning to them."[104] Mark's meaning, Donahue suggests, can be found in his attention to Jesus as the eschatological Son of Man, namely, the suffering Jesus who will come in glory to judge his opponents and gather the elect.[105] Mark has worked the so-called passion predictions together "into a pattern of suffering, judgment and salvation of the elect."[106] In addition, "the meaning of Christological titles is held in suspension until the trial scene. . . . No Christological title is made *publicly* and *accepted as such* by Jesus until the trial scene."[107] Thus, the Jesus who suffers as Christ and Son of God will return as the glorious Son of Man.

---

100. Ibid., 108–9.

101. Ibid., 109.

102. Ibid.

103. Donahue, *Are You the Christ?* For a brief summary of Donahue's work, see Naluparayil, *Identity of Jesus*, 30–32.

104. Ibid., 95.

105. Ibid., 181.

106. Ibid., 191.

107. Ibid., 181; emphasis in original.

Gerhard Dautzenberg has likewise built his understanding of Mark's christology around the concept of Son of Man.[108] He observes the convergence of christological titles in the trial scene of 14:61–62, a passage he labeled "the deciding point of the passion story."[109] The titles Messiah and Son of the Blessed come as a result of those in the story, that is, they are confessional titles used by characters in the story and as such speak to the earthly ministry of Jesus.[110] Yet Son of Man is not confessional in that sense because it appears only on the lips of Jesus and carries with it notions of eschatological judgment. This eschatological answer, which includes both condemnation and vindication, encompasses the total ministry of Jesus (not simply his earthly ministry) and prepares for his eschatological coming.[111]

Son of Man, as the culminating christological title, has had its opponents. The work of Kingsbury (which will be summarized below) held that it was not a confessional title in Mark and therefore it contributes nothing to the question of Jesus' identity in the Gospel.[112] Similarly, Cilliers Breytenbach suggests that the Son of Man sayings must be interpreted in light of the Son of God and Messiah statements, not the other way around.[113] Kazmierski, whose work focused on Son of God in Mark, has been critical of this school for similar reasons.[114]

## Christologies Based on Structure

Rather than focusing on titles (i.e., Son of God) or christological motifs (i.e., messianic secret), several scholars study Mark's christology from the perspective of structural markers in the Gospel itself. Thus far in our survey, we have observed several scholars who have focused on structural

---

108. Dautzenberg, "Zwei Kompendien." I am indebted to Naluparayil (*Identity of Jesus*, 32–33) for his cogent summary of Dautzenberg's position.

109. Dautzenberg, "Zwei Kompendien," 25–26; Naluparayil, *Identity of Jesus*, 32.

110. Dautzenberg, "Zwei Kompendien," 31.

111. Ibid., 29.

112. Kingsbury, *Christology of Mark's Gospel*, 166. For his most recent thoughts on Mark's use of Son of Man, see "The Christology of Mark and the Son of Man," in *Unity and Diversity in the Gospels and Paul*.

113. Breytenbach, "Grundzüge markinischer Gottessohn-Christologie." See also Naluparayil, *Identity of Jesus*, 33.

114. Kazmierski (*Son of God*, 160) notes: "The implication is not therefore that Mark has used the Son of man traditions to interpret those of the Son of God, but rather the exact opposite."

concerns as they developed their view of Mark's christology (e.g., Vielhauer, Steichele). They mostly, however, identified structural issues to confirm their christological views. In this section, what sets these works apart from others is that it is the structure of the narrative itself that gives rise to the overall christology of the Gospel. The work of three scholars fit this category, Michael Theobald, Klaus Scholtissek, and C. Clifton Black.

As the subtitle to his article suggests, Michael Theobald argues that the christology of Mark's Gospel is ascertainable because of the "polar structure" (*polaren Struktur*) of the narrative.[115] The two poles of the Markan narrative are (1) the powerful deeds of the historical Jesus, and (2) the kerygmatic reference to his passion (death, resurrection, and second coming), each of which is found in three central passages of the Gospel, 8:29–31; 9:7–13; and 14:61–62.[116] The titles Messiah and Son of God represent the first pole, that of the powerful deeds of Jesus because these deeds signal the in-breaking of the coming kingdom.[117] The title Son of Man represents the kerygmatic proclamation of the death, resurrection, and *parousia* of Jesus, which is the inaugural element of the kingdom's coming.[118] The titles associated with Jesus' powerful deeds—what some might call the confessional titles—always come *von außen* ("from the outside") while the kerymatic Son of Man description is an *Innenansicht* ("interior opinion") from the Markan Jesus.[119]

Theobald argues that none of these titles is meant to correct another title or even the Markan community's understanding of them. Rather, the polar structure is present in order to build to a climax in the final pole (14:61–62) those "confessions" that were developed in the previous central passages.[120] The two poles act in a reciprocal manner in that both aid in interpreting the other—Messiah/Son of God (confessional dealing with powerful deeds of the historical Jesus) and Son of Man (interior opinion of the Christ of faith). For Theobald, the climax comes in the latter, the so-called Son of Man christology.[121]

115. Theobald, "Gottesohn und Menschensohn."
116. Ibid., 39–40. See also Naluparayil, *Identity of Jesus*, 33.
117. Theobald, "Gottesohn und Menschensohn," 55–66.
118. Ibid., 41.
119. Ibid.
120. Ibid., 45.
121. Ibid., 73. On this point, Naluparayil (*Identity of Jesus*, 34n195) adds: "The 'Polar Christology,' in the final analysis turns out to be a 'Son of Man Christology' because the Son of Man seems to be getting more importance. He prefers to speak of Jesus' identity as the Son of Man identity . . . Moreover, he asserts that Jesus is the Son of God, because

The Turning Point in the Gospel of Mark

Klaus Scholtissek distances himself from the polar christology of Theobald and chooses to see Mark's christology as an integration of the christological titles in the narrative.[122] His focus can still be regarded as structural in nature as opposed to titular since he bases his understanding not on a specific passage (as Theobald) but rather on overarching motifs that pair Mark's understanding of Jesus with other key aspects in the Gospel. These overarching pairs are (1) christology and eschatology; (2) Son of God and Kingdom of God; and (3) the messenger (Jesus) and the message (gospel).[123] Christology and eschatology are brought together in the narrative through the authority of Jesus, which is authenticated by the mighty deeds of Jesus. These mighty deeds serve a dual purpose according to Scholtissek. On the one hand, they draw people into the kingdom; on the other hand they generate questions about Jesus' authority. In this way, the second motif, Son of God and Kingdom of God, is brought together since the present aspect of the kingdom is presented through the miracles of the Son of God while the future aspect of the kingdom is linked with the coming of the Son of Man.[124] The messenger Jesus and the message of the kingdom come together in the narrative when people exhibit faith, something that is available to the reader of Mark's Gospel after the resurrection. Scholtissek's christology plays off Mark's eschatology. Through the categories of eschatology, kingdom, and message one comes to understand the proper identity of Jesus.

Black, in an essay introduced in chapter 4, suggests that the Gospel has a tripartite structure composed of Jesus' (1) baptism (1:9–11); (2) transfiguration (9:2–8); and (3) death (15:33–41).[125] He observes that scholars have observed these three events but they "have not always been correlated with the interpretive care that they invite."[126] In fact, he suggests that the three events "beg joint consideration as mutually interpretive" because of the following five features.[127] First, their location is critical. The transfigura-

---

of his being the Son of Man . . . As a result, the polarity is broken and is faded away in favour of the 'Son of Man Christology.'"

122. Scholtissek, "Sohn Gottes," 88. For a helpful summary of Scholtissek's work, see Naluparayil, *Identity of Jesus*, 35–36.

123. Ibid., 68–90.

124. Ibid., 73–74.

125. Black, "The Face Is Familiar," 35.

126. Ibid., 35.

127. Ibid.

*Converging Lines in Markan Christology*

tion narrative sits at the (almost) dead center of the Gospel, flanked as it were with two bookends, the baptism scene at the beginning, the crucifixion scene at the end. Second, all three scenes "are drenched in imagery that is apocalyptic or revelatory."[128] Third, Mark's narrative thread, that is, the way the narrative links the three episodes together, is important commentary on how Mark wanted to show the interrelationship of the three scenes. Fourth, the nature of Jesus as God's Son is affirmed in all three episodes, a claim that Black holds is comparatively rare in the Gospel. Finally, the three episodes have primarily been understood christologically, that is, as an element in understanding Mark's portrait of Jesus and the kingdom. However, the three scenes "are no less significant for construing Mark's presentation of *God*" also—especially since in the first two scenes (1:11 and 9:7) God is the speaker. To Black, "if we want to learn something about God in Mark's Gospel, attention must be paid to him who is identified as God's Son."[129]

This last assertion means that Black is as equally concerned with theological matters in the Gospel of Mark as with christological concerns. This, as has been noted by Donahue and others, is a neglected factor in the study of Mark's Gospel.[130] But because Black's insistence that God and Jesus are inextricably linked in the narrative, it is appropriate to look at the christological issues he raises in his analysis of the tripartite structure of Mark's Gospel.

Without restating what I have already said about Black's structure in Chapter Four, let me emphasize a few features related to how this structure contributes to Black's understanding of Mark's christology. The first feature is Black's attention to the "confessions" that occur in each of the three scenes. For Black they share a common, formulaic structure.

---

128. Ibid.

129. Ibid., 36; emphasis in original.

130. Donahue, "Neglected Factor." See also, Kingsbury, "'God' within the Narrative World of Mark"; and Driggers, *Following God through Mark*.

The Turning Point in the Gospel of Mark

| Baptism (1:11) | Transfiguration (9:7) | Crucifixion (15:39) |
|---|---|---|
| A "You are my Son, B the beloved, C in whom I am well pleased" | A "This is my Son, B the beloved: C Listen to him." | A "Truly, B this man C was God's son." |

*Table 7*

The most significant difference in the above analysis lies in the third passage, the declaration of the Centurion (15:39). For Black, while the syntactical elements may be dissimilar, the pattern is the same with the first two.[131] This pattern helps to draw these three scenes together and each relates important information concerning Jesus (and God) to the reader. But how does the intervening narrative draw together things in such a way that the three scenes are mutually interpreted? And how does this mutual interpretation reveal the essence of Jesus (and God) in the Markan narrative? The thread, for Black, is seen in the notion of following. Throughout the Gospel, disciples are asked to follow Jesus (e.g., 1:16–20; 2:14; 3:13–19; 6:6b-13, 30; 8:34–38). In the Markan narrative, everyone, including Jesus, must ultimately become a follower of God. But not all do become followers in Mark's Gospel. Why? Black's answer is: "Through Jesus, God outruns everyone in Mark."[132] Indeed, in Mark's Gospel, God is "elusive," unable of being figured out or grasped. Though Black never says so explicitly, the same is true with Mark's presentation of Jesus (as God's Son): just as the Father is elusive, so is Mark's presentation of the Son. The tripartite structure gives us "hints" of his identity, but none of the three is fulfilling in that sense. Black's tantalizing title is appropriate to conclude—Jesus' (and God's) face is familiar (because of the narrative), I just can't place it (because of God's mysterious revelation).[133] As we shall see in the subsequent section, these christologies based on structural issues raise points similar to my reading of Mark's narrative.

131. Ibid., 44.
132. Ibid., 45.
133. Ibid. Black cites approvingly the work of Burkill (*Mysterious Revelation*).

## Teacher/Prophet

### *Jesus as Teacher*

As we have seen, Divine Man christology dominated much of the first half of the twentieth century. As its foundations began to crack, other christologies became prominent because of a number of factors, one being the decreasing dependence on purely historical-critical methodology. The rise of redaction and literary criticism gave rise to the so-called "corrective" christologies of Weeden and Perrin but it also allowed scholars to look at Mark's presentation of Jesus through new lenses. One such lens was explored by Eduard Schweizer in the 1960s and early 1970s. Schweizer's analysis centered on the role of Jesus as teacher in the Gospel of Mark.[134]

Schweizer was heavily dependent on redaction criticism. He observed numerous places in the Gospel that betrayed the influence of an editor. In those passages, Schweizer observed the curious feature that most (if not all) the occurrences of διδάσκω and cognate words are ascribed to Jesus. This led him to conclude that, for Mark, Jesus' distinctiveness lies in the frequency of his teaching.[135] Schweizer emphasized the nature of Jesus as teacher but downplayed the actual content of this teaching. Thus, for Schweizer, Mark was not interested in the substance of his teaching, only that his teaching (and miracles, etc.) proved his authority—an authority that could only be derived from the notion that he was "God's holy messenger."[136]

Reactions to Schweizer's focus on Jesus as an authoritative teacher were mixed. Some held that "teacher" cannot really be applied to christological matters; it is descriptive of Jesus' activity and cannot contribute to what Oscar Cullmann called "the Christological problem."[137] Others took issue with the Schweizer's claim that Mark was not concerned with the

---

134. Schweizer's works that speak to this element of Markan Christology are Schwiezer, "Ammerkungen"; "Zur Frage des Messiasgeheimnisses bei Markus"; and *Good News According to Mark*.

135. Schweizer, "Ammerkungen," 93–95. See also, Jacobs, "Mark's Jesus," 63.

136. Ibid., 51.

137. Cullmann, *Christology of the New Testament*, 5–6. One of Cullmann's fundamental texts as he constructs his Christology is Mark 8:27–29, a portion of our "twin pericopae." On the point about why teacher is an inappropriate designation in answering the "christological problem" (which was for him the answer to the question "Who is Jesus?" by addressing not the nature of Jesus, but his function), he states, "Therefore, the designation of Jesus as 'Rabbi' or 'Teacher' or 'Physician' (titles certainly important for describing the life of Jesus) is not important for the Christological problem."

content of Jesus' teaching.[138] Several interpreters, however, embraced the notion of Jesus as teacher and held it the central feature of Mark's presentation of Jesus.[139] Two names are generally associated with this view, Paul J. Achtemeier and Vernon K. Robbins.

In an essay published in the *Catholic Biblical Quarterly*, Achtemeier examined Mark's use of four words that occur a total of 38 times in the narrative: (1) the noun διδάσκαλος, (2) its Semitic equivalent, ῥαββί, (3) the verb διδάσκω, and (4) the noun διδαχή, which describes the act of teaching.[140] He concluded that "one of Mark's intentions was to establish the idea that Jesus was preeminently a teacher."[141] However, that emphasis is clearly shared with Matthew and Luke. Is there any other matter that Mark emphasizes, with respect to Jesus as teacher, which neither the Gospels according to Matthew nor Luke emphasizes? Achtemeier answers this question in the affirmative by suggesting that Mark's constant highlighting of Jesus as a miracle-worker was unique, primarily because "Mark makes clear that Jesus' teaching shares the same power as his miracles. Indeed, they seem to be essentially the same activity."[142] In other words, "the intention of Mark's Christological discussion thus appears to be the establishment of Jesus as teacher, whose power as teacher is made visible in his acts as miracle-worker."[143]

---

138. See, for example, Evans, *Beginning of the Gospel*, 46.

139. Meye, *Jesus and the Twelve*, 46–47; Egger, *Frohbotschaft und Lehre*, 159–60; and Achtemeier, "Reflections on Marcan Christology."

140. Achtemeier, "Reflections on Marcan Christology," 465–81. He lists the twelve occurrences of the noun διδάσκαλος in their redactional categories: (1) miracle stories (4:38; 5:35; 9:17); (2) Jesus "sayings" (9:38; 10:17, 20; 10:35); (3) pronouncement stories (12:14, 19, 32); (4) *chreia* (13:1); and (5) traditional saying regarding the Last Supper (14:14). Similarly, with the exception of 6:30; 7:7; 12:14; 14:49, the verb διδάσκω appears as editorial compositions (1:21, 22; 2:13; 4:1, 2; 6:2, 6, 34; 8:31; 9:31; 10:1; 11:17; 12:35). The noun διδαχή ("teaching") occurs five times, four of which are redactional (1:22, 27; 4:2, 12:38) while the fifth he holds as traditional (11:18; but "may equally well be editorial"). The Hebrew "Rabbi" occurs four times in Mark (9:5; 10:51; 11:21; and 14:45).

141. Ibid., 476.

142. Ibid., 478. Broadhead (*Teaching with Authority*, 208–10) also picks up the role of Jesus' miracles in Mark's Christology. Broadhead's work, along with his other two works on Markan Christology, will be dealt with below in the material dealing with narrative approaches.

143. Ibid., 480. Perhaps I should also mention that Boring ("Christology of Mark") picked up on Achtemeier's emphasis on Jesus as teacher/miracle-worker and sought to show how Mark used "teacher" as a bridge between the more common titles of Christ, Son of God, and Son of Man. For Boring, the crucial piece of evidence was the frequency

The second prominent advocate for seeing Mark's Jesus primarily as a teacher is Vernon K. Robbins.[144] Robbins's work on Mark's Gospel straddles three areas of academic scholarship—socio-rhetorical criticism, comparative literature, and structural analysis. Such areas provide the background for his innovative work, published in 1984 as *Jesus the Teacher: A Socio-Rhetorical Interpretation of Mark*.[145] As I described in chapter 1, Robbins based his formal structure of the Gospel on repetition and progression, which led him to suggest the rubric "three-step progression" to the Gospel.[146] The Greek antecedent of this repetition could be found in Xenophon's *Memorabilia*, while the prophetic literature of the Hebrew Bible (especially the narratives of Elijah and Elisha) provided the Jewish antecedent.[147] The pattern that develops in the Gospel of Mark, based on this progression, is: (1) Jesus goes to a new place with his disciples; (2) he engages in a special situation of interaction; and (3) as a result of this interaction he summons his disciples anew.[148] "These three-step progressions show Jesus 'repeating his identity . . . under changing situations.'"[149] Thus, using this pattern, the formal structure of the Gospel looks likes this, with the "changing identity" of Jesus noted.[150]

---

with which Mark used "teacher" and "teaching" in the Gospel. Teacher (the noun) is used twelve times, more than either "Christ" (seven times) or "Son of God" (nine times, including 1:1 and the veiled references to "son" in 12:6 and 13:32), and, if the four additional occurrences of the Hebrew equivalent are included, even more than "Son of Man" (fourteen times). When the verb "teach" and the noun "teaching" are added to the evidence, they are "proportionately speaking, far more than any of the other Gospels." Boring suggests that the repeated reference to Jesus as teacher is a hermeneutical device employed by Mark to aid in the interpretation of christological matters "expressed in ancient and alien categories into a new cultural setting." In other words, Jesus as "teacher" (a commonly understood term or idea by the Markan community) would aid Mark's intentions of presenting Jesus as "Christ," "Son of God," and "Son of Man" ("indispensable categories of christological confession for Mark" according to Boring), which were likely foreign concepts to Mark's readers.

144. In addition to those already mentioned, the following scholars have picked up on the notion of Jesus as teacher in Mark's Gospel: Stein, "'Redaktionsgeschichtlich' Investigation of a Markan Seam"; Schierse, "Das Christusbild"; and Graudin, "Jesus as Teacher."

145. Robbins, *Jesus the Teacher*.

146. Ibid., 19–27.

147. Ibid., 53–73.

148. Ibid., 25.

149. Ibid.

150. Ibid., 27.

The Turning Point in the Gospel of Mark

>   Introduction: Jesus and the Baptist (1:1–13)
>   - Jesus and the Gospel of God (1:14—3:6)
>   - The Healing Son of God (3:7—5:43)
>   - The Rejected Prophet (6:1—8:26)
>   - The Suffering, Dying, Rising Son of Man (8:27—10:45)
>   - The Authoritative Son of David (10:46—12:44)
>   - The Future Son of Man and the Dying Messiah-King (13:1—15:47)
>
>   Conclusion (16:1–8)

Though Robbins believed that though Mark presents Jesus in ever-changing circumstances, the structure of the Gospel presents his basic identity as "a disciple-gathering teacher."[151] But what about the other dimensions—the attributes of Jesus that emerge under changing situations? According to Robbins:

> When new attributes of Jesus emerge in new situations, a qualitative progression occurs that unfolds attributes of Jesus' thought and activity which the reader may not have anticipated at the beginning but which the reader accepts as appropriate when they emerge. In this manner, the author molds the folklore of early Christian groups into a unified presentation of 'the gospel of Jesus Christ, the Son of God.' In Mark, the 'gospel of God' is transformed into a biographical account of a prophet-teacher who embodies wisdom and power and transmits his mode of thought and action to a select group of disciple-companions who associate with him.[152]

Thus, these other attributes, as illustrated in the outline above, are additional features of Jesus' basic role as "teacher-Messiah who transmits a system of thought and action to a group of disciple-companions that he gathers around him."[153]

---

151. Ibid., 47.

152. Ibid. Others join Robbins in noting the biographical nature of the Gospel and its emphasis on Jesus as teacher. See esp. Botha, "Die dissipels in die Markusevangelie." On the nature of the Gospels as biography, see Burridge, *What Are the Gospels?*

153. Robbins, *Jesus the Teacher*, 48. See also, Naluparayil, *Identity of Jesus*, 37.

## Jesus as Prophet

There are three references of prophet in the Gospel of Mark (6:4, 15; 8:28). Two of these instances are of reactions of others to Jesus; only in 6:4 is the word προφήτης used by Jesus and here it is an implied reference ("a prophet is not without honor except in his hometown"). Therefore, it would appear difficult to base an entire christology on such few references. Rather than attempt this, however, some have combined the notions of teacher (rabbi) and prophet. One early voice to explore this connection was Charles Harold Dodd. In that work, he observed the similarities of Jesus both to a Jewish rabbi and to an OT prophet.[154] Howard Clark Kee, who held that Mark's understanding of Jesus was that of an agent for establishing the New Covenant, later developed this view.[155] Kee notes: "Mark's favourite designation for Jesus is teacher, as we have noted. Yet Jesus does not appear as a rabbinic interpreter of the scriptures, but as a charismatic, divinely authorized spokesman for God. . . Jesus is a charismatic prophet whose words and works are self-authenticating."[156] In a subsequent work (an essay entitled "Christology in Mark's Gospel"), Kee distances himself somewhat from this single-minded view of Jesus as prophet-teacher.[157] Rather, he holds that Mark is consistently presenting Jesus in opposition to a whole range of options open to Judaism (he does not consider Greco-Roman options) in the first century.[158] Kee continues to uphold the notion that Jesus is to be identified with the New Covenant of the OT—and in that sense Jesus' mission is messianic; however, he suggests that Mark wants his readers to grasp that none of the traditional terms (e.g., Messiah; Son of God; Son of Man; Son of David; King of Israel; Teacher/Prophet) or expectations have a fixed meaning. "All must be reassessed in light of the transformation through Jesus of understanding of the divine purpose and of God's expectations for his people in the New Age."[159]

According to Richard Horsley, the issue for Jesus' contemporaries was less a question of "does Jesus fit the model of eschatological prophet," but

---

154. Dodd, "Jesus as Teacher and Prophet," 57, 66. See also, Naluparayil, *Identity of Jesus*, 36; and Jacobs, "Mark's Jesus," 65.

155. Kee, *Community of the New Age*, 116.

156. Ibid., 117.

157. Kee, "Christology in Mark's Gospel."

158. Ibid., 200.

159. Ibid., 206.

rather "since this fellow is obviously a prophet, what sort of prophet is he?"[160] Arguing from a socio-historical methodology, Horsley posits that the first-century evidence does not support the standard dichotomy of Jewish prophet—eschatological prophet or "prophet like Moses."[161] These were not important factors in the Jewish literature of the day, according to Horsley's survey of first-century authors. Instead, the two distinctive types of prophets, to which the Markan audience would have looked at Jesus, were (1) oracular prophets (like Elijah and Elisha of the OT) and (2) prophets who led movements (the great "liberators" of Israel, like Moses and Joshua).[162] Thus, though Horsley's work is far from a "Christology of Mark's Gospel," he does posit (by inference) that early Christians would have embraced the notion of Jesus as prophet, explicitly what type of prophet (oracular; liberator) is left open for interpretation.

## Other Markan Christologies

### Shepherd

I am not aware of any scholar who has posited that the overriding christology of Mark's Gospel should be put under the heading "Shepherd." The word, as a title applied to Jesus, occurs only once in the narrative (14:27).[163] Matera, however, observes that "Mark portrays Jesus as Israel's Shepherd king in the feeding of the 5000" in 6:34, a passage that recalls Ezekiel 34, where God is portrayed as looking for the scattered sheep.[164] Similarly, "Mark's use of προάγω in 14:28 and 16:7 also portrays Jesus as a shepherd, 'going before' his disciples."[165] While Matera is not presenting or even sug-

---

160. Horsley, "Two Types of Popular Prophets," 435.

161. Ibid., 463.

162. Ibid., 437. On this point, see his later work, "A Prophet Like Moses and Elijah."

163. Boring, "Christology of Mark," 149.

164. Matera, "Transcending Messianic Expectations," 206, n.13. Kee ("Christology in Mark's Gospel," 196) builds on this "scattered" image by indicating, "The image of the community as the scattered flock of God's people appears at two crucial points in Mark: at 6:34, in connection with the story of the feeding of the 5000, and at 14:27 in Gethsemane, just before his arrest."

165. Ibid. One also wonders if the so-called wilderness motif might strengthen this point. Exodus 3:1 connects ἔρημος and πρόβατα (see also Ezek 36:37–38). On the meaning of προάγω, see Best, *Following Jesus*, 199–203. On the wilderness theme in Mark, see Mauser, *Christ in the Wilderness*.

gesting a full-blown Markan christology (he does that in *New Testament Christology*, a work that will be presented below), he does offer another possibility, though hardly one that would be considered Mark's overriding christological theme.

## Son of David

In the Gospel of Mark, Son of David is not a prominent title for Jesus, it occurs only twice in the narrative (10:47–48; 12:35–37) and generally carries messianic overtones.[166] Few scholars would dispute that what Mark seemed to deemphasize, Matthew has taken over and made it a key element of his Gospel. However, not all scholars think Mark has downplayed the image of Son of David. Hooker, for example, writes: "It is true that in Mark's eyes 'Son of David' is not an adequate title for Jesus (12.35–7), but it is typical of Mark's irony that the blind should see more than those with sight, and the title points forward to the story of the triumphal entry into Jerusalem which immediately follows."[167] Such a sentiment is a far cry from making Son of David the primary christological title of the Markan narrative. My investigation, indeed, found no scholar since 1900 that made Son of David the overarching concern of Mark when it came to Jesus' identity.

Stephen H. Smith, however, does argue that Son of David in Mark's Gospel plays a more significant role in the Gospel than is generally recognized.[168] His reasoning is as follows. Though the title itself appears infrequently, one complete section of the narrative (10:46–12:44) is dominated by what he calls "Son of David activity."[169] Son of David is downplayed in people's minds while reading the Gospel; however, it must be remembered that Mark "confines the Son of David activity to the environs of Jerusalem,"

---

166. Boring ("Christology of Mark," 149) includes it in the "Others" category of his appendix of christological titles in Mark, occurring at 10:47–48 and 12:35–37. France (*Gospel of Mark*, 423) observes, "This is the only time when Jesus is addressed as υἱὲ Δαυίδ, and nothing in this gospel (unlike Mt. 1:1–17, 20) has prepared us for this specific title. For Jewish people it would be functionally equivalent to Χριστός, but the voicing of David's name increases the loading of royal and nationalistic ideology which it carries." See also Moloney, *Gospel of Mark*, 208–9, esp. nn. 197–98.

167. Hooker, *Gospel According to Saint Mark*, 253.

168. Smith, "Function of the Son of David Tradition."

169. Ibid., 523. Smith acknowledges the two passages where the term Son of David is mentioned (10:47–48; 12:35–37), but also includes 11:9–10 in his analysis since the Son of David concept of David messiahship is present.

but in Mark's narrative (contra the Gospel according to John), Jesus makes only one visit to Jerusalem, which is in the last week of Jesus' life.[170] "[S]o it is clear that the Son of David concept could not have been introduced prior to his entry into Judea (10:1)."[171] This domination of "Son of David activity" in 10:46—12:44 makes the title a "low-key term" in the Gospel.[172] By "low-key," Smith means that the phrase is void of all political overtones and instead carries ethical overtones. "Thus, for Mark, the lordship of Jesus (and hence his authority) is presented as the ultimate authority behind the advice of the Evangelist to his community that it, too, should thread an ethical, not a political path."[173] So, for Smith, the infrequency of the title does not mean that it is nonetheless unimportant in the Gospel. However, he would not embrace Son of David as *the* Christology of the Gospel despite its significance as Jesus draws near to and enters Jerusalem (10:46—12:44).

## Methodological Interlude: The Move from Redaction to Narrative Criticism

Our survey thus far has focused on seven dominant christologies of Mark's Gospel in the last one hundred years: (1) Messiah and Messianic Secret; (2) Divine Man; (3) Son of God; (4) Son of Man; (5) christologies based on structure; (6) Prophet/Teacher; and (7) others. The majority of those surveyed above approach Mark's christology from the perspective of redactional criticism, that is, each author attempts to isolate material infused into the traditional material by Mark in hopes that such evidence might betray Mark's theological convictions and/or purposes.[174] In my opinion, Perrin serves as the quintessential "bridge" figure between redactional interests and literary or narratological interests. His work in the early 1970s (cut short by his untimely death) was already presenting literary concerns in conjunction with redactional ones, and others, including his own students, moved the literary study of the NT texts (especially the Gospels) forward

---

170. Ibid.
171. Ibid.
172. Ibid.
173. Ibid., 539.
174. There are, of course, some voices in the above survey that do not approach Mark's Christology from a redactional perspective. For example, many would argue that Wrede predates what is typically held to be redaction criticism, while Robbins, Peace, and Black would fit more appropriately in the narrative criticism category.

in many respects.¹⁷⁵ It is only natural, then, that this final section should conclude with a brief section on the christology of Mark's Gospel from a narrative-critical perspective.

## Narrative Christologies of Mark's Gospel

Just as a historical/redactional survey on Markan christology must be selective, so also must a discussion of narrative christologies of the Gospel. There are a number of works dealing with Mark's Gospel from this perspective and since the Gospel itself is interested in the question "Who then is this?" (4:41), hardly any article, monograph, or commentary will leave out christological concerns. My selection principle here is to focus on what I deem to be important works on Mark's narrative, either because of their perspective (i.e., plot, characterization, etc.) or because of their contribution to the theology/christology of the Gospel (i.e., the substance of what they hold the narrative to be saying about Jesus).¹⁷⁶

### *Robert C. Tannehill and the Plot of Mark's Gospel*

Tannehill is considered by many to be the father of narrative criticism, especially as it is applied to the Gospel of Mark. His 1977 essay focused on the plot of the Markan narrative since "the study of character (not in the sense of inner qualities but in the sense of defining characteristics as presented in the story) can only be approached through the study of plot."¹⁷⁷ This attention to plot development causes him to see three major sections in the "unified narrative," each offering connecting thread of purpose and development (which he labels "narrative lines").¹⁷⁸

---

175. Even Perrin's primer on redaction criticism, which included an example of redaction criticism at work (*What is Redaction Criticism?*, 51–57) paid attention to narrative issues. See also his NT introduction (Perrin, *The New Testament*, 143–67). Of Perrin's students who took on narrative methodologies (in whole or in part), see esp. Tolbert, *Sowing the Gospel*; Robbins, *Jesus the Teacher*; and Kelber, *Mark's Story of Jesus*.

176. I have dealt with narrative-critical methodology, in general, in prior chapters (e.g., chapters 2 and 4).

177. Tannehill, "Mark as Narrative Christology," 58. For a summary of Tannehill's Christology, see Jacobs, "Mark's Jesus," 76–77.

178. Tannehill, "Mark as Narrative Christology," 60.

## The Turning Point in the Gospel of Mark

The first major section (1:1–8:26) focuses on the commission of Jesus—a commission that essentially defines Jesus' role as directed by the divine voice in 1:11, in which Jesus is called God's beloved son.[179] "Jesus' basic role is that of eschatological salvation bringer."[180]

In the second major section (8:27–10:52), Jesus' relationship to his disciples (which is introduced in the first section, but obscure at best according to Tannehill) becomes dominant.[181] Jesus' disciples, through Peter, appear to overcome their lack of perception highlighted in the opening section, but "the narrative sequence makes clear that a major problem remains."[182] That major problem involves the fate of Jesus, a fate that is announced in the passion predictions, which most importantly "announces a program of action which will be carried out in the rest of the narrative."[183] This section of the narrative produces a strange disclosure (10:45), according to Tannehill: "Jesus, renouncing all concern for life and power, goes to the cross in service of others. Strangely, this death brings life."[184]

The final section of Mark's narrative (11:1–16:8) emphasizes the task of Jesus' opponents and brings together in climactic fashion the three major lines in the Gospel (the commission of Jesus, the commission of disciples, the task of the opponents) for Tannehill.[185] Here the plot involves several literary features, such as irony, paradox, and enticement to false hopes, each of which provides a lens into Mark's presentation of Jesus. The identity of Jesus comes into focus in his final confrontation with opponents, the trial scene. There Jesus affirms the very images that are seemingly in conflict with the whole messianic theme, "just at the most disadvantageous time," and lays claim to these titles "as he goes to his death."[186] Thus, Tannehill can conclude: "The study of Mark as narrative reveals more unity and art in this Gospel than is commonly recognized. These appear as we consider the narrative lines which flow from the commissions or tasks of major characters and groups in the Gospel. . . .

---

179. Ibid., 61.
180. Ibid., 63.
181. Ibid., 72.
182. Ibid.
183. Ibid.
184. Ibid., 76.
185. Ibid., 77.
186. Ibid., 87.

Studying Mark as narrative Christology provides a deeper understanding of the meaning and function of Mark's presentation of Jesus Christ."[187]

## Jack Dean Kingsbury and the Characterization of Jesus in Mark

"Characterization refers to the way a narrator brings characters to life in a narrative."[188] Kingsbury, without ever employing the word "characterization," presents a narrative-critical rendering of Jesus, whom Kingsbury calls "the protagonist in Mark's story."[189] Kingsbury's goal was to "explore the christology of Mark with an eye to the motif of the secret of Jesus' identity.[190] To do this, he combined several common features of narrative criticism (point of view, structure, themes) with an examination of the christological titles in the Gospel. Studying the titles alone was considered insufficient, but still an "indispensable part" of such an investigation.[191]

Kingsbury's major christological titles are Messiah, King of the Jews, Son of David, Son of God, and Son of Man.[192] The first four titles comprise a group for Kingsbury, a group that the narrative correlates into a presentation of Jesus as the Davidic Messiah-King, the royal son of God.[193] The latter term, Son of God, is the only title in the Gospel that transcends human beings and human characters in the narrative, making it the preeminent title for Jesus in the Gospel.[194] In contrast, Son of Man "is neither 'messianic' in nature nor is it used to inform the reader or any character in Mark of the identity of Jesus."[195] Its function is different: rather than a title revealing something of Jesus' nature, for Kingsbury it is a "technical term"

---

187. Ibid., 89.

188. Rhoads, Dewey, and Michie, *Mark as Story*, 98. On characterization of Jesus in Mark's Gospel, see esp. Danove, "Rhetoric'"; and Johnson, "Characterization of Jesus in Mark."

189. Kingsbury, *Christology of Mark's Gospel*, ix, 51. (The Roman numeral references refer to the preface to the paperback edition.)

190. Ibid., 52.

191. Ibid., 53.

192. Ibid., 55.

193. Ibid., 142.

194. Ibid.

195. Ibid., x, 174.

that bears a precise meaning within the story world of Mark.[196] Son of Man functions in the Markan narrative as a pointer to Jesus' divine authority in the face of opposition.[197] "The overall impact of this title upon Mark's story is that it underlines the twin elements of conflict with the 'world' and of vindication in the sight of the 'world' at the Parousia."[198]

## Elizabeth Struthers Malbon and Enacted/Deflected/ Reflected/Refracted Christology

Elizabeth Struthers Malbon presents her narrative analysis of Mark's christology using five rubrics: (1) enacted; (2) projected; (3) deflected; (4) refracted; and (5) reflected.[199] Mark's narrative discloses information about Jesus by the actions he initiates, which is seen in the first third of the narrative (1:1–8:26) through his teaching, preaching, healings, and exorcisms (35, 37), and in the latter third (11:1–16:8) in his willingness to undergo suffering with an intervening middle section (8:27–10:52) focused on the preparation of Jesus' disciples for the decisive shift that takes place beginning in Mark 11.[200] The resulting christology (which she calls "the christological surprise") is "the powerful one who teaches and heals with God's authority accepts his suffering and death at human hands as the will of God."[201] Against Kingsbury she claims Mark's stress is not on the identity of Jesus, but rather upon the implication of this enacted christology—Jesus' message of the nearness of the kingdom (1:15) is good news for both Jew and Gentile.[202]

Projected christology is what the narrator and other characters in the story say about Jesus.[203] The narrator speaks of Jesus primarily in titles, es-

196. Ibid., xi.

197. Ibid., 174.

198. Ibid. On the conflict notion, see Kingsbury, *Conflict in Mark*.

199. Malbon's program is set out in four articles: (1) "The Christology of Mark's Gospel: Narrative Christology and the Markan Jesus"; (2) "'Reflected Christology': An Aspect of Narrative 'Christology' in the Gospel of Mark"; (3) "Narrative Christology and the Son of Man: What the Markan Jesus Says Instead"; and (4) "Markan Narrative Christology and the Kingdom of God." These four essays are now included in Malbon, *Mark's Jesus*.

200. Malbon, "Christology of Mark's Gospel," 36.

201. Ibid.

202. Ibid., 37.

203. Malbon ("'Reflected Christology,'" 128) puts Kingsbury and his focus on christological titles in this category.

pecially with the opening line: Jesus is the Christ, the Son of God (1:1), the latter of which the narrator affirms in 1:11 and 9:7 by means of the divine voice and in 15:39 by means of the centurion's confession. In Malbon's understanding, however, Jesus deflects (hence deflective christology) much of what is said about him (i.e., he never accepts the titles given to him, such as the demon's announcement that he is the Holy One of God or Peter's confession that he is the Messiah).[204] "The Markan Jesus consistently deflects honor away from himself and toward God."[205] Instead, Jesus changes or refracts these statements by others by including his own perspective about himself, especially the notion of Son of Man, and about God. This christology she calls refracted christology.[206] Finally, how what other characters do in response to these refracted statements makes for her reflected christology. This final category is best seen in the minor characters of the narrative that serve as exemplars of Jesus' words and deeds to the rest of the characters in the narrative.[207]

## Edwin K. Broadhead and Titular Christology

Broadhead prefers the phrase titular christology rather than christological titles because "there are no titles which are inherently and unambiguously Christological; they become so only within defined social and literary contexts."[208] In effect, then, titles are part of a more complex narrative analysis of texts, namely that of characterization. With respect to the Markan narrative, Broadhead examines sixteen titles found in the Gospel: Jesus the Nazarene; Prophet; the Greater One; Priest; King; the Teacher; Shepherd; the Holy One of God; the Suffering Servant of God; Son of David; Son of God; Son of Man; Lord; Christ; the Risen One; and the Crucified One.[209] The case Broadhead desires to make is that Mark does not simply import

---

204. Ibid., 136. It is this deflected Christology that likely gave rise to the so-called "messianic secret," according to Malbon ("Christology of Mark's Gospel," 38).

205. Malbon, "Christology of Mark's Gospel," 41.

206. Malbon, "Narrative Christology and the Son of Man," 374.

207. Malbon, "'Reflected Christology,'" 136.

208. Broadhead, *Naming Jesus*, 28. This work is part of a larger christological investigation by the author. See Broadhead, *Teaching with Authority*; and *Prophet, Son, Messiah*.

209. Broadhead does not necessarily capitalize all the titles in his work. For several of them, Jesus is never directly called this title (e.g., priest, shepherd). I capitalize them here only to preserve their titular nature.

a few prepackaged titles and insert them into his narrative. Rather, Mark shapes and reshapes these images "into a stream of titular christology."[210]

Broadhead categorizes Mark's shaping of these titles in four groupings: (1) embedded titles; (2) framework titles; (3) climactic titles; and (4) extending titles. Embedded titles are images embedded into the story line of the Gospel and give substance to the story of Jesus. Some embedded terms, such as Holy One of God, Greater One, and Son of David, make a limited contribution to Mark's overall plot. Other images (e.g., Prophet, Priest, Teacher, Shepherd, Suffering Servant; Lord) exert more influence over the narrative flow of the Gospel.

Framework titles function as introductory and concluding markers; in other words, they frame or provide a grid from which to read the narrative.[211] The titles Messiah and especially Son of God function in this way since at least the latter is found in 1:1 and 15:39.

Similarly, "some titles gather the focus of the entire story into a climactic confession."[212] Mark's use of Christ and Son of God in 14:61–62 functions in this manner, says Broadhead, though in this case they could also be part of a larger framing device. One unambiguous example of a climactic title in Mark is the description of Jesus as the Crucified One (16:6). This title "consummates the name of Jesus within this story . . . this is his story, this is his destiny, this is his name."[213]

Broadhead's final category for titular christology is that of extending titles. Extending titles are those titles found in the narrative that are present primarily to point beyond itself to something else in the story.[214] For example, the description of Jesus as the Risen One (in 14:28) is meant to be a bridge that allows the reader to move ahead in the story. Similarly, the Son of Man titles functions in this manner in the narrative. In the Gospel, Son of Man "points to a reality which stands at some distance, both temporally and ideologically, from the realms of the story. At some point in the future and under the sovereign authority of God, the Son of Man will come with power and glory. This promise explodes the bounds of the story and leaves open the final destiny of its participants."[215]

210. Broadhead, *Naming Jesus*, 159.
211. Ibid., 165.
212. Ibid., 166.
213. Ibid., 158.
214. Ibid., 166.
215. Ibid.

Therefore, in Broadhead's estimation, focusing on the christological titles (as one might do in systematic theology) is the wrong approach since it assumes a certain understanding of each title would be held constant by Mark.[216] Titular christology, on the other hand, permits the reader of Mark's narrative to see how Mark shaped and reshaped these "known" christological images as he presented his characterization of Jesus.

## Jacob C. Naluparayil and Plot, Point of View, and Characterization

The purpose of Naluparayil's work on Mark's christology analyzes three narrative elements, plot, point of view, and characterization, each of which points to the fact that in the Markan narrative "Jesus is the Son of Man on earth."[217] The interaction of the three narrative elements can be summarized briefly in the following manner: (1) The development of plot with its corresponding affective response in the reader displays that Jesus is the divine Son of Man whose "way" is entrusted to the reader, who in effect is asked to follow in the same way; (2) the points of view of God, Jesus, and the narrator (as it relates to the identity question) converge, providing affirming evidence that Jesus is the Son of Man on earth; and (3) a study of the divine traits of Jesus leads Naluparayil to conclude that the Son of Man operates as the name of the divine person present in Jesus of Nazareth.[218]

Not all NT scholars will agree with Naluparayil's conclusions. However, it should be noted that like many of the scholars who have articulated a Son of Man christology under redaction-critical methodologies (e.g., Donahue), Naluparayil has constructed a similar understanding employing narrative elements, especially those of plot, point of view, and characterization. Second, Naluparayil has observed a feature that will play into my observations later, namely, that of convergence. He suggests that the points of view of God, Jesus, and the narrator converge to present a unified picture of Jesus in the Markan narrative. I have suggested (and will articulate later) that Mark's three christological designations converge and provide a key to understanding the identity question. Finally, Naluparayil's discussion of

---

216. Examples of "Christological Titles" used by Broadhead include Cullmann, *Christology of the New Testament*; Hahn, *Titles of Jesus in Christology*; and Fuller, *Foundations of New Testament Christology*.

217. Naluparayil, *Identity of Jesus*, 554.

218. Ibid., 550–52.

plot concentrates not only on the constitutive elements of the narrative but also on how Mark brings the reader into the plot by encouraging him/her to adopt a "way" similar to Jesus. As we have seen, regardless of how hard one may try to isolate the christological question in Mark, the discipleship issue is never far away.

## *Frank J. Matera's Literary-Historical Analysis of Mark's Gospel*

Frank Matera's monograph on NT christology was written under the assumption that readers "learn how the writers of the New Testament understand the person and work of Jesus Christ by paying attention to the explicit and implicit stories of Christ in the New Testament. These stories provide the literary-historical framework within which readers can understand (1) Jesus' relationship to God and humanity; (2) the significance of his life, death, and resurrection; and (3) the titles attributed to him."[219] This literary-historical focus causes him to look closely at Mark's presentation of Jesus in the narrative. For Matera, Mark's story is simply told in two narrative parts: (1) Jesus is the Messiah, the Son of God (1:15–8:26); (2) whose destiny is the fate of the Son of Man and that fate involves suffering/death, resurrection, and glorious return (8:31–16:8). However, even if Mark's story is simple, Mark's christology is elusive; in what sense is Jesus the Messiah, the Son of God?[220]

The meaning of Messiah (and Son of God, Son of Man) is found in the story Mark tells, according to Matera.[221] That story shows a Messiah that is the Spirit-anointed Son of God who proclaims the arrival of the kingdom in word and action. Jesus performs healings, exorcises demons, and teaches the masses about this kingdom through parables. Most importantly, Jesus gives his life as a ransom for the many, including Gentiles. "Having suffered, died, and risen from the dead, he will return as the glorious Son of Man."[222] For Matera, Jesus is the Messiah because he is the Son of God.[223] This sonship depiction is developed in the story by means of secrecy motif, which he associates with "the messianic secret." "The real secret, however, con-

---

219. Matera, *New Testament Christology*, 3.
220. Ibid., 6.
221. Ibid., 24.
222. Ibid., 24–25.
223. Ibid., 25.

cerns Jesus' sonship rather than his messiahship."[224] No human character recognizes Jesus' true identity until the Roman centurion (15:39)—and his confession occurs after the death of Jesus. "Jesus' death, then, paradoxically reveals his divine sonship."[225]

Son of Man, a phrase central to Mark's presentation of Jesus, is "the most enigmatic term in the Gospel," Matera notes.[226] It is not confessional in the sense that the others are, such as Peter confessing Jesus as Messiah (8:29) or the Roman soldier exclaiming, "Truly this was the Son of God" (15:39). Jesus alone uses the term and its function in the narrative is to describe Jesus' destiny.[227] This destiny involves suffering and death, but also resurrection and a glorious return at the end of the ages to gather the elect of God.[228] "For Mark, Jesus is the Messiah, the Son of God, because he fulfills the destiny of the Son of Man."[229] Mark's christology may be presented using these three titles, but it is through the story that the titles derive meaning.

## I. Howard Marshall and Mark's Theological Story

The goal of I. Howard Marshall, in his *New Testament Theology*, is to describe and analyze the theologies of the NT books and their authors and to see whether there is a unified theology of the NT.[230] Marshall begins with the Gospel writers, Mark in particular, because they go "back to the beginning of how the early Christians came to believe . . . about Jesus."[231] Mark's story of Jesus (what Marshall calls his theological story) functions as an explanation that shows how Jesus presented himself and how his followers came to understand who he was and what his mission entailed.[232]

Mark's theological story is summarized by Jesus' message of the kingdom of God (1:14–15); for it is in establishing the kingdom that is Jesus'

---

224. Ibid.
225. Ibid.
226. Ibid., 26.
227. Ibid.
228. Ibid.
229. Ibid.
230. Marshall, *New Testament Theology*, 47.
231. Ibid., 58.
232. Ibid. In this it is easy to see how historical questions get intermingled with narratological ones.

destiny, that is how he will "carry out his mission for God."²³³ But Jesus' message of the kingdom, albeit vitally important for understanding the ministry of Jesus, took a backseat to Mark's determination to "present the role and the identity of Jesus rather than his message."²³⁴ This blending of message (i.e., kingdom) and messenger (i.e., Jesus) produces several key theological themes according to Marshall (kingdom of God, who Jesus is, the mighty works, the future of the kingdom and the Messiah, responses to Jesus), none of which is more important than the second—who Jesus is.²³⁵ "The Messiah and the kingdom are correlative, and Mark concentrates on the Messiah."²³⁶

Marshall focuses on three christological titles in the Gospel to describe the substance of Jesus' identity according to Mark: Christ, Son of God, and Son of Man.²³⁷ The first term, Messiah, carries "kingly associations" and indicates that it is this person "through whom God establishes his kingdom."²³⁸ The title Son of God, which culminates with the centurion's confession (15:39) suggests "the closeness of Jesus as the divine agent of God" and "brings out more deeply who the Messiah is."²³⁹ The last term, Son of Man, while "enigmatic," is "essential to an understanding of Jesus."²⁴⁰ For Marshall, it is the preferred term for use in statements regarding Jesus' suffering and death and functions as a self-designation for Jesus and messianic in nature.²⁴¹ Therefore, "the main theme of the Gospel is the identity of Jesus in his relationship to the kingdom of God."²⁴² There is (1) the recognition of Jesus as the Messiah and Son of God, his mighty works and preaching showing evidence of the kingdom; and (2) there is

---

233. Ibid., 59. Rhoads, Dewey, and Michie (*Mark as Story*, 104), in their focus on the narrative feature of Mark's characterization of Jesus, reach similar conclusions. For them, Jesus is "given the authority by God to inaugurate a rule that will eventually culminate in the restoration of all creation."

234. Ibid., 60.

235. Ibid., 81. The quote is: "Who Jesus is takes priority over his message of the kingdom."

236. Ibid.

237. Ibid., 82–83. He indicates (p. 82) that Son of David is "tantamount to Messiah and is associated with the mighty works of healing the blind."

238. Ibid., 82.

239. Ibid., 82–83.

240. Ibid., 85.

241. Ibid.

242. Ibid., 91.

*Converging Lines in Markan Christology*

reference that the Messiah (Son of Man?) must suffer and be raised, and the attendant implications this has for his followers/disciples.²⁴³ Throughout the Gospel, Marshall recognizes, there is a tension: the Messiah (and his followers) must suffer; yet somehow it is through this suffering that the kingdom comes.

## *Morna D. Hooker on Mark's Purpose*

The final narrative-critical examination we shall undertake is a recent essay by Morna Hooker (though to be fair, this is far from a comprehensive treatment of Markan christology from a narrative perspective).²⁴⁴ She presents her understanding of the christology of Mark's Gospel by examining four matters: the Prologue, God's kingdom, Mark's story, and Mark's purpose. Hooker sees the Prologue as containing essential information about Jesus and his ministry. The opening line contains the key: the beginning of the gospel of Jesus Christ, which can mean either "the gospel proclaimed *by* Jesus Christ" or "the gospel *about* Jesus Christ."²⁴⁵ She claims it is both since the message Jesus preached (that the kingdom is near) is, in fact, about Jesus himself.²⁴⁶ Mark's prologue clearly functions as "the key to his Gospel," she argues, "for it provides readers with essential information as to how his Gospel should be read."²⁴⁷

The message Jesus preached, namely, the message concerning the kingdom of God, is presented in her second major section. Jesus, she suggests, announces that God's rule has drawn near in four passages in the Gospel, the first three of which are on the lips of Jesus: 1:14–15 (the proclamation of Jesus); 9:1 (Jesus' announcement to his followers); 14:25 (Jesus' words at Passover meal); and 15:43 (the narrator's description of Joseph of Arimathea). As Hooker states: "It is not clear whether Mark believes that with Jesus' resurrection the kingdom of God has arrived in power or is himself still waiting for the kingdom's coming. What *is* clear, however, is that all three announcements of the coming kingdom are linked in Mark's Gospel with revelations of Jesus' identity as God's Son [cf. 1:11; 9:7; 15:39].... And while all three revelations occur in passages that refer to Jesus as Messiah

---

243. Ibid.
244. Hooker, "Christology of Mark's Gospel."
245. Ibid., 81; emphasis in original.
246. Ibid.
247. Ibid., 83.

## The Turning Point in the Gospel of Mark

(1:1; 8:29; 14:61–62; 15:2, 18, 26, 32), it is clear that, for the evangelist, Jesus is supremely the *Son of God*."[248]

The third section of Hooker's essay deals with Mark's story, which she claims is "full of christological significance."[249] She lays out the basic storyline in eight segments: scenes of authority (1:14—3:35); Jesus' teaching (4:1–34); miracle stories (4:35—6:13); John the Baptist and Jesus (6:14–29); further miracle stories (6:30—8:26); the truth about Jesus (8:27—10:52); further scenes of authority (11:1—12:37); and the passion narrative (14:1–47).[250]

The final section—entitled Mark's Purpose—begins with this statement: "Mark's Gospel is the Gospel about Jesus Christ, and so it is christological from beginning to end. The greatest puzzle is *why* the evangelist decided to write it!"[251] Hooker here suggests four possible reasons why Mark wrote this story, three of which are directly related to christological concerns (and the fourth is tangentially related). Let me begin with the one that is not directly related to christological concerns. Hooker observes that one possible reason why Mark wrote this Gospel relates to Mark's interest in discipleship. It is possible, she suggests, that the readers of Mark's Gospel were struggling to grasp Jesus as a suffering Messiah (a christological issue indeed). The necessity of Jesus' suffering is clearly presented in the Gospel, coming to a climax as it were in the crucifixion. Jesus' death was a given to those reading the Gospel. "The meaning of Christian discipleship, however, was *not* a given fact."[252] It is possible that Mark wrote this Gospel with the notion of suffering both as a description of Messiah Jesus and to demonstrate that Christian discipleship would also involve a similar path. "Was [Mark's] book primarily intended to remind its hearers of the implications of Christian discipleship?"[253]

Hooker's three other possible purposes of Mark's Gospel relate more directly to Mark's christology. She first asks the question: "Is Mark

---

248. Ibid., 86–87; emphasis in original.

249. Ibid., 87.

250. Ibid., 87–94. She curiously does not include the Olivet Discourse of Mark 13 in her analysis and mentions the epilogue of 16:1–8 in one sentence: "All that is needed to round off the story is a brief epilogue in 16:1–8, which tells the women that he has been raised and summons his disciples once again to follow him" (94).

251. Ibid., 94; emphasis in original.

252. Ibid., 96; emphasis in original.

253. Ibid.

countering an alternative Christology?"[254] Here she presents much of what has been addressed above—the "Divine Man" christology being replaced by the notion of Jesus as the suffering Son of Man (e.g., Weeden). She also touches on the "corrective christology" of Perrin (though she does not refer to Perrin's works directly). Also included is a brief presentation of Joseph B. Tyson's work on the Son of David. All of these "correctives" present inadequate responses to Jesus, she suggests.[255]

More acceptable to Hooker is the notion of Jesus as Son of God. As she states it: "It is difficult to know precisely what Mark is attacking [e.g., the so-called corrective christologies]. But what is he affirming? Clearly, he is affirming that Jesus is the Son of God."[256] But what does this phrase mean? Without expounding in detail, she offers the following four points concerning the meaning of Son of God in Mark and thereby his purpose in writing. First, in Mark's narrative, sonship is both linked with obedience to God and with suffering. Second, the narrative presents the power at work within Jesus as the Holy Spirit. Third, the whole of Jesus' earthly ministry is seen to be the fulfillment of God's purpose as depicted in the OT prophets and in Jesus' own proclamation of the kingdom. Finally, Jesus himself speaks of his vocation as the Son of Man.[257]

Hooker's "final piece of the puzzle" is the issue of the messianic secret.[258] Hooker notes that the issues surrounding the secret are complex and occur at many levels (i.e., historical, redactional, etc.). Her interest, as is ours, relates to Mark's use of the secrecy motif. She, like Luz (whom she does not cite), separates the commands to silence regarding Jesus' identity from those commands that are linked with healings/miracle stories. However, in the end, for Hooker the messianic secret "is the equivalent of the Johannine 'My hour has not yet come' statements."[259]

> During Jesus' ministry many things are hidden—not only from the crowds but also from the disciples. Only with the crucifixion and resurrection does full understanding finally come. For Mark, 'the messianic secret' is, perhaps, some explanation for Israel's failure to recognize here Messiah. It is also a pointer to the true

254. Ibid., 95.
255. Ibid., 96.
256. Ibid.
257. Ibid., 97.
258. Ibid.
259. Ibid., 98.

> meaning of being a disciple…above all [it] is a pointer to the truth about Jesus—a truth that so many fail to grasp, but which is spelled out for us at the beginning of the Gospel in the prologue, in the middle at the Transfiguration, and at the end in the words of the centurion. It serves to nudge Mark's readers in the ribs, as if to say: "And you, of course, because I have let you into the secret, will understand precisely what this means!"[260]

So, from Hooker's most recent work on Mark, it is hard to tell where she stands on the question of Markan christology from a narrative perspective. She holds high the "revelation" (her word) of Jesus as Son of God. Yet she closes her essay on the enigmatic secret motif, which for her functions similar to a Johannine σημεῖον. The secret points to beyond itself. But to what does it point in the narrative? She claims the reader knows enough, that this Gospel is about/of Jesus Christ.

## Conclusion

As one might expect, these narrative christologies have each taken one (or in some cases more than one) element of narrative criticism and examined Mark's presentation accordingly. Tannehill's work focused on Mark's plot and concluded that Mark's presentation of Jesus could be summarized using the theme of commissioning. Kingsbury worked within the characterization framework and argued that Mark's Jesus should be seen as the Davidic Messiah-King, who is the Son of God. Struthers Malbon turned her attention to the narrator and isolated where Jesus enacted, deflected, reflected, or refracted statements about himself and his work.

With Broadhead's work, a familiar phrase in the study of theology, "Christological Titles," was amended to "titular christology" so that the emphasis was on how Mark used and/or redeployed these titles for his own use rather than in a standard meaning brought into the Markan story. Naluparayil attempted to address three narrative elements, plot, point of view, and characterization, all of which he claimed pointed to one fact: Mark saw the Son of Man in Jesus of Nazareth. Frank Matera, similarly, sees the whole of Mark's narrative as essential for understanding Mark's particular presentation of Jesus. For him, like Broadhead, titles are important since Mark's christology is presented using these titles. But, for Matera, it is only through the storyline that the titles become meaningful. As he put it, "The Christology is

---

260. Ibid.

in the story, and through the story we learn to interpret the titles."[261] Marshall emphasized this storyline also, concluding that Mark's presentation of Jesus is interwoven with Jesus' preaching of the kingdom. Because Son of Man is the most enigmatic of the titles used for Jesus in the Gospel, it must be primary. Perhaps he concludes this since the kingdom is likewise enigmatic in Mark's Gospel. Finally, the recent work of Morna Hooker focused the attention of Gospel research once again on the issue of Mark's purpose. Like Marshall, she is content to connect kingdom language and christological concerns. But in the end, it is Mark's secrecy motif that dominates the narrative.

Markan christology since 1900 has come full circle. What began with Wrede and the so-called messianic secret now comes back in narrative form as an issue of the secrecy motif. Perhaps Luz had it right more than thirty years ago: the messianic secret is still a mystery.[262] Yet this analysis has proved helpful, especially Hooker's concluding observations. She (along with others) referred to several issues that I maintain are crucial in grasping Mark's presentation of Jesus; namely, the significance of the story line of Mark, a story that at its core presents the message of the Kingdom of God. This kingdom message is both Jesus' message, that is he the one proclaiming it, and that message in turn concerns Jesus (that is, it is about him). Whatever else Hooker's analysis shows, it speaks of the all-important titles of Messiah, Son of God, who is (by self-declaration) Son of Man. Now, it is my turn to articulate my understanding of Mark's presentation of Jesus.

## CONVERGING LINES IN MARKAN CHRISTOLOGY

As the survey of narrative christologies suggest, one's reading of the Markan narrative tends to embrace one particular christology, such as Son of God (Kingsbury) and downplay the others. Seldom have scholars attempted to construct a christology of the Gospel of Mark holding in tension more than one title or designation of Jesus.[263] Yet I have suggested that Markan christology is best understood as one where the notions of Messiah, Son of God, and Son of Man are preserved.

---

261. Matera, *New Testament Christology*, 26.
262. Luz, "Secrecy Motif and Marcan Christology," 75.
263. As I will note below, Matera's appears to be the closest.

## The Turning Point in the Gospel of Mark

Much of my analysis has been dependent upon the so-called narrative flow in chapter 1, which is presented in Appendix 1. In the discussion of this, it was noted that Mark's Gospel is a balanced Gospel. For example, the primary teaching part of the narrative (the so-called parable chapter of Mark 4) occurs approximately one-fourth of the way into the narrative. Similarly, approximately three-fourths of the way into the narrative another key teaching section is presented (the so-called Olivet Discourse).[264]

Three features of my narrative flow play into the author's christology. The first is the primary importance of the central section of the Gospel, especially the turning point of 8:27–9:13. The image that I have used is that of Janus, where Peter's declaration of Jesus as Messiah faces back to the Prologue and affirms the narrator's opening line (1:1) and thus serves as a mid-course conclusion to the Gospel. Second, the divine voice declares Jesus as "the beloved son" in 9:7, which faces the climactic declaration by the centurion in 15:39. The remaining designation of Jesus in the twin pericopae is Jesus' own description of himself in Son of Man language (8:31, 38; 9:9). Thus, in a way, the Janus image affirms the tripartite structure of the Gospel—a face looking backward to the first third (especially the Prologue), a face looking forward to the climactic third (the Passion Narrative), and a face looking inward, that is, at Jesus' self description.

Further examination of this tripartite structure reveals that in each of the three movements, the three designations (Messiah, Son of God, and Son of Man) are present. I have suggested that their presence raises important narrative-critical elements worthy of attention. These elements include (1) convergence; (2) clusters; (3) repetition; and (4) foreshadowing. I will address these narrative elements in more detail. But first I will look at the meaning of Messiah, Son of God, and Son of Man in the Markan narrative.

---

264. Felix Just (in the online resource entitled "New Testament Statistics") observes that there are 11,304 words in the Gospel of Mark (1:1—16:20). By my count, there are 181 words in 16:9-20 in the NA28 (including those the editors chose to include in brackets). Subtracting the 181 from Just's total equates to 11,123 words in the Gospel (1:1—16:8). Taking the total number of words (11,123) and dividing by fifteen chapters (Mark 16:1-8 contains only 135 words) equals an average of 741.53 words per chapter. Using this statistic, the so-called Parable Chapter occurs at the 20 percent mark in the Gospel (a little shy of ¼ of the way through). Similarly, the Olivet Discourse occurs at the 80 percent mark in the Gospel (a little more than ¾ of the way through). These calculations, of course, are not precise and are only meant to substantiate my claim that the two main teaching discourses occur at *approximately* ¼ and ¾ of the way in the Gospel.

## Messiah in Mark's Gospel

The term ὁ χριστός occurs seven times in the Gospel of Mark (1:1; 8:29; 9:41; 12:35; 13:21; 14:61; 15:32). Some interpreters like Donald Juel nevertheless refer to it as the "preeminent title" in the Gospel.[265] While the term's lexical definition, "anointed one," is straightforward, its relationship to the Palestinian notion of Messiah, from which ὁ χριστός is often translated, is less clear.[266]

In the OT, the term and title "Messiah" refers to a political and religious leader appointed by God and was applied primarily to a king or a priest and occasionally to a prophet.[267] Typically, this notion of messiah is coupled with the idea of an eschatological agent sent by God at the end time.[268] As Fitzmyer has observed, one or more of these features were highlighted during the Second Temple period and beyond, yet "one must stress that the expectation of a Jewish Messiah was not one form, for we have seen that the expectation envisaged at times a kingly and a priestly figure, a Messiah of Aaron and a Messiah of Israel, a Messiah of David and a Messiah of Joseph (or Ephraim)."[269] To the Jewish mind, this priest-king would come as a deliverer bringing economic, political, and spiritual peace and prosperity to the nation. The concept of deliverance gave rise to messianism, a slippery term meant to denote the final consummation of history.

NT writers applied this understanding of Messiah to a single individual that had already appeared in human history, Jesus of Nazareth. Jesus' mission, as has been discussed, was to introduce or usher in the kingdom of God, which most believed would include a spiritual kingdom in addition to a political or socioeconomic one. However, it is difficult if not unwise to group all NT writers into a single category when discussing Messiah and messianism. In fact, as Charlesworth has observed, "It is inappropriate to speak of a single normative stream of Judaism in the postexilic period or

---

265. Juel, "Origin of Mark's Christology," 450. The accusative χριστόν is found at 1:34 in a few MSS (B L W Θ $f^1$ 28 33$^{vid}$565 2427) and versions (Latin, Syriac, and Coptic).

266. Fitzmyer, *One Who Is to Come*, viii.

267. Charlesworth, "Preface," in *The Messiah*, xv. See also Fitzmyer, *One Who Is to Come*, 11.

268. Fitzmyer, *One Who Is to Come*, 2.

269. Ibid., 182. Among the Qumran scrolls that speak of two Messiahs, see esp. 1QS 9:10–11 and CD 19:35—20:1. For a helpful discussion on this point, see Collins, *Scepter and the Star*, 74–101.

throughout the period of the Second Temple."[270] With such ambiguity, how should we understand Mark's use of the title as he applied it to Jesus?

Of the seven uses in Mark's Gospel, four are not used in direct reference to Jesus but rather are attributed by Jesus to refer to something else (and in one case by the chief priests).[271] In 9:41, Jesus speaks of the consequences of "bearing the name of Christ" (*RSV*); in 12:35, Jesus taught in Temple by asking the rhetorical question, "How can the scribes say that the Messiah is the son of David?"; in 13:21, in the discourse on the Mount of Olives, Jesus speaks of the Messiah and false messiahs; and in 15:32, the chief priests ridicule the crucified Jesus by proclaiming "let the Messiah, the king of Israel, come down from the cross." The remaining three instances of ὁ χριστός (1:1; 8:29; 14:61) are important for developing Mark's understanding of Jesus as the Messiah.

The contexts of the remaining occurrences of ὁ χριστός have been mentioned and need not be recounted here. There are, however, three points I wish to make regarding the notion of Messiah in these passages. First, it may be remembered that Morna Hooker observed that Son of God and kingdom of God are paired at the beginning (Son of God, 1:1, 11; kingdom of God, 1:15), middle (Son of God, 9:7; kingdom of God, 9:1), and end (Son of God, 15:39; kingdom of God 15:43).[272] It should also be noted that these three references to Messiah (1:1; 8:29; 14:61) occur within a few verses of the kingdom of God (1:15; 9:1; 14:25) as well. I suggest this clustering of christological titles along with the content of Jesus' preaching (i.e., the kingdom of God) provides narrative evidence of Mark's intentional design about the identity of Jesus. Second, as previously noted the confession of Peter ("You are the Messiah") points backward and forward (in a Janus-like manner) affirming the narrative intent of Mark. The Janus motif enables the careful reader to observe something that is telling not only for Mark's presentation of Jesus as Messiah but also for Mark's overall presentation of Jesus. It is only in 14:61 that Jesus affirms this designation.[273] In 1:1 the

---

270. Charlesworth, "Preface," in *The Messiah*, xv.

271. In saying this, I am not saying that these four references do not contribute to Mark's presentation of Jesus. These verses do indeed aid considerably in understanding Mark's presentation of Jesus. However, since at least the latter three speak of Messiah and another christological notion (Son of David; false messiahs; King)—and not the dominating images of Son of God and Son of Man—a detailed discussion of them is unwarranted. On these verses, see the major commentators.

272. Hooker, "Mark's Parables of the Kingdom."

273. Boring, "Christology of Mark," 129.

narrator relates this to the reader. In 8:29 Peter declares Jesus as Messiah. There is a progression as the narrator's views give way to a character in the story, which in turn is confirmed (in the narrative) by Jesus' unequivocal affirmation. In other words, the first mention of ὁ χριστός is declared by someone outside the story (the narrator). The second mention is spoken by someone in the narrative (Peter). The final occurrence occurs on the lips of the subject himself (Jesus).

So what does this mean for Mark's presentation of Jesus? From the perspective of this Janus reading of the narrative, I believe that Mark would respond by stating that the Messiah is Jesus, the Son of God, whose mission was to proclaim to Jew and Gentile alike the coming of God's kingdom. I concur with Matera: "In other words, Mark would define messiahship in terms of Jesus, rather than define Jesus in terms of messiahship. Although Jesus does not fulfill traditional messianic expectations, his life and ministry are the norm for defining what it means to be God's anointed one."[274]

## Son of God in Mark's Gospel

As has already been mentioned, Son of God as a designation for Jesus occurs at least eight times in the Gospel of Mark.[275] Two of these instances (1:11 and 9:7), the divine voice from heaven declares Jesus to be his "beloved son." In two other places (3:11; 5:7) demons identify Jesus as God's son ("Son of God" in 3:11 and "Son of the Most High" in 5:7) and while their declarations hardly could be considered "confessions" in the sense of a confession of one's faith, there is a sense that the narrator is using these designations to alert the reader that those in the spirit world possess a correct understanding of Jesus.[276] In one instance, the phrase ὁ υἱὸς τοῦ εὐλογητοῦ ("Son of the Blessed One," 14:61) is used as a substitute for ὁ υἱός τοῦ θεοῦ. The shortened "the Son" occurs in 13:32 and is present in allegorical fashion ("a beloved son") in 12:6, the so-called parable of the vineyard. The only time a human being confesses Jesus as Son of God occurs in 15:39 in the climatic scene of the Passion Narrative.

Leaving aside the questionable occurrence in the opening line of 1:1 (discussed below), Mark's first use of the Son of God occurs at the baptismal

274. Matera, *New Testament Christology*, 25.

275. The undisputed references are: 1:11; 3:11: 5:7; 9:7; 12:6; and 15:39. Some MSS include it at 1:1 (discussed below).

276. Matera, *New Testament Christology*, 25.

scene in 1:9–11. There, as Jesus is coming up out of the water, a voice from above declares, "You are my beloved Son; with you I am well pleased." As most commentators note, this phrase evokes two passages from the OT (and provides an allusion to a third passage). The first passage in which the divine voice evokes is Ps 2:7, where Yhwh says to the king, "You are my son" (LXX: υἱός μου εἶ σύ). Similarly, the voice echoes Isa 42:1, a passage where Yhwh declares, "Behold my servant, whom I uphold, my chosen, in whom my soul delights."[277] Finally, Mark's addition of the word "beloved" could cause many readers familiar with the Jewish Scriptures to be reminded of Gen 22:2, where Abraham is instructed to take his "beloved Isaac" up the mountain to be sacrificed (λαβὲ τὸν υἱόν σου τὸν ἀγαπητὸν ὃν ἠγάπησας τὸν Ισαάκ). In the Markan story, a dove descends on Jesus, symbolic of the bestowal of the Spirit, which is also present in Isaiah 42 and Genesis 22.

Adela Yarbro Collins has argued that the allusions to Psalm 2 and Isaiah 42, along with the descent of the Spirit, carried messianic connotations at the time Mark was written.[278] Her reasoning for this stems from 1QS 9:10–11 where the Messiah of Israel is likely understood as the eschatological Davidic king whose arrival is predicted in other texts from Qumran, such as the so-called Messianic Apocalypse (4Q521). Based on these OT references and allusions, the notion of Son of God appears to be coupled with Messiah in the mind of Mark.[279]

Before going further in the examination of Son of God in Mark, I must address the opening line of the Gospel and the text-critical issue of the variant readings concerning υἱοῦ θεοῦ. Frequently in scholarly circles the issue has been oversimplified into a choice between two variant readings, those witnesses that include the words "Son of God" and those witnesses that do not. N. Clayton Croy, however, suggests that there are at least nine variants for 1:1. These nine can be catalogued as follows:[280]

---

277. The translation is from the MT. The LXX renders the phrase: Ιακὼβ ὁ παῖς μου, ἀντιλήψομαι αὐτοῦ· Ισραηλ ὁ ἐκλεκτός μου, προσεδέξατο αὐτὸν ἡ ψυχή μου.

278. Collins, "Son of God among Jews," 408.

279. As Matera (*New Testament Christology*, 25) notes: "Jesus is the Messiah because he is the Son of God (*huios tou theou*). While it does not appear that Jesus' contemporaries employed 'Son of God' as a messianic title, it is clearly employed as such in Mark's Gospel."

280. Croy, "Where the Gospel Text Begins," 107–8.

| | Variant | Translation | Witness(es) |
|---|---|---|---|
| 1. | ἀρχὴ τοῦ εὐαγγελίου | "The beginning of the Gospel" | Irenaeus[gr, lat 1/3] Epiphanius |
| 2. | ἀρχὴ τοῦ εὐαγγελίου Ἰησοῦ | "The beginning of the Gospel of Jesus" | MS 28* |
| 3. | ἀρχὴ τοῦ εὐαγγελίου Ἰησοῦ χριστοῦ | "The beginning of the Gospel of Jesus Christ" | ℵ* Θ 28^c cop[sa, ms] arm geo[1] Origen[gr, lat] (several other Fathers) |
| 4. | ἀρχὴ τοῦ εὐαγγελίου Ἰησοῦ χριστοῦ υἱοῦ θεοῦ | "The beginning of the Gospel of Jesus Christ, Son of God" | ℵ[1] B D L W 2427 |
| 5. | ἀρχὴ τοῦ εὐαγγελίου Ἰησοῦ χριστοῦ υἱοῦ τοῦ θεοῦ | "The beginning of the Gospel of Jesus Christ, Son of [the] God" | A Δ f[13] 33 180 205 565 579 597 700 892 1006 1010 1071 1243 1292 1342 1424 1505 *Byz* [E F G[supp] H Σ] *Lect* eth geo[2] slav |
| 6. | ἀρχὴ τοῦ εὐαγγελίου Ἰησοῦ χριστοῦ υἱοῦ τοῦ κυρίου | "The beginning of the Gospel of Jesus Christ, Son of the Lord" | 1241 |
| 7. | *Initium evangelii domini nostri Iesu Christi filii Dei* (which Croy presupposes in Greek was: ἀρχὴ τοῦ εὐαγγέλιου κυρίου ἡμῶν Ἰησοῦ χριστοῦ υἱοῦ θεοῦ) | "The beginning of the Gospel of our Lord Jesus Christ, the Son of God" | Vg[mss] |

|   | **Variant** | **Translation** | **Witness(es)** |
|---|---|---|---|
| 8. | Syriac version which Croy presupposes in Greek was εὐαγγέλιον τοῦ κυρίου Ἰησοῦ χριστοῦ | "The Gospel of the Lord Jesus Christ" | syr^pal |
| 9. | Arabic translation of the *Diatessaron*, which Croy presupposes the Greek was ἀρχὴ τοῦ εὐαγγελίου Ἰησοῦ τοῦ υἱοῦ τοῦ θεοῦ τοῦ ζῶντος | "The beginning of the Gospel of Jesus, the Son of the living God" | Arabic preface to Tatian's *Diatessaron* |

*Table 8*

Numerous commentators note the difficulties associated with this text-critical issue.[281] Many suggest it is simply too hard to chose.[282] Others argue that the context of the remainder of the narrative suggests that Son of God is original. Many resort to the sentiment, "If it was not original, it should have been." Peter M. Head, in an insightful essay published in *New Testament Studies*, opts for the shorter reading (number three above).[283] His reasoning includes the external evidence of the variant MSS and internal evidence of the text. In terms of external evidence, Head notes the three major options commonly cited (numbers 3, 4, and 5 above) and writes, "Since 1:1 is not found in any papyri texts (nor the early Syriac), the place of the Fathers is very important in assessing the early distribution and dating of the readings."[284] Primarily Western witnesses attest to the longer reading,

---

281. See esp. Globe, "Caesarean Omission"; Head, "A Text-Critical Study of Mark 1:1"; and Collins, "Establishing the Text."

282. The majority of commentators opt for inclusion: France, *Gospel of Mark*, 49–51; Donahue and Harrington, *Gospel of Mark*, 60; and Moloney, *Gospel of Mark*, 29 esp. n.11.

283. Head, "A Text-Critical Study of Mark 1:1," 621–29.

284. Ibid., 624.

while earlier and more diverse witnesses from the patristic period support the shorter reading.[285] Thus, though he concludes that the evidence is not totally conclusive, Head suggests that the external evidence points to the shorter reading. From the perspective of internal evidence, Head examines the Markan text from the perspective of Markan style and scribal habits. The presence of the Son of God theme indeed is a significant element in Mark's theology. With respect to scribal habits, many interpreters suggest that one explanation for the shorter reading was scribal confusion in the *nomina sacra*. The most common argument is that a scribe must have confused the similar endings of the last four words (ΙΥΧΥΥΥΘΥ) and omitted the last four letters by *homoioteleuton*. Head argues that this is highly unlikely since one does not "expect errors due to tiredness in the first verse of a work."[286] Thus, Head concludes, "This scenario [the shorter reading] is more plausible than any other, it accounts for the other variants, and fits what we know of scribal habits and the tendency of the gospel traditions."[287] Head's argument on this text-critical issue is persuasive.

But what does this decision have to do with understanding Mark's use of Son of God in the narrative? If the Janus image has been a helpful device for understanding Mark's turning point in the narrative, then perhaps it can aid in our attempt to ascertain the meaning of Son of God in the Markan story. As we have argued, Peter's confession of Jesus as Messiah in 8:29 looks backward to the Prologue (and the opening line of 1:1) and brings the discussion to a mid-course conclusion. Similarly, the divine voice from heaven in 9:7 echoes another voice, which reveals similar information to the reader about Jesus, namely, he is God's beloved Son. In a way, the Janus image works for both Messiah and Son of God; in terms of Son of God, the declaration in 1:11 is privileged information for the narrator's audience (as opposed to the characters in the story as Matera argues). In 9:7, the inner circle of disciples is privy to hearing virtually the same declaration as the audience has heard. From the narrative-critical perspective, the storyteller has emphasized one crucial element in the story, the identity of Jesus as God's beloved Son, and he has done so through an interesting narrative technique.

Yet, the Janus image also looks forward from 9:7. First, at the trial scene in 14:61–62, the High Priest asks Jesus whether he is Son of the Blessed One. Jesus unequivocally responds ἐγώ εἰμι (14:62). Mark's placement of

285. Ibid.
286. Ibid., 629.
287. Ibid.

this "confession" is meant to have Jesus affirm or agree to the same points as the others in the narrative: the narrator (1:11); the demons (3:11; 5:7); God (1:11; 9:7). In addition, it is found within a few words of the other two key christological identification markers in the Gospel, Messiah and Son of Man. All three of these images occur at strategic places in the narrative.

Yet there is one additional place in the narrative where Son of God is mentioned. It occurs in the Passion Narrative, after Jesus' own agreement before the high priest. In 15:39, a Roman soldier, upon seeing the manner of Jesus' death declares, "Truly this man was the Son of God." In the narrative, this is the only time that a human being confesses Jesus as Son of God. In a way, it stands outside the tripartite structure I have mentioned because it is outside the narrative. As Malbon and others have noted, it is only the "minor characters" in the Markan narrative that exhibit the kind of faith that Mark desires his readers to have after reading his story.[288] He has shown that Jesus is God's Son (1:11; 3:11; 5:7; 9:7; 14:61). Now, after Jesus' death (not before), a character in the story (and not one of the disciples) speaks the truth. "Jesus' death, then, paradoxically reveals his divine sonship. Because of Jesus' death, disciples begin to understand that divine sonship exercises its power in weakness. The true Son of God does not save himself but waits for, and trusts in, God to save him."[289] Mentioning weakness leads us to the final significant christological designation, the suffering Son of Man.

## Son of Man in Mark's Gospel

The Son of Man, as a reference to Jesus, occurs fourteen times in the Gospel of Mark (2:10, 28; 8:31, 38; 9:9, 12, 31; 10:33, 45; 13:20; 14:21 [*bis*]; 14:41, 62). As discussed in chapter 4, Mark applies the phrase to Jesus in three ways: (1) in reference to his earthly ministry (2:10, 28; 10:45); (2) to refer to his suffering (8:31; 9:12, 31; 10:33; 14:21 [*bis*], 41); and (3) to speak of his exalted state (8:38; 9:9; 13:26; 14:62).[290] Another way of categorizing these sayings is to consider them as statements concerning (1) Jesus' earthly activity (2:10, 28); (2) the suffering of the Son of Man (8:31; 9:9, 12, 31; 10:33,

---

288. Malbon, *In the Company of Jesus*, 189–225. See also, Williams, *Other Followers of Jesus*.

289. Matera, *New Testament Christology*, 25.

290. Fitzmyer, "'Son of Man' Philologically Considered," 143–60.

45; 14:21 [*bis*], 41); and (3) the future coming of the Son of Man (8:38; 13:26; 14:62).²⁹¹

The background of this phrase is Aramaic and scholars generally look to Dan 7:13–14 for background.²⁹² In Daniel 7, the prophet speaks of his vision, which included the following: "I saw One like a son of man coming, on the clouds of heaven; When he reached the Ancient One and was presented before him, He received dominion, glory, and kingship; nations and peoples of every language serve him. His dominion is an everlasting dominion that shall not be taken away, his kingship shall not be destroyed" (*NAB*). Some scholars are quick to note Mark's reference is not precisely that of Daniel's. Daniel saw "one like a son of man"; Mark uses "the son of man."²⁹³ Ignoring that, however, the verbal connections are otherwise striking.²⁹⁴ As Simon Gathercole writes, "The connections between Daniel 7:13–14 and Mark are therefore fairly conclusive."²⁹⁵

However, not all scholars are so quick to conclude that Daniel 7 is the background without considering the Similitudes of *1 Enoch*. In *1 Enoch* 46:1, the Son of Man figure is described as one "whose face had the appearance of a man." Similarly, in 62:3, the Son of Man is referred to with terms reminiscent of a judge. Some scholars, especially those focusing on Mark's future statements concerning the Son of Man (8:38; 13:26; 14:62) argue against any Danielic background to Mark. The question seems to boil down to whether in Mark the Son of Man sayings speak of judgment or are simply eschatological in another sense.²⁹⁶

As Hooker has observed, the first two Son of Man sayings in Mark's Gospel (2:10, 28) are meant to depict Jesus as acting with authority, the kind of authority that the Danielic Son of Man is given in 7:13 ("He received

---

291. Matera, *Kingship of Jesus*, 100. The literature on Son of Man is vast. In addition to those referred to earlier and in prior chapters, see also Hay, "The Son of Man in Mark 2:10 and 2:28" and Cheroke, "Is Mark 2, 10 a Saying of Jesus?"

292. One dissenting voice on the Danielic background of this phrase is Goulder ("Psalm 8 and the Son of Man") who argues the origin of the title is Psalm 8, not the Aramaic *bar' nash* or the Son of Man conception in Daniel 7.

293. On this, see Casey, "Some Approaches to the Son of Man Problem," 33.

294. On this, see Shepherd, "Daniel 7:13 and the New Testament Son of Man."

295. Gathercole, "Son of Man in Mark's Gospel," 368. Gathercole (p. 371) goes on to say that Daniel 7 is not the sole source of the imagery of Son of Man for Mark. He suggests that Mark gathers additional scriptural evidence from Isaiah 53 and Psalm 110.

296. Collins, *Scepter and the Star*, 177. See also, Matera, *Kingship of Jesus*, 108.

dominion").²⁹⁷ The authority Jesus is given in Mark 2 is twofold: first, he is given the power to forgive sins (2:10); then, he is given the status of being lord over the Sabbath (2:28). Both of these verses (and their narrative contexts) show that this is the present ministry of Jesus on earth. He was given an authority normally reserved for God. Unfortunately, the religious leaders rejected Jesus for claiming this authority.

Paradoxically, as the narrative progresses, it becomes known that Jesus' suffering and death was the "intention of the Son of Man in his mission."²⁹⁸ In other words, the authoritative Son of man instructs his followers that this is his mission and it is only through this mission that God will be glorified.²⁹⁹ The central verse in this line of thinking is 10:45, which speaks of the Son of Man serving rather than being served. When authority is bestowed, one would think that one would be served from that point forward. However, with Mark's portrayal of Jesus, it is the other way around. Jesus' authority is "not a self-serving authority, but a self-effacing authority."³⁰⁰ The irony is that though the disciples have been instructed about this authority and the eventuality of suffering and death, they completely misunderstand it. Mark does not want the reader to follow the same steps as those disciples in the story, so he includes 10:45 as a "correcting measure," a measure that points back to the earlier Son of Man sayings (2:10, 28) and forward to the Passion Narrative, especially the Last Supper.³⁰¹

The final classification of the Son of Man sayings focuses on the future coming of the Son of Man. Again, it is difficult to know whether these future-oriented sayings are meant to connote judgment or something else (or a combination of both). If the background to Mark's use of the Son of Man sayings is Daniel 7, as I believe it is, then Dan 7:14 mentions that the Son of Man receives glory and kingship. But in Daniel this occurs after a period of intense suffering (Dan 7:25–27). So also in Mark, Jesus as the Son of Man endures suffering (leading to death) only to be assured of his vindication by

---

297. Hooker, *Son of Man in Mark*, 81.

298. Gathercole, "Son of Man in Mark," 366.

299. On Jesus' own understanding of the Son of Man, see Moloney ("*Constructing Jesus* and the Son of Man," esp. 737–38).

300. Matera, *Kingship of Jesus*, 102–3.

301. Dowd and Malbon, "Significance of Jesus' Death in Mark," 281n33. Interestingly, Dowd and Malbon see 10:45 in a Janus-like fashion also: "The saying looks both backward and forward in the Markan narrative."

## Converging Lines in Markan Christology

God in the future.[302] The precise time frame of this vindication is unclear in the Gospel. Is it at the resurrection? The *parousia*? Or both?[303]

I have suggested that 9:1 provides a clue into all of this. Rather than forcing a horizon on the narrative—the Transfiguration, crucifixion, resurrection, or *parousia*—Mark presents fulfillment of the promise of 9:1 (and thus of God's vindication of the Son) in a progressive and elastic manner. God, as the ultimate exonerator of Jesus (and therefore of followers), will not allow him to taste (γεύσωται) death until the Kingdom of God comes in (eschatological) power. Regardless of when this might take place, the fact is that vindication will occur. The emphasis is that Mark presented Jesus as the Danielic Son of Man and the entire narrative points to this. Gathercole summarizes this point nicely: "The narrative pattern which holds the Son of Man sayings together is: *the authoritative Son of Man revealed – the authority of the Son of Man rejected – the authority of the Son of Man vindicated*. Each of these elements, as we have seen, is derived primarily, though not exclusively, from Daniel 7."[304]

We have observed that Mark's use of Son of Man is different that that of Messiah or Son of God in that it is the only "title" in the Gospel that is not confessional. No character is the story exclaims, "You are the Son of Man." Some might argue that it should not be placed on the same level of importance as the other confessional titles. I disagree. Mark's purpose in writing this Gospel has been to present his understanding of Jesus. We have called this the identity question. An element of identity includes his role in the future, that is, his destiny. Jesus' destiny involves vindication by God, the gathering the elect of heaven in power and glory, and a never-ending rule of God's kingdom.

---

302. Kingsbury ("The Christology of Mark and the Son of Man," 69): "Jesus refers to himself as 'the Son of Man' not to attribute to himself a messianic title of majesty, but solemnly and forcefully to claim for himself vindication in fulfillment of Old Testament prophecy."

303. For a view of the resurrection as the time frame, see France, *Jesus and the Old Testament*, 139–48; France, *Gospel of Mark*, 341–43, 530–37; and Wright, *Jesus and the Victory of God*, 341, 360–67. For those who see it at the *parousia*, see esp. Marshall, "The Parousia in the New Testament"; and Adams, "Coming of the Son of Man in Mark's Gospel."

304. Gathercole, "Son of Man in Mark," 372; emphasis in original.

## Convergence, Clusters, Repetition, and Foreshadowing in Mark's Gospel

There are three key elements or textual clues of the Markan narrative that cause one to see the importance of the twin pericopae of 8:27–9:13 in isolating Mark's presentation of Jesus: convergence and/or clusters of key themes or titles, repetition, and foreshadowing.

### *Convergence*

In an essay on the christology of Luke-Acts, Luke Timothy Johnson argues that the character of Jesus is constructed by the Gospel's author by means of textual clues in the narrative itself. These textual clues include what a character says about himself, what others in the narrative say about that character, and what the narrator says about the character. "The more rounded and complex a character within a narrative, the more difficult it is to reduce its presentation to a simple formula." In complex character presentations, such as Mark's depiction of Jesus, the "more different kinds of evidence from different kinds of discourse and from different angles of vision converge, the more likely it is that a characterization is worth considering." Mark's repeated presentation of Jesus as Messiah, Son of God, and Son of Man meets this test of convergence.[305]

### *Clusters*

In a separate article on the theology of the canonical Gospels, Johnson offers an intriguing suggestion regarding the study of the NT texts namely, the clustering of compositions for analytical purposes.[306] For Johnson, as long as clusters of canonical compositions are temporary, tentative, and heuristic, employing them enables a conversation to occur and this conversation can offer readers a way to appreciate what texts have in common and how they differ.[307] In developing this clustering notion, Johnson is applying the idea to compositions as a whole. I believe there is similar value in taking a similar approach within a narrative, namely, looking for clusters of

---

305. Johnson, "Christology of Luke-Acts," 54.
306. Johnson, "Does a Theology of the Canonical Gospels Make Sense?"
307. Ibid., 96.

topics, themes, and/or ideas from within a single composition to apply to common features and dissimilar features.

## *Repetition*

Janice Capel Anderson suggests that the Gospel of Matthew is "a complex narrative web spun with numerous verbal repetitions. . . . It contains key words and phrases which readers must interpret to weave their own webs of meaning."[308] Such repetitions occur not only in the Gospel of Matthew, but in the Gospel of Mark as well. As noted, the repetition of key christological titles in strategic places in the narrative further suggests that these titles present the key to understanding Mark's christology.

## *Foreshadowing*

Charles H. Lohr, in discussing Matthew's narrative, argues that authors or presenters "had to prepare the hearer for what was to come in order to unify the composition."[309] Foreshadowing is one such preparation. From the perspective of the Markan narrative, I will argue that Mark's use of the three christological titles contained progressive foreshadowing techniques that enabled the readers to grasp Mark's true intentions.

## CONCLUSION

In this chapter, I set out to do three things: to survey Markan Christology since 1900; to examine the key notions of Jesus as Messiah, Son of God, and Son of Man, and to present the reasons why I see these three images converging in the Gospel. My survey of Markan scholarship indicated that most interpreters choose one dominant christological image to the exclusion of others. This is true whether one is working from within a historical-critical perspective or a narrative-critical one. Second, the meaning of Mark's key christological images is a bit clearer when one understands that Mark is attempting to hold all three in tension, hoping that readers will see Jesus as the long-awaited Messiah, the royal Son of God, whose destiny is to fulfill the role of the Danielic Son of Man. In some ways, each image connects to

---

308. Anderson, *Matthew's Narrative Web*, 11.
309. Lohr, "Oral Techniques in the Gospel of Matthew," 411–12.

and with Jesus' preaching of the coming kingdom of God. Finally, Messiah, Son of God, and Son of Man are the dominant christological themes in the Gospel because they converge at critical places in the narrative. Mark has highlighted this convergence using a number of narrative techniques aimed at helping the reader see his true intentions. In the concluding chapter, I will set forth the reasons for this convergence.

# 6
# Conclusion

IN THE PRECEDING CHAPTERS, I have made it clear that I believe the turning point of the Gospel is found in not one but two pericopae in Mark's central section, Peter's confession (8:27—9:1) and the Transfiguration (9:2-13). I have employed the notion of Janus as a heuristic device to attempt to get at Mark's true purpose in writing. The Janus image helps readers see the backward and forward nature of 8:27—9:13. This feature enables readers to grasp that Mark wanted his readers to understand Jesus as the anointed one of God, who through his vindication as Son of God would fulfill the destiny of the (suffering) Son of Man. I have argued that structurally the three images of Messiah, Son of God, and Son of Man converge at the beginning, middle, and end of the narrative and that this placement enables readers to see Mark's true intention in writing. What I have not done is set forth the reasons for this convergence. I wish to do so now by articulating four theses.

## THESIS 1

*Mark's images of Messiah, Son of God, and Son of Man are the key christological terms in the Gospel because the cluster of these three images converge at strategic places in the narrative (in Aristotelian terms: the complication phase (1:1—8:26); the turning point (περιπέτεια; 8:27—9:13); and the final phase (14:1—16:8).*

Mark's presentation, as I have described, could be viewed as follows:

## The Turning Point in the Gospel of Mark

Beginning, Prologue and Beyond
- Christ/Messiah (1:1)
- Son of God (1:11)[1]
- Son of Man (2:10, 28)

Middle, the Turning Point
- Messiah (8:29)
- Son of God (9:7)
- Son of Man (8:31, 38; 9:9, 12)

End, the Passion Narrative
- Messiah (14:61–62)
- Son of God (or of the Blessed One, 14:61–61; 15:39)
- Son of Man (14:62)

There are several narrative features worthy of attention here. The first is clustering. As noted in chapter 5, clustering involves the grouping together of key ideas in order to highlight their importance. In Mark's case, he has grouped the terms Messiah, Son of God, and Son of Man together at strategic places in the narrative to aid readers in grasping the particular picture of Jesus he wishes to portray. The second narrative feature is convergence. As Johnson has suggested, the more an analysis depends on the convergence of evidence, the more adequate the presentation will be. In the Markan narrative, the christological images converge three separate times. Would a serious reader (or listener) to the narrative not begin to think, "I have heard this before?" Lastly, Mark employs a technique that I believe makes this convergence unmistakable, especially to the reader of the narrative (as opposed to listener). This feature involves the gradual narrowing of the convergence of christological images between pericopae.[2]

In the first third of the narrative, Mark presents Jesus as Messiah in 1:1, Son of God in 1:11, and Son of Man in 2:10, 28. The first two images occur within a single pericope, the Prologue (1:1–13). But the Son of Man image

---

1. As mentioned in chapter 5 (Table 8), some MSS include the phrase υἱοῦ θεοῦ at 1:1.

2. One phrase used by Matera (*New Testament Christology*, 10) when discussing the first half of the Gospel suggests this: "As each stage unfolds, the Markan narrator builds up the character of Jesus, episode by episode, so that by the end of the narrative readers arrive at the whole truth about Jesus' identity."

*Conclusion*

occurs several pericopae later (nine paragraphs separate 1:11 and 2:10 in NA²⁷). However, in the so-called middle section, the three images are present in adjacent pericopae (i.e., the twin pericopae of Peter's confession and the Transfiguration).³ In the Passion Narrative, the three images occur in a single dialogue, (14:61–62) with the Centurion's confession (15:39) serving as the climactic moment in the crucifixion scene.

Before moving to the second thesis, another attendant factor needs mentioning. Many of the other scholars who have observed the significance of Messiah, Son of God, and Son of Man usually choose one as the dominant theme or image. For example, Kingsbury noted many of the same things we have noted here regarding Messiah and Son of God (he did not hold Son of Man as high as the other two), but he eventually argued that royal Son of God was the overarching title in the Gospel.⁴ Similarly, Marshall stresses the importance of Messiah, Son of God, and Son of Man but appears to opt for Son of Man because it best presents Jesus as "the messiah who must suffer."⁵ The same sort of thing could be said of most of the others that were surveyed in the first part of chapter 5. The point is this: when the convergence issue is taken seriously, readers are in a better position to hold all three christological titles in tension. No one title assumes priority over the other. Mark, in my opinion, wanted to readers to see Jesus as all three (Messiah, Son of God, Son of Man), not one to the exclusion (or reduction) of the other.⁶

## THESIS 2

*The convergence of christological titles occurs near references to the kingdom of God. Narratively speaking, this assists in connecting the identity of Jesus with the message he preached.*

This was already seen previously in our discussions of Hooker's work on the parables (chapter 2 as we discussed possible turning points) and Marshall's

---

3. There is only one paragraph (the single verse paragraph of 9:1) in the twin pericopae that does not contain one of these images.

4. Kingsbury, *Christology of Mark's Gospel*, 173. For his recent thoughts on the Son of Man in Mark, see "The Christology of Mark and the Son of Man."

5. Marshall, *New Testament Theology*, 86.

6. The scholar who exemplifies this best, in my opinion, is Matera (*New Testament Christology*, 24–26).

work on the theological story of Mark (chapter 5). Hooker argued that Jesus' kingship and his relationship to God as beloved Son are linked in the Gospel. Her reasoning for this is that references to the kingdom of God occur at three key places in the narrative, the beginning (1:15), middle (9:1), and end (14:25) (her descriptions).[7] These three kingdom references occur in close proximity to disclosures of Jesus being the Son of God (1:11; 9:7; 15:39—and we could add 14:61). Marshall observed a similar connection ("the Messiah and the kingdom are correlative") but settled for emphasizing the messenger over the message.[8]

The phenomenon that Hooker observed dealt with the connection of the Son of God references and the kingdom of God. But it can be argued that all three christological images (Messiah, Son of God, and Son of Man) are present at or near references to the kingdom. The following outlines this:

|  | **Beginning** | **Middle** | **End** |
|---|---|---|---|
| **Christology** | 1:1 Messiah | 8:29 Messiah | 14:61 Messiah |
|  | 1:11 Son of God | 9:7 Son of God | 14:61 Son of God |
|  |  | 8:31, 38; |  |
|  | 2:10, 28 Son of Man | 9:10, 12 Son of Man | 14:62 Son of Man |
| **Kingdom of God** | 1:15 | 9:1 | 14:25 |

*Table 9*

---

7. Hooker, "Mark's Parables of the Kingdom," 82.
8. Marshall, *New Testament Theology*, 81.

*Conclusion*

Because of the issues discussed above, especially those related to the coming of the Son of Man, matters of the kingdom are applicable to all three christological notions not simply Son of God.

## THESIS 3

*The so-called Janus effect is seen in multiple ways regarding the christology of Mark's Gospel.*

In previous chapters, I argued that the Roman deity Janus could be used as a heuristic device to enable readers to see Mark's true intention, the identity of Jesus and the reality of that identity for followers. The Janus image suggested that Peter's confession faced backward to the Prologue (specifically 1:1) and affirmed Jesus as Messiah. Similarly, the divine voice of 9:7 faced forward to the Passion Narrative and foreshadowed the centurion's confession in 15:39. In the middle of Peter's voice and the Divine voice stands Jesus' self-declarations as Son of Man.

This heuristic device, however, can be applied to each of the christological titles as well. Using the twin pericopae as the turning point and employing the narrative techniques discussed in chapter 5 (clustering, convergence, foreshadowing, retrospection), each of the three key christological titles point backward and forward in the narrative. The image of Messiah, as has already been noted, points back to the opening line of the Gospel (1:1), but it also points forward to the trial scene (14:61–62). Likewise, Son of God, which I argued points forward in the narrative to the culminating confession in 15:39, also points backward to the baptism and the divine voice's declaration ("You are my beloved son; with you I am well pleased"). Son of Man, the most difficult of the christological declarations, does the same. If we employ the analysis of Son of Man mentioned above (especially with the notions of authority and future glory), then the four references to Son of Man in the twin pericopae function in similar manner. Jesus' statement in 8:31 reminds the reader of his authority as Son of Man and points backward to 2:10, 28. The Son of Man references in 8:38, 9:9, 12 speak of the future glory of the Son of Man and thus point forward to 14:62, which contains another "future-oriented" saying about the Son of Man. In short, the Janus image as a heuristic device can be employed in a macro manner or in micro ways. This micro function can be visualized in this manner:

The Turning Point in the Gospel of Mark

| **Beginning** | **Twin Pericopae** | **Ending** |
|---|---|---|
| Messiah (1:1) | ◀ Messiah (8:29) ▶ | Messiah (14:61–62) |
| Son of God (1:11) | ◀ Son of God (9:7) ▶ | Son of God (14:61; 15:39) |
| Son of Man (2:10, 28) | Son of Man &#124; 8:38 ▶ <br> ◀ 8:31 &#124; 9:9, 12 ▶ | Son of Man (14:62) |

*Table 10*

## THESIS 4

*Though Jesus' identity may be known through Mark's narrative (employing these narrative devices), there remains something elusive about Jesus, the kingdom, and God.*

Matera observes that simplicity of Mark's story does not negate the fact that its christology is elusive.[9] Similarly, Moloney has called Mark's narrative a "subversive narrative."[10] Black suggests that Mark's story of Jesus is a story that begs the reader to explore the God who "outruns everyone in Mark."[11] One reason for this elusive nature of Jesus (and the gospel message itself) is due to the ambiguity in the opening line: ἀρχὴ τοῦ εὐαγγελίου Ἰησοῦ Χριστοῦ [υἱοῦ θεοῦ] (the beginning of the gospel of Jesus Christ [Son of God]). What beginning? The beginning of Jesus' life? The beginning of

---

9. Matera, *New Testament Christology*, 6.

10. Moloney, *Gospel of Mark*, 16. Moloney's quote is: "Whatever the first readers knew of the life-story of Jesus of Nazareth was subverted by the Markan story. They were not familiar with this plot: Jesus' presence in Galilee, his single journey to Jerusalem to be rejected, tried, and crucified, the resurrection, and the surprising silence of the women."

11. Black, "The Face Is Familiar," 45.

*Conclusion*

Mark's story? What does "the beginning" mean? Similarly, what gospel? Is it the gospel preached by Jesus (the genitive being translated as a subjective)? Or does the phrase mean the gospel about Jesus, that is, the gospel concerning Jesus (the genitive being translated as an object). Is it possible that Mark intended both? I am persuaded that Mark the storyteller has left this element unresolved in his narrative. Mark's story is the beginning of the "good news" message of Jesus. He knew the message would continue (and was continuing indeed as he wrote). Likewise, he knew the story of this Messiah, Son of God, whose destiny is that of the Son of Man, had to begin somewhere. So he began it with references to the OT. And what about the genitive phrase? Could Mark be thinking both—the gospel about Jesus was Jesus' message? Given what I have written about the connections between kingdom language and christology in the narrative, one would think the answer to such a question would be yes. Try as we may, arriving at conclusive answers to questions concerning Jesus, God, and the kingdom in Mark remain beyond our grasp as readers. Perhaps this is because God is beyond our grasp. Has not the Markan narrative shown that "the way" of a disciple includes faith? There are some things that a reader of the Gospel of Mark must take on faith and that would include the very nature of the Gospel's subject matter.

Mark set out to answer the question "Who then is this?" (4:41). His answer is that he God's anointed son whose future role will be that of Son of Man, who must first suffer but will then usher in the kingdom in power. Mark's subordinate purpose—what does this mean for a disciple—is that one should after calculating the cost, have faith and follow Jesus. Does Mark intend that disciples will understand everything about the One behind whom they follow? No, in some ways his presence (and his identity) remains forever elusive.

## The Turning Point in the Gospel of Mark

Perhaps I should give Black the last word:[12]

> For when we speak of Mark's Jesus—his baptism, transfiguration, death and resurrection; his gospel of the kingdom and way of discipleship; all of the religious and cultural definitions exploded by the Messiah's apocalypse—are we not probing, at bottom, a particular theology of divine presence and its 'mysterious revelation"? Are we not invited by this evangelist to reconsider where God is truly found and, in the process of that search, to discover what the true God looks like—the One whose power is revealed in power's renunciation, whose glory is cloaked in suffering self-abnegation? . . . [T]heology is not an inquiry that pursues the divine as an object, but rather, a clarification and communication of the inherently mysterious operation by which God pursues and transforms humanity into the *imago Dei*. Writ large across Scripture, exemplified by the Second Gospel, that divine pursuit is utterly free, uncontrollably gracious, ever present yet forever elusive.

---

12. Ibid., 45–46.

# Appendix 1
## The Narrative Flow of the Gospel of Mark

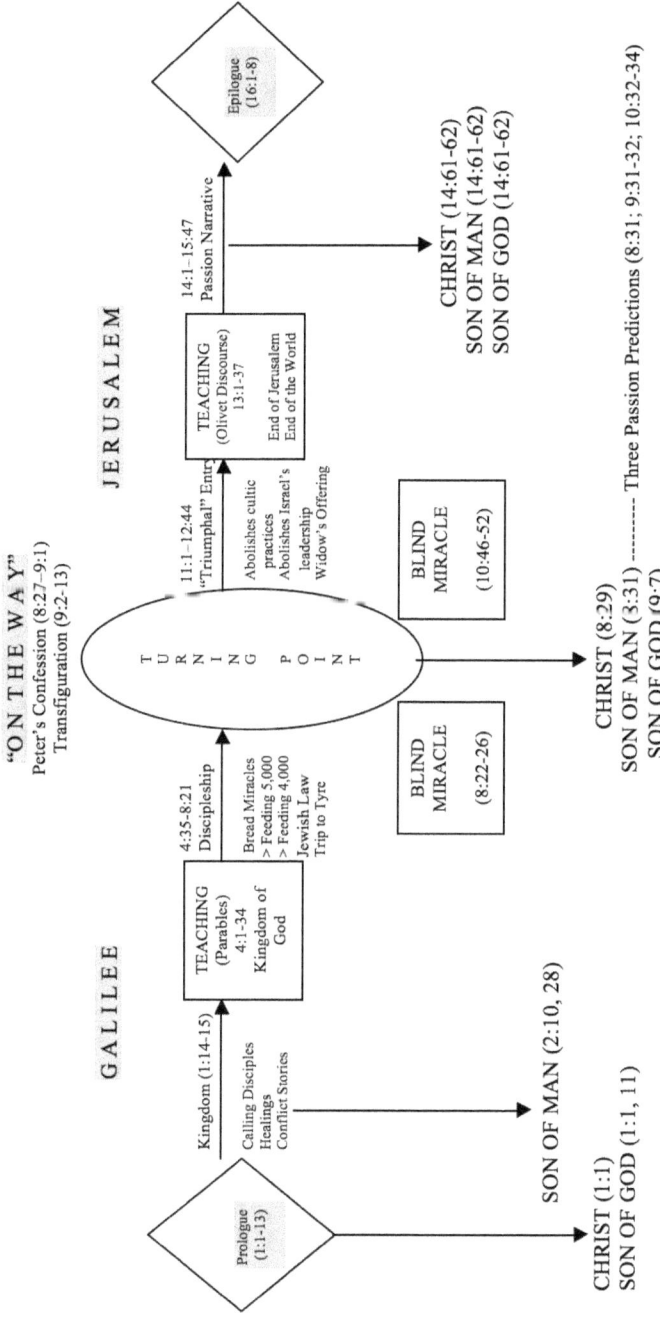

237

# Appendix 2

Summary of Major Commentators and Mark's "Turning Point"[1]

| Commentator (with Series noted where applicable) | 8:21 | 8:26 | 8:30 | Other |
|---|---|---|---|---|
| A. Kuby | × | | | |
| F. G. Lang | × | | | |
| E. LaVerdiere | × | | | |
| J. Marcus (AB) | × | | | |
| C. Myers | × | | | |
| D. Senior & C. Stuhlmueller | × | | | |
| L. Williamson (Interpretation) | × | | | |
| E. Bickerman | | × | | |
| R. Bultmann | | × | | |
| C. E. B. Cranfield (GCTC) | | × | | |
| A. Y. Collins (Hermeneia) | | × | | |

1. The verse demarcations indicate where the commentators believe a major section to *end*. For the majority of commentators, the "watershed" event of Peter's confession (8:29) occurs after the major break of 8:26. A few see Peter's confession as a turning point, but choose to divide the material somewhere other than 8:26.

*Appendix 2*

| **Commentator** *(with Series noted where applicable)* | 8:21 | 8:26 | 8:30 | Other |
|---|---|---|---|---|
| J. G. Cook (SBL Semeia Studies) | | × | | |
| J. R. Donahue & D. J. Harrington (SP) | | × | | |
| J. R. Edwards (PNTC) | | × | | |
| C. A. Evans (WBC) | | × | | |
| C. Focant | | × | | |
| R. T. France (NICGT) | | × | | |
| R. Fowler | | × | | |
| R. A. Guelich (WBC) | | × | | |
| D. R. A. Hare (Westminster Bible Companion) | | × | | |
| M. D. Hooker (BNTC) (also, "Mark's Parables of the Kingdom") | | × | | 9:1/9:7 (??) |
| M. Horstmann | | × | | |
| S. E. Johnson (HNTC) | | × | | |
| J. D. Kingsbury | | × | | |
| E. Klostermann (HNT 3) | | × | | |
| E. Lohmeyer (MeyerK 2) | | × | | |
| D. Lührmann (HNT 3) | | × | | |
| C. S. Mann (AB) | | × | | |
| D. Nineham (Pelican) | | × | | |

*Appendix 2*

| Commentator *(with Series noted where applicable)* | 8:21 | 8:26 | 8:30 | Other |
|---|---|---|---|---|
| N. Perrin/D. Duling | | × | | |
| R. Pesch (HTKNT) | | × | | |
| V. Robbins | | × | | |
| K. L. Schmidt | | × | | |
| E. Schweizer | | × | | |
| A. Stock | | × | | |
| H. B. Swete | | × | | |
| V. Taylor | | × | | |
| B. van Iersel | | × | | |
| P. Vielhauer | | × | | |
| B. Witherington | | × | | |
| A. Culpepper (Smyth & Helwys Bible Commentary) | | | × | |
| S. Dowd (Reading the New Testament) | | | × | |
| L. Hurtado (NIBC) | | | × | |
| F. J. Moloney | | | × | |
| R. H. Gundry | | | | Nowhere |
| J. Painter (NT Readings) | | | × | 8:11—10:52 |

241

# Appendix 3

## Mark 8:27-38

---

27 **Καὶ** ἐξῆλθεν ὁ Ἰησοῦς καὶ οἱ μαθηταὶ Αὐτοῦ εἰς τὰς κώμας Καισαρείας τῆς Φιλίππου· καὶ ἐν τῇ ὁδῷ ἐπηρώτα τοὺς μαθητὰς αὐτοῦ λέγων αὐτοῖς· τίνα με λέγουσιν οἱ ἄνθρωποι εἶναι;

28 οἱ δὲ εἶπαν αὐτῷ λέγοντες [ὅτι] Ἰωάννην τὸν βαπτιστήν, καὶ ἄλλοι Ἠλίαν, ἄλλοι δὲ ὅτι εἷς τῶν προφητῶν.

29 καὶ αὐτὸς ἐπηρώτα αὐτούς· ὑμεῖς δὲ τίνα με λέγετε εἶναι; ἀποκριθεὶς ὁ Πέτρος λέγει αὐτῷ· **σὺ εἶ ὁ χριστός**.

30 καὶ ἐπετίμησεν αὐτοῖς ἵνα μηδενὶ Λέγωσιν περὶ αὐτοῦ.

31 **Καὶ** ἤρξατο διδάσκειν αὐτοὺς ὅτι δεῖ τὸν υἱὸν τοῦ ἀνθρώπου πολλὰ Παθεῖν καὶ ἀποδοκιμασθῆναι ὑπὸ Τῶν πρεσβυτέρων καὶ τῶν ἀρχιερέων καὶ τῶν γραμματέων καὶ ἀποκτανθῆναι καὶ μετὰ τρεῖς ἡμέρας ἀναστῆναι·

32 καὶ παρρησίᾳ τὸν λόγον ἐλάλει. καὶ προσλαβόμενος ὁ Πέτρος αὐτὸν ἤρξατο ἐπιτιμᾶν αὐτῷ.

33 ὁ δὲ ἐπιστραφεὶς καὶ ἰδὼν τοὺς μαθητὰς αὐτοῦ ἐπετίμησεν Πέτρῳ καὶ λέγει· ὕπαγε ὀπίσω μου, σατανᾶ, ὅτι οὐ φρονεῖς τὰ τοῦ θεοῦ ἀλλὰ Τὰ τῶν ἀνθρώπων.

34 **Καὶ** προσκαλεσάμενος τὸν ὄχλον σὺν τοῖς μαθηταῖς αὐτοῦ εἶπεν αὐτοῖς· εἴ τις θέλει ὀπίσω μου ἀκολουθεῖν, ἀπαρνησάσθω ἑαυτὸν καὶ ἀράτω τὸν σταυρὸν αὐτοῦ καὶ ἀκολουθείτω μοι.

35 ὃς γὰρ ἐὰν θέλῃ τὴν ψυχὴν αὐτοῦ σῶσαι ἀπολέσει αὐτήν· ὃς δ' ἂν ἀπολέσει τὴν ψυχὴν αὐτοῦ ἕνεκεν ἐμοῦ καὶ τοῦ εὐαγγελίου σώσει αὐτήν.

36 τί γὰρ ὠφελεῖ ἄνθρωπον κερδῆσαι τὸν κόσμον ὅλον καὶ ζημιωθῆναι τὴν ψυχὴν αὐτοῦ;

37 τί γὰρ δοῖ ἄνθρωπος ἀντάλλαγμα τῆς ψυχῆς αὐτοῦ;

38 ὃς γὰρ ἐὰν ἐπαισχυνθῇ με καὶ τοὺς ἐμοὺς λόγους ἐν τῇ γενεᾷ ταύτῃ τῇ μοιχαλίδι καὶ ἁμαρτωλῷ, καὶ ὁ υἱὸς τοῦ ἀνθρώπου ἐπαισχυνθήσεται αὐτόν, ὅταν ἔλθῃ ἐν τῇ δόξῃ τοῦ πατρὸς αὐτοῦ μετὰ τῶν ἀγγέλων τῶν ἁγίων.

*Appendix 3*

## Mark 9:1

9:1 Καὶ ἔλεγεν αὐτοῖς· ἀμὴν λέγω ὑμῖν ὅτι εἰσίν τινες ὧδε τῶν ἑστηκότων οἵτινες οὐ μὴ γεύσωνται θανάτου ἕως α‡ν ἴδωσιν τὴν βασιλείαν τοῦ θεοῦ ἐληλυθυῖαν ἐν δυνάμει.

## Mark 9:2-13

9:2 Καὶ μετὰ Ἡμέρας ἓξ παραλαμβάνει ὁ 'ιησοῦς τὸν Πέτρον καὶ τὸν 'ιάκωβον καὶ τὸν 'ιωάννην καὶ ἀναφέρει αὐτοὺς εἰς ὄρος ὑψηλὸν κατ' ἰδίαν μόνους. καὶ μετεμορφώθη ἔμπροσθεν αὐτῶν,

3 καὶ τὰ ἱμάτια αὐτοῦ ἐγένετο στίλβοντα λευκὰ Λίαν, οἷα γναφεὺς ἐπὶ τῆς γῆς οὐ δύναται οὕτως λευκᾶναι.

4 καὶ ὤφθη αὐτοῖς 'ηλίας σὺν Μωϋσεῖ καὶ ἦσαν συλλαλοῦντες τῷ 'ιησοῦ.

5 καὶ ἀποκριθεὶς ὁ Πέτρος λέγει τῷ 'ιησοῦ· ῥαββί, καλόν ἐστιν ἡμᾶς ὧδε εἶναι, καὶ ποιήσωμεν τρεῖς σκηνάς, σοὶ Μίαν καὶ Μωϋσεῖ μίαν καὶ 'ηλίᾳ μίαν.

6 οὐ γὰρ ᾔδει τί ἀποκριθῇ, ἔκφοβοι γὰρ ἐγένοντο.

7 καὶ ἐγένετο νεφέλη ἐπισκιάζουσα αὐτοῖς, καὶ ἐγένετο φωνὴ Ἐκ τῆς νεφέλης· **οὗτός ἐστιν ὁ υἱός μου ὁ ἀγαπητός**, ἀκούετε αὐτοῦ.

8 καὶ ἐξάπινα περιβλεψάμενοι οὐκέτι οὐδένα εἶδον ἀλλὰ Τὸν 'ιησοῦν μόνον μεθ' ἑαυτῶν.

9 Καὶ καταβαινόντων αὐτῶν ἐκ τοῦ ὄρους διεστείλατο αὐτοῖς ἵνα μηδενὶ Ἃ εἶδον διηγήσωνται, εἰ μὴ Ὅταν ὁ υἱὸς τοῦ ἀνθρώπου ἐκ νεκρῶν ἀναστῇ.

10 καὶ τὸν λόγον ἐκράτησαν πρὸς ἑαυτοὺς συζητοῦντες τί ἐστιν τὸ ἐκ νεκρῶν ἀναστῆναι.

11 Καὶ ἐπηρώτων αὐτὸν λέγοντες· ὅτι λέγουσιν οἱ γραμματεῖς ὅτι 'ηλίαν δεῖ ἐλθεῖν πρῶαπ

12 ὁ δὲ ἔφη αὐτοῖς· 'ηλίας μὲν ἐλθὼν πρῶτον ἀποκαθιστάνει πάντα· καὶ πῶς γέγραπται ἐπὶ τὸν υἱὸν τοῦ ἀνθρώπου ἵαπ ολλὰ Πάθῃ καὶ ἐξουδενηθῇ;

13 ἀλλὰ Λέγω ὑμῖν ὅτι καὶ 'ηλίας ἐλήλυθεν, καὶ ἐποίησαν αὐτῷ ὅσα ἤθελον, καθὼς γέγραπται ἐπ' αὐτόν.

# Bibliography

Abrams, Meyer Howard. "Plot." In *A Glossary of Literary Terms*, 159. 6th ed. Fort Worth: Harcourt Brace Jovanovich, 1993.
Abrahams, Israel. "After Six Days." *HTR* 8 (1915) 94–121.
Achtemeier, Paul J. "'And He Followed Him' Miracles and Discipleship in Mark 10:46–52." *SBLSS* 11 (1978) 115–45.
———. "'He Taught Them Many Things': Reflections on Marcan Christology." *CBQ* 42 (1980) 465–81.
———. *Mark*. Proclamation Commentaries: The New Testament Witnesses for Preaching. Philadelphia: Fortress, 1975.
———. "Toward the Isolation of Pre-Markan Miracle Catenae." *JBL* 89 (1970) 265–91.
Adams, Edward. "The Coming Son of Man in Mark's Gospel." *TynBul* 56 (2005) 39–61.
Agua, Agustín, del. "The Narrative of the Transfiguration as a Derashic Scenification of a Faith Confession (Mark 9.2–8 Par)." *NTS* 39 (1993) 340–54.
Aland, Kurt. *Synopsis Quattuor Evangeliorum: Locis Parallelis Evangeliorum Apocryphorum et Patrum Adhibitis Edidit*. 15th ed. Stuttgart: Deutsche Bibelgesellschaft, 1996.
Ambrozic, Aloysius M. *The Hidden Kingdom: A Redaction-Critical Study of the References to the Kingdom of God in Mark's Gospel*. CBQMS 2. Washington, DC: Catholic Biblical Association, 1972.
Anderson, Janice Capel. *Matthew's Narrative Web: Over, and Over, and Over Again*. JSNTSup 91. Sheffield: JSOT Press, 1994.
Anderson, Janice Capel, and Stephen D. Moore. *Mark & Method: New Approaches in Biblical Studies*. Minneapolis: Fortress, 1992.
Arav, Rami, and Richard A. Freund. *Bethsaida: A City by the North Shore of the Seas of Galilee*. Kirksville: Thomas Jefferson University Press, 1995.
Aristotle. *The "Art" of Rhetoric*. Translated by John Henry Freese. LCL 22. Cambridge, MA: Harvard University Press, 1926.
Auer, Johann. "Die Bedeutung der Verklärung Christi für das Leben des Christen und für die Kirche Christi." In *Mysterien des Lebens Jesu und die christliche Existenz*, 146–76. Aschaffenburg: Pattloch, 1994.
Aune, David E. "The Problem of the Messianic Secret." *NovT* 11 (1969) 1–31.
Baarlink, Heinrich. *Anfängliches Evangelium: Ein Beitrag zur näheren Bestimmung der theologischen Motive im Markusevangelium*. Kampen: Kok, 1977.
Bacon, Benjamin W. *The Beginnings of Gospel Story: A Historico-Critical Inquiry into the Sources and Structure of the Gospel according to Mark with Expository Notes upon the Text, for English Readers*. Modern Commentary. New Haven: Yale University Press, 1909.
Baldinger, Kurt. *Semantic Theory: Towards a Modern Semantics*. Oxford: Blackwell, 1980.

# Bibliography

Barton, Stephen C. "The Transfiguration of Christ according to Mark and Matthew: Christology and Anthropology." In *Auferstehung—Resurrection: The Fourth Durham-Tübingen Research Symposium "Resurrection, Transfiguration, and Exaltation in Old Testament, Ancient Judaism, and Early Christianity (Tübingen, September 1999)*, edited by Friedrich Avemarie and Hermann Lichtenberger, 231–46. WUNT 135. Tübingen: Mohr/Siebeck, 2001.

Basser, Herbert W. "The Jewish Roots of the Transfiguration." *Bible Review* 14 (1998) 30–35.

Bauckham, Richard. "For Whom Were the Gospels Written?" In *The Gospels for All Christians: Rethinking Gospel Audiences*, edited by Richard Bauckham, 9–48. Grand Rapids: Eerdmans, 1998.

Beare, F. W. *The Earliest Records of Jesus*. New York: Abingdon, 1962.

Beasley-Murray, George R. *Jesus and the Kingdom of God*. Grand Rapids: Eerdmans, 1986.

Beavis, Mary Ann. *Mark's Audience: The Literary and Social Setting of Mark 4.11–12*. JSNTSup 33. Sheffield: JSOT Press, 1989.

Beck, Norman A. "Reclaiming a Biblical Text: The Mark 8:14–21 Discussion about Bread in the Boat." *CBQ* 43 (1981) 49–56.

Becker, Matthew L. "Schweitzer's Quest for Jesus and Paul." *Concordia Journal* 28 (2002) 409–30.

Beiler, Ludwig. *Theios Anēr: Das Bild des "Göttlichen Menschen" in Spätantike und Früchristentum*. 2 vols. Vienna: Höfels, 1935–1936.

Beker, J. Christiaan. *Paul the Apostle: The Triumph of God in Life and Thought*. Philadelphia: Fortress, 1980.

Berlin, Adele. *Poetics and Interpretation of Biblical Narrative*. Bible and Literature. Sheffield: Almond, 1983.

Best, Ernest. *Disciples and Discipleship: Studies in the Gospel according to Mark*. Edinburgh: T. & T. Clark, 1986.

———. *Following Jesus: Discipleship in the Gospel of Mark*. JSNTSup 4. Sheffield: JSOT Press, 1981.

———. *Mark: The Gospel as Story*. Edinburgh: T. & T. Clark, 1983.

———. "Peter in the Gospel according to Mark." *CBQ* 40 (1978) 547–58.

Betz, Hans Dieter. *Christology and a Modern Pilgrimage: A Discussion with Norman Perrin*. N.p.: SBL, 1971.

———. "Jesus as Divine Man." In *Jesus and the Historian: Written in Honor of Ernest Cadman Colwell*, edited by Thomas F. Trotter, 114–33. Philadelphia: Westminster, 1968.

Bickermann, Elias. "Das Messiasgeheimnis und die Komposition des Markusevangeliums." *ZNW* 22 (1923) 122–46.

Bilezikian, Gilbert G. *The Liberated Gospel: A Comparison of the Gospel of Mark and Greek Tragedy*. Baker Biblical Monograph. Grand Rapids: Baker, 1977.

Bird, Michael F. "The Crucifixion of Jesus as the Fulfillment of Mark 9:1." *TJ* 23 (2003) 23–36.

Black, C. Clifton. *The Disciples according to Mark: Markan Redaction in Current Debate*. JSNTSup 27. Sheffield: JSOT Press, 1989.

———. "The Face Is Familiar—I Just Can't Place It." In *The Ending of Mark and the Ends of God: Essays in Memory of Donald Harrisville Juel*, edited by Beverly Roberts Gaventa and Patrick D. Miller, 35–50. Louisville: Westminster John Knox, 2005.

———. *Mark: Images of an Apostolic Interpreter*. Studies on Personalities of the New Testament. Minneapolis: Fortress, 2001.

———. "The Quest for the Markan Redactor: Why Has It Been Pursued, and What Has It Taught Us?" *JSNT* 22 (1989) 19–39.

Black, Matthew. "The Son of Man Problem in Recent Research and Debate." *BJRL* 45 (1962/63) 57–65.

Blackburn, Barry L. "Divine Man." In *Dictionary of Jesus and the Gospels*, edited by Joel B. Green et al., 189–92. Downers Grove: InterVarsity, 1992.

Blank, Josef. *Der Jesus des Evangeliums*. Entwürfe zur biblischen Christologie. Münich: Kösel, 1981.

———. "Die Sendung des Sohnes: Zur christologischen Bedeutung des Gleichnisses von den bösen Winzern Mk 12, 1–12." In *Neues Testament und Kirche: Festschrift für Rudolf Schnackenburg*, edited by Joachim Gnilka, 11–41. Freiburg: Herder, 1974.

Blatherwick, David. "The Markan Silhouette?" *NTS* 17 (1971) 184–92.

Blomberg, Craig L. *Jesus and the Gospels: An Introduction and Survey*. Nashville: Broadman & Holman, 1997.

Boers, Hendrikus. "Reflections on the Gospel of Mark: A Structural Investigation." In *SBLSP* 1987, 255–57. Missoula: Scholars, 1987.

Bolt, Peter G. *The Cross from a Distance: Atonement in Mark's Gospel*. New Studies in Biblical Theology 18. Downers Grove: InterVarsity, 2004.

———. *Jesus' Defeat of Death: Persuading Mark's Early Readers*. SNTSMS 125. Cambridge: Cambridge University Press, 2003.

———. "Mark's Gospel." In *The Face of New Testament Studies. A Survey of Recent Research*, edited by Scot McKnight and Grant R. Osborne, 391–413. Grand Rapids: Baker Academic, 2004.

Boomershine, Thomas R. "Peter's Denial as Polemic or Confession: The Implications of Media Criticism for Biblical Hermeneutics." *SBLSS* 39 (1987) 47–68.

Borg, Marcus J. "An Appreciation for Albert Schweitzer." In *The Quest of the Historical Jesus: First Complete Edition*, edited by John Bowen, vii–xi. Fortress Classics in Biblical Studies. Minneapolis: Fortress, 2001.

Boring, M. Eugene. "The Christology of Mark: Hermeneutical Issues for Systematic Theology." *SBLSS* 30 (1985) 125–53.

———. "Mark 1:1–15 and the Beginning of the Gospel." *SBLSS* 52 (1991) 43–81.

Borsch, Frederick Houk. *The Son of Man in Myth and History*. Philadelphia: Westminster, 1967.

Borrell, Augusti. *The Good News of Peter's Denial: A Narrative and Rhetorical Reading of Mark 14:54.66–72*. International Studies in Formative Christianity and Judaism 7. Atlanta: Scholars, 1998.

Botha, Peter J. J. "Die dissipels in die Markusevangelie." DD proefskrif, Universiteit van Pretoria, 1989.

Bowman, John. *The Gospel of Mark: The New Christian Jewish Passover Haggadah*. SPB 8. Leiden: Brill, 1965.

Boyer, J. L. "The Classification of Infinitives: A Statistical Study." *Grace Theological Journal* 6 (1985) 3–27.

Branscomb, B. H. *The Gospel of Mark*. MNTC. London: Hodder and Stoughton, 1937.

Breytenbach, Cilliers. "Grundzüge markinischer Gottessohn-Christologie." In *Anfänge der Christologie*, edited by Henrich Paulsen and Cilliers Breytenbach, 169–84. Göttingen: Vandenhoeck & Ruprecht, 1991.

## Bibliography

Broadhead, Edwin K. *Mark*. Readings: A New Biblical Commentary. Sheffield: Sheffield Academic, 2001.

———. *Naming Jesus: Titular Christology in the Gospel of Mark*. JSNTSup 175. Sheffield: Sheffield Academic, 1999.

———. *Prophet, Son, Messiah: Narrative Form and Function in Mark 14-16*. JSNTSup 97. Sheffield: JSOT Press, 1994.

———. "Reconfiguring Jesus: The Son of Man in Markan Perspective." In *Biblical Interpretation in Early Christian Gospels*, edited by Thomas Hatina, 1:18-30. LNTS 304. London: T. & T. Clark, 2006.

———. *Teaching with Authority: Miracles and Christology in the Gospel of Mark*. JSNTSup 74. Sheffield: JSOT Press, 1992.

Brower, Kent. "Mark 9:1: Seeing the Kingdom in Power." *JSNT* 6 (1980) 17-41.

Brown, Raymond E. *The Death of the Messiah: From Gethsemane to the Grave: A Commentary on the Passion Narratives in the Four Gospels*. 2 vols. New York: Doubleday, 1994.

———. *An Introduction to the New Testament*. ABRL. New York: Doubleday, 1997.

Brown, Raymond E., et al. *Peter in the New Testament: A Collaborative Assessment by Protestant and Roman Catholic Scholars*. New York: Paulist, 1973.

Bryan, Christopher. *A Preface to Mark: Notes on the Gospel in Its Literary and Cultural Settings*. New York: Oxford University Press, 1993.

Bryant, Jo-Ann A. *Dialogue and Drama: Elements of Greek Tragedy in the Fourth Gospel*. Peabody, MA: Hendrickson, 2004.

Bultmann, Rudolf. *History of the Synoptic Tradition*. Translated by J. Marsh. Peabody, MA: Hendrickson, 1963. Originally published as *Geschichte in der Synoptischen Tradition*, 5th ed. (Göttingen: Vandenhoeck & Ruprecht, 1921).

———. *Primitive Christianity in its Contemporary Setting*. Translated by Reginald H. Fuller. Cleveland: World, 1956.

———. *Theology of the New Testament*. Translated by Kendrick Grobel. 2 vols. New York: Scribner's Sons, 1951, 1955.

Bundy, Walter E. "Dogma and Drama in the Gospel of Mark." In *New Testament Studies: Critical Essays in New Testament Interpretation, with Special Reference to the Meaning and Worth of Jesus*, edited by Edwin Prince Booth, 70-75. New York: Abingdon-Cokesbury, 1942.

Burch, Ernest W. "Tragic Action in the Second Gospel: A Study of the Narrative of Mark." *JR* 11 (1931) 346-58.

Burger, Klaus. "Die Königlilchen Messiastraditionen des Neuen Testaments." *NTS* 20 (1973-74) 1-44.

———. "Zum Problem der Messianität Jesu." *ZTK* 71 (1974) 1-30.

Burkett, Delbert R. *The Son of Man Debate: A History and Evaluation*. SNTSMS 107. Cambridge: Cambridge University Press, 2000.

Burkill, T. A. *Mysterious Revelation: An Examination of the Philosophy of St. Mark's Gospel*. Ithica: Cornell University Press, 1963.

Burridge, Richard A. "About People, by People, for People: Gospel Genre and Audiences." In *The Gospel for All Christians: Rethinking the Gospel Audiences*, edited by Richard Bauckham, 113-45. Grand Rapids: Eerdmans, 1998.

———. *What Are the Gospels: A Comparison with Graeco-Roman Biography*. SNTSMS 70. Cambridge: Cambridge University Press, 1992. Rev. ed. Grand Rapids: Eerdmans, 2004.

Cahill, Michael. *The First Commentary on Mark: An Annotated Translation*. New York: Oxford University Press, 1998.

———. "The Identification of the First Markan Commentary." *RB* 101-2 (1994) 258-68.

Caragounis, Christopher C. *The Son of Man: Vision and Interpretation*. WUNT 38. Tübingen: Mohr/Siebeck, 1986.

Carré, Henry Beach. "The Literary Structure of the Gospel of Mark." In *Studies in Early Christianity*, edited by Shirly Jackson Case, 105-26. New York: Century, 1928.

Carrington, Philip. *The Primitive Christian Calendar: A Study in the Making of the Markan Gospel*. Cambridge: Cambridge University Press, 1952.

Carson, Donald A., et al. *An Introduction to the New Testament*. Grand Rapids: Zondervan, 1992.

Casey, Maurice. *Son of Man: The Interpretation of and Influence of Daniel 7*. London: SPCK, 1980.

Casey, P. M. "Method in our Madness, and Madness in their Methods: Some Approaches to the Son of Man Problem in Recent Scholarship." *JSNT* 42 (1991) 17-43.

Ceresko, Anthony R. "Janus Parallelism in Amos's 'Oracles Against the Nations' (Amos 1:3-2:16)." *JBL* 113 (1994) 485-90.

Chapman, Dean W. *The Orphan Gospel: Mark's Perspective on Jesus*. Biblical Seminar 16. Sheffield: JSOT Press, 1993.

Chatman, Seymour. *Story and Discourse: Narrative Structure in Fiction and Film*. Ithaca, NY: Cornell University Press, 1978.

Charlesworth, James H. *The Messiah: Developments in Earliest Judaism and Christianity*. The First Princeton Symposium on Judaism and Christian Origins. Minneapolis: Fortress, 1992.

Cheroke, Christian P. "Is Mark 2, 10 a Saying of Jesus?" *CBQ* 22 (1960) 369-90.

Chilton, Bruce D. "The Son of Man: Human and Heavenly." In *The Four Gospels 1992*, edited by Frans van Segbroeck et al., 1:203-18. BETL 100. Leuven: Leuven University Press, 1992.

———. "The Transfiguration: Dominical Assurance and Apostolic Vision." *NTS* 27 (1980) 115-24.

Christensen, Duane L. "Janus Parallelism in Genesis 6:3." *HS* 27 (1986) 20-24.

Chronis, Harry L. "To Reveal and to Conceal: A Literary-Critical Perspective on 'the Son of Man' in Mark." *NTS* 51 (2005) 459-81.

Collins, Adela Yarbro. *The Beginning of the Gospel: Probings of Mark in Context*. Minneapolis: Fortress, 1992.

———. "Daniel 7 and Jesus." *Journal of Theology (United Theological Seminary)* 93 (1989) 5-19.

———. "Establishing the Text: Mark 1:1." In *Texts and Contexts: Biblical Texts in Their Textual and Situational Contexts: Essays in Honor of Lars Hartman*, edited by Tord Fornberg and David Hellholm, 117-27. Oslo: Scandinavian University Press, 1995.

———. *Is Mark's Gospel a Life of Jesus? The Question of Genre*. Milwaukee: Marquette University Press, 1990.

———. *Mark: A Commentary*. Hermeneia. Minneapolis: Fortress, 2007.

———. "Mark and His Readers: The Son of God among Greeks and Romans." *HTR* 93 (2000) 85-100.

———. "Mark and His Readers: The Son of God among Jews." *HTR* 92 (1999) 393-408.

———. "The Origin of the Designation of Jesus as 'Son of Man.'" *HTR* 80 (1987) 391-407.

## Bibliography

Collins, John J. *Daniel: A Commentary on the Book of Daniel.* With an essay, "The Influence of Daniel on the New Testament," by Adela Yarbro Collins. Hermeneia. Edited by Frank Moore Cross. Minneapolis: Fortress, 1993.

———. *The Scepter and the Star: The Messiahs of the Dead Sea Scrolls and Other Ancient Literature.* ABRL. New York: Doubleday, 1995.

———. "The Son of Man in First-Century Judaism." *NTS* 38 (1992) 448–66.

Cook, John G. *The Structure and Persuasive Power of Mark: A Linguistic Approach.* SBLSS. Atlanta: Scholars, 1995.

Cranfield, Charles E. B. *The Gospel according to St. Mark.* Cambridge Greek Testament Commentary. Cambridge: Cambridge University Press, 1959.

Crawford, Barry S. "Near Expectations in the Sayings of Jesus." *JBL* 101 (1982) 225–44.

Crossan, John Dominic. *Four Other Gospels.* Minneapolis: Winston, 1985.

Croy, N. Clayton. *The Mutilation of Mark's Gospel.* Nashville: Abingdon, 2003.

———. "Where the Gospel Text Begins: A Non-Theological Interpretation of Mark 1:1." *NovT* 43 (2001) 105–27.

Cuddon, John Anthony. "Turning Point." In *A Dictionary of Literary Terms*, revised by C. E. Preston, 950. 4th ed. Oxford: Blackwell, 1998.

Cullmann, Oscar. *The Christology of the New Testament.* Translated by Shirley C. Guthrie and Charles A. M. Hall. Rev. ed. Philadelphia: Westminster, 1963.

———. *Peter: Disciple, Apostle, Martyr: A Historical and Theological Study.* Philadelphia: Fortress, 1953.

Culpepper, Alan R. *Anatomy of the Fourth Gospel: A Study in Literary Design.* Philadelphia: Fortress, 1983.

———. *Mark.* Smyth & Helwys Bible Commentary. Macon: Smyth & Helwys, 2007.

———. "Mark 10:50: Why Mention the Garment?" *JBL* 101 (1982) 131–32.

———. "The Passion and Resurrection in Mark." *RevExp* 75 (1978) 583–600.

Currie, Stuart Dickson. "Isaiah 63:9 and the Transfiguration in Mark." In *Austin Seminary Bulletin: Faculty Edition* 82 (1966) 7–34.

Dahl, Nils A. "A Neglected Factor in New Testament Theology." *Reflections* 75 (1975) 5–8. Repr., *Jesus the Christ: The Historical Origins of Christological Doctrine*, edited by Donald H. Juel, 153–63. Minneapolis: Fortress, 1991.

Danove, Paul. *Linguistics and Exegesis in the Gospel of Mark: Application of a Case Frame Analysis and Lexicon.* JSNTSup 218. Sheffield: Sheffield Academic, 2001.

———. "The Rhetoric of the Characterization of Jesus as the Son of Man and Christ in Mark." *Bib* 84 (2003) 16–34.

Dart, John. *Decoding Mark.* Harrisburg, PA: Trinity, 2003.

Dautzenberg, Gerhard. "Elija im Markusevangelium." In *The Four Gospels 1992*, edited by Frans van Segbroeck et al., 2:1077–94. BETL 100. Leuven: Leuven University Press, 1992.

———. "Zwei unterschiedliche 'Kompendien' markinischer Christologie: Überlegungen zum Verhältnis von Mk 15,39 zu Mk 14,61f." In *Evangelium Jesu Christi heute verkündigen*, edited by B. Jendorff and G. Schmalenberg, 17–32. Geißen: Selbstverlag des Fachbereichs, 1989.

Davies, W. D. and Dale C. Allison, Jr. *A Critical and Exegetical Commentary on the Gospel according to St. Matthew.* 3 vols. ICC. Edinburgh: T. & T. Clark, 1998, 1991, 1997.

deSilva, David. *An Introduction to the New Testament: Contexts, Methods, and Ministry Formation.* Downers Grove, IL: InterVarsity, 2004.

Dewey, Joanna. "The Gospel of Mark as an Oral-Aural Event: Implications for Interpretation." In *The New Literary Criticism and the New Testament*, edited by Elizabeth Struthers Malbon and Edgar V. McKnight, 145–63. JSNTSup 109. Sheffield: Sheffield Academic, 1994.

———. "Mark as Interwoven Tapestry: Forecasts and Echoes for a Listening Audience." *CBQ* 53 (1991) 221–36.

———. *Markan Public Debate: Literary Technique, Concentric Structure, and Theology in Mark 2:1–3:6*. SBLDS 48. Chico, CA: Scholars, 1980.

———. "Oral Methods of Structuring Narrative in Mark." *Int* 43 (1989) 32–44.

———. "The Survival of Mark's Gospel: A Good Story?" *JBL* 123 (2004) 495–507.

Dibelius, Martin. *From Tradition to Gospel*. New York: Scribner's Sons, 1934. Originally published as *Formgeschichte des Evangeliums* (Tübingen: Mohr/Siebeck, 1919).

Dodd, Charles Harold. "Jesus as Teacher and Prophet." In *Mysterium Christi*, edited by G. K. A. Bell and D. Adolf Deissmann, 57–66. Christological Studies by British and German Theologians. London: Longmans & Green, 1930.

Donahue, John R. "A Neglected Factor in the Theology of Mark." *JBL* 101 (1982) 563–94.

———. *Are you the Christ? The Trial Narrative in the Gospel of Mark*. SBLDS 10. Missoula: Scholars, 1973.

———. "Recent Studies on the Origin of 'Son of Man' in the Gospels." *CBQ* 48, no. 3 (1986) 484–96.

Donahue, John R., and Daniel J. Harrington. *The Gospel of Mark*. SP 2. Collegeville, MN: Liturgical, 2002.

Dowd, Sharyn E. "The Gospel of Mark as Ancient Novel." *Lexington Theological Quarterly* 26 (1991) 53–59.

———. *Reading Mark: A Literary and Theological Commentary on the Second Gospel*. Reading the New Testament. Macon, GA: Smyth & Helwys, 2000.

Dowd, Sharyn E., and Elizabeth Struthers Malbon. "The Significance of Jesus' Death in Mark: Narrative Context and Authorial Audience." *JBL* 125 (2006) 271–97.

Driggers, Ira Brent. *Following God through Mark: Theological Tension in the Second Gospel*. Louisville: Westminster John Knox, 2007.

Duling, Dennis C. *The New Testament: History, Literature, and Social Context*. Belmont, CA: Wadsworth, 2003.

Duling, Dennis C., and Norman Perrin. *The New Testament: Proclamation and Parenesis, Myth and History*. 3rd ed. Fort Worth: Harcourt Brace, 1994.

Dungan, David L. *A History of the Synoptic Problem: The Canon, the Text, the Composition, and the Interpretation of the Gospels*. ABRL. New York: Doubleday, 1999.

Dunn, James D. G. *Jesus Remembered: Christianity in the Making*. Vol. 1. Grand Rapids: Eerdmans, 2003.

Ebeling, H. J. *Das Messiasgeheimnis und die Botschaft des Marcus-Evangelisten*. BZNW 19. Berlin: de Gruyter, 1939.

Edwards, James R. *The Gospel according to Mark*. Pillar New Testament Commentary. Grand Rapids: Eerdmans, 2002.

———. "Markan Sandwiches: The Significance of Interpolations in Markan Narratives." *NovT* 31 (1989) 193–216.

Egger, Wilhelm. *Frohbotschaft und Lehre: Die Sammelberichte des Wirkens Jesus im Markusevangelium*. Frankfurt: Knecht, 1976.

Ehrman, Bart D. *Peter, Paul, & Mary Magdalene: The Followers of Jesus in History and Legend*. Oxford: Oxford University Press, 2006.

# Bibliography

Elliott, J. Keith. *The Language and Style of the Gospel of Mark: An Edition of C. H. Turner's 'Notes on Marcan Usage' Together with Other Comparable Studies.* Leiden: Brill, 1993.

———. "The Middle of ἀποκρίνομαι." *ZNW* 96 (2005) 126–28.

Elwell, Walter A., and Robert W. Yarbrough. *Encountering the New Testament: A Historical and Theological Survey.* Grand Rapids: Baker, 1998.

Evans, Craig A. "How Mark Writes." In *The Written Gospel*, edited by Markus Bockmuehl and Donald A. Hagner, 135–48. Cambridge: Cambridge University Press, 2005.

———. *Mark 8:27—16:20.* WBC 34B. Dallas: Nelson, 2001.

Evans, Craig A., and Peter W. Flint. *Eschatology, Messianism, and the Dead Sea Scrolls.* Studies in the Dead Sea Scrolls and Related Literature. Grand Rapids: Eerdmans, 1997.

Evans, Craig F. *The Beginning of the Gospel.* London: SPCK, 1968.

Farmer, Willliam R. *The Synoptic Problem: A Critical Analysis.* New York: Macmillan, 1964.

Fish, Stanley. *Is There a Text in This Class? The Authority of Interpretive Communities.* Cambridge, MA: Harvard University Press, 1980.

Fitzmyer, Joseph A. "4Q246: The 'Son of God' Document from Qumran." *Bib* 74 (1993) 153–74.

———. *The Gospel according to Luke (I-IX): Introduction, Translation, and Notes.* AB 28. Garden City, NY: Doubleday, 1981.

———. "The New Testament Title 'Son of Man' Philologically Considered." In *A Wandering Aramean: Collected Aramaic Essays*, 143–60. Chico, CA: Scholars, 1979.

———. *The One Who Is to Come.* Grand Rapids: Eerdmans, 2007.

Fleddermann, Harry T. "The Central Question of Mark's Gospel: A Study of Mark 8:29." PhD diss., Graduate Theological Union, 1978.

Focant, Camille. *The Gospel according to Mark: A Commentary.* Translated by Leslie Robert Keylock. Eugene, OR: Pickwick, 2012.

Fowler, Alistair. *Kinds of Literature: An Introduction to the Theory of Genres and Modes.* Oxford: Clarendon, 1982.

Fowler, Robert M. *Let the Reader Understand: Reader-Response Criticism and the Gospel of Mark.* Minneapolis: Fortress, 1991.

———. *Loaves and Fishes: The Function of the Feeding Stories in the Gospel of Mark.* SBLDS 54. Chico, CA: Scholars, 1981.

France, R. T. *The Gospel of Mark: A Commentary on the Greek Text.* NIGTC. Grand Rapids: Eerdmans, 2002.

———. *Jesus and the Old Testament: His Application of Old Testament Passages to Himself and His Mission.* London: Tyndale, 1971.

Freytag, Gustav. *Freytag's Technique of the Drama: An Exposition of Dramatic Composition and Art: An Authorized Translation from the 6th German Edition.* Translated by Elias J. MacEwan. 3rd ed. Chicago: Griggs, 1985. Originally published as *Die Technik des dramas* (Leipzig: Hirzel, 1911).

Fuller, Reginald. *The Foundation of New Testament Christology.* London: Lutterworth, 1965.

Gathercole, Simon. "The Son of Man in Mark's Gospel." *ExpTim* 115 (2004) 366–72.

Genette, Gérard. *Narrative Discourse. An Essay in Method.* Translated by Jane E. Lewis. Ithaca, NY: Cornell University Press, 1980.

Globe, Alexander. "The Caesarean Omission of the Phrase 'Son of God' in Mark 1:1." *HTR* 75 (1982) 209–18.

Gnilka, Joachim. *Das Evangelium nach Markus.* Vol. 2 EKKNT 2. Zürich: Benzinger, 1979.
Goodacre, Mark. *The Case Against Q: Studies in Markan Priority and the Synoptic Problem.* Harrisburg, PA: Trinity, 2002.
Gould, Ezra P. *A Critical and Exegetical Commentary on the Gospel according to St. Mark.* ICC. New York: Scribner's Sons, 1896.
Goulder, Michael. "Psalm 8 and the Son of Man." *NTS* 48 (2002) 18-29.
Grant, Frederick C. *The Earliest Gospel: Studies of the Evangelic Tradition at Its Point of Crystalization in Writing.* New York: Abingdon-Cokesbury, 1943.
―――. *The Growth of the Gospels.* 1857. Repr., New York: Abingdon, 1933.
Graudin, Arthur F. "Jesus as Teacher in Mark." *Concordia Journal* 3 (1977) 32-35.
Green, Joel B. "The Challenge of Hearing the New Testament." In *Hearing the New Testament: Strategies for Interpretation,* edited by Joel B. Green, 1-9. Grand Rapids: Eerdmans, 1995.
―――. *Hearing the New Testament: Strategies for Interpretation.* Grand Rapids: Eerdmans, 1995.
Greeven, Heinrich. "Nochmals Mk 9:1 in Codex Bezae (D, 05)." *NTS* 23 (1977) 305-8.
Griesbach, Johann Jakob. *Synopsis Evangeliorum Matthaei Marci et Lucae una cum iis Joannis pericopis quae omnino cum caeterorum evangelistarum narrationibus conferendae sunt.* 3rd ed. Halle: Officina libraria curtiana, 1809. English translation, "A Demonstration That Mark Was Written after Matthew and Luke." In *J. J. Griesbach: Synoptic and Text-critical Studies 1776-1976,* edited by B. Orchard and T. R. W. Longstaff, 103-35. Cambridge: Cambridge University Press, 1977.
Griffin, William S. "Seeing and Perceiving: The Narrative Rhetoric of a Theme in Mark 15:20b-41." PhD diss., Graduate Theological Union, 1996.
Grundmann, Walter. *Das Evangelium nach Markus.* Zweite Auflage. THNT. Berlin: Evangelische, 1959.
Guelich, Robert. "The Gospel Genre." In *Das Evangelium und die Evangelien. Vorträge vom Tübinger Symposium 1982,* 183-220. WUNT 28. Tübingen: Mohr/Siebeck, 1983.
―――. *Mark 1:1―8:26.* WBC 34A. Dallas: Word, 1989.
Gundry, Robert H. *Mark: A Commentary on His Apology for the Cross.* Grand Rapids: Eerdmans, 1993.
―――. "A Rejoinder to Joel F. Williams's 'Is Mark's Gospel an Apology for the Cross?'" *Bulletin for Biblical Research* 12 (2002) 123-39.
Guthrie, Donald. *New Testament Introduction.* Downers Grove, IL: InterVarsity, 1970.
Guttenberger, Gundrum. "Why Caesarea Philippi of all Sites? Some Reflections on the Political Background and Implications of Mark 8:27-30 for the Christology of Mark." In *Zwischen den Reichen: Neues Testament und Römische Herrschaft,* 119-29. Tübingen: Francke, 2002.
Hagner, Donald A. *Matthew 14-28.* WBC 33B. Dallas: Word, 1995.
Hahn, Ferdinand. *The Titles of Jesus in Christology: Their History in Early Christianity.* Translated by H. Knight and G. Ogg. London: Lutterworth, 1969.
Hall, David R. *The Gospel Framework: Fiction or Fact? A Critical Evaluation of Der Rahmen der Geschichte Jesu by Karl Ludwig Schmidt.* Carlisle: Paternoster, 1998.
Hanson, James S. *Endangered Promises: Conflict in Mark.* SBLDS 171. Atlanta: SBL, 2000.
Hare, Douglas R. A. *Mark.* Westminster Bible Companion. Louisville: Westminster John Knox, 1996.
―――. *The Son of Man Tradition.* Minneapolis: Fortress, 1990.

# Bibliography

Harrington, Daniel J. "The Gospel according to Mark." In *NJBC*, edited by Raymond E. Brown et al., 596–629. Englewood Cliffs, NJ: Prentice-Hall, 1990.

Hartman, Louis F. *Book of Daniel: A New Translation with Notes and Commentary on Chapters 1–9*. Introduction and Commentary on chapters 10–12 by Alexander A. DiLella. AB 23. Garden City, NY: Doubleday, 1978.

Hatina, Thomas R. *Biblical Interpretation in Early Christian Gospels: Volume 1: The Gospel of Mark*. LNTS 304. Edinburgh: T. & T. Clark, 2006.

———. *In Search of a Context: The Function of Scripture in Mark's Narrative*. JSNTSup 232/Studies in Scripture in Early Judaism and Christianity 8. Sheffield: Sheffield Academic, 2002.

Hauck, D. Friedrich. *Das Evangelium des Markus (Synoptiker I)*. THKNT. Leipzig: Deichertsche, 1931.

Hay, Lewis S. "Mark's Use of the Messianic Secret." *JAAR* 35 (1967) 16–27.

———. "The Son of Man in Mark 2:10 and 2:28." *JBL* 89 (1970) 69–75.

Head, Peter M. "A Text-Critical Study of Mark 1:1 'The Beginning of the Gospel of Jesus Christ.'" *NTS* 37 (1991) 621–29.

Healy, Mary E. "Behind, in Front of . . . or Through the Text? The Christological Analogy and the Lost World of Biblical Truth." In *"Behind" the Text: History and Biblical Interpretation*, edited by Craig Bartholomew et al., 181–95. Scripture & Hermeneutics Series 4. Grand Rapids: Zondervan, 2003.

Heil, John Paul. *The Gospel of Mark as a Model for Action: A Reader-Response Commentary*. New York: Paulist, 1992.

———. "A Note on 'Elijah and Moses' in Mark 9, 4." *Bib* 80 (1995) 115.

———. *The Transfiguration of Jesus: Narrative Meaning and Function of Mark 9:2–8, Matt 17:1–8 and Luke 9:28–36*. AnBib 144. Rome: Editrice Pontificio Istituto Biblico, 2000.

Henderson, Susan Watts. *Christology and Discipleship in the Gospel of Mark*. SNTMS 135. Cambridge: Cambridge University Press, 2006.

Hendrick, Charles W. "The Role of 'Summary Statements' in the Composition of the Gospel of Mark: A Dialog with Karl Schmidt and Norman Perrin." *NovT* 26 (1984) 289–311.

Hengel, Martin. *The Son of God*. Translated by John Bowen. Philadelphia: Fortress, 1976. German original, Tübingen: Mohr/Siebeck, 1975.

———. *Studies in the Gospel of Mark*. Translated by John Bowen. Eugene, OR: Wipf and Stock, 1985. German original, "Probleme des Markusevangeliums." In *Das Evangelium und die Evangelien*, edited by Peter Stuhlmacher, 221–65. WUNT 28. Tübingen: Mohr/Siebeck, 1983.

Herron, Robert W., Jr. *Mark's Account of Peter's Denial of Jesus: A History of Its Interpretation*. Lanham, MD: University Press of America, 1991.

Hess, Richard S., and M. Daniel Carroll R. *Israel's Messiah in the Bible and the Dead Sea Scrolls*. Grand Rapids: Baker, 2003.

Higgins, Angus John Brockhurst. *The Son of Man in the Teaching of Jesus*. SNTSMS 39. Cambridge: Cambridge University Press, 1980.

Hirsch, E. D. *Validity in Interpretation*. New Haven: Yale University Press, 1967.

Hoffeditz, David M. "A Prophet, a Kingdom, and a Messiah: The Portrayal of Elijah in the Gospel in Light of First-Century Judaism." PhD diss., University of Aberdeen, 2000.

———. "A Prophet, a Messiah, and a Kingdom: The Portrayal of Elijah in the Gospel of Mark." Paper presented at the annual meeting of the Evangelical Theological Society, Atlanta, GA, November 19, 2003, 1–32.

# Bibliography

Hoffeditz, David M., and Gary E. Yates. "*Femme Fatale* Redux: Intertextual Connection to the Elijah/Jezebel Narratives in Mark 6:14–29." *BBR* 15, no. 2 (2005) 199–221.

Holladay, Carl H. *Theios Aner in Hellenistic Judaism: A Critique of the Use of this Category in New Testament Christology*. Missoula: Scholars, 1977.

Holtzmann, Heinrich Julius. *Die synoptischen Evangelien: Ihr Ursprung und geschichtlicher Charakter*. Leipzig: Engelmann, 1863.

Hooker, Morna D. *Beginnings: Keys That Open the Gospels*. Harrisburg, PA: Trinity, 1997.

———. *The Gospel according to St. Mark*. BNTC. London: A. & C. Black, 1991.

———. "Mark's Parables of the Kingdom." In *The Challenges of Jesus' Parables*, edited by Richard N. Longenecker, 79–101. Grand Rapids: Eerdmans, 2000.

———. "The Son of Man and the Synoptic Problem." In *The Four Gospels 1992*, edited by Frans van Segbroeck et al., 1:189–201. BETL 100. Leuven: Leuven University Press, 1992.

———. *The Son of Man in Mark: A Study of the Background of the Term "Son of Man" and Its Use in St. Mark's Gospel*. Montreal: McGill University Press, 1967.

———. "'What doest thou here, Elijah': A Look at St. Mark's Account of the Transfiguration." In *Glory of Christ in the New Testament: Studies in Memory of George Bradford Caird*, edited by L. D. Hurst and N. T. Wright, 59–70. Oxford: Clarendon, 1987.

———. "'Who Can This Be?' The Christology of Mark's Gospel." In *Contours of Christology in the New Testament*, edited by Richard N. Longenecker, 79–99. McMaster New Testament Studies. Grand Rapids: Eerdmans, 2005.

Horbury, William. *Jewish Messianism and the Cult of Christ*. London: SCM, 1998.

———. "Jewish Messianism and Early Christology." In *Contours of Christology in the New Testament*, edited by Richard N. Longenecker, 3–24. Grand Rapids: Eerdmans, 2005.

———. "The Messianic Associations of 'The Son of Man.'" *JTS* 36 (1985) 34–55.

Horsley, Richard A. *Hearing the Whole Story: The Politics of Plot in Mark's Gospel*. Louisville: Westminster John Knox, 2001.

———. "'Like One of the Prophets of Old': Two Types of Popular Prophets at the Time of Jesus." *CBQ* 47 (1985) 435–63.

———. "A Prophet Like Moses and Elijah: Popular Memory and Cultural Patterns in Mark." In *Performing the Gospel: Orality, Memory, and Mark*, edited by Richard A. Horsley et al., 166–90. Minneapolis: Fortress, 2006.

Horsley, Richard A., et al. *Performing the Gospel: Orality, Memory, and Mark*. Minneapolis: Fortress, 2006.

Hultgren, Arland J. *The Parables of Jesus: A Commentary*. Grand Rapids: Eerdmans, 2000.

Humphrey, Hugh. *He is Risen? A New Reading of Mark's Gospel*. New York: Paulist, 1992.

Hurtado, Larry W. "Following Jesus in the Gospel of Mark—and Beyond." In *Patterns of Discipleship in the New Testament*, edited by Richard N. Longenecker, 9–29. McMaster New Testament Studies. Grand Rapids: Eerdmans, 1996.

———. *Lord Jesus Christ: Devotion to Jesus in Earliest Christianity*. Grand Rapids: Eerdmans, 2003.

———. *Mark*. NIBC. Peabody, MA: Hendrickson, 1983.

Inch, Morris A. *Exhortations of Jesus according to Matthew and Up from the Depths: Mark as Tragedy*. Lanham, MD: University Press of America, 1997.

Iverson, Kelly R., and Christopher W. Skinner. *Mark as Story: Retrospect and Prospect*. Resources for Biblical Studies 65. Atlanta: SBL, 2011.

Jacobs, M. M. "Mark's Jesus through the Eyes of Twentieth Century New Testament Scholars." *Neot* 28 (1994) 53–85.

## Bibliography

Jeremias, Joachim. *The Parables of Jesus*. Translated by S. H. Hooker. New York: Scribners & Sons, 1963.

Johnson, David H. "The Characterization of Jesus in Mark." *Didaskalia* 10 (1999) 79–92.

Johnson, Earl S. "Mark 15, 39 and the So-Called Confession of the Roman Centurion." *Bib* 81 (2000) 406–13.

Johnson, Luke Timothy. "The Christology of Luke-Acts." In *Who Do You Say That I Am? Essays on Christology*, edited by Mark Allan Powell and David R. Bauer, 49–65. Louisville: Westminster John Knox, 1999.

———. "Does a Theology of the Canonical Gospels Make Sense?" In *The Nature of New Testament Theology*, edited by Christopher Rowland and Christopher M. Tuckett, 93–108. Malden, MA: Blackwell, 2006.

———. *The Gospel of Luke*. SP 3. Collegeville, MN: Liturgical, 1991.

———. *The Writings of the New Testament: An Interpretation* (with the assistance of Todd C. Penner). Rev. ed. Minneapolis: Fortress, 1999.

Johnson, Sherman E. *A Commentary on the Gospel according to St. Mark*. BNTC. London: Black, 1960.

Juel, Donald H. *The Gospel of Mark*. IBT. Nashville: Abingdon, 1999.

———. *Mark*. ACNT. Minneapolis: Fortress, 1990.

———. *A Master of Surprise: Mark Interpreted*. Minneapolis: Fortress, 1994.

———. *Messiah and Temple: The Trial of Jesus in the Gospel of Mark*. SBLDS 31. Missoula: Scholars, 1977.

———. *Messianic Exegesis: Christological Interpretation of the Old Testament in Early Christianity*. Philadelphia: Fortress, 1988.

———. "The Origin of Mark's Christology." In *The Messiah: Developments in Earliest Judaism and Christianity*, edited by James H. Charlesworth, 449–59. First Princeton Symposium on Judaism and Christian Origins. Minneapolis: Fortress, 1992.

Just, Felix. "New Testament Statistics." Catholic Resources. http://catholic-resources.org/Bible/NT-Statisics-Greek.htm.

Kähler, Martin. *The So-Called Historical Jesus and the Historic, Biblical Christ*. Philadelphia: Fortress, 1964.

Kazmierski, Carl R. *Jesus, the Son of God: A Study of the Markan Tradition and Its Redaction by the Evangelist*. FB 33. Würzburg: Echter, 1979.

Keck, Leander E. "The Introduction to Mark's Gospel." *NTS* 12 (1965–66) 352–70.

———. "Mark 3:7–12 and Mark's Christology." *JBL* 84 (1965) 341–58.

———. *Who Is Jesus? History in Perfect Tense*. Studies on Personalities of the New Testament. Minneapolis: Fortress, 2001.

Kee, Howard Clark. "Christology in Mark's Gospel." In *Judaisms and Their Messiahs at the Turn of the Christian Era*, edited by Jacob Neusner et al., 187–208. Cambridge: Cambridge University Press, 1987.

———. *Community of the New Age: Studies in Mark's Gospel*. 1977. Repr., Macon, GA: Mercer University Press, 1983.

Kelber, Werner H. *The Kingdom in Mark: A New Place and a New Time*. Philadelphia: Fortress, 1974.

———. *Mark's Story of Jesus*. Philadelphia: Fortress, 1979.

———. *The Oral and Written Gospel: The Hermeneutics of Speakers and Writing in the Synoptic Tradition, Paul, and Q*. Philadelphia: Fortress, 1983.

Kermode, Frank. *The Genesis of Secrecy: On the Interpretation of Narrative*. Cambridge, MA: Harvard University Press, 1979.

# Bibliography

Kilgallen, John J. "Mk 9:1—the Conclusion of a Pericope." *Bib* 63 (1982) 81–83.
Kim, Seyoon. *"The 'Son of Man'" as the Son of God.* WUNT 30. 1983. Repr., Grand Rapids: Eerdmans, 1983.
Kingsbury, Jack Dean. "The Christology of Mark and the Son of Man." In *Unity and Diversity in the Gospels and Paul: Essays in Honor of Frank J. Matera*, edited by Christopher W. Skinner and Kelly R. Iverson, 55–70. Atlanta: SBL, 2012.
———. *The Christology of Mark's Gospel*. Philadelphia: Fortress, 1983.
———. *Conflict in Mark: Jesus, Authorities, Disciples*. Minneapolis: Fortress, 1985.
———. "The 'Divine Man' as the Key to Mark's Christology—The End of an Era? *Int* 35 (1981) 243–57.
———. "'God' Within the Narrative World of Mark." In *The Forgotten God: Perspectives in Biblical Theology*, edited by A. Andrew Das, and Frank J. Matera, 75–89. Louisville: Westminster John Knox, 2002.
Kloppenborg, John S. *Q, the Earliest Gospel: An Introduction to the Original Stories and Sayings of Jesus*. Louisville: Westminster John Knox, 2008.
Klostermann, Erich. *Das Markusevangelium*. HNT 3. Tübingen: Mohr/Siebeck, 1950.
Koester, Helmut. "History and Development of Mark's Gospel (from Mark to Secret Mark and 'Canonical' Mark)." In *Colloquy on New Testament Studies: A Time for Reappraisal and Fresh Approaches*, edited by B. Corley, 33–57. Macon, GA: Mercer University Press, 1983.
Kraftchick, Steven J. "Facing Janus: Reviewing the Biblical Theological Movement." In *Biblical Theology: Problems & Prospects*, edited by Steven J. Kraftchick et al., 54–77. Nashville: Abingdon, 1995.
Kselman, John S. "Janus Parallelism in Psalm 75:2." *JBL* 121 (2002) 531–32.
Kümmel, Werner G. *Introduction to the New Testament*. 2nd English ed. Nashville: Abingdon, 1986.
Lafontaine, René and Pierre Mourlon Beernaert. "Essai sur la structure de Marc 8:27—9:13." *Recherches de Science Religieuse* 57 (1969) 543–61.
Lagrange, Marie-Joseph. *Évangile selon Saint Marc*. Ebib. Paris: Gabalda, 1947.
Lambrecht, Jan. "A Note on Mark 8.38 and Q 12.8–9." *JSNT* 85 (2002) 117–25.
———. "Q-influence on Mark 8:34; 9:1." In *Logia: les paroles de Jesus—the sayings of Jesus*, 277–304. BETL 59. Leuven: Leuven University Press, 1982.
———. "Redaction and Theology in *Mk.*, IV." In *L'Évangile selon Marc: Tradition et Rédaction*, edited by M. Sabbe, 269–307. BETL 34. Leuven: Leuven University Press, 1974.
Lane, William L. *The Gospel according to Mark*. NICNT 2. Grand Rapids: Eerdmans, 1974.
———. "*THEIOS ANÊR* Christology and the Gospel of Mark." In *New Dimensions in New Testament Study*, edited by Richard N. Longenecker and Merrill C. Tenney, 144–61. Grand Rapids: Zondervan, 1974.
Larsen, Kevin W. "'Do You See Anything?' (Mark 8:23): Seeing and Understanding Jesus: A Literary and Theological Study of Mark 8:22–9:13." PhD diss., Catholic University of America, 2002.
———. "The Structure of Mark's Gospel: Current Proposals." *Currents in Biblical Research* 3, no. 1 (2004) 140–60.
LaVerdiere, Eugene. *The Beginning of the Gospel: Introducing the Gospel according to Mark*. 2 vols. Collegeville, MN: Liturgical, 1999.
Lee, Dorothy A. *Transfiguration*. New Century Theology. London: Continuum, 2004.
Lee, J. A. L. "Some Features of the Speech of Jesus in Mark's Gospel." *NovT* 27 (1985) 1–26.

*Bibliography*

Lee, Robert G. "Thinking the Things of God: A Literary Study of Mark 8:27–9:13." PhD diss., Graduate Theological Union, 1995.

Levine, Amy-Jill. *A Feminist Companion to St. Mark*. Feminist Companion to the New Testament and Early Christian Writings 2. Cleveland: Pilgrim, 2004.

Lewis, Philip B. "Indications of a Liturgical Source in the Gospel of Mark." *Encounter* 39 (1978) 385–94.

Liefeld, Walter L. "Theological Motifs in the Transfiguration Narrative." In *New Dimensions in New Testament Study*, edited by Richard N. Longenecker and Merrill C. Tenney, 162–79. Grand Rapids: Eerdmans, 1974.

Lightfoot, R. H. *The Gospel Message of St. Mark*. Oxford: Clarendon, 1950.

Lindars, Barnabas. *Jesus Son of Man: A Fresh Examination of the Son of Man Sayings in the Gospels in Light of Recent Research*. Grand Rapids: Eerdmans, 1984.

Lohmeyer, Ernst. *Das Evangelium des Markus*. 17th ed. KEK. 2 vols. Göttingen: Vandenhoeck & Ruprecht, 1959.

Lohr, Charles H. "Oral Techniques in the Gospel of Matthew." *CBQ* 23 (1961) 403–55.

Lührmann, Dieter. *Das Markusevangelium*. HNT 3. Tübingen: Mohr/Siebeck, 1987.

Luz, Ulrich. "Das Geheimnismotiv und die markinische Christologie." *ZNW* 56 (1965) 9–30.

———. *Matthew 8–20: A Commentary*. Hermeneia. Minneapolis: Fortress, 2001.

MacDonald, Dennis R. *The Homeric Epics and the Gospel of Mark*. New Haven: Yale University Press, 2000.

———. "Secrecy and Recognitions in the *Odessey* and Mark: Where Wrede Went Wrong." In *Ancient Fiction and Early Christian Narrative*, edited by Ronald F. Hock et al., 139–53. SBLSymS 6. Atlanta: Scholars, 1998.

Malbon, Elizabeth Struthers. "Echoes and Foreshadowings in Mark 4–8: Reading and Rereading." *JBL* 112, no. 2 (1993) 211–30.

———. *Hearing Mark: A Listener's Guide*. Harrisburg, PA: Trinity, 2002.

———. *In the Company of Jesus: Characters in Mark's Gospel*. Louisville: Westminster John Knox, 2000.

———. "The Major Importance of the Minor Characters in Mark." In *The New Literary Criticism and the New Testament*, edited by Elizabeth Struthers Malbon and Edgar V. McKnight, 58–86. JSNTSup 109. Sheffield: Sheffield Academic, 1994.

———. "Markan Narrative Christology and the Kingdom of God." In *Literary Encounters with the Reign of God*, edited by Sharon Ringe and H. C. Paul Kim, 177–93. FS Robert C. Tannehill. New York: T. & T. Clark, 2004.

———. *Mark's Jesus: Characterization as Narrative Christology*. Waco: Baylor University Press, 2009.

———. "Narrative Christology and the Son of Man: What the Markan Jesus Says Instead." *Biblical Interpretation* 11 (2003) 372–85.

———. "Narrative Criticism: How Does the Story Mean?" In *Mark and Method: New Approaches in Biblical Studies*, edited by Janice Capel Anderson and Stephen D. Moore, 23–49. Minneapolis: Fortress, 1992.

———. *Narrative Space and Mythic Meaning in Mark*. New Voices in Biblical Studies. San Francisco: Harper & Row, 1986.

———. "'Reflected Christology': An Aspect of Narrative 'Christology' in the Gospel of Mark." *Perspectives in Religious Studies* 26 (1999) 127–45.

―――. "Text and Context: Interpreting the Disciples in Mark." SBLSS 62 (1993) 81–102. Repr., In the Company of Jesus: Characters in Mark's Gospel, 100–130. Louisville: Westminster John Knox, 2000.

Malbon, Elizabeth Struthers, and Edgar V. McKnight. The New Literary Criticism and the New Testament. JSNTS 109. Sheffield: Sheffield Academic, 1994.

Malley, Edward J. "The Gospel according to Mark." In JBC, edited by Raymond E. Brown et al., 21–61. Englewood Cliffs, NJ: Prentice-Hall, 1968.

Maloney, Elliott C. Jesus' Urgent Message for Today: The Kingdom of God in Mark's Gospel. New York: Continuum, 2004.

Malul, Meir. "Janus Parallelism in Biblical Hebrew: Two More Cases (Canticles 4, 9.12)." BZ 41 (1997) 246–49.

Mann, C. S. Mark: A New Translation with Introduction and Commentary. AB 27. Garden City, NY: Doubleday, 1986.

Mansfield, M. Robert. "Spirit and Gospel" in Mark. Peabody, MA: Hendrickson, 1987.

Marcus, Joel. "Blanks and Gaps in the Markan Parable of the Sower." Biblical Interpretation 5 (1997) 247–62.

―――. Mark 1–8: A New Translation with Introduction and Commentary. AB 27. New York: Doubleday, 1999.

―――. Mark 8–16: A New Translation with Introduction and Commentary. AB 27A. New Haven: Yale University Press, 2009.

―――. "Mark 9, 11–13: As It Has Been Written." ZNW 80 (1989) 42–63.

―――. "Mark 14:61: 'Are You the Messiah-Son-of-God?'" NovT 31 (1989) 125–41.

―――. The Mystery of the Kingdom of God. SBLDS 90. Atlanta: Scholars, 1986.

―――. The Way of the Lord: Christological Exegesis of the Old Testament in the Gospel of Mark. Louisville: Westminster John Knox, 1992.

Marshall, Christopher D. Faith as a Theme in Mark's Narrative. SNTSMS 64. Cambridge: Cambridge University Press, 1989.

Marshall, I. Howard. Commentary on Luke: A Commentary on the Greek Text. NIGTC. Grand Rapids: Eerdmans, 1978.

―――. New Testament Theology: Many Witnesses, One Gospel. Downers Grove, IL: InterVarsity, 2004.

―――. "The Parousia in the New Testament—and Today." In Worship, Theology and Ministry in the Early Church: Essays in Honor of Ralph P. Martin, edited by Michael J. Wilkins and T. Paige, 194–211. JSNTSup 87. Sheffield: Sheffield Academic, 1992.

Martin, Ralph P. Mark: Evangelist and Theologian. Exeter: Paternoster, 1972.

Martínez, Florentino García, and Eibert J. C. Tigchelaar. The Dead Sea Scrolls Study Edition. 2 vols. Grand Rapids: Eerdmans, 2000.

Marxsen, Willi. Mark the Evangelist: Studies on the Redaction History of the Gospel. Translated by James Boyce, Donald Juel, and William Poehlmann with Roy A. Harrisville. Nashville: Abingdon, 1969.

Matera, Frank J. "The Incomprehension of the Disciples and Peter's Confession (Mark 6:14–8:30)." Bib 70 (1989) 153–72.

―――. The Kingship of Jesus. SBLDS 66. Chico, CA: Scholars, 1982.

―――. New Testament Christology. Louisville: Westminster John Knox, 1999.

―――. "The Prologue as the Interpretive Key to Mark's Gospel." JSNT 34 (1988) 3–20.

―――. "Transcending Messianic Expectations: Mark and John." In Transcending Boundaries: Contemporary Readings of the New Testament, edited by Rekha

## Bibliography

Chennattu and Mary L. Coloe, 201–216. Biblioteca di Scienze Religiose 187. Rome: Libreria Ateneo Salesiano, 2005.

———. *What Are They Saying About Mark?* New York: Paulist, 1987.

Mauser, Ulrich. *Christ in the Wilderness: The Wilderness Theme in the Second Gospel and Its Basis in the Biblical Tradition.* SBT 39. London: SCM, 1963.

McCurley Jr., Foster R. "'And After Six Days' (Mark 9:2): A Semitic Literary Device." *JBL* 93 (1974) 67–81.

McDermott, John M. "Gegenwärtiges und kommendes Reich Gottes." *Internationale katholische Zeitschrift "Communio"* 15 (1986) 142–44.

McKinnis, Ray. "An Analysis of Mark X 32–34." *NovT* 18 (1976) 81–100.

McKnight, Edgar V. "Form and Redaction Criticism." In *The New Testament and Its Modern Interpreters*, edited by Eldon Jay Epp and George W. MacRae, 149–79. Bible and Its Modern Interpreters 3. Atlanta: Scholars, 1989.

———. *What Is Form Criticism?* GBS. Philadelphia: Fortress, 1969.

Meadors, Edward P. *Jesus: The Messianic Herald of Salvation.* Peabody, MA: Hendrickson, 1997.

Meier, John P. *A Marginal Jew: Rethinking the Historical Jesus.* 4 vols. ABRL. New York: Doubleday, 1991–2009.

Metzger, Bruce M. *A Textual Commentary on the Greek New Testament.* 2nd ed. Stuttgart: Deutsche Bibelgesellschaft, 1994.

Meye, Robert P. *Jesus and the Twelve.* Grand Rapids: Eerdmans, 1968.

Meyer, Marvin. "Taking Up the Cross and Following Jesus: Discipleship in the Gospel of Mark." *Calvin Journal of Theology* 37 (2002) 230–38.

Miller, Susan. "The Kingship of Jesus: The Use of the Combat Myth in Mark's Portrayal of Jesus' Death." Paper presented at the annual meeting of the Mark Group of the SBL, San Antonio, TX, November 22, 2004, 1–16.

Minor, Mitzi. *The Spirituality of Mark: Responding to God.* Louisville: Westminster John Knox, 1996.

Moeser, Marion C. *The Anecdote in Mark, the Classical World and the Rabbis.* JSNTSup 227. Sheffield: Sheffield Academic, 2002.

Moloney, Francis J. *Beginning the Good News: A Narrative Approach.* Collegeville, MN: Liturgical, 1995.

———. "Constructing Jesus and the Son of Man." *CBQ* 75 (2013) 719–38.

———. "The End of the Son of Man?" *The Downside Review* 98 (1980) 280–90.

———. *The Gospel of Mark: A Commentary.* Peabody, MA: Hendrickson, 2002.

———. *Mark: Storyteller, Interpreter, Evangelist.* Peabody, MA: Hendrickson, 2004.

———. "Narrative Criticism of the Gospels." In *"A Hard Saying": The Gospel and Culture,* 85–105. Collegeville, MN: Liturgical, 2001.

———. "The Vocation of the Disciples in the Gospel of Mark." In *"A Hard Saying": The Gospel and Culture,* 53–84. Collegeville, MN: Liturgical, 2001.

Montague, George T. "Hermeneutics and the Teaching of Scripture." *CBQ* 41 (1979) 1–17.

Moore, Stephen D. *Literary Criticism and the Gospels: The Theoretical Challenge.* New Haven: Yale University Press, 1989.

Morgan, Robert and John Barton. *Biblical Interpretation.* Oxford: Oxford University Press, 1988.

Moses, A. D. A. *Matthew's Transfiguration Story and Jewish-Christian Controversy.* JSNTSup 122. Sheffield: Sheffield Academic, 1996.

Mounce, William D. *The Morphology of Biblical Greek: A Companion to the Basics of Biblical Greek and Analytical Lexicon of the Greek New Testament*. Grand Rapids: Zondervan, 1994.

Myers, Ched. *Binding the Strong Man: A Political Reading of Mark's Story of Jesus*. Maryknoll, NY: Orbis, 1988.

Naluparayil, Jacob C. *The Identity of Jesus in Mark: An Essay on Narrative Christology*. AnBib 49. Jerusalem: Franciscan, 2000.

Nardoni, Enrique. "A Redactional Interpretation of Mark 9:1." *CBQ* 43 (1981) 365-84.

Neirynck, Frans. *Duality in Mark: Contributions to the Study of the Markan Redaction*. Rev. ed. with supplemental notes. Leuven: Leuven University Press, 1988.

———. "Introduction: The Two-Source Hypothesis." In *The Interrelations of the Gospels*, edited by David L. Dungan, 3-22. BETL 95. Leuven: Leuven University Press, 1990.

———. "Minor Agreements Matthew-Luke in the Transfiguration Story." In *Evangelica: Gospel Studies*, edited by Frans van Segbroeck, 797-810. BETL 60. Louvain: Peeters, 1982.

Neusner, Jacob, et al. *Judaisms and their Messiahs at the Turn of the Christian Era*. Cambridge: Cambridge University Press, 1987.

Nineham, Dennis E. *The Gospel of St. Mark*. PNTC. New York: Seabury, 1963.

Noegel, Scott B. "Janus Parallelism in Job and Its Literary Significance." *JBL* 115 (1996) 313-20.

———. *Janus Parallelism in the Book of Job*. JSOTSup 223. Sheffield: Sheffield Academic, 1996.

Öhler, Markus. "Die Verklärung (Mk 9.1-8). Die Ankunft der Herrschaft Gottes auf der Erde." *NovT* 38 (1996) 197-217.

Osborne, B. A. E. "Peter: Stumbling-block and Satan." *NovT* 15 (1973) 187-90.

Painter, John. *Mark's Gospel: Worlds in Conflict*. New Testament Readings. London: Routledge, 1997.

Peace, Richard V. *Conversion in the New Testament: Paul and the Twelve*. Grand Rapids/ Cambridge: Eerdmans, 1999.

Perrin, Norman. "The Christology of Mark: A Study in Methodology." *JR* 51 (1971) 173-87.

———. "Composition of Mark 9:1." *NovT* 11 (1969) 67-70.

———. "The Creative Use of the Son of Man Tradition by Mark." *USQR* 23 (1967-68) 237-65.

———. *The Kingdom of God in the Teaching of Jesus*. London: SCM, 1963.

———. "The Modern Interpretation of the Parables of Jesus and the Problem of Hermeneutics." *Int* 25 (1971) 131-48.

———. *The New Testament: An Introduction: Proclamation and Parenesis, Myth and History*. New York: Harcourt Brace Jovanovich, 1974.

———. "Toward and Interpretation of the Gospel of Mark." In *Christology and a Modern Pilgrimage: A Discussion with Norman Perrin*, edited by Hans Dieter Betz, 1-78. N.p.: SBL, 1971.

———. *What Is Redaction Criticism?* GBS. Philadelphia: Fortress, 1969.

Perrin, Norman, and Dennis C. Duling. *The New Testament: An Introduction: Proclamation and Parenesis, Myth and History*. 2nd ed. New York: Harcourt Brace Jovanovich, 1982.

Perry, B. E. *The Ancient Romances: A Literary-Historical Account of Their Origins*. Berkeley: University of California Press, 1967.

## Bibliography

Pesch, Rudolf. *Das Markusevangelium*. 2 vols. HTKNT II 1–2. Freiburg: Herder, 1976–1977.

———. "Das Messiasbekenntnis des Petrus, Mk 8:27–30." *BZ* 18 (1974) 20–31.

———. "Die Verleugnung des Petrus: Mk 14:54, 66–72 (und Mk 14:26–31)." In *Neues Testament und Kirche*, 42–62. Freiburg: Herder, 1974.

———. *Naherwartungen: Tradition und Redaktion in Mk 13*. Düsseldorf: Patmos, 1968.

Petersen, Norman R. "The Composition of Mark 4:1–8:26." *HTR* 73 (1980) 185–217.

———. "'Literarkritik,' the New Literary Criticism and the Gospel according to Mark." In *The Four Gospels 1992*, edited by Frans van Segbroeck et al., 2:935–48. BETL 100. Leuven: Leuven University Press, 1992.

Peuch, Émile. "Messianism, Resurrection, and Eschatology at Qumran and in the New Testament." In *The Community of the Renewed Covenant: The Notre Dame Symposium on the Dead Sea Scrolls*, edited by Eugene Ulrich and James VanderKam, 235–56. Christianity and Judaism in Antiquity 10. Notre Dame: University of Notre Dame Press, 1994.

Powell, Mark Allan. "Narrative Criticism." In *Dictionary of Biblical Interpretation*, edited by John H. Hayes, 2:201–4. Nashville: Abingdon, 1999.

———. *What Is Narrative Criticism?* GBS. Minneapolis: Fortress, 1990.

Pryke, E. J. *Redactional Style in the Marcan Gospel: A Study of Syntax and Vocabulary as Guides to Redaction in Mark*. Cambridge: Cambridge University Press, 1978.

Purcell, Nicholas. *The Oxford Classical Dictionary*. 3rd ed. Oxford: Oxford University Press, 1999.

Quesnell, Quentin. *The Mind of Mark: Interpretation and Method through the Exegesis of Mark 6, 52*. AnBib 38. Rome: Pontificio Instituto Biblico, 1969.

Räisänen, Heikki. *The "Messianic Secret" in Mark*. Translated by Christopher M. Tuckett. Studies of the New Testament and Its World. Edinburgh: T. & T. Clark, 1990.

Reardon, Bryan P. *Collected Ancient Greek Novels*. Berkeley: University of California Press, 1989.

Reardon, Patrick Henry. "The Cross, Sacraments and Martyrdom: An Investigation of Mark 10:35–45." *St. Vladimir's Theological Quarterly* 36 (1992) 103–15.

Redlich, E. B. *Form Criticism: Its Value and Limitations*. London: Duckworth, 1939.

Reedy, Charles J. "Mk 8:31—11:10 and the Gospel Ending: A Redaction Study." *CBQ* 34 (1972) 188–97.

Reimarus, Hermann Samuel. *Fragments*. Translated by R. S. Fraser. Edited by Charles H. Talbert. Philadelphia: Fortress, 1970. German original, 1778.

Reitzenstein, Richard. *Hellenistische Wundererzählungen*. Darmstadt: Wissenschaftliche Buchgesellschaft, 1910.

Renan, J. Ernest. *The Life of Jesus*. London: Trebner, 1864. Originally published as *Vie de Jésus* (Paris: Lévy, 1863).

Rendsburg, Gary. "Janus Parallelism in Gen 49:26." *JBL* 99 (1980) 291–93.

Rhoads, David. "Narrative Criticism and the Gospel of Mark." *JAAR* 50 (1982) 411–34.

———. "Narrative Criticism: Practices and Prospects." In *Characterization in the Gospels: Reconceiving Narrative Criticism*, edited by David Rhoades and Kari Syreeni, 254–85. JSNTSup 184. Sheffield: Sheffield Academic, 1999.

———. *Reading Mark: Engaging the Gospel*. Minneapolis: Fortress, 2004.

Rhoads, David and Donald Michie. *Mark as Story: An Introduction to the Narrative of a Gospel*. Philadelphia: Fortress, 1982.

Rhoads, David, et al. *Mark as Story: An Introduction to the Narrative of a Gospel.* 2nd ed. Minneapolis: Fortress, 1999.

———. *Mark as Story: An Introduction to the Narrative of a Gospel.* 3rd ed. Minneapolis: Fortress, 2012.

Riddle, Donald W. "The Martyr Motif in the Gospel according to Mark." *JR* 4 (1924) 397–410.

Rimmon-Kenan, Shlomith. *Narrative Fiction: Contemporary Poetics.* 2nd ed. New Accents. New York: Routledge, 2002.

Robbins, Vernon K. *Exploring the Texture of Texts: A Guide to Socio-Rhetorical Interpretation.* Valley Forge, PA: Trinity, 1996.

———. *Jesus the Teacher: A Socio-Rhetorical Interpretation of Mark.* Philadelphia: Fortress, 1984.

———. "Orality, Literacy, Memory, and Mark." In *Performing the Gospel: Orality, Memory, and Mark*, edited by Richard A. Horsley et al., 125–46. Minneapolis: Fortress, 2006.

———. "Socio-Rhetorical Criticism: Mary, Elizabeth and the Magnificat as a Test Case." In *The New Literary Criticism and the New Testament*, edited by Elizabeth Struthers Malbon and Edgar V. McKnight, 165–209. JSNTS 109. Sheffield: Sheffield Academic, 1994.

———. "Summons and Outline in Mark: The Three-Step Progression." *NovT* 23 (1981) 97–114.

Rollmann, H. "Wrede, Friedrich Georg Eduard William." In *Dictionary of Biblical Interpretation*, edited by John H. Hayes, 2:659–61. Nashville: Abingdon, 1999.

Roskam, Hendrika N. *The Purpose of the Gospel of Mark in Its Historical and Social Context.* NovTSup 114. Leiden: Brill, 2004.

Rowe, Robert D. *God's Kingdom and God's Son: The Background of Mark's Christology from Concepts of Kingship in the Psalms.* AGAJU 50. Leiden: Brill, 2002.

Sabin, Marie Noonan. *The Gospel according to Mark.* New Collegeville Bible Commentary 2. Collegeville, MN: Liturgical, 2006.

———. *Reopening the Word: Reading Mark as Theology in the Context of Early Judaism.* Oxford: Oxford University Press, 2002.

Sanday, William. "The Injunctions to Silence in the Gospels." *JTS* 5 (1904) 321–29.

Schaberg, Jane. "Daniel 7, 12 and the New Testament Passion-Resurrection Predictions." *NTS* 31 (1985) 208–22.

Schierse, Franz J. "Das Christusbild im Markusevangelium." *BK* 27 (1972) 114–16.

Schmidt, Karl Ludwig. "Die Stellung der Evangelien in der allgemeinen Literaturgeschichte." In *ΕΥΧΑΡΙΣΤΗΡΙΟΝ: Studien zur Religion und Literatur des Alten und Neuen Testaments: Hermann Gunkel zum 60 Geburtstag*, edited by Emil Balla and Hans Schmidt, 50–134. FRLANT 19.2. Göttingen: Vandenhoeck & Ruprecht, 1923.

———. *Der Rahmen der Geschichte Jesu: Literarkritische Untersuchungen zur ältesten Jesusüberlieferung.* Berlin: Trowitzsch, 1919.

Schnackenburg, Rudolf. *The Gospel of Matthew.* Translated by Robert R. Barr. Grand Rapids: Eerdmans, 2002.

Schnelle, Udo. *The History and Theology of the New Testament Writings.* Translated by M. Eugene Boring. Minneapolis: Fortress, 1998.

Scholtissek, Klaus. "Der Sohn Gottes für Reich Gottes." In *Der Evangelist als Theologe*, edited by T. Söding, 63–90. Studien zum Markusevangelium. SBS 163. Stuttgart: Katholisches Bibelwerk, 1995.

# Bibliography

Schweitzer, Albert. *Das Messianitäs- und Leidensgeheimnis: Eine Skizze des Lebens Jesu*. Tübingen: Mohr/Siebeck, 1901.

———. *The Mystery of the Kingdom of God: The Secret of Jesus' Messiahship and Passion*. Translated by Walter Lowrie. New York: Schocken, 1964.

———. *The Mysticism of Paul the Apostle*. Translated by W. Montgomery. London: A. & C. Black, 1931.

———. *The Quest of the Historical Jesus: First Complete Edition*. Edited by John Bowen. Fortress Classics in Biblical Studies. Minneapolis: Fortress, 2001. Originally published as *Von Reimarus zu Wrede: eine Geschichte der Leben-Jesu-Forschung* (Tübingen: Mohr/Siebeck, 1906, 1913, 1950).

Schweizer, Eduard. "Ammerkungen zur Theologie des Markus." In *Neotestamentica: Deutsche und Englische Aufsätze*, edited by Eduard Schweizer, 93–104. Zürich: Zwingli, 1963.

———. *The Good News according to Mark*. Translated by Donald H. Madvig. Richmond, VA: Knox, 1970.

———. "The Portrayal of the Life of Faith in the Gospel of Mark." *Int* 32 (1978) 387–99.

———. "Zur Frage des Messiasgeheimnisses bei Markus." *ZNW* 56 (1965) 1–8.

Scott, M. Philip. "Chiastic Structure: A Key to the Interpretation of Mark's Gospel." *BTB* 15 (1985) 17–26.

Senior, Donald and Carroll Stuhlmueller. *The Biblical Foundation for Missions*. Maryknoll, NY: Orbis, 1984.

Shepherd, Michael B. "Daniel 7:13 and the New Testament Son of Man." *WTJ* 68 (2006) 99–111.

Shepherd, Tom. *Markan Sandwich Stories: Narration, Definition, and Function*. Andrews University Seminary Doctoral Dissertation Series 18. Berrien Springs, MI: Andrews University Press, 1993.

———. "The Narrative Function of Markan Intercalations." *NTS* 41 (1995) 522–40.

Sergeant, John. *Lion Let Loose: The Structure and Meaning of St. Mark's Gospel*. Carlisle: Paternoster, 1992.

Shiner, Whitney T. *Follow Me! Disciples in Markan Rhetoric*. SBLDS 145. Atlanta: Scholars, 1995.

———. *Proclaiming the Gospel: First-Century Performance of Mark*. Harrisburg, PA: Trinity, 2003.

Simonsen, Hejne. "Mark 8:27–10:52 i Markusevangeliets komposition." *DTT* 27, no. 2 (1964) 83–99.

Sjöberg, Erik. "בן אדם and בר אנש im Hebräischen und Aramäischen." *AcOr* 21 (1950–53) 57–65.

———. *Der verborgene Menschensohn in den Evangelien*. Lund: Gleerup, 1955.

Slomp, J. "Are the Words 'Son of God' in Mark 1:1 Original?" *BT* 28 (1977) 143–50.

Smith, Morton. "The Origin and History of the Transfiguration Story." *USQR* 36 (1980) 39–44.

Smith, Robert Harry. "Wounded Lion: Mark 9:1 and Other Missing Pieces." *CTM* 11 (1984) 333–49.

Smith, Stephen H. "A Divine Tragedy: Some Observations on the Dramatic Structure of Mark's Gospel." *NovT* 37 (1995) 209–31.

———. "The Function of the Son of David Tradition in Mark's Gospel." *NTS* 42 (1996) 523–39.

Smyth, Herbert Weir. *Greek Grammar*. Cambridge, MA: Harvard University Press, 1920.

Spence, F. Scott. "The Transfiguration of Jesus: Narrative Meaning and Function of Mark 9:2-8, Matt 17:1-8 and Luke 9:28-36." *CBQ* 63 (2001) 746-48.
Ssebadduka, George William. "'Rabbi, It Is Good That We Are Here': Moses, Elijah, and John in Mark's Transfiguration Story (9:2-8)." PhD diss., Marquette University, 1995.
Stamps, Dennis L. "Rhetorical and Narratological Criticism." In *Handbook to Exegesis of the New Testament*, edited by Stanley E. Porter, 219-39. Leiden: Brill, 1997.
Standaert, Benoît H. M. G. M. *L'Évangile selon Marc: Composition et genre littéraire*. Brugge: Sint-Andriesabdij, 1978.
Steichele, Hans-Jörg. *Der leidende Sohn Gottes*. Biblische Untersuchungen 14. Regensburg: Pustet, 1980.
Stein, Robert H. "Is the Transfiguration (Mark 9:2-8) a Misplaced Resurrection-Account?" *JBL* 95 (1976) 67-81.
———. "The 'Redaktionsgeschichtlich' Investigation of a Markan Seam (Mc 1:21f.)." *ZNW* 61 (1970) 70-94.
Stock, Augustine. *The Call to Discipleship: A Literary Study of Mark's Gospel*. GNS 1. Wilmington< DE: Glazier, 1982.
———. "Chiastic Awareness and Education in Antiquity." *BTB* 14 (1984) 23-27.
———. "Hinge Transitions in Mark's Gospel." *BTB* 15 (1985) 27-31.
———. *The Method and Message of Mark*. Wilmington, DE: Glazier, 1989.
Strauss, David F. *The Life of Jesus Critically Examined*. Translated by G. Eliot. Philadelphia: Fortress, 1846. Originally published as *Das leben Jesu: kritisch bearbeitet* (Tübingen: Osiander, 1835-1836).
Strecker, Georg. "The Passion- and Resurrection Predictions in Mark's Gospel (Mark 8:31; 9:31; 10:32-34)." *Int* 22 (1968) 421-44. Originally published in *ZTK* 64 (1967) 16-39.
———. "Zur Messiasgeheimnistheorie im Markusevangelium." *SE* III, TU 88 (1964) 87-104. Repr., "The Theory of the Messianic Secret in Mark's Gospel." In *The Messianic Secret*, edited by Christopher M. Tuckett, 49-64. Issues in Religion and Theology 1. Philadelphia: Fortress, 1983.
Strickert, Fred. *Bethsaida: Home of the Apostles*. Collegeville, MN: Liturgical, 1998.
Swartley, Willard M. "The Structural Function of the Term 'Way' (Hodos) in Mark's Gospel." In *The New Way of Jesus: Essays Presented to Howard Charles*, edited by William Klassen, 73-86. Newton, KS: Faith and Life, 1980.
Swete, Henry Barclay. *The Gospel according to St. Mark: The Greek Text with Introduction Notes and Indices*. 3rd ed. London: Macmillan, 1913.
Talbert, Charles H. *What is a Gospel? The Genre of the Canonical Gospels*. Philadelphia: Fortress, 1977.
Tannehill, Robert C. "The Disciples in Mark: The Function of a Narrative Role." *JR* 57 (1977) 386-405.
———. "The Gospel of Mark as Narrative Christology." SBLSS 16 (1979) 57-95.
———. "Reading It Whole: The Function of Mark 8:34-35 in Mark's Story." *Quarterly Review* 2 (1982) 67-78.
———. *The Sword of His Mouth*. SBL Semeia Supplements 1. Missoula: Scholars, 1975. Repr., Eugene, OR: Wipf and Stock, 2003.
Taylor, Vincent. *The Gospel according to St. Mark: The Greek Text with Introduction, Notes, and Indexes*. 2nd ed. London: Macmillan, 1966.
———. "The Origin of Mark's Passion Sayings." *NTS* 1 (1954-55) 159-67.

## Bibliography

Telford, William R. *The Interpretation of Mark*. Issues in Religion and Theology 7. Edinburgh: T. & T. Clark, 1995.

———. *Mark*. NTG. Sheffield: Sheffield Academic, 1997.

———. *The Theology of the Gospel of Mark*. New Testament Theology. Cambridge: Cambridge University Press, 1999.

Terrin, Samuel. *The Elusive Presence: The Heart of Biblical Theology*. Religious Perspectives 26. San Francisco: Harper & Row, 1978.

Theobald, Michael. "Gottesohn und Menschensohn: Zur polaren Struktur der Christologie im Markusevangelium." SNTU 13 (1988) 37–79.

Thiselton, Anthony C. "'Behind' and 'In Front Of' the Text: Language, Reference and Indeterminacy." In *After Pentecost: Language & Biblical Interpretation*, edited by Craig Bartholomew et al., 97–120. Scripture & Hermeneutics 2. Grand Rapids: Zondervan, 2001.

———. *New Horizons in Hermeneutics*. Grand Rapids: Zondervan, 1992.

———. *Thiselton on Hermeneutics: Collected Works with New Essays*. Grand Rapids: Eerdmans, 2006.

———. *The Two Horizons: New Testament Hermeneutics and Philosophical Description*. 2nd ed. Grand Rapids: Eerdmans, 1993.

Thrall, Margaret E. "Elijah and Moses in Mark's Account of the Transfiguration." NTS 16 (1970) 305–17.

Tiede, David L. *The Charismatic Figure as Miracle Worker*. New York: Scholars, 1972.

Tillesse, G. Minnette, de. *Le secret messianique dans l'Evangile de Marc*. LD 47. Paris: Cerf, 1968.

Tödt, Heinz Eduard. *The Son of Man in the Synoptic Tradition*. New Testament Library. Translated by Dorothy M. Barton. London: SCM, 1965.

Tolbert, Mary Ann. "The Gospel of Mark." In *The New Testament Today*, edited by Mark Allan Powell, 45–56. Louisville: Westminster John Knox, 1999.

———. *Sowing the Gospel: Mark's World in Literary-Historical Perspective*. Minneapolis: Fortress, 1989.

Trimaille, Michel. "Le Récit de la Transfiguration comme récit interprétif: Marc 9, 1–13." In *Temps de la lecture*, 163–72. Paris: Cerf, 1993.

Trites, Allison A. "The Transfiguration of Jesus: The Gospel in Microcosm." EvQ 51 (1979) 67–79.

Truitt, Danny P. "The Function of Elijah in the Markan Messianic Drama." PhD diss., Baylor University, 1993.

Tsumura, David Toshio. "Janus Parallelism in Hab. III 4." VT 54 (2004) 124–28.

———. "Janus Parallelism in Nah 1:8." JBL 102 (1983) 109–11.

Tuckett, Christopher M. "Introduction: The Problem of Messianic Secret." In *The Messianic Secret*, edited by Christopher M. Tuckett, 1–28. Issues in Religion and Theology 1. London: SPCK, 1983.

———. *The Messianic Secret*. Issues in Religion and Theology 1. London: SPCK, 1983.

———. "The Present Son of Man." JSNT 14 (1982) 58–81.

———. "The Son of Man and Daniel 7: Q and Jesus." In *Source: Sayings Source Q and the Historical Jesus*, 371–94. Leuven: Leuven University Press, 2001.

VanderKam, James. "Messianism in the Scrolls." In *The Community of the Renewed Covenant: The Notre Dame Symposium on the Dead Sea Scrolls*, edited by Eugene Ulrich and James VanderKam, 211–34. Christianity and Judaism in Antiquity 10. Notre Dame: University of Notre Dame Press, 1994.

Vanhoozer, Kevin J. *Is There a Meaning in This Text? The Bible, The Reader, and the Morality of Literary Knowledge.* Grand Rapids: Zondervan, 1998.
van Eck, Ernst and Andries G. van Aarde. "A Narratological Analysis of Mark 12:1-12: The Plot of the Gospel in a Nutshell." *Hervormde Teologiese Studies* 45 (1989) 778-800.
van Iersel, Bas M. F. *Mark: A Reader-Response Commentary.* Translated by W. H. Bisscherrux. JSNTSup 164. Sheffield: Sheffield Academic, 1998.
―――. *Reading Mark.* Translated by W. H. Bisscherrux. Collegeville, MN: Liturgical, 1988.
van Oyen, Geert. "Intercalations and Irony in the Gospel of Mark." In *The Four Gospels 1992: Festschrift Frans Neirynck*, edited by Frans van Segbroeck et al., 2:949-74. BETL. Leuven: Leuven University Press, 1992.
Vena, Osvaldo D. "The Rhetorical and Theological Center of Mark's Gospel." In *Los Caminos inexhauribles de la Palabra (las Relecturas creativas en la Biblia y de la Biblia*, 327-45. Buenos Aires: Lumen, 2000.
Vermes, Geza. *Jesus the Jew.* New York: Harper, 1979.
―――. "The Use of נש בר / נשא בר in Jewish Aramaic." Appendix E in Matthew Black, *An Aramaic Approach to the Gospels and Acts*, 310-30. 3rd ed. Oxford: Clarendon, 1967.
Via, Dan O. *The Ethics of Mark's Gospel in the Middle of Time.* Philadelphia: Fortress, 1985.
―――. *Kerygma and Comedy in the New Testament.* Philadelphia: Fortress, 1975.
Vielhauer, Phillip. "Erwägungen zur Christologies des Markusevangeliums." In *Zeit und Geschichte*, edited by Erich Dinkler, 155-69. Tübingen: Mohr, 1964.
―――. *Geschicte der urchristlichen Literatur. Einloitung in das Neue Testament, die Apokryphen und die Apostolischen Väter.* Berlin: de Gruyter, 1975.
Vines, Michael E. *The Problem of Markan Genre: The Gospel of Mark and the Jewish Novel.* SBLAB 3. Atlanta: SBL, 2002.
von Martitz, Peter Wülfing. "υἱός υἱοθεσία," *TWNT.* 8:335-40.
Voster, Willem. "The Characterization of Peter in the Gospel of Mark." *Neot* 21 (1987) 57-75.
Waetjen, Herman C. *A Reordering of Power: A Sociopolitical Reading of Mark's Gospel.* Minneapolis: Fortress, 1989.
Westerholm, Stephen. *Perspectives Old and New on Paul: The "Lutheran" Paul and His Critics.* Grand Rapids: Eerdmans, 2004.
Wallace, Daniel B. *Greek Grammar Beyond the Basics: An Exegetical Syntax of the New Testament.* Grand Rapids: Zondervan, 1996.
Watson, Duane F. "Rhetorical Criticism, New Testament." In *Dictionary of Biblical Interpretation*, edited by John H. Hayes, 2:399-402. Nashville: Abingdon, 1999.
Watson, Francis. "The Quest for the Real Jesus." In *The Cambridge Companion to Jesus*, edited by Markus Bockmuehl, 156-69. Cambridge: Cambridge University Press, 2001.
Watts, Rikki E. *Isaiah's New Exodus in Mark.* WUNT 2, 88. 1997. Repr., Grand Rapids: Baker Academic, 2000.
Weeden, Theodore J. "The Heresy That Necessitated Mark's Gospel." *ZNW* 59 (1968) 145-58.
―――. *Mark: Traditions in Conflict.* Philadelphia: Fortress, 1971.
Weiss, Bernhard. *The Life of Jesus.* Translated by John Walter Hope. 3 vols. Edinburgh: T. & T. Clark, 1883-1909. Originally published as *Das Leben Jesu*, 2 vols. (Berlin: Hertz, 1882).
Weiss, Johannes. *Das Leben Jesu.* 2 vols. Berlin: Herz, 1882, 1884.

# Bibliography

Weizsäcker, Karl Heinrich. *Untersuchungen üuber die Evangelische Geschichte, ihre Quellen und den Gang ihrer Entwicklung.* Gotha: Besser, 1864.

Wenham, David and Moses, A. D. A. "'There Are Some Standing Here . . .'": Did They Become the 'Reputed Pillars' of the Jerusalem Church? Some Reflections on Mark 9:1, Galatians 2:9 and the Transfiguration." *NovT* 36 (1994) 146–63.

Wetter, Gillis Petersson. *"Der Sohn Gottes": Eine Untersuchung über den Charakter und die Tendenz des Johannes Evangeliums: Zugleich ein Beitrag zur Kenntnis der Heilandsgestalten der Antike.* Göttingen: Vandenhoeck & Ruprecht, 1916.

Whitaker, Robyn. "Rebuke or Recall? Rethinking the Role of Peter in Mark's Gospel." *CBQ* 75 (2013) 666–82.

Wiarda, Timothy. "Peter as Peter in the Gospel of Mark." *NTS* 45 (1999) 19–37.

Williams, Joel F. "Is Mark's Gospel an Apology for the Cross?" *Bulletin for Biblical Research* 12 (2002) 97–122.

———. *Other Followers of Jesus: Minor Characters as Major Figures in Mark's Gospel.* JSNTSup 102. Sheffield: JSOT Press, 1994.

Williamson, Lamar. *Mark.* IBC. Louisville: John Knox, 1983.

Witherington, Ben C., III. *The Gospel of Mark: A Socio-Rhetorical Commentary.* Grand Rapids: Eerdmans, 2001.

———. "Transfigured Understanding—A Critical Note on Mark 9:2–13 as a Parousia Preview." *Ashland Theological Journal* 24 (1992) 88–91.

Wrede, William. *The Messianic Secret.* Translated by J. C. G. Greig. Cambridge: Clark, 1971. Originally published as *Das Messiasgeheimnis in den Evangelien* (Göttingen: Vandenhoeck & Ruprecht, 1901).

Wright, N. Thomas. *Jesus and the Victory of God.* Vol. 2 of *Christian Origins and the Question of God.* Minneapolis: Fortress, 1996.

———. *The New Testament and the People of God.* Vol. 1 of *Christian Origins and the Question of God.* Minneapolis: Fortress, 1992.

———. *The Resurrection of the Son of God.* Vol. 3 of *Christian Origins and the Question of God.* Minneapolis: Fortress, 2003.

Wuellner, Wilhelm. "Where is Rhetorical Criticism Taking Us?" *CBQ* 49 (1987) 448–63.

Ziesler, J. A. "Transfiguration Story and the Markan Soteriology." *ExpTim* 81 (1970) 263–68.

www.ingramcontent.com/pod-product-compliance
Lightning Source LLC
Chambersburg PA
CBHW070239230426
43664CB00014B/2352